ISBN 978-1-331-96165-9
PIBN 10260293

This book is a reproduction of an important historical work. Forgotten Books uses state-of-the-art technology to digitally reconstruct the work, preserving the original format whilst repairing imperfections present in the aged copy. In rare cases, an imperfection in the original, such as a blemish or missing page, may be replicated in our edition. We do, however, repair the vast majority of imperfections successfully; any imperfections that remain are intentionally left to preserve the state of such historical works.

1 MONTH OF
FREE
READING

at

www.ForgottenBooks.com

By purchasing this book you are eligible for one month membership to ForgottenBooks.com, giving you unlimited access to our entire collection of over 1,000,000 titles via our web site and mobile apps.

To claim your free month visit:
www.forgottenbooks.com/free260293

English
Français
Deutsche
Italiano
Español
Português

www.forgottenbooks.com

Mythology Photography **Fiction**
Fishing Christianity **Art** Cooking
Essays Buddhism Freemasonry
Medicine **Biology** Music **Ancient**
Egypt Evolution Carpentry Physics
Dance Geology **Mathematics** Fitness
Shakespeare **Folklore** Yoga Marketing
Confidence Immortality Biographies
Poetry **Psychology** Witchcraft
Electronics Chemistry History **Law**
Accounting **Philosophy** Anthropology
Alchemy Drama Quantum Mechanics
Atheism Sexual Health **Ancient History**
Entrepreneurship Languages Sport
Paleontology Needlework Islam
Metaphysics Investment Archaeology
Parenting Statistics Criminology
Motivational

DIARY

OF

RALPH THORESBY, F.R.S.

AUTHOR OF THE TOPOGRAPHY OF LEEDS.,

(1677—1724.)

NOW FIRST PUBLISHED FROM THE ORIGINAL MANUSCRIPT,

BY THE REV. JOSEPH HUNTER, F.S.A.

IN TWO VOLUMES.

VOL. I.

LONDON:

HENRY COLBURN AND RICHARD BENTLEY,
NEW BURLINGTON STREET.
1830.

LONDON:
PRINTED BY SAMUEL BENTLEY,
Dorset-street, Fleet-street.

PREFACE.

RALPH THORESBY was the son of Mr. John Thoresby, by Ruth his wife, a daughter of Mr. Ralph Idle, whose residence was at Bulmer, an agricultural village, about ten miles north of York. He had numerous relations both on his father's and his mother's side, all of whom appear in the genealogical tables, which he has introduced into his " Topography of Leeds."

John Thoresby was the son of a Leeds merchant, who was a member of the Corporation, and was a native of that town. At the commencement of the civil wars, his father would have sent him to Holland, but he preferred to remain in England, and to serve in the Parliament army. He was an officer under Fairfax, with whom he coincided in principle, both religious and political.

When the wars were over, he settled as a merchant at Leeds, and there his son Ralph was born, on the 16th of August, 1658.

One of the most amiable features in the character of the son, was his filial piety. There was an unusual strength of attachment as well as community of sentiment. Both were deeply religious; both had a strong attachment to pursuits, which now are called antiquarian. The foundation of the Museum, which made the name of Thoresby celebrated, not only in England, but over the continent of Europe, was laid by the father, in the purchase, for a considerable sum, of the coins and medals collected by Stonehouse, and the family of Fairfax.

By the death of an elder brother at twelve years of age, Ralph became the eldest son of his father. At the Grammar-school in Leeds, he acquired a knowledge of the Latin and Greek languages, which was eminently useful to him in the studies to which he afterwards devoted his attention.

His father intended that he should succeed him as a merchant; and with this view he was sent, when eighteen years old, (1677,) to the house of a relation in London.

At this period the Diary commences; and from

this period till near the time of his death, we possess in the present work so ample and minute an account of his life, including his studies, his literary friendships, his religious history, his temporal concerns, as to render it unnecessary to do more than to point out the more remarkable æras.

July 1678, to February 1679, he was in Holland to complete his mercantile education. From this time to the end of his life, he was a resident of Leeds.

October 31, 1679. The sudden death of his father devolved the concerns and cares of the whole family upon him. He undertook to proceed with the business left by his father, in whose house he continued to reside, and had a younger brother and sister in household with him.

1683. He was prosecuted as a Non-conformist.

1684. He took up his freedom in the Eastland and Hamburgh Companies.

1685, February 25. He married Anna Sykes, a daughter of Richard Sykes, of Ledsham in Yorkshire, one of the Lords of the Manor of Leeds.

1689. In conjunction with Mr. Ibbetson, he erected a mill for the preparing of rape-oil, at

Sheepscar, near Leeds; in which, as well as in his other mercantile concerns, he had little, or rather no, success.

1690. His acquaintance commenced with Mr. Archdeacon Nicolson, afterwards Bishop of Carlisle; an eminent antiquarian scholar: and about this time his mind began to be determined towards the design, which he afterwards accomplished, of preparing a Topographical Account of the Parish of Leeds.

1692. About this time, the museum of coins, prints, autographs, &c. collected by himself and his father, began to attract the public attention, and to be an object of curiosity to strangers visiting Leeds.

1697. He was elected a Fellow of the Royal Society, and some of his communications appeared in their Transactions. In this year he was also elected an Assistant, or Common-Councilman, in the Corporation of Leeds.

1699. He finally abandoned his connection with the Dissenters.

1704. In great perplexity concerning his temporal affairs. About this time he seems to have retired from business, with a very small competency, and to have devoted himself to his Museum, his literary pursuits, and his religious duties.

1715. He published his Topographical Survey of the Parish of Leeds, the result of many years' enquiry and study : to which he annexed a Descriptive Catalogue of the Curiosities in his Museum.

1724. He published his History of the Church of Leeds. The latest date in his Diary, is September 13, in this year.

What little remains of his history, may be given in the words of Dr. Whitaker, who, a century after its original publication, gave to the world, a second edition of his Topography of Leeds, with a Life of the Author prefixed.*

" In the month of October 1724, he was suddenly seized by a paralytic stroke, from which he so far recovered as to speak intelligibly and walk without help. There is also a letter extant written by him in this melancholy state, and complaining, though with great patience and submission, of his feelings : thus he languished till the same month of the following year, when he received a second and

* The information from which this Life was composed, is chiefly to be found in a Life of Thoresby, written by his eldest son, and printed in the " Biographia Britannica," p. 3931-3943.

final shock from the same disease, which put an end to his life, October 16th, 1725, in the sixty-eighth year of his age.   He was interred with his ancestors in the choir of the parish church, close to the column which separates the chancel from the north transept, and has now lain a century without any memorial from the piety of his friends, or the gratitude of his townsmen.".

When it was once proposed to erect a monument to his memory, the following inscription was prepared for it by the same writer who has done so much justice to his memory in the life from whence the above extract is made :

H. S. E.

RADULPHUS. JOH. F. THORESBY, S. R. S.

Patriarum historiarum ac præsertim
hujus Municipii et Ecclesiæ,
quas felici solertiâ indagavit,
peritissimus:

Hæc studia, vitæ simplicis et innocuæ oblectamina,
immensâ adeo supellectile antiquitatum
accendit, fovitque,
ut nemo non magnis opibus auctus,
quæ nostro vix mediocres contigerant,
Museo Thoresbeiano
Seu nummis veterum, seu rebus in quovis genere perraris,
aut par aut proximum quidquam
eo sæculo ostendisset.

Thoresby left his wife surviving, and two sons and a daughter, the survivors of ten children. Both the sons were clergymen. Ralph, the elder, died Rector of Stoke Newington, in 1763. Richard, the younger, had the church of St. Catherine, Coleman-street, and died 1774. Both the brothers owed their preferment to Bishop Gibson, their father's friend. The daughter married Mr. John Wood, and had a son named Ralph, who died in 1781, and is supposed to have been the last surviving descend-ant of this learned, judicious, and religious anti-quary.*

WORKS OF THORESBY.

DUCATUS LEODIENSIS; or the Topography of the antient and populous Town and Parish of Leedes, and parts adjacent in the West Riding of the County of York. With the Pedigrees of many of the Nobility and Gentry, and other matters relat-

* A Correspondent of the *Gentleman's Magazine* (vol. liii. p. 322) who appears to be well-informed, says that the Rector of Newington certainly died without issue ; but that he had been informed that Richard, the younger son, had two sons and a daughter ; that the two sons were in the Black-Hole at Calcutta, where one of them died.

ing to those parts, extracted from Records, Original Evidences and Manuscripts. By Ralph Thoresby, F.R.S. To which is added, at the request of several learned persons,

[MUSEUM THORESBYANUM, or] A Catalogue of his Museum, with the Curiosities Natural and Artificial, and the Antiquities; particularly the Roman, British, Saxon, Danish, Norman, and Scotch Coins, with Modern Medals. Also a Catalogue of Manuscripts of the various Editions of the Bible and of Books published in the infancy of the art of printing: with an Account of some unusual accidents that have attended some persons, attempted after the method of Dr. Plot. London. Folio, 1715.

VICARIA LEODIENSIS: or the History of the Church of Leedes in Yorkshire. Containing an account of the Learned Men, Bishops, and Writers, who have been Vicars of that populous parish; with the Catalogues of their Works, printed and manuscript, &c. London, 8vo. 1724.

These were the only separate publications. But nearly the whole of the additions to the account of Yorkshire, in Bishop Gibson's edition of Camden, were by Thoresby. He has several letters in the

Transactions of the Royal Society. A portion of his intended Historical work on Leeds, but which would in fact have been an History of the West Riding of Yorkshire, is printed in the notes to his Life in the Biographia. Dr. Calamy received from him memoirs of many of the Puritan ministers of Yorkshire. There is a valuable contribution of his to our Glossarial Literature in the Letters of Ray, published after his death by Derham. Much of the original matter in Stevens' additions to the Monasticon, he received from Thoresby; and in the works of Obadiah Walker, Bishop Nicolson and Hearne, are frequent acknowledgments of literary favours which these distinguished scholars received from him.

At the present day, the inhabitants of such a town as Leeds would scarcely allow a Museum like that of Thoresby to be removed and dispersed; but he died in a less scientific and less curious age than the present, and his collection was gradually dismembered, till what remained of it was sold by public auction, in March 1764, at a distance from the town of which it had long been the pride and ornament. Thoresby's Collection of Letters from Celebrated Persons found its way to its proper depository, the

British Museum, where are also some of his Biographical Collections. But it is not known what was
the fate of his own Correspondence in the general
and total wreck, or of his Diary, a more sacred relic.
While it is uncertain whether they were suffered to
be sold with the rest of his manuscripts, it is certain
that they were allowed to pass into the hands of
parties who had no natural connexion with the man
whose most secret history and most sacred sentiments
those leaves contained. Some of the volumes of the
Diary, and many of the Correspondence, are, it is
feared, irrecoverably lost. Those out of which the
present publication has arisen, were discovered some
years ago, lying neglected in a garret in the city.
From this obscure repository they were rescued by
a gentleman to whom the public owes many such
obligations, my friend William Upcott, Esq. of the
London Institution, who was permitted to add them
to his splendid and almost unrivalled collection of
autograph remains of celebrated men. It is Mr.
Upcott who now permits the public to share in the
curious information contained in them ; and in the
interesting views which they present of the life of
one of the fathers of English Topography, and of

that numerous and increasing family so well known amongst us under the name of the Collectors.*

It will be perceived that the series both of the Diary and Correspondence is broken. This is of less consequence in the Correspondence, where each letter may be regarded as distinct from the rest. The chasms are, except in one instance, supplied in this publication from a Review of his life, a manuscript also in possession of Mr. Upcott. This was written at different periods, usually after intervals of eight or ten years. The good man had his Diary before him, and he selected from it the principal circumstances, forming out of them a continued narrative of his life, and adding notices of his then present sentiments respecting them. I once thought of printing the Review entire; but there is much of it which is too personal and tedious; it is not continued beyond the year 1714; and for the greater part of the time over which it extends, we possess the Diary itself.

* While this work was in the press, another volume, containing two portions of the Diary, was discovered in the library of Christ's Hospital. I owe thanks to Robert John Tennant, Esq. of Trinity College, Cambridge, for having directed my attention to it; and to the Rev. Mr. Greenwood, the head master, for having assisted in obtaining the use of it for this publication.

The keeping a register of facts and feelings was a part of the religious exercise of the good and serious of those times; and in this light Thoresby seems to have regarded the labour to which he voluntarily submitted himself. He seems to have regarded it as a religious duty to make this record; for from the day when he commenced his Diary, till he was disabled by age and infirmity, I believe, if we had the manuscripts complete, we should find that there is not a single day in his life for which he has not accounted. In his mind, also, the keeping of this register was associated with the religious regard which he ever cherished for the memory of his excellent father: for it was at his suggestion that the Diary was originally commenced, and he had himself set the example of the practice. The letter in which he urged this exercise on his son, who was then in London, is found attached to the fly-leaf of the first volume: and with this letter the preface may be brought to a close.

SON RALPH,   Leeds, 15th Aug. 1677.

I WROTE two or three lines to my cousin, by Mr. Hassle, and at the bottom of that shred of paper

two lines to you, and expected two or three words
from you with my cousin's letter this last post, but
I suppose you had written by the carrier. Remember what I advised you, to be always employed in
some lawful employment or other; sometimes in
hearing good sermons, wherein you will have many
opportunities; sometimes in attending my cousin at
the Hall, and helping to lift or remove cloth, or any
such thing wherein you can be useful or serviceable;
sometimes in writing or drawing prospects (which
will be a pleasant and innocent recreation), as that
of the Monument, or of Bedlam, which might be
taken very well in the middle of Moorfields; and I
would have you, in a little book, which you may
either buy or make of two or three sheets of paper,
take a little journal of any thing remarkable every
day, principally as to yourself, as, suppose, Aug. 2.
I was at such a place; (or) I omitted such a duty;
(or) such a one preached from such a text, and my
heart was touched; (or) I was a negligent hearer, (or)
otherwise, &c. I have thought this a good method
for one to keep a good tolerable decorum in actions,
&c. because he is to be accountable to himself as
well as to God, which we are too apt to forget : but

I have not room to say much.   Remember me to all the good family where you are, and to Mr. Thomas Dickenson, and with my love to and prayers for yourself, I am

Your truly loving father,

JOHN THORESBY.

CORRIGENDUM.

Vol. 1. p 179. l. 6. place a comma after *senior*.

DIARY

OF

RALPH THORESBY.

A.D. 1677.

Sept. 2. Die Dom. Mr. Slater* preached from Acts v. 4, whence he proved the Holy Ghost to be God. Afternoon, Mr. Keeling, from Prov. iv. 23, showed very well how we ought to keep our hearts, especially from our own corruptions, which, like a leak in a ship, though there was no rock to split upon, would, without care, sink us to all eternity.

* Thoresby was now in London, where he was living in the family of Mr. John Dickenson, of whom he says in the *Review*, that "he was a holy and humble Christian, his wife also very pious; and so was her ingenious sister Mrs. Madox, all now at rest in Christ, but their posterity remain, eminent here and at Coningsberg." Mrs. Madox was mother of Madox the Exchequer Antiquary.

He also says, that the order of the family was most regular and excellent: that they were great frequenters of sermons and lectures;

3. I was at Mr. Lawrence's* at the Fast for the Fire. Oh, that there was a heart in me seriously to set about (what he exhorted to) the great work of repentance and reformation !

9. Die Dom. Mr. Ralphson (though to me incognito, else I have a charge from my good Father not to hear him, as a person less orthodox)† preached

---

and it may be mentioned, as a trait of the manners of the times, that on other evenings of the week their young inmate was accustomed to read History for the amusement of the family, but on Saturday evenings nothing but Divinity appeared. They were members of a nonconformist congregation, assembling at a chapel in Crosby-square. Mr. Slater, the pastor, had left the Church when the Act of Uniformity placed it on its present basis. He lived till 1705. An account of him may be found in Calamy, the instructive and, on the whole, very fair and impartial biographer of the Clergy who at that period found it their duty to withdraw from the stations which they held in the Church. Mr. Keeling was another.

The disposition of Thoresby's mind to antiquarian and historical enquiry manifested itself at this period of his life. He employed himself in attempts at making drawings of tombs and buildings: he copied engraved portraits: he took notes in most of the churches, especially of Protestant Benefactors. This last was through life a very favourite subject. He himself tells us, that the tauntings of some writers of the Romish Church, as if little had been done in England since the Reformation under the impulses of piety and charity, first put him upon the work.

* Edward Lawrence, formerly of Magdalene College, Cambridge. See Calamy : *Account, &c.* p. 557.

† The real name of this nonconforming minister was Jeremiah Marsden, one of several sons, all ministers, of an old Puritan minister in Yorkshire, well known to Thoresby's family. His name was amongst those who were charged by an accomplice with some insurrectionary movements in October 1663. The affair is still spoken of as The Farnley-wood Plot, from the woods of Farnley near Leeds, in which the deluded persons assembled. It has lately been recalled to notice by the publication of the exparte statements of the accomplice before the magistrate. Many were executed. Marsden fled to London ; and no vigilant search being made after him, was allowed

for Mr. S. from Psalm xxxvii. 5, A Christian ought
to live a dependent life upon Christ. Mr. Keeling
from 1 Cor. vii. 29, What would the damned give
for a little time, and yet how hardly are we prevailed
with to redeem this time. At night Mr. Baker,
from Matth. xii. 39, showed that most of our words,
if rightly considered, are idle words, because, though
perhaps they have no direct tendency to evil, yet
they are not edifying.

13. Mr. Baxter* showed, that God gives graces
and gifts for the good of his Church; private persons
as well as ministers should improve them to that
purpose; and that we should labour to prevent
ignorance, pride, and hypocrisy, as very dangerous
though common evils.

15. At home most of the day, reading in Mr.
Clark's History, Mirror, and Persecutions.

16. Die Dom. Mr. Ralphson preached again for
Mr. S. from Amos iii. 7, but not to my great satisfaction, seeming, though covertly, to infuse his own
principles.

---

under his assumed name, to suffer no more than was inflicted in
common upon the nonconforming ministers. He left behind him a
Memoir of his own life, which he entitled *Contemplatio Vitæ Misera-
bilis.* Calamy had the use of it. He died in Newgate in 1684.

In the *Review*, Thoresby speaks of him as being at this time "a
plausible and popular preacher;" and says, that "he was attended by
a numerous auditory." Calamy says nothing of the suspicion at
which Thoresby hints, that he was less orthodox than the nonconforming ministers in general were, but only that "he was inclined to
the notions of the Fifth Monarchists."—*Account,* &c. p. 796.

R ichard Baxter, one of the most eminent of the nonconforming
divines.

18. At the Glasshouse Lecture, forenoon, though it was thronged:* could hear little: at home in the afternoon.

22. I was most part at home, but might have improved time better than I did; towards night, I went with Elkana Boyse to Southwark to see the elephant, &c.

23. Die Dom. Dr. Owen preached very well of the power of Christ; but was sore thronged, that I could neither write nor hear very well.

24. Forenoon spent in doing little or nothing; after dinner went with Mr. T. D. to see the tombs in Westminster Abbey. No quality is exempted from death.

28. Most of the forenoon was near the Temple, where was a terrible fire: it was almost quenched ere I got thither; but yet to me it was so dreadful, that I can scarce suppress the terrible idea of it, especially thinking upon the miserable condition of several grievously wounded, and one laid upon the grass sadly mangled, his face and head so dreadfully burnt, broken, and mishapen, that it could scarcely be perceived to be a face. I saw a man pass his hand from the broken skull through his very mouth, which, with all the aggravating circumstances, struck

---

* Thoresby affected to use the uncouth but forcible expressions of his native tongue. Of the Glasshouse Lecture, I can discover no particular account; but it must have been one of several supported at that time by the nonconforming clergy. He afterwards speaks of hearing Dr. Bates, who was one of them, at the Glass-House.

such a terror into my mind, that I fear, if left to my own poor strength, would have prejudiced me.

29. I spent too much time vainly at home and abroad; was a great part of the day at Guildhall. In the chapel, Dr. Bell preached very honestly for love and amity amongst Christians ; and though we cannot close with their opinions, yet should respect their persons.

30. Die Dom. Mr. Thomson preached (Zach. ii. 10,) that the Lord will take away his staff of beauty, even his word and ordinances, from those that will not be fed by them. Mr. Buck preached very well from 1 Thess. iii. 3, concerning the afflictions of God's people. He was a very young person, and yet preached excellently, which affected me extremely ; and sadly reproved my loss of time that he should be fit so notably to teach others, and I be not fit to hear, much less practise aright.

Oct. 1. Most part of the forenoon at Guildhall, to see the Sheriffs in their pomp and splendid gallantry go to take the oath at Westminster, &c. All the afternoon at home with Mrs. Mitley and Mrs. M. Madox, helping them in cutting paper, &c.

2. Forenoon, heard Dr. Owen preach at Pinnershall ; but to my shame may I confess how many thoughts and imaginations were in me. After dinner, went to the Strand to inquire after crayons, but in vain.

3. Went thither again about crayons, and got

sixty, a set, for 2*s.* 6*d.* and several in besides. Rest of the day at home.

4. At the Hall* in the forenoon, at a fast afterward.

6. At home all day, drawing a picture, writing, and reading; but yet, alas! how little of this time is spent in matters of eternal concernment.

8. At home all the day, mostly imitating a picture—Joseph and his Mistress.

9. Dr. Jacomb, at Pinners-hall, showed, from Job xi. 7, it is impossible for a finite creature to comprehend an infinite God : we ought to bless God for the little knowledge we may have of him, but where he sees good to conceal himself, we should not be sinfully curious. The rest of the day at home drawing. Evening, the Tuesday-night meeting at our house. Mr. Darrington repeated an excellent sermon of Mr. West's: it is a hard matter to perform any good duty and not to overvalue it, but the best are unable to save us, nor were they appointed by God for that end.

16. Mr. Baxter, from the eighth commandment, showed very well the different sorts of stealing : when they overreach in their bargains; entice others to game to get their money; when servants or others are not true in their accounts, but take of their masters' money to maintain their lewd courses; when children get any thing surreptitiously from their parents, &c. These are all forbid, as well as

* Blackwell-hall.

downright stealing.   Afternoon, at Westminster Abbey, transcribing some epitaphs.

20. Called up in the night with the alarm of fire; went with Mrs. M. to give the best assistance we could to a friend without Bishopsgate.

22. Forenoon at home; after, walked to Newington to see the church, and the eminent Dr. Manton's funeral, who, being deservedly styled the King of Preachers, was attended with the vastest number of ministers of all persuasions, &c. that ever I saw together in my life.*

23. Forenoon heard Dr. Bates at Pinners-hall. He showed that it is a duty to exercise faith and patience in our greatest troubles.

28. Die Dom. Mr. Ralphson made a sermon, but, in my opinion, none of the best. His subject should have been, that sufferings precede the glory of God's children; he more than hinted at Christ's personal reign.   Afternoon, Mr. White,† from Phil. ii. 12, showed very well the freeness and immensity of God's grace, but that we should work out our own salvation with fear and trembling; for the operation of God's power and grace do not exclude our industry.

29. I was to see the Lord Mayor's show, where I got a sight of the King, Queen, Duke of York,

---

* In the *Review,* he says, the Ministers walked in pairs, a Conformist and a Nonconformist.

† Jeremiah White, who had been Cromwell's household chaplain. He was preaching at this time on what was, through life, his favourite subject.

Prince of Orange and Princess, Lady Anne, many of the nobility, &c., and have great cause to bless God for preserving me from imminent danger, a great part of the lofts we stood upon falling down, but, through mercy, I got away before the end came down.

31. Mr. Lawrence showed very well the excellency and necessity of Christ's Love.   Afternoon at Hyde Park, to see the soldiers train before the King.

Nov. 2. At the monthly fast, where Dr. Jacomb, from 1 Cor. x. 13, showed very well that God doth not chastise his people according to what he is able, they deserve, or their enemies desire, but in measure, according to his own good pleasure.

4. Die Dom.   Mr. Taylor, from 1 Tim. iv. 18, showed that the refusal of Christ, as he is offered in the Gospel, doth expose sinners to eternal punishment.   Mr. ——, from Matt. xvi. 18, confuted the Popish tenet of Peter's being the foundation of their Popes, and showed that Christ himself is the rock upon which the true church is so built, as that the gates of hell shall not prevail against it.

5. Mr. Lawrence, from Isaiah xxvii. 23, showed very well that God will have a special care and providence in all ages.   Evening, to see the fire-works, &c.

7. All, or most of the day, imitating the pictures of Huss and Jerome of Prague.

8. At the Hall, and at home making Luther and Zuinglius's pictures.

10. At Guildhall hearing some causes tried, and at home made Knox's picture.

13. At Westminister Hall to see the Judges, &c. and at home making Beza's picture, &c.

20. Dr. Bates preached at the Glasshouse, of the New-birth; but I could scarcely hear anything. Rest of the day writing part of a sermon, &c.

27. Mr. Jenkins preached from 2 Cor. ii. 14. In the afternoon at the Tower, to see the French Ambassador's entrance in state, &c.

Dec. 4. Dr. Bates showed, that in a true Christian there must be a perseverance to the end in well doing. At home rest of day. Evening, at the private Meeting, where Mr. West's sermon concerning the knowledge of God was repeated :* he knows himself and every creature, all the good and evil done in the world, the end thou hast in all duties, &c.

25. Cousin D. was pleased to go along with me to several churches to see the tombs, &c.; after dinner to see Cousin Ibbetson, &c.

29. Forenoon at home, writing, &c.; after dinner, at Lord Privy Seal's in Drury Lane, with a letter to Mr. Hurst.

A. D. 1678.

Jan. 1. At the Fast all day. Mr. Lye prayed and preached very well from 1 Cor. xi. 28, showing that Examination is every one's duty. Mr. Slater

---

* It was read from the notes of some private person who heard it. These meetings for repetition formed part of the Puritan religious discipline.

prayed. Mr. Vincent preached from Psalm cxlvi. **10**, that God is the God of Sion ; a glorious and merciful God.

3. Forenoon at home writing, after at Cripplegate Church; vid. a Collection of Epitaphs, for those eminent historians, Fox and Speed.

19. I cannot omit to insert, that on Thursday night, about two or three o'clock, there was a most terrible storm of rain, hail, and violent winds, accompanied with such dreadful thunder and lightning, that some started up half distracted, thinking it to be the day of judgment; it was indeed the most formidable, unparallelled tempest that ever I knew ; the wind blustering and beating great hailstones with such force against the windows and walls as did awaken very hard sleepers with fear.

22. With Mr. Stretton* at a lecture in Cornhill Church, where Mr. Moore, the Lord Chancellor's

---

* Mr. Stretton was one of the confidential friends of Thoresby. Many of his letters will appear among the Correspondence. Their acquaintance began in Thoresby's youth, when Mr. Stretton came to reside at Leeds, as one of the pastors of the Nonconformists of that town, who in 1672, erected the Chapel on the Mill Hill. Mr. Stretton had been educated in New College, Oxford, and was settled at Petworth, in Sussex, when the Act of 1662 required terms of conformity with which he could not comply. He was brought into Yorkshire by Lord Fairfax, the Sir Thomas Fairfax of the Civil wars, in whose family he resided as household Chaplain till the death of his lord, in 1671. Mr. Stretton resided at Leeds five years, during which period there must have been very frequent intercourse between him and the family of Thoresby, who formed part of the congregation of the new chapel, and took a very active share in all its concerns. In 1677, the year in which the Diary commences, Mr. Stretton removed to London,

Chaplain,* from those words, "I can do all things through Christ that strengthens me;" showed very well that Arminianism is heretical, contrary to the Scripture, &c. Afternoon at the Tower to see the crown, armoury, &c. with my cousin Dickenson, to whom I am daily more obliged for repeated favours.

24. Both parts of day at Blackwell-hall; at noon at Bow Church to see Dr. Sancroft confirmed Archbishop of Canterbury. (I think) Dr. Tillotson preached.

Feb. 7. At the Hall all day. Evening, to see them make glasses, &c. which is very ingenious and curious.

10. Die Dom. Mr. Slater, from Psalm ii. 7, showed that the decrees of God do not hinder second contingent causes; they do not discharge man's duty; he must not neglect the means appointed for safety of either soul or body, upon pretence that his time or salvation is decreed of God. Afternoon,

---

where he continued during the remainder of his life, exercising the duties of his ministerial office among the Nonconformists, and bearing his share of the hardships to which they were exposed. He died in 1712.

The Letters which will be hereafter given, illustrate his character and history, and whoever wishes to know more concerning him, may consult Calamy, *Account,* &c. p. 676.

* This was Dr. John Moore, afterwards Bishop of Ely, who was celebrated as a preacher, and truly eminent as a scholar and divine. His name is connected most honourably with the history of literature in England, by the noble library which he collected; bought after his death by King George I. and presented to the University of Cambridge.

Mr. Slater, from Ephes. i. **11,** showed that predestination is of God; and though we should not pry too curiously into it, yet it ought to be preached and maintained, because it is commanded by God, and is so profitable to clear the Deity of Christ, to comfort saints, humble them and excite their love to God, promoting holiness, and procuring patience under afflictions. Then showed what predestination was: it is eternal, flows from the free-will of God, goes down to particular persons, and makes no difference till effectual calling, &c.

12. At Pinners-hall, to hear Dr. Bates; but the place so thronged, that I could hear little.

16. At Westminster, to buy some pictures, &c. After, with Mr. Jos. Wilson, and providing for a Northern journey.

19. At Westminster, the Exchanges and several places, to buy pictures and tokens for relations.

21. Mr. Baxter did very well explain Matth. xxv. 1, 2, &c. opening the customs of the Jews at the solemnization of marriage, &c. and why the kingdom of heaven is likened to ten virgins, and then excellently showed the glorious joys and blessedness of heaven. At the Hall, and within writing and providing for a journey.

22. Left, I think, the finest city in the world, an obliging kind family, &c. where all imaginable advantages for soul and body; but returning home to the dearest, most affectionate, and best of fathers, which doth more than counterbalance all else. Came from London to Royston, wherein experienced the goodness of God, in preservation from innumerable evils.

23. Die Dom. Constrained utterly against my mind to travel from Royston to Stamford, though the Lord's day; but either do so, or be left upon the road about a hundred miles from home and not knowing a foot of the way.

24. From Stamford to Tuxford, and

25. From Tuxford home: all along having large experience of the goodness of God, in preservation from so many evils as might justly have befallen me.

26, 27, 28. In converse with friends and perusing some papers.

March 2. At home righting my papers, &c. that came by London carrier.

3. Die Dom. Mr. Kay,* from Heb. iv. last verse, showed very well that it is a necessary duty to pray with a holy confidence, but that cannot be if we live in the commission of any known sin: we must pray for nothing but what is agreeable to the will of God: our prayers should be affectionate,

---

* The nonconformity of Thoresby was never so decided that he forbore to attend the public services of the Church. We find him almost uniformly, at this period of his life, attending on the Sundays the services of both Conformist and Nonconformist ministers. It is to be observed, that in Thoresby's time there were two churches at Leeds; the parish-church in which were the Vicar and a Lecturer, and St. John's Church, which had been founded in the time of Thoresby's grandfather, by John Harrison, a name held in great veneration at Leeds. Mr. Milner was at this period the Vicar, Mr. Benson the Lecturer, and Mr. Kay the Minister of St. John's.

&c. At noon, Mr. Sharp* showed very well, from 1 Cor. i. 30, that Christ is made wisdom to us by God to salvation, which he improved for reproof and for instruction.

8. Perusing some old parchments with cousin Joshua Thoresby, at home, &c.

15, 16. Both days within, taking down the pictures, beds, &c. in order to the workmen's pulling down the chimneys, to build them more safely, conveniently, &c. of brick.†

29. At Wakefield, but sold nothing.

April 24. A day of humiliation. Mr. Sharp, from

---

* Mr. Sharp was the minister of the Dissenting congregation on Mill Hill. Thoresby appears to have had a very strong attachment to him, and the highest possible admiration of his ministerial abilities. We shall often meet with his name as we proceed.

He had been educated in Clare Hall, Cambridge, partly under Tillotson. He had some preferment in the Church, when the Act of Uniformity compelled him to retire to a private station. He lived with his father, who was the head of the family of the Sharps of Little Horton, in the neighbourhood of Bradford, pursuing his studies diligently till 1672, when the severity of the measures taken to prevent the consolidation of a nonconformist religious interest being a little relaxed, he began to preach in his own house and at Morley. In 1677, he succeeded Mr. Stretton as pastor of the Leeds Presbyterian Nonconformists, and that society had the benefit of his labours till his death in 1693. Thoresby has left a very affecting account of the last moments of Mr. Sharp, of whom, in his *Review*, he says that " he was a most instructive, moving, learned, yet constant preacher," and calls him, it does not appear for what reason, " the honour and reproach of Leeds!"

† At this house, which was in Kirk Gate, Thoresby had his Museum, and spent the whole of his life. It may be seen in the View of Leeds, given in the *Ducatus*, distinguished from the other buildings by a small turret. The house was built by his grandfather, in the reign of James I. when, as he says in his *Review*, " brick was scarcely known at Leeds."

Joel ii. 12, preached suitably for the occasion; showing, that the way to prevent judgments is by repentance.

25, 26, 27. All days at home with the workmen, being from morning to night with them, ever since their coming.

May 12. Mr. Kay, from Rev. ii. 2, treated of Excommunication, showing that it was of divine institution, and practised by the Church in all ages, and should strictly be put in execution against the wicked.

26. Die Dom. Mr. Milner* preached very well; but Mr. Kay, in my slender opinion, too fawningly to please some, showing the ignorance, pride, &c. of heretics. Mr. Sharp, from 1 Cor. i. 30, showed some excellent marks to know whether Christ be our sanctification or not. Can we endure to be searched by God? do we labour to avoid sin? are we truly humble?

June 16. Die Dom. Mr. Kay showed there is no Church without imperfection, and therefore a madness to separate on that account. Afternoon he

---

* Of Mr. Milner, the Vicar, Thoresby has himself given a Memoir in the *Vicaria Leodiensis*, in which he has manifested the esteem in which he held his memory. Mr. Milner held the Vicarage of Leeds till 1689, when, declining to take the oaths to the new Government, he gave up his preferment, and retired to St. John's College, Cambridge, where he died.

Thoresby has recorded in the Preface to the *Ducatus*, that his desire to enquire into the history and antiquities of his native town, was excited when a school-boy, by a remark introduced into a sermon by Mr. Milner, who said that the town was mentioned by the venerable Bede, near a thousand years ago. The allusion must have been to the well-known passage, in which he speaks of the *Regio Loidis*.

preached from ditto text showing, (Rev. ii. 3,) that there is no person so pure but God can see sin in him, instanced in Moses, David, Solomon, Lot, Job, &c. which may teach the best patience in affliction, and the greatest saints have need of mercy. Mr. Sharp, from 1 Cor. i. 30, showed, that if Christ be not our sanctification, it will cause dreadful pangs of conscience in those mansions of torments; to consider the grace we have slighted, the convictions we have stifled, the reproofs we have neglected: this is the time of grace, if we expect salvation; it should raise the heirs of heaven from the dunghill of this world; most live and grow downwards, fixed to the earth as trees, scarce live the life of a moral heathen, much less a sanctified Christian.

17. And so to the end of this month, so thronged for the greatest part with the workmen, and preparing for a voyage, that neglected diary, &c. for which I desire to be humbled.

July 4. I came with my father for Hull, and had a very good journey.

5. Forenoon viewing the town, and with friends, &c. most of the day; about six o'clock came aboard Thomas Scheman's vessel, was a little sick and then somewhat better again.

6. All day at sea, and mostly very sick, but had a very good wind and fair weather.

7. Die Dom. Upon our voyage all day, but through sea-sickness and the depravity of my heart, had not such holy thoughts as ought to have been in

one that has so many mercies daily bestowed upon him. About noon we were encompassed with land, which quitted me of my sickness. About six we arrived at Rotterdam, having had a very prosperous voyage, being but forty-eight hours exactly from Hull to Rotterdam.

8. Most of this week walking about the city, observing their customs, which at first seemed mighty strange, differing so very much from my own country's; not neglecting to look into a book for the language, and being very intent upon it, may perhaps say, without a boast, that I did not slip much time (knowing that it might be but short and was very chargeable in Holland) without observing something or other ; and, if the praises of all the family were not *ex dentibus*, made a considerable progress, which I hope is not noted through pride or vain glory, but somewhat to curb that extremity of ill-conceit which my natural temper inclines me to entertain of every thing I am concerned in, even to the suppressing of endeavours, as impossible (for me) to attain to eminency in any thing that is commendable.

14. Die Dom. Mr. Maden preached twice at the English Church, very well, showing there is mercy in God for penitent sinners, to prevent despair, and *per contra*, there is justice and severity in God to revenge himself of every evil work. At night, I could not but with sorrow observe one sinful custom of the place ; it being customary for all sorts to

profane the Lord's-day, by singing, playing, walking, sewing, &c., which was a great trouble to me,
because they profess the name of Christ, and are of
the Reformed Churches.

16. At Cousin Milner's packhouse before noon,
helping with the cloth, &c.

17. Former part of the day at home, and with
Mr. Charles Greenwood, &c.; about four, took a waggon (with cousin Joseph Milner) for Turgow, and
from thence in the night-boat, where we lay con-
tentedly upon fresh straw, with much company, all
night to Amsterdam, which we discerned.

18. This morning, spent the whole day in company and viewing that famous town, wherein the
stately Stadthouse (having abundance of excellent
workmanship upon very rich marble, black, white,
curiously speckled, &c.) was most remarkable.

19. All this day observing things most remarkable, as the Great Church, the wine-fat, &c.

20. We came this morning, by waggon, to Haar-
lem, a pretty neat town, where (*ut dicitur*) printing
was first invented: from thence, by boat, to Leyden;
the boat is covered, to secure from the injury of
weather, &c., and is drawn by a horse, that goes by
the water-side, and has a cord fastened to it. At
Leyden, we saw the Physic Garden, stocked with
great variety of foreign trees, herbs, &c., and the
Anatomy Theatre, which has the skeletons of almost
all manner of beasts, rare as well as common, and
human of both sexes, &c. There is a most curious

collection of rarities, heathen idols, Indian arrows, garments, armour, money, &c. *Vide* the printed catalogue.

21. Die Dom. An English Minister preached, but very slenderly, I thought, considering it is an university. After dinner we returned, per boat, by way of Delft, (a very pretty town, in the great church whereof we saw the stately monument for Admiral Van Tromp,) to Rotterdam, where we safely arrived this night, being hasted, and thereby constrained to travel upon the Lord's-day, because of the arrival of a ship from England, of considerable concerns, for cousin Milner.

23. At cousin Milner's packhouse, and at the great church, taking Admiral De Witt's epitaph.

24. A little at the packhouse, mostly at home, and at Delfthaven, to see the town, and a fair there.

25. At home most of the day, writing to my dear father, and imitating Mr. Burroughs' picture, &c.

28. (Aug. 7, *stilo novo.*) Die Dom. The Scots Minister, from Ephes. ii. 13, showed very well that unconverted persons are far from Christ, &c.

29. With Mr. Morrison, and at Scheidam with cousin Milner, &c. to bespeak my schoolage and tabling at Mr. Puslewitt's.

Aug. 1. (11th *stilo novo.*) I came to Scheidam, and was boarded at Mr. Puslewitt's, in order to my learning Dutch, &c.

14. Die Dom. I was at the Dutch church at

Scheidam, but could not understand any thing; was not so careful of my thoughts, words, and deeds, as I ought to have been; too compliant with the vices of the place, in not so strictly observing the Sabbath.

15. I went to Mr. William Brents, schoolmaster, in order to my learning the Dutch lingua.

21. Die Dom. At church, but not to the increase of my knowledge. Oh that I may learn to set a watch over my heart! and resolve, Deo juvante, not to yield to the great sin of profaning the Lord's-day.

22, 23, 24, 25, 26, 27. Most of time at school.

28. Die Dom. The Scheidam minister, 'Sam. xv. 16, applied it almost word for word, in reference to a day of thanksgiving for the peace, and the Prince's deliverance, being in great danger by a Frenchman, who came full butt upon him, but was slain by the Heer. So urged they should solicit the Prince for the future not to be too venturesome, and if his valour would not willingly permit it, they should even make him swear he would not expose his Royal person, lest the lamp of Israel should be put out.

29. I went to see the Kirmis at Rotterdam, and was at the fair.

Sept. 1. At school before noon; afternoon at Rotterdam, alone on foot, both going and coming, about six English miles.

4. Die Dom.   At home in the forenoon, at church after.

8. At school in the forenoon, then went to the Maiz-key, and endeavoured to take a prospect of Scheidam.

11. Die Dom.   At church both parts of the day, but could not understand much.

13. Forenoon at school, then writing to my father, was afterwards at the Bove's house, where I first saw the notable invention of a mill to churn abundance of milk at once, and took a rude draught of it.

19 and 20. Both days at school, to understand Dutch, and learn their way of cyphering ; I would hope not inconsiderably.

30. At the school both parts of the day ; the peace was proclaimed from the Stadthouse, and order given that a day should be observed to praise the Lord for it.

Oct. 1. At school forenoon ; after at home writing, and imitating some Dutch money.

2. Die Dom.   At church both parts of the day, the minister pressing it very earnestly upon the people to observe the Lord's-day better, not to go walking, &c., as is too usual with them.

5. This being the day of thanksgiving for the peace, I was at church both parts of the day. Both the ministers showed. very well that it is an unspeakable blessing to have peace, they should therefore be duly thankful for it, and walk worthy of it,

reforming their lives and conversations, else God may have given it in anger. " This people will not be reformed, therefore I will give them over to their own wicked hearts, &c."

12. Being the Verke-mart, was in the town, observing the customs, &c.; after dinner walked to Kettle, to see that town, and one custom of the boors' merriment. *Felix quem faciunt, &c.*

15. At Rotterdam, to buy some things, where found Mrs. Greenwood very ill; and upon my return, Mrs. Helena Puslewitt so at home, taken suddenly.

18. At Rotterdam, to consult cousin Milner, and to fetch home Mrs. Puslewitt from one sick relation (Mrs. G.) to another, her daughter being dangerously ill.

21. At school both parts of the day, though not very well, finding myself somewhat aguishly inclined; at night at church, but what, by reason of the quivering and dithering of my body, and the depravedness of my heart, I could not understand any thing to purpose.

22. Most of the day at home, not caring, or rather daring, to stir out yet.

23. Die Dom. I was at church both ends of day, the minister pressing very earnestly that we should look after the *unum necessarium :* coming home, found Mrs. Helena very ill, near death as we thought, and thereupon at her mother's (a good old gentlewoman, who was a nurse to me in a strange

land in my sickness,) request, went hastily to Rotterdam, about a special concern relating to Mrs. Helena, that she durst not entrust any other with the knowledge of. Returned again, per water, the same night, but suppose increased my indisposition.

24. Yet at school all day, loth to lose more time than I needs must.

25. Somewhat ill with the growings of the ague, which increased all this week, that I stirred not out, (but a little on Saturday,) being very ill, not only with the dithering, but a violent pain in the back of my head, insomuch that I could not turn it without great torment ; but they seldom came together.

30. Die Dom. I had a very sick day altogether. This morning, about nine o'clock, died Mrs. Helena Puslewitt, a well-accomplished young gentlewoman, who had never seen England, yet could have spoke the language as well as if born in it.

Nov. 2. Was pretty hearty, not troubled with the pain in my head ; accompanied the corpse to the grave.

3. At home forenoon ; after, at Rotterdam for a letter from dear father ; now the ague has changed its course, coming in the nights, and being indifferently well on the days.

6. Die Dom. Very ill most of the day, sweating much in bed till four o'clock.

7. Somewhat better.

8. Indifferently when up, but, by reason of bad nights, lost a great part of the forenoon.

9. At Rotterdam, to try the benefit of a walk.

10. Was finely all the day.

13. Die Dom.   Very badly all day, and now the distemper increased daily; so that I was advised to go for Rotterdam, there to have the advice of some able physician, who gave me several bitter potions, which yet nothing assuaged the illness, which grew to such a height, that without help, (and great trouble and pain besides,) I could neither go to bed, nor get up.   I had extremely bad nights, generally lying awake the greatest part of them, and tossing so violently, that it forced such an unmeasurable sweat from me, as is almost inconceivable to those that saw it not; insomuch, as not the sheets only, but blankets and rug, were daily dried by the fire; which violent sweating so weakened me, that I could scarce get up stairs, nor sometimes go over the room without help.   But after about a fortnight's physic, the ague changed, first its hours, and then the day, coming every other day; but then the fit was more violent than before, because two conjoined in one.   So it continued very sore for a week longer, when, by advice, I came for England, it being hoped that my native air, and other means used, might, if any thing, recover me.

On Monday morning, very early, I came from Rotterdam in Mr. George Brook's vessel, and that day was reasonably well till towards evening that we got to sea, where I was extremely sick, but the ague did not disturb me, being expelled by vomiting, which was so terrible for a long time, that it would force my clothes open with the violence of it.   The next day there was very uncertain weather, for the wind that was right for us at first, was turned quite contrary, and was so fickle, that in a few hours it was in all or most of the quarters of the compass; whereupon the Captain, foreseeing the danger, thought to have returned for Holland, and accordingly made a retrograde motion for two or three leagues, but seeing no probability to reach land, with desperate hazard turned about again for England; when quickly after there was no wind at all, but a wonderful calm, which did precede a most terrible storm; for, about four or five o'clock at night, there arose a sudden violent wind, which was the more dangerous because we were, by this time, got partly upon the shore of England, and so in much more danger of the sands and rocks.   They were particularly afraid of a dangerous sand in Yarmouth Roads, whereupon they hoisted up sails a great way southward, and were after, by the extremity of the tempest, driven many degrees northward; and in conclusion, so violently tossed, that the mariners themselves knew not where we were, and as a considerable aggravation, the ship-master was surprised with a sudden and seemingly mortal sickness, that for many hours he was not able to come above deck, or be any ways assisting, &c.   But lest we should be dashed in pieces, we were constrained to let down anchor, even where we supposed ourselves upon a

sand, which we feared, upon the ebbing of the
water, would discover itself to our ruin ; but there
was no other way but by faith to anchor our hopes
upon God. The ship was but crazy, and wanted
several (five or six) inches ballast, which they durst
not stay to take in, for fear of being frozen up. (I
am myself an eye-witness that if the night before
they had not hauled her up to the head, we had
been surrounded with a considerable thick ice, though
there was none to be seen the evening before) ; besides, she was a very high-built vessel, all which
made against us. She was by the storm blown on
one side, so that innumerable boisterous waves did
literally pass over my head ; and thus, for about sixteen hours, we lay in a full expectation of shipwreck,
which nothing but a miraculous deliverance from
God could free us from. The seamen, like Job's
comforters, one following another with evident signs
of ruin, that we lay gasping as it were at the gates
of death a long and dark winter's night, knowing
nothing but we were upon ———— Sand all the
while. The storm abated nothing all night, nor
most of the next day, and the dreadful darkness continued till almost noon. Next day, at noon, we
hoisted up sail, and saw land ; and, which infinitely
more affected me, the Ram in the Bush,—I mean a
delicate large ship, in this very tempestuous storm,
dashed in pieces upon that very sand, which we supposed had been our death-bed, all the night. The
goods were floating upon the sea, two of the masts

broken down by the tempest, a third standing for us to look upon as a monument of God's distinguishing mercy to us. The poor comfortless creatures held out a flag for help,-but alas! I was told that without manifest hazard, or rather certain ruin, we could not do them any good. But afterwards their lives were given them, for a prey; the next (and last vessel this year) from Rotterdam, espied a small flat-bottomed vessel aboard her, and which doubtless first brought off the passengers. The storm not being quite overcome, we were still in danger; and it was Thursday night, very late, ere we arrived at Hull. But, blessed be God! that we did then, even beyond our expectations, land in England; and I desire to own it as an additional mercy, that I had not one fit of the distemper all the time.

On Friday, at Hull. Though crazy, yet had not a fit of my Dutch distemper; but the next day it was redoubled, being very violent, and so it continued every other day for about a fortnight, all the while I was at Hull, which I thought a tedious time without a sight of my dear father; who, alas! knew not where I was, at sea or land, in England or Holland. But I desire to be thankful, that the letter from Rotterdam, which gave account of my setting forth, came not to hand till a letter of my safe arrival was first read, which had been an insupportable terror to my compassionate father, who was extremely full of fears, alarms, and disturbances during that storm, though he knew nothing of my being in it.

Immediately upon receipt of my letter, my good father came in person to Hull ; and what a meeting we had shall never be forgotten by me, who am infinitely unworthy of so good and affectionate a parent, who, though full of rhetoric at other times, could not express his joy otherwise than by tears, (not usual from a soldier) and embraces which would have moved an adamant.

From Hull, we came by coach to York,* and thence on horseback to Leeds ; and, though weak and crazy, yet not by much so ill as was feared. When at home, it came, though gently, every other day almost for a month, but at length upon means (especially camphor and elixir proprietatis) it was quite overcome.

A.D. 1679.

Mar. 2. Die Dom. Mr. Sharp from Matt. xii. 18, showed that we should imitate Christ in showing judgment to others ; long for the calling of the Jews, and fulness of the Gentiles : afterwards rid with much company to York, supposing it an act both of necessity and mercy.

3. Made appearance for the election of the Lord Clifford and Lord Fairfax, as Parliament-men for the County; after dinner rid, to Bulmer, to visit relations.

---

* The following extract from the *Review* is illustrative of the state of society at this period, in respect of the facilities for moving from place to place. " The stage-coaches being given over for this winter, he hired one to conduct me safe; though it proved a mortification to us both, that he was as little able to endure the effeminacy of that way of travelling, as I was at present to ride on horseback."

4. Returned home.

9 and 10. At home both days, imitating Mr. Calamy and Mr. Caryl's pictures: Oh, that I could as well follow their heavenly directions!

April 11. Was a day appointed by Parliament for humiliation and prayer.

17. Went along with my dear father towards Newcastle, and so to Rock and Berwick, experiencing all along the goodness of God in our preservation.

26. We returned safe home, *Laus Deo!*

June 1. Die Dom. Mr. M. made a passing mean sermon, and, as far as I could judge, out of spite, to render Protestant Dissenters odious; and the discourse was much more inconvenient considering the present face of things.

17. Went to the Spaws,* and stayed till Saturday. I went to Knaresborough to see St. Robert's Chapel in the Rock, (of which see my Collections, &c.) and the admirable petrifying well.

25. Taking the inscriptions upon some monuments in Halifax Church.

26. Mostly at Mr. Brearcliff's, and viewing the Antiquities of the place, as the View-tree, with the haliȝ ꝼæx, &c. (vid. Cam. Brit.) and Johannes de Sacro-bosco's hill, &c.†

---

* Now better known by the name of Harrowgate.

† In the *Review,* Thoresby speaks of his journey thus: " I should not mention a short journey to Halifax, but for the sake of my old friend Mr. Brearcliffe, the antiquary, who showed me the tree whereupon tradition says the Virgin's head was hung, whose *holy hair* gave denomination to the town ; and, with more certainty, the hill whereupon the celebrated Johannes de Sacro Bosco made his celestial obser-

July 11. Morning transcribing and epitomizing the famous Lord Bacon's life, &c. ; most of the day busy with the hay : by a good Providence thereby avoiding the Feast at Hunslet (whither I was invited by Uncle Idle) which ended in great discontents, troubles, and misunderstandings betwixt two brothers, T. and M. I. The Lord reconcile them ! &c.

Aug. 4. Perusing Dubartas, translated by Sylvester.

5. The Lives of Walter and Robert Devereux, Earls of Essex : both days very cloudy and rainy, being the Apertio Portarum.

7. All day writing Memoirs of Sir Francis Walsingham, Sir Philip Sydney, Sir Francis Drake.

8. Of Sir Walter Raleigh; rest of day with Mr. Illingworth, (late President of Emanuel College)* who dined here, &c.

9. Writing memoirs of Sir Thomas Overbury and Camden.

vations." Brearcliffe was an apothecary at Halifax, and made a few collections for the history of the place, which were lost before 1710. He died in 1682. Thoresby remembered this early friend when he published the *Vicaria,* and speaks of him as " that industrious and (which is infinitely better) religious antiquary." The spirit of just scepticism and of critical enquiry, which has made its way into the study of topographical antiquities, would have led this early antiquarian and his zealous pupil to have rejected at once both the fables with which they amused themselves. Mr. Watson has shown that there is no reason to suppose that de Sacro Bosco had any connection with Halifax : but it was reserved for a later and abler antiquary to destroy the foundation of the story of the Virgin and the Holy Hair, by bringing to light the true etymology of the name of Halifax.

* This was another of Thoresby's acquaintance among the Nonconforming Ministers. Wherever his name occurs in Thoresby's Papers, it is generally accompanied with the addition of " late Pre-

11. Collecting Memoirs of Bishop Andrews, and Mr. Sutton.

12. Of Dr. Donne, and Sir Henry Wotton; and at Uncle's with Mr. Illingworth.

14. At home all day writing, viz. George Duke of Buckingham, and some of Dr. Wild's Poems; which pious and ingenious poet died this last week, at London.*

26. All day within: and most of it was reading the Trials of the Popish Conspirators. Blessed be God, for disappointing their wicked enterprises!

Sep. 13. Went with my dear father to York, and from thence to Bulmer.

14. Die Dom. Mr. Hasle endeavoured (though, alas, slenderly in comparison of the teaching we eujoy) to show the mercy of God towards his creatures.

15. Was up by three in the morning for York, where the Lords Fairfax and Clifford joined for Knights of the Shire; Sir John Kay opposed; 'twas put to the poll in the country.

I took the inscription upon Mrs. Middleton's (a great benefactress) hospital, and returned safe home.

18, 19, 20. All the days with the workmen at the

---

sident, &c.;" but Calamy, who gives some account of him, speaks of him only as Fellow. See *Account*, p. 84. *Continuation*, p. 116.

* In the declined taste in English Poetry, when the fresh and living stream of poesy which had flowed in the Elizabethian reign was entirely neglected, such writers as Dr. Wild had a high degree of celebrity, and their works constituted the staple of the readers of Poetry. In a Manuscript Obituary of a contemporary and friend of Thoresby his death is thus noticed: " 1679. Dr. Robert Wild, of Oundle, *our famous English Poet*, died, of two or three hours' sickness, about August 17, aged 69."

garden; in the evenings, mostly perusing Clarke's Martyrology, and epitomizing most of the Lives adjoined; viz. Dr. Collet, Bishops Coverdale and Sands, Mr. Greenham, &c.

25, 26, 27. With the workmen all day : evening generally transcribing Memoirs of Mr. Bennet, Lambert, Barns, &c.

Oct. 13. Attending the funeral of Mr. Samuel Bradley; dead in the prime of his days. Mr. Benson, 1 Cor. xv. last verse, treated of the immortality of the soul. At night, reading the Sad Estate of Francis Spira.

Nov. 5. Mr. Sharp from Psm. cxxiv. 6, showed very well that we have infinite reason to bless God for his deliverances to this sinful nation, &c. But, alas! these national mercies, for which I desire to bless God, are all embittered by my personal affliction, that dispensation which even presses me down to the very pit; a lamentable affliction that has laid my superlative comfort in the dust.

6, &c. Spent the latter part of this week, as the beginning, and as the end of the last, in weeping, lamentation, and mourning for my inestimable loss of the best of fathers.

12. As to my health, which was not only impaired but almost destroyed by continued and excessive mourning for my irreparable loss; it is now much better, the pains of the stone and strangury (which till then I never knew the terrors of,) are abated.

12. At the funeral of my cousin Robert Cloudsley, who lived to a good old age and died happily; he much lamented the death of my dear father, and though weak yet came to comfort me, and when urged to take gloves refused, saying, he should be heartily sorry to live so long in this world as to wear them.*   Oh, happy men, that thus die in the Lord!

25. Mr. Sharp, Jer. xxx. 7, showed, that it is really to be feared there is a great day coming upon us of these lands, that, in all probability, may exceed in terror that of the Jews; cruelty being then in its infancy, which is now strangely improved.   Now the reasons why such sad and terrible days may be expected are, 1st. Because it hath been the lot of all the Protestant Churches in the nations about us, the Netherlands, Valteline, Savoy, the whole Empire, Germany, Bohemia, Ireland, Scotland, and why should impenitent England be left unpunished? the very dregs seem to be reserved for us.   2d. None of the neighbouring nations have enjoyed those mercies that we have.   Such famous, faithful ministers; such multitudes of professors; such uninterrupted prosperity; such wonderful discoveries, and yet we walk unworthily, which argues that God

---

* The name of Cloudsley became extinct at Leeds, by the death, without issue, of Mr. Benjamin Cloudsley in 1753.   Thoresby's grandmother was of this family; and the Editor of this Diary would be permitted to add, that by descent from the Cloudsleys he can claim for himself a distant consanguinity with the Topographer of Leeds.

designs rather to pluck us down than build us up.
3rd. The schisms, heresies, divisions amongst us
testify against us, and forego our ruin, as in Jerusalem before its desolation, in Germany before those
wars, and in France before the terrible massacres:
Rev. Moulin complaining that the ministers had
forsaken old truths, and affected new niceties in
religion. 4th. We have not been profited by the
judgments already inflicted upon us; the pestilence
that swept away thousands, and the destroying hand
of God in our own families have yet left us an impenitent people. How few have heard the voice of
the rod! the generality, instead of repenting, impute
all to the fanatics, and then *Christiani ad Leones*,
fine and confine, raise, ruin, banish them. Lastly,
things seem at present to ripen towards utter confusion, and hasten fast to the greatest day that ever
was foretold by the slaying of the two witnesses.

A. D. 1680.

Jan. 1. Mr. Sharp, from Jer. xxx. 7, showed what
reason we have to expect and therefore provide for
such a day as the Prophet speaks of: how many
present themselves as a new year's gift to Satan by
their vain mirth and jollity upon this day, which
custom was derived from the Heathens, who then
sacrificed to their idol Janus: but we should labour
to present ourselves as a spotless sacrifice to God.

14. At court most of the forenoon about the poor
pensioners' business, for whose advantage my dearest

father was pleased to take the trouble of being treasurer. Dined with several friends at old cousin Milner's, rejoicing with him for his son's return; but came away timely, being to give in the accounts at the Mayor's, which I did accordingly, and Mr. L. was substituted in my father's place.

22. At Wakefield, returned early, but in a sad, melancholy and troubled humour, the remembrance of my inexpressible loss seizing deeply upon my spirits; went to bed with wet cheeks and a sad heart, dreamed troublesomely and somewhat remarkably about following my dear father to his long home.

24. After dinner rode to Beeston to see the most dreadful spectacle that was ever beheld in these parts. Mr. Scurr, his mother, and a maid servant, every one burnt to death last Thursday, at night between eleven and one o'clock, but whether accidentally, or designedly by the malice of some, (whom perhaps he was in suit with) is yet uncertain. The old gentlewoman was most burnt; her face, legs, and feet quite consumed to ashes, the trunk of her body much burnt, her heart hanging as a coal out of the midst of it! Part of his face and arms, with the whole body unburnt, but as black as the coals, his hands and feet quite consumed. Very little of the maid was to be found, only I saw her head; a most piteous sight! Some observe all their skulls are broken, as it were, in the same place, which causes some to suspect it is wilfully done; but if so,

the Lord will reveal it, so that in all probability those inhuman murderers may have their deserts in this life.*

25. Die Dom.   Mr. Kay, Coloss. iii. 12, discoursed very well of good works : though faith be the life of the soul, yet good works are as the breath by which it is perceived ; and showed, as a motive to charity, that to lay it out upon pious occasions is the only means to secure any thing to us : we shall never be poorer for what is expended in pious uses. Mr. Whateley, late minister of Banbury, eminent for his charity, seriously protested, that after he begun his charitable course he had much increased his estate ; formerly he was often forced to borrow 10*l.* and could not make both ends of the year meet, but after could have lent 100*l.*, and imputed it to the blessing of God upon his charity—he gave the tenth part, both of his spiritual and temporal means, to the poor.   The other instance was Dr. Hammond, that worthy assertor of alms, who was taxed for rather overdoing in pity and compassion, yet increased so that he died worth 1500*l.* &c.   Mr. Sharp, Matthew xii. 21.

Feb. 7. Perusing authors concerning Bradford the meekest, and Ridley the learnedest Marian martyr.

9. Mostly employed with aunt Alice ; went to

---

* These suspicions were but too well founded. Thoresby, as we shall see, was present at the execution of one of the murderers. Mr. Scurr had been the minister at Beeston during the Commonwealth. A particular account of this tragical event may be read in the *Loidis and Elmete* of Dr. Whitaker, p. 102.

Wakefield with her, and thence with cousin Benjamin Wordsworth to Swaith Hall.

11. Rid with cousins to Barnsley.

12. To Wakefield, and so, *Laus Deo!* returned well home again; but though very kindly entertained and reasonably cheerful when abroad, yet a trouble, sorrow, and a deep sense of my present doleful, fatherless condition almost overwhelmed me at my return, mourning heavily all night long, and,

13. This day likewise, even to excess, and the prejudice of health.

March 4. At Wakefield, but returned soon to Holbeck, and found uncle much better, *Laus Deo!* Perusing of Philpot, &c. Lord! imprint the good examples of thy faithful servants so fully in my mind, that I may imitate them in my life; and if that bloody religion should, as a plague for our sins, be again established in these lands, good Lord! for Christ's sake, strengthen me by thy grace, that if thou callest for it, I may cheerfully suffer for thy name and truth's sake.

10. About six this morning, my dear uncle Thomas Idle departed this life, changing this frail for an immortal, glorious life: it was the greatest satisfaction imaginable to me to observe, as his bodily strength decayed, so his faith increased; expressing himself very feelingly and comfortably, that he was even unwilling to abide any longer in this world, that was so full of trouble and sorrow; and protesting, and it was (as himself said) no time to

dissemble at death, that to his knowledge he had never in his whole life wronged any man. He carried himself with extraordinary patience; and my good aunt Lucy coming in, he shook her by the hand, blessing God for that grace of patience now in his greatest extremity, saying, that all his life long he dreaded the want of patience to undergo these pangs of death. But now he was very remarkable for it, called his children and myself, gave good advice, testifying his great love and affection to me, &c. He called for all the servants, and gave them seasonable advice.

12. All day at Holbeck, assisting to my utmost at dear uncle's funeral; but such vast multitudes, what bidden and what unbidden, that abundance of confusion must unavoidably happen. (Of 130 dozen of cakes not one left.)

14. Die Dom. Mr. Kay, Coloss. iii. 15. Mr. Sharp from . . . preached extraordinarily well, as a funeral sermon for dear uncle; but extreme sorrow, partly for uncle, but most violent in remembrance of my dear father, would not permit me to write. He showed, that it is the greatest comfort and support under the afflicting hand of God, to consider that Christ will bring with him, at the great day, all our dear relations that now sleep with him.

20. Reading a funeral Sermon for the Countess Dowager of Warwick, (deceased April, 1679,) a most virtuous, religious lady: I was mightily taken with her pious Diary, religious life, heavenly meditations, &c.

26. A great part of the day with Dr. Johnston, of Pontefract, who gave me good advice as to my health, and encouragement as to my studies; was pleased to adopt me his son as to antiquities.*

* This is the first occurrence of a name of great note in that department of historical literature, in which the name of Thoresby has a conspicuous place. Johnston had succeeded to Dodsworth as the *princeps* of Yorkshire collectors; and, after the manner of the old alchymists, he adopts this young and zealous aspirant as his *son*. There was something in the character and conduct of Johnston which diminished the respect to which his zeal and assiduity might have entitled him. Thoresby intimates that this adoption was not a pure instance of disinterested regard, or even of that exultation which is sometimes felt, when one who has laboured hard in some peculiar department of literature, meets with a rising genius in his own line. But there is a pleasure in observing how, for the perfecting of designs which require the combined labours of several minds and those existing in successive generations, that advantage may be taken of facilities of obtaining knowledge which are offered at one period and denied at another, Nature raises a succession of men with predispositions which appear to be irresistible, to enquiries which, to the common mind, appear the least inviting. Dodsworth was born in 1585. Johnston in 1627. Thoresby in 1658. The æras of Torre and De la Pryme nearly correspond with that of Thoresby. Burton and Drake were later. But after Johnston, there was no one whose ambitiou reached to the illustration of the whole of that great county, till Brooke, who was born in 1748, and who brought as much enthusiasm and knowledge, and more of taste, to the office, than any who had laboured before him.

The name of Dr. Johnston will often occur in the Diary, and many of his letters will be found among the Correspondence. A few notices of his varied and unhappy life, chiefly collected from unpublished sources of information, may here with propriety be annexed.

His father, a native of Scotland, was a minister in the English church, and, at the time of his death, the rector of Sutton-upon-Derwent. He seems to have resided at one period of his life at Reedness, in the marshy parts of Yorkshire; for there, I believe, Dr. Nathaniel Johnston was born, and that he was baptized in the church of Whitgift. Early in life he married and settled at Pontefract, in the practice of the profession of medicine, to which he had been edu-

31. At Woodkirk, Howley Hall, and Batley
Church, writing the epitaph of the famous Sir John
Savile.

cated; and at Pontefract, a place peculiarly adapted to stimulate and
to encourage a spirit of antiquarian research, he continued to reside
during the long period of his abode in Yorkshire. His wife was a
daughter and co-heiress of the Cudworths, of Eastfield, in the parish
of Silkston, an ancient family of the better sort of yeomanry, or the
lesser sort of gentry. His practice was extensive, lying amongst the
superior gentry of the West Riding. But an attachment to historical research seems to have gradually weaned him from his profession; and he did not find, like his more illustrious contemporaries
Mead and Sloane, that it was possible to be successful and eminent
in both.

I have seen nothing to show the precise period of his leaving Yorkshire: but he went to reside in London, and there he was for ever
giving out that he had methodized his Collections for the History of
the County, and intended to publish them. The work was to be in
ten volumes. De la Pryme thus speaks of him in his MS. Diary,
under November 11, 1696:—" Dr. Johnston, after thirty years' labour in writing his History of Yorkshire, gives us now some hopes to
see it brought to light. The Doctor is exceeding poor; and one
chief thing that has made him so was this great undertaking of his.
He has been forced to skulk a great many years, and now he lives
privately with the Earl of Peterborough, who maintains him. He
dares not let it be openly known where he is!" The Earl of Peterborough was the Antiquarian Earl, whom, perhaps, he assisted in the
composition of the History of the House of Mordaunt. From this
obscurity he seems not to have emerged; and I had in vain sought
for the year of his decease, till I found in an obscure memorandum
of Thoresby, that he died in 1705.

It is remarkable that the published writings of Dr. Johnston show
so little of the curious line of research in which he was so long employed. They are dull, not because they are composed of a dry detail of facts, but from the absence of facts. His History of Yorkshire,
if we may judge by the specimen of it to be found among the *Miscel-
laneous Tracts* of Bowyer, the learned Printer, would have abounded
in detached facts; but there would have been little of inference, or
of the *callida junctura*. Of his manuscript remains, much may be
seen in Dr. Bernard's *Catalogue of the Manuscripts of England;* in
Mr. Gough's *British Topography*, and in Mr. Nichols's *Literary Anec-*

April 4. Die Dom.   Mr. Kay, Colos. iii. **16,** showed, that we ought to attend to the word of God with reverence and attention ; to hearing it preached and reading it ; but most persons let their Bibles lie moulding, like old almanacks, whilst play-books and romances are worn out with their diligent perusal.

5. Making ready writings, &c. for the North ; after dinner set forth with uncle Michael Idle, and got well to Boroughbridge.

6. Thence to Northallerton, and so to Darlington, expecting there to have met with Captain Widdrington.

7. Up early in the morning to Durham, and so having dispatched that business with him, and visited relations, got well to Newcastle.   Newcastle was the place formerly much delighted in, and earnestly desired, for my dear relations there ; but now, it is an aggravation to my sorrow, to remember past comforts and present slights.

8. Returned from Newcastle to Darlington, and thence to Topcliffe ; and next day,

9. Home.   I found my poor desolate family all

dotes and *Illustrations of Literary History.*   There was once a scheme for placing them in the Library attached to the Minster at York ; but it was at a time when there was little of the spirit of historical curiosity among the Yorkshire gentry, and they were suffered to pass into private hands.   The purchaser was a man who knew how to value them, and who saw that their only value to himself or to the world, would arise out of the use of them for purposes of topographical illustration.   It is to be regretted, that a spirit like his has not always presided over these remains.

well; but, alas! the fresh remembrance of our un-
utterable loss is most bitter, and almost insupportable.

13. At the stationer's, &c.; afterwards with Mr.
B. D. collecting for worthy Mr. Sharp; ditto at
Holbeck, &c.

20. Most of the day with some York friends at
Lawyer Bathurst's, &c.; spent too much time idly,
neither reading nor writing.

25. Die Dom.   Mr. Kay, Colos. iii. 16, 17, showed the necessity of singing psalms; but though it
has formerly been the constant practice of this family, and I hope in time will be again, yet, I must
confess the neglect of it now, it being an aggravation of sorrow, and bringing my inexpressible loss
more freshly to remembrance. Methinks, I hear
his very voice, that with renewed pangs I am constrained to crouch to the bottom of the pew, and
there vent my sorrow in plenty of tears; so that,
never yet, to my shame do I record it, was I able to
sing one line in public or private.

28. From morning to evening with Bulmer friends
at Holbeck, writing about the appraisement, &c.,
thereby missing a good lecture sermon, though sore
against my mind.

30. Some miles out of town at noon; spent rest
of the day with uncles at Alderman Hicks', but the
conclusion of the day was very bad, with hasty
words, and falling out betwixt relations, and though
not much concerned myself, yet was much troubled

for others; and now the loss of that blessed peacemaker is sadly evident, who, with admirable prudence, prevented such clashings.

May 1. I rid to York with uncle Jeremiah and cousin Susan of Holbeck, and from thence to Bulmer, and though late, got well thither.

2. Die Dom. Mr. Hasle preached honestly, but, in my slender judgment, far off so well and learnedly as he, whose worthy labours we usually enjoy : spent too much of the day in frivolous visits and discourse, more fit for any other than the Sabbath-day. Evening, very happily lighted upon a sermon of worthy Mr. Sharp's, that I had writ for cousin Eliz. Idle, repeated it with joy, and retired into the garden, where 1 had more satisfaction in half an hour's meditation, &c. than in all the day besides.

3. At Stittenham, the ancient seat of the Gowers, a knightly family.

4. Rid with uncle Idle and cousin Myers (the lord of that manor,) to Allerthorp : learnt a piece of law from a learned charge given the jury by Mr. Langley; was nobly entertained, and had pleasure enough, but none so great or refreshing as the happy discourse in our return with good cousin Myers, who declared his very heart to me, and was very importunate for direction about the main business. I was extremely glad to hear such discourse, and as my love to him is infinitely increased upon this account, the Lord grant that both our affections may be increased heaven-wards.

5. I returned to York, consulted Lawyer Rookby* about the northern business, dined at cousin Thoresby's, got well home, and in good time.

6. Went to Wakefield; had nothing of business; under some discouragements from want of trade.

17. Began our northern journey, had uncle Michael Idle's company, and carried pretty sister Abigail (her dear father's picture) along with me, and got safe to Darlington, forty long miles, and yet she not at all weary.

19. From Newcastle we rid to Morpeth, and thence to Alnwick, where we lodged.

20. Rid to my estate at Rock, dispatched our business, though in haste, and returned to Alnwick again that day.

21. From thence to Newcastle, where, having stayed three or four hours, we rid to Durham; there I got a sight again of my poor sister. Natural affections wrought sore, and she could not forbear weeping at our parting, which made my very heart bleed within me, and my too violent affections were so strong, that I think I slept not an hour all night, the inconveniences whereof I found the next day.

22. From thence to Northallerton, and having dried us there (it being a most stormy rainy day,) to Boroughbridge, where lodged all night.

23. Die Dom. Rid to Aldborough to church, where a young man treated of the Sacrament, alas!

---

* Afterwards Sir Thomas Rokeby, and a Judge.

very obscurely, full of high words, to a poor un-
learned congregation ; but this was the best we
could have in these parts. It was my great trouble
that, because of the bad weather, and worse way, we
could not reach home yesterday ; but imagining I
might spend the evening in some good manner there
with my desolate family, and being sensible of the
many inconveniences that would certainly attend us
at the inn, in profane company, was willing to ride
home after sermon, but was troubled to find my expectations in some measure frustrated, by the unseasonable visit of some, neither relations, nor very
great friends.

24. Spent most of this day in advising about
affairs, visiting some friends, having others to dine
with me ; so that too much of the time was spent in
idle, unprofitable talk.

25. About some necessary, though small occasions, in the forenoon ; but too much precious time
spent afterwards in visits, and converse with friends,
though, blessed be God ! not in bad company.

27. Rid to Wakefield, had some little business,
but was rather too compliant in the company.

29. Very busy in the forenoon, writing to London
and to the North, and sending away some cloth, per
carrier ; but the latter part of the day not so well
employed ; for, coming home from a visit, unhappily
found some company, (by the means of my house-
keeper, cousin S. I.) to my great dissatisfaction, too
merry for our circumstances, too many profane

words, and much precious time spent idly if not sinfully.

30. Die Dom. In the morning under much trouble and dissatisfaction for the aforementioned business, the remembrance whereof was very bitter and accompanied with great plenty of tears.

31. Most of the day within, imitating the picture of the virtuous Lady Mary, Countess Dowager of Warwick:

June 1. At home till five, writing and abbreviating the life of that incomparable lady; and here I cannot but record my hopes are that I have found considerable advantage by reading and epitomising the lives of pious and religious persons.

2. Mr. Sharp dined with me, for whose pious advice I hope I shall have cause to bless God to all eternity.

3. Within till five, epitomizing Bishop Cousins's life and drawing his picture; he was a noble benefactor, and I hope a more sincere Protestant than some would insinuate.

4. At Mr. Milner's at a conference in order to the sacrament.

12. Morning we set forwards, viz. uncle M. Idle, cousin S. Idle and maid, with myself; got well to Bawtree, where lodged.

13. Die Dom. Rid thence to Tuxford (though I thought it had not been so far) and there heard Mr. Charlesworth, who made a very honest though not very elegant discourse; and thence rid to

Newark : the maid unfortunately got a grievous fall ; perhaps we may read the crime, travelling upon the Lord's-day, in the punishment, but was not much worse.

14. Thence to Wansford, near which town a cart driving furiously down the hill, hit the maid's horse and caught hold of her clothes, but got her not under the wheel, though at the very door of death : thence to Stamford, and so to Stilton, where we lodged.

15. Thence to Royston, and thence to Ware, where stayed all night.

16. To London by noon. Afternoon at Captain Widdrington's about the business which chiefly occasioned this journey.

17. Heard the famous Mr. Baxter preach, was pleased with the very sight of that worthy good man, but lost the advantage of his sermon by business and diversions ; was at Captain W.'s and then at Westminster.

20. Die Dom. Heard Mr. Slater in the forenoon, and Mr. Stretton in the evening ; but, alas, being involved in so much business and company, had not the time, or rather improved it not so well as to write the heads, whereby lost most of the advantage.

21 to 26. Every day employed either about my concerns at Rock with Captain Widdrington, or visits at Mr. Stretton's and good cousin Dickenson's, or buying books and pictures of good or great persons, and can better acquit myself for going with

good company to see Paradise, where multitudes of
beasts and birds are lively represented both in shapes
and notes, than in going to see a play, whither curiosity carried me, but fear brought me back.   It was
the first, and I hope, will be the last time I was
found upon that ground.

27. Die Dom.   Heard the famous Dr. Stillingfleet in the forenoon; Mr. Pemberton in the afternoon, and Mr. Stretton in the evening; but, as last
Lord's-day, lost most of the advantage for want of
writing the heads.

Most of this week spent in business with Captain
Widdrington, Sir Richard Stott, &c. the rest in
visits, buying things, transcribing monuments in
Westminster Abbey, in which I can better excuse
myself than in staying so late on Saturday night at
Captain Widdrington's, where was too great plenty
of the strongest liquors, which afflicted me by their
conquest of my friend, which being partly on my
account, I desire may be for my humiliation.

July 4. Die Dom.   Went to Newington-green to
hear Mr. Joseph Boyse preach, which I rejoiced in as
the first-fruits of our generation ;* he showed very
accurately our happiness under the Gospel in com-

---

* Boyse and Thoresby were born at Leeds in the same year. He
was educated for the ministry, among the Nonconformists, in the
academy which was conducted by Richard Frankland, one of the
silenced ministers. He was afterwards of Dublin, minister of a dissenting congregation there, and the author of many controversial
works, a catalogue of which may be seen in the " Biographia." Many
of his letters to Thoresby will appear in the Correspondence.

parison of those under the law. I came back with ditto, good friend, to hear Mr. Charnock and Mr. Stretton in the evening, from whom and family, especially my dearest cousin, I parted with a sad heart.

5. Came from London to Cambridge, where observed some stately buildings and curious libraries.

6. From Cambridge to Bridge Casterton.

7. Thence to Barnby-moor, and,

8. Thence home.

9. At Mr. Boyse's, and about some necessary affairs; but in the evening much disturbed by the ingratitude of some persons, that I expected better things from.

10. Writing letters about some urgent business; at Holbeck with Aunt; and other visits took up the rest of the day.

17. Writing, and taken up with stating Rock accounts. Lord, help me to be the better for the greater plenty and prosperity that I enjoy; and not like the worldling, either to set my heart thereon, or be more negligent in spiritual things.

18. Die Dom. Mr. Sharp, Psalm cxxii. 6. Shake off your security; never since the establishment of Protestancy amongst us, was there such grounds of fear. Be of public spirits; look up to the gasping estate of the Protestant religion with an affected eye. 1. Consider the example of God's children in all ages. David, in his greatest agonies for those two great sins, Psalm li, cries out " Lord, build up

the walls of Jerusalem.   2. Consider your near relation to Jerusalem : all our private cases, like as the several cabins in a ship, are interested in the Church's prosperity.   Jerusalem's cause is the cause of God, and therefore it shall certainly prevail at last.   Who so hard-hearted as not to throw in some prayers to the churches; who cannot bestow a benevolence of tears, or levy a subsidy of sighs for Jerusalem's sake?

19.   Forenoon, with J. Robinson, about Northern tenants, and writing to Captain Widdrington, Cousin Dickenson, &c.   After dinner, at Mr. Murfield's with young Mr. W. ; and evening with other company about some business, which, notwithstanding, was put off till

20.   At Widow D.'s, lent out some money ; afterward, with the said Londoner, and at Alderman Sykes'; but alas! spent the whole day in visits, &c.

21.   Afternoon, at Mr. Morris's banquet, had some learned company, the Vicar and two antiquaries, that made the entertainment abundantly more acceptable.

24.   Writing *ut prius*, and with my kind friend, Mr. Henry Fairfax, having the honour to be sent for by my Lord Fairfax and Squire Palmes, who expressed great kindness to me for my dear father's sake :—the Lord give me wisdom in all things.

27.   About some business all day till four, and then took horse with Uncle T. to York, and so to Stitnam that night.   Blessed be God for his preservation! the waters being very great and dangerous.

28. Forenoon, looking over Sir Thomas Gore's library, the best furnished with ancient fathers and commentators, both Popish and Protestant, upon the Scriptures, of any that I have seen;* the rest were mostly on Medicine, for which Sir Thomas was justly famous.   Then at Bulmer, to visit relations there; designed home, but was beat back by a violent shower, which wetted me through all in a small time.

29. Came from Bulmer to York ; after business dispatched, went to the Hall, where one Twing, a Popish priest, was upon his trial, found guilty and condemned accordingly, but not upon the account of religion, but treason,—saying at a consult at Sir Tho. Gascoyne's, at Barnbow, that if they lost this opportunity of killing the King they could never expect such another.   After at the Minster, transcribing the monuments of Archbishops Hutton, Matthews, and Frewin.   Evening, to see the Manor.

30. Dispatched my business; went to the hall where Lawyer Ingleby was tried, but before concluded,† took horse and got very well home.

Aug. 1. Die Dom.   Mr. ——— from a good text, " Cease to do evil, learn to do well :" made no extraordinary matter ; declaring positively, in many per-

---

* Sir Thomas Gower, the second Baronet, grandfather to the first Lord Gower. Stittenham has long been abandoned by its native lords.

† Ingleby, more lucky than Thweng, was acquitted. He was made one of the Barons of the Exchequer, by King James, in the year of the Revolution.

sons' sentiments, for downright Arminianism. Mr.
Kay, jun. in the afternoon, made a better discourse
from Prov. xxviii. 14, showing, that though nothing
can be hid from the all-seeing eye of God, yet poor
sinful creatures are too apt to endeavour it the best
they can. Mr. Sharp, Hos. xiv. 4, made an excellent discourse, showing that sin is the soul's sickness,
and Christ alone can be the soul's physician :—for use ;
no wonder then, that God is angry with these nations
so full of backsliders. It was the observation of a
famous Scotchman, which though at first it look like
a scandal, will upon a serious consideration be too
evident a truth ; that there can be no doctrine so
monstrous, but it will find its followers in England ;
the newer the doctrine, the nearer they think themselves to Heaven ; and, indeed, most are too like
sheep in this respect, that are observed to eat most
greedily of the grass that rots them.

11. Writing to London ; sent for out ; (as part of
yesterday forenoon ;) endeavouring to make peace betwixt Cousin Ibbetson, of London, and Cousin Cloudsley, of Leeds, which I hope was effected, so that we
all dined together at Cousin C's.

12. Almost all the day transcribing my dear Uncle
Thomas Idle's Will, especially what relates to his
benefaction to Holbeck Chapel.

15. Die Dom. Mr. Milner, vicar, preached extraordinary well from Jonah ii. 2, showing that our
prayer must be fervent, if we would prevail for mercy.
If all Conformists preached thus, excellent, sound

divinity, and practical, as this good man, who could be against hearing them? But, alas! in the afternoon, Mr. Medcalf made sad dull, nay, I doubt, profane matter of it; using malicious expressions to render the poor Nonconformists ridiculous, &c. " Do but hire a stage," saith he, " and I will find the actors; the precise fellow, that like the Pharisees, delight in long prayers, &c. and felt the pulse of a holy sister." Mr. Sharp did excellently improve his former doctrine, that those that seek the Lord shall find; by way of reproof: 1. to those that cannot seek God, they are so ignorant: 2. those that will not serve God, let things go which way they will: 3. those that spend their time in seeking other things, and so continue till the cold grave devour their body, and hot Tophet burn their soul: 4. seekers of pleasure: 5. those that desire the name, rather than the thing; religion being now-a-days too like a dial; when the sun shines, all will look upon it, but when that is down, all is done: those hypocrites are (as one glosses upon it) the freeholders of hell.

16. Morning, writing the heads of yesterday's excellent sermons, and reading the admirable letter of the pious Countess of Warwick to the Lord Berkeley. Lord, help me to follow such excellent directions!—was in a contemplative humour; much affected that this very day completes twenty-two years since I came into this sinful world; was afterwards about some business, and was much troubled at the anger I was oppressed with, by the uncivil and unjust carri-

age of one I expected his principles should have
taught better.` Oh, the various crosses that attend
us in this world! I have lost this friend by too
great kindness : I had both money and a friend, but
now can procure neither in that place.

20. Writing to the North, and to Cousin Dickenson of London. Evening took horse, and rid with
Cousin Ruth to Pannel, whither, though late enough,
and in the dark, we got very well.

21. Went early to the Spaws ; drank of both waters freely, and hope for benefit by them.

22. Die Dom. Designed for Knaresborough Church,
but prevented by the effect of the waters.

23. Drunk the waters before noon ; after rid to
ditto Church, and took the inscriptions of the monuments of the Slyngsbys ; much pleased with the
serious humour of one, where, above all, stood an
angel, with a trumpet, calling *Venite ad judicium.*
Under the name and titles of the Knight in his
winding-sheet, *Omnia Vanitas!*

24. Drinking the waters ; rest of day in company, mostly with Dr. Hook's son and daughter,
walking, &c.

25. Drinking the waters early, and returned to
hear Mr. Sharp's lecture ; afterwards visiting Mr.
W.'s, and a-walking with Mr. Wispelaer, and spent
most of the day in that manner, which I hope may
be for my health ; but must be cautious, lest I
gratify the flesh to the detriment of the spirit.

26. Rid to Wakefield, and returned well in good

time; the greater mercy, because in the evening was such thunder and lightning as would have startled the stoutest heart, so extremely violent, and after such a dreadful manner, as some in a fright were ready to judge the approach of the day of doom, and accompanied with such a quantity of rain, that, having my boots on, was forced to wade to the midleg hy the houses, where is no water at other times, in my return from Mr. E. H.'s.

28. Writing to London, and with tenants; but chiefly epitomizing the life of that Pillar of Justice, Judge Nichols; but I doubt my affections are too much bent upon books, which, though not unlawful, yea, in some respects commendable in themselves, yet I am afraid an immoderate love to them doth withdraw my affections too much from more practical duties.

31. After dinner had the honour of a visit from Mr. Henry Fairfax and Mr. Corlas; (the virtuous Lady Barwick's* chaplain ;) was much satisfied with their excellent company.

September 1.　Mr. Sharp's lecture; showing, that the time of a people's enjoying the means of grace is their morning, and fitly compared thereunto, in

---

* The relict of Sir Robert Barwick, of Tolston, Recorder of York, and daughter of Walter Strickland, of Boynton, Esq. Her only son was drowned in the Wharf, anno 1666, in the prime of life, and her only surviving daughter was married to Henry, the fourth Lord Fairfax, of Cameron. Thoresby often speaks gratefully of the respect which was shown him by the whole family of Fairfax. Lady Barwick died at the age of 81, October 4, 1682.

respect of its imperfection in respect of heaven, which is the day, and its shortness. Showed far- ther, that the more light God doth vouchsafe, the shorter usually the time is: the old world had 120 years, but those in the wilderness only forty; and so less and less; and our light appears to be very excellent,—a clear light, far excelling even that of the Jews, which was clouded till Christ's coming, with mysterious ceremonies; and much clearer than most or all the world's,—a great part of which is clouded with thick mists of antichristian supersti- tion; but now, if we improve not this, our sins, of all others, will be most inexcusable, and we shall be the greatest reproach to the ways and truth of God, and to our own souls, which was the second doctrine: that if this morning be mispent, it shall quickly be turned into night, which was evinced from many sad examples; even Jerusalem herself, of which God had said that place should be his rest, yet for her slighting the Gospel, is become desolate. So all those famous Asian Churches, mentioned in the Revelations, those of Corinth, Coloss, Ephesus, &c. all which once enjoyed the same glorious light of the Gospel, and had as sober, serious professors as Eu- rope can now boast of; and yet, alas! for this very sin, they are all desolate, and become the habitation of the destroying Turk. And what now shall be said to England I know not, only this, Be not high- minded, but repent; for the Gospel is a mercy too precious to be abused and trampled under foot by

unworthy professors.   God will not lend it as outward mercies of health, wealth, &c. to the slighters
of it, but will certainly remove it far from us ; for
it is nothing but just with God to turn the light of
a people into darkness when they reject it, which is
the crying sin of this land: to say nothing of any
public, our own defections are very ominous.   It has
been impartially observed, that ever since the first
Reformation in Edward the Sixth's time, there has
been a decay of love to the truth in sincerity ; but
farther, though there has been a decrease for these
130 years, yet it has been much more evident these
last thirty years ; so that, upon a serious consideration, we have great cause to fear that God will remove the light of his rejected Gospel from amongst
us, the signs whereof are clear, even as the natural sun.   1. You know it always sends its beams
westward, and so this Sun of Righteousness, it began to show its lustre in Jewry, eastward from
us, and so came westward to the Churches of Asia,
where it stayed for a time ; thence to the Grecian
Churches farther west, where it shone somewhat
longer ; and from thence to Italy and Spain, where
it was soon overshadowed with idolatry and superstition ; then the light broke forth in a happy Reformation in Germany, still more westward ; and so
came at last, in its full lustre, to these our nations ;
and now, whether it shall go from us to America
and the West Indies, God himself knows best :
however, this is certain, that the Gospel must be

preached even to them, that the light thereof may shine through the whole world.   2. Shadows grow longer towards night, and is it not thus with us?   I am sure the shadows of religion increase more than the substance, so that there is little else than the shadow of it amongst us.   3. Toward night it grows cold; and so doth the love of many, nay most, towards the ways of God.   Professors of old have even been sick of love to the Ordinances; but now, those meetings that used to be spent in bewailing their wants and directing one another heavenwards, are usually taken up in scurrilous discourse, drinkings, &c. 4. Towards night men can outstare the sun, the too common practice of many now-a-days, that practice contrary to what they know to be right and true. 5. Towards night persons grow more sleepy; and do not most live a sleepy, secure life, as though they had made a covenant with death, and feared no danger from God's severe justice?   All that is spoken to them is as stories told to a sleeping man; and should any one be asked when he goes out here, what he hath heard? perhaps they might say, a good sermon, holy matter: but alas! how little would be fully remembered, and how much less practised!   6. Wild beasts (seducers) stir out and devour towards night.   7. Men set up candles, and how many false pretended lights have lately been set up amongst us; and, lastly, men choose new things with us, as in the Egyptian darkness men know not which way to go, some to Quakerism,

Anabaptism, Antinomianism, and they will not leave
their Dalilahs, their beloved errors. . Alas! how we
should lament the loss of the sun in the firmament,
though but for three or four days; but if this
glorious Sun of Righteousness withdraw its light,
it will not be for such a short time, and this will
certainly be, if we repent not. Our morning will
be turned into night: whence this third doctrine,
that a serious consideration of the swift motion of
our time should be an effectual motive to repentance.
Who is there that seriously thinks upon the shortness of life and length of eternity, the shortness of
the day and length of the night, but would look
about for help in time? Oh! the madness of those
who are notionally convinced of the truth of all
this, yet will not regard,—will have excuses. Come
to a young man :—well, it is too soon for him—he
must now enjoy himself. "Rejoice," saith the wisest
man, "in the day of thy youth, before the evil days
come," &c. Well, after a few years, the young man
is grown up to manhood : repentance then comes to
claim its promise. Oh! now? not now! he was
never more busy in all his life ; he is now entering
upon the world, must take care for an estate —he
that provides not for his wife and children is worse
than an infidel; but come in his old age, and then
he will certainly repent and turn. Suppose him
well stricken in years ;—well, then it is too troublesome, he hath pangs enough to grapple with ; he
hopes God will be merciful, and not damn his own

workmanship, and so alas! is miserably deluded till too late. . . . . After dinner, rode with Squire Fairfax, Mr. Corlass, Mr. E. Hickson, and Mr. Wispelaer to Bradford; was to visit Mr. Waterhouse,* &c., and to my exceeding satisfaction, Mr. Corlass prayed in the family. I have not in my life been so pleased with a journey; such duties being too frequently omitted by the best upon the road.

2. Morning, my dear friend prayed again very fervently; I was greatly pleased, that being so many young men on travel, we should so happily agree in the best things. Rode to Little Horton, and dined with Mr. Sharp, that holy angelical man; was much in his library. Evening, returned home, but was wet to the very skin by a terrible thunder shower, the most violent, I think, that has often been known.

13. Set forward, though melancholy, and all alone, towards Durham, baited at Northallerton, and got well to Darlington.

14. Got to Durham pretty early; and found my poor sister, and all relations, pretty well.

15. Enjoyed the converse of friends; then dined at Cousin Walker's; went afterwards to see the Abbey; viewed the exceedingly rich copes and robes, was troubled to see so much superstition re-

---

* Jonas Waterhouse, a moderate Nonconformist, of whom there is some account in Calamy; to which I add, the result of recent researches into the history of the numerous family of the name, that he was the son of Henry Waterhouse of Tooting, in Surrey, to which place this part of the family of Waterhouse of Halifax had migrated.

maining in Protestant Churches; tapers, basins, and richly embroidered I.H.S. upon the high altar, with the picture of God the Father, like an old man; the Son, as a young man, richly embroidered upon their copes. Lord, open their eyes, that the substance of religion be not at length turned into shadows and ceremonies!

16. Advising with Aunt, &c.; returned from Durham to Allerton, and thence to Topcliffe, though late enough.

17. From Topcliffe returned to my desired home.

23. At Wakefield, and thence at the earnest entreaty of Mr. Wispelaer, (of the same Romish persuasion) rid to Aunt Thoresby's, at Snidall, but got well home again that night.

25. Set forward very early in the morning with Mr. Robert Hickson; had a very rainy morning; wet to the skin, before we reached Wentbrig, where we stayed some while: thence by Doncaster to Bawtry, and so to Gainsborough at night; but in the way had to ferry over the Trent, and had many rivulets to ride over within evening, but without any damage.

26. Went early in the morning to the Church; transcribed some epitaphs; then heard an honest sermon, and then rid three miles to Knaith, to the Lady Willoughby's of Parham, in expectation of an extraordinary sermon, and so it proved, indeed; but in the worst sense, full of nothing in the world but railleries against Protestant Dissenters, who, in his opinion,

were far more dangerous enemies than the Papists; was much troubled at our disappointment, and to see the house so sadly degenerated so shortly after the Lord's death, who had the repute of a most honest, worthy, judicious, and religious Lord; we rid from thence over the noted heath to the ancient city of Lincoln, whither we got well, though late in the evening.

27. Got up early to view the town, and chiefly the Cathedral, an ancient and stately fabric, where by the assistance of one Clark, a poor but ingenious man, I transcribed not only the modern, but the names and some inscriptions of the ancient Bishops' tombs; thence we travelled to Sleeforth, where we baited, and in the church I found and transcribed the monuments of the Carrs; thence to . . .

28· From thence to . . . . but in the church was no monument; but Mr. North, the minister, had given Mr. Mede's Works, whence I transcribed his Epitaph; from thence (for we would not venture to ride the washes, which are dangerous at best) we rid to Wisbeach, an ancient and large market-town, having in it a bishop's house and a fair church, but no monuments of antiquity. For Mr. R.'s, &c. *vide* p. 93, which I transcribed, not without difficulty, through the ignorance and impudence of the sexton, who took me for a Papist. But we found much civility from two gentlemen related to Mr. Hickson, so we stayed all night; in the evening we heard a good honest sermon from one Mr. Howe, which was some satisfaction for the smallness of the journey this day.

29. This morning, before we left Wisbeach, I had
the sight of an hygre, or eager, a most terrible flush
of water, that came up the river with such violence
that it sunk a coal vessel in the town, and such a
terrible noise that all the dogs in it snarl and bite at
the rolling waves, as though they would swallow up
the river; the sight of which (having never seen the
like before) much affected me, each wave surmount-
ing the other with an extraordinary violence. From
Wisbeach we rid to Setcha, a small country village,
but much noted for the beast fair, all the closes
round the town for a considerable distance being
spread over with beasts from Scotland, &c. : and (if
not too light an observation in this place) for the
common country proverb, Setcha has but thirteen
houses and fourteen cuckolds; true enough in the
former part, but I charitably hope false in the latter.
From thence we rid to Lynn, three miles off, a
stately great town, with many churches but few
monuments; and it being late I transcribed none,
though the chief reason was because I could attain
the knowledge of few or no considerable benefactors.
Here I saw the famous cup which King John gave
to the town, which is preserved with great honour
and veneration, and it being the new Mayor's festival, I had not the sight of it only, but the honour
to have it brought me by the Mayor himself, who
(when according to the ancient custom I had taken
off the cover) drunk his Majesty's health in sack,
and then turned one part of the bottom of the cup

to himself and the other to me, and so having received it, drank to another gentleman after the same
manner.

30. Before four, in a cold frosty morning, I took
horse, and having raised the people at the city-gate,
I went along with my guide, (having left Mr. Hickson at Lynn,) to . . . . , fourteen miles off, and
thence alone through many country towns, but none
of any note, till I came at noon to that ancient,
famous, and stately city of Norwich, where the first
thing I observed, as I rid along, was the manner of
building not only many houses, but churches, of
flint; some flint alone, others flint and stone, or
brick mixed, and the east end of the town-house is
very curiously chequered with squared flints and
brick.   Christ's church, or the cathedral, is a stately
building, and kept in very good repair and order,
whence I transcribed many curious monuments of
ancient and some modern bishops; and in a very
pretty chapel adjoining, of that late worthy divine
Bishop Reynolds' foundation : and having thus spent
the afternoon abundantly to my satisfaction, I eujoyed in the evening the company of some acquaintance, &c., and early next morning took coach for
London.   The first place we baited at was . . . .,
whence, in the adjoining church, I had the epitaph
of Sir Francis Bickley, famous for his numerous
posterity ; and thence to . . . ., where we dined,
but there were no monuments in the church ; thence

over a great spacious heath, many miles long and broad, where we had a fine prospect of Ely Minster, to . . . .; and thence to Newmarket, where we had the honour to see his Majesty and the Duke of York ; thence over the spacious heath to Stour-bridge, where the noted yearly fair is, where we had the prospect of two churches in one church-yard, built by two sisters ; and thence to Cambridge, where we lodged at night.   Early next morning we mounted Gogmagog hills, whence in a very misty unhealthy morning, we came to . . . ., where we baited ; thence we past by the greatest house in England, viz. Audley-end, a vast building, or rather town walled in ; it is adorned with so many cupolas and turrets above, walks and trees below, as render it a most admirably pleasant seat : thence we came to Saffron Walden, in Essex, where grows that costly flower, which teaches them to rise early ; for they must either be up before the sun to take the seeds, or they lose the prize : from thence to . . . ., where we dined, and from thence to Hogsden, three miles from Ware, and seventeen from London, which appeared but short, because of the pleasantness of the way, almost like a continued town or street.   I got safe to London that night. . . .   This evening, though very late, I went to Mr. Stretton, from Bishopsgate to Holborn, and there, alas ! received the sad tidings of my poor cousin, Sus. Idle's reso-lution, to bestow herself upon one Stubbs, altogether

unworthy of so virtuous a young woman, whom I
cordially love, for her goodness, much above the
common pitch of this age.

Oct. 13. All or most of the day in buying
several things, seeking funeral sermons, lives, and
pictures of eminent persons.

15. Morning, inquiring for Mr. Hickson, sen.;
then went by water to Westminster with cousin R.
Idle, bought some pictures, and, upon return, found
my fellow-traveller, and stayed with him till late.

16. Die Dom. Mr. H. being gone ere I called, I
returned back to the Dutch church, but understood
not so much as I expected, because of the great
echo that church makes. As the custom is, after
sermon, sung a psalm, wherein I joined them with
great satisfaction, understanding then what I read
and sung; after dinner, with M. R. H., went up to
Mr. Stretton's, had some discourse with him, and
then returned to the Dutch church.

17. Went to Whitehall with Mr. R. H., and saw
the Duke of Monmouth, who was somewhat indisposed, yet, by means of Mr. Skinner, we were admitted into the bed-chamber, when he discoursed
pretty freely; and, understanding by Mr. R. H.,
that we came from Leeds, the great clothing-place,
he answered, with a smile, we were not for popery
there,* no more than they in the West, alluding to

---

* This is a curious testimony. The poor Duke of Monmouth was
now practising on these simple people from Leeds the Achitovelian
policy, which, in less than five years, involved him in destruction:—
"Surrounded

his extraordinary kind entertainment there (as in the public news); then we called at Mr. Fairfax's, to see my Lord and him.

18. To take leave of Mr. Stretton . . . .; was at the other end of the town about a horse, &c. Evening, took leave of my good cousin Dickenson and family, who has approved himself the most faithful, cordial, true-hearted friend, I ever met with in London, and indeed equal to the best I have in the world, which true testimony I purposely mention, as a note of gratitude.

19. Morning, departed from the metropolis of

" Surrounded thus with friends of every sort,
Deluded Absalom forsakes the court :
Impatient of high hopes, urged with renown,
And fired with near possession of a crown.
The admiring crowd are dazzled with surprise,
And on his goodly person feast their eyes;
His joy concealed, he sets himself to show ;
On each side bowing popularly low :
His looks, his gestures, and his words he frames,
And with familiar ease repeats their names.
Thus formed by nature, furnished out with arts,
He glides unfelt into their secret hearts.
Then, with a kind compassionating look,
And sighs, bespeaking pity e'er he spoke,
Few words he said ; but easy those, and fit,
More slow than Hybla drops, and far more sweet.
" ' *I mourn, my countrymen, your lost estate,*
Though far unable to prevent your fate :
Behold a banished man, for your dear cause
Exposed a prey to arbitrary laws !
Yet, oh ! that I alone could be undone,
Cut off from empire, and no more a son !
Now all your liberties a spoil are made,
Egypt and Tyrus intercept your trade,
And Jebusites your sacred rites invade.' "

this island, and one of the most famous cities in the world, to Tottenham High Cross, where is an ancient built column, erected in the full road: thence to Waltham, where is a most curious stately cross, erected by King Edward I. in memory of his beloved Queen Eleanor; it is adorned with the well-cut statues of several saints, kings, queens, &c.: thence to Edmonton, where, in the midst of the town, is a fair conduit, in the form of a woman, with a pitcher under her arm, whence continually issueth a stream of water: thence to Hogsden, where is an ancient house, with stately turrets, and a curious garden, with the best and largest pine-trees I have seen: thence to Ware, twenty miles from London, a most pleasant road in summer, and as bad in winter, because of the depth of the cart-ruts, though far off as bad as thence to Buntingford and Puckeridge, and part of the way to Royston, though we got well thither.

20. From thence, early in the morning (long before day) to Godmanchester, a great town, and almost joined to a greater, Huntingdon, a county town; but there we stayed not but rid on by two very delicate stately buildings to Stamford, and thence two miles further to Bridge Casterton, where we lodged all night.

21. As early up again, and passed safely the great common, where Sir Ralph Wharton slew the high-wayman, and Stonegate Hole, a notorious robbing place, by Grantham, the church whereof is reported

to have the highest steeple in England; to Newark, a garrison in the late war for King Charles I., where, in the ruins of the old castle, I saw the place where my grandfather was kept prisoner; within two miles of which, through a too passionate respect to, and fear of, Mr. Hutton (who promised to meet at night the rest of the company), I left the road and lost the company, who designed for Barnby-moor; but the way and weather being very bad, Mr. Hutton (for whose sake, lest he should receive any damage, being too full of drink, I had left the other company) would not stir a foot farther than Tuxford, so that I had to ride alone eight tedious long miles, in a place easy enough to mistake the way in, especially in a dark evening, over Shirewood Forest; but through the mercy of a good God, I got safe to my designed stage, and before the rest of the company.

22. Thence to Bawtry: to my no small joy now got into my native country again. From that Millstone town to Doncaster, and thence by Ferrybridge to Brotherton, where I visited old Mrs. Rayner, being my great grandfather's father's third wife, now a great age, having lived to see many of her grandchildren's grandchildren. It was somewhat late ere I got home.

23. Die Dom. Mr. Sharp, from Acts xxvi. 8, showed that Jesus Christ, by the ministry of the word, brings liberty to those that are captives to the power of Satan. By nature, we are in the power

of Satan, and how great that is, is clear from Scripture.   He is called the God of this world, and that
is the highest power.   Consider his natural power
as a fallen angel, and then his regal power as chief
of the spirits, and you will find them great ; but
sometimes he has a greater power given him by
God : 1. Over the bodies of men, as many examples
in history, and some in our own memories do clearly
evince.   2. Sometimes to inflict distempers upon
them, as in Job's case.   3. To torment their bodies,
as in bewitched persons ; and, lastly, sometimes to
take away life from the body, as in witches, that
have made a formal contract with the Devil.   But
God seldom allows him this immediate power on the
bodies of his children.   But though these examples
of his power over men's bodies are very dreadful,
even to make our hair stand on end at the reading thereof, many whereof are contained in a book
called the Theatre of God's Justice, yet this is nothing to the design he hath upon, and power over
the souls of men..   1. By a tempting power to sin ;
he being a spirit can approach nearer the souls of
men.   2. By a deluding power.   3. By a tyranniz-
ing power over all, and even a ruling power over
the wicked. . . . . . Afternoon, I went to church,
but could have wished myself at home, a stranger
preaching very meanly.   I was especially vexed at
these words, " Precise persons now-a-days will cry
out of innocent plays and honest comedies, &c.,
when in the mean time themselves are the greatest

actors in the world." A speech, in my opinion, very unbecoming a minister of the Gospel at any time, much more in the pulpit, leading to the encouragement of those insatiable devourers of precious time.

24. Morning writing to London; but most of the day abroad visiting friends, and discoursing Mr. Kay and Mr. B. Dixon (a faithful friend) concerning the London business.

27. (Our fair-day,) being the last day (last year) that I enjoyed the invaluable happiness of my dear father's prayers, directions, society, &c.; the reflections upon the severe Providence of God in depriving us of so every way useful a person to Church and State, and the unspeakable loss to this poor desolate family almost overwhelmed me; the violence of natural affections, augmented with the sense of the displeasure of God for my sins, the occasion of so severe a dispensation, was so extreme, that such rivers of tears issued from my eyes, as almost deprived me of the use of them; the smart and pain scarce suffering me to open them, accompanied with such an exceeding pain in my head, as made me doubt what the issue would be; which sorrow (though the pain abated) continued the next,

28th, day, so that I refused all consolation; would not stir into town, but retired, spending the time in bitterness and lamentation for my unspeakable loss,— a mercy to his pious soul, yet a judgment upon me!

'Nov. 1. Thinking to have got up by six, was mistaken; rose so early, that I had read a chapter be-

fore it chimed four; spent most of the time in reading my dear father's diary.   I entered into a resolution,—to redeem more time, particularly to retrench
my sleeping time, and getting an alarm put to the
clock, and that set at my bed's head, to arise every
morning by five, and first to dedicate the morning (as
in duty obliged) to the service of God, by reading and
prayer; to spend some hours in writing and collecting remarks upon the lives and deaths of the saints
and servants of God in most, or all ages; and I have
thoughts, and some glimmering hope to bring down
a continued series of all the heroes, both spiritual and
temporal, since the very first planting of Christianity
in this our island.

2. This morning again I got up sooner than I designed, having read a chapter before four; till day,
writing into a book the inscriptions I had taken from
some monuments in London.

3. Most of the day transcribing some observations
upon the lives and deaths of some great persons, out
of Lloyd's Memoirs.

5. Morning, preparing charcoal and powder for a
ship of war; then heard Mr. Sharp, who made an
excellent discourse, and suitable to the deliverance
vouchsafed our ancestors upon this day; in the evening, full of company, to see the ship discharged.

6. Morning, writing to Durham and Newcastle;
afternoon, spent rather too much time abroad, though
not in bad company, or I hope bad discourse, though
much in controversy about Con. and Nonconformity.

7. Die Dom.　Mr. Naylor made such a discourse as I am apt to believe, was never preached in the New church since it was built, so full of rancour against poor Dissenters.

10. Morning, writing; and surprised with the death of honest Mr. Robert Myrfield, as courteous and well humoured a person, as the town of Leeds afforded; lamented the loss of him, being also a serious Christian, and willing to do any kindness that lay in his power.

15. Writing in the morning; but spent most of the day in visits, especially Mr. Naylor, with design of discourse about his sermon.

22. In the house all day, sorting the effigies of many worthy persons, to place them according to their several centuries in my collection.

Dec. 2. Afternoon with some company to perform the usual ceremony of going to drink with cousin Fentons, at Woodhouse Hill, where stayed late enough though not so late as some, being resolute against drinking, having observed the bad consequence.

6. Writing some Collections till noon from five in the morning, (having procured an alarm to the clock,) designing to prosecute my former resolutions not to sleep away so much of my precious time, but endeavour to improve it to what advantage I can, which I have the more need to do considering the frequent summons to many persons—more likely for life than myself, as J N. at whose funeral I was.

9. Up *ut prius*, writing till noon, then dined at uncle Idle's; thence sent for by Mr. B. D.*; writing till nine in the evening the public donations, gifts to the poor, lecturer, free-school, highways, &c. designed to be engrossed upon a table, and hung up in the church, which, good design my dear father was very earnest in prosecuting many years ago, but prevented by the iniquity of some great persons, who had of the poor's money in their hands.

13. Arranging the pictures of many noted persons, in order to fix them methodically into the book.

16. Lost too much of the morning; most of the day pasting the collection of pictures, and placing them according to their several generations.

21. Came from Snidall with cousin and Mr. Wispelaer; dined at Dr. Neale's,† and stayed there rather too long at play, to the loss of too much precious time.

27. Morning set forward with friends for the North; got well to Rippon, and thence, though some miles in the dark, without harm to Catterick.

28. Thence to Piercebridge and Bishops Aukland; transcribed the epitaph of Bishop Cousins, interred in a stately chapel of his own foundation;

* Mr. Bryan Dixon, of Hunslet Lane, an intimate and faithful friend of Thoresby, who says of him in the *Ducatus*, that he was "a curious florist in his younger days, and an useful retriever of ancient scripts in his elder years, whereby some benefactions have been recovered, and some secured."—p. 103.

† Dr. George Neale, a physician then practising at Leeds.

thence to Durham, without prejudice, though the ways very deep and the night dark.

29. Dined at cousin Walker's, and stayed most of the day there, with relations.

31. Rid with cousins to Newcastle.

A. D. 1681.

January 1. Afternoon returned to Durham.

2. Die Dom. In the forenoon went to the Minster; was somewhat amazed at their ornaments, tapers, rich embroidered copes, vestments, &c. Dr Brevin, a native of France, discoursed of the birth of Christ; went after to Shinkley, and heard a discourse from Mr. Dixon, Colos. iii. 3.

3. Rid with relations to cousin Paxton's, at Shinkley; dined there, and returned safe to Durham.

5. Set forwards pretty early; found the ways worst at first, but afterwards tolerable, so got well to Burniston, where I found a pretty new Hospital, erected 1680, by Dr. Robinson; writ thence an inscription, *vide* my Collections.

7. Most of the day about some little business, and visiting some friends, and in the evening, some that scarce deserve the name, considering their carriage and designs.

8. Up writing post letters about earnest business to London, Durham, &c. and afterwards several more to drapers, by the carriers; afternoon disposing the effigies of eminent divines, and pasting them

into my collection; evening at neighbour W. A.'s for an hour, then catechised the children, &c.

9. Die Dom. Mr. Sharp, from Matthew v. 4, had a good discourse concerning true mourning; was upon an use of reproof to such as are so far from mourning, that they spend their time in foolish merriment and jollity; showing that mirth, as it is an affection of the mind, and created by God, is very good, and commanded in Scripture, and what many of the saints of God, in all ages, have not only allowed, but praised, and have themselves been highly commended for such a cheerful spirit, thereby taking off the scandal, that *spiritus Calvinisticus est spiritus melancholicus;* but it is to be condemned when God calls for mourning, &c.

11. Up before four, writing till eight; then about the History of the Ancient Britons till three; then abroad for argent.

13. Lay till five; writing till eight, and so till noon; then at the funeral of Mr. Robert Ibbetson; then at Mr. B. D.'s about pious donations, writing them in order to their being fixed in the Church.

14. Mr. Sharp had an affecting discourse from the Revelations, " Behold, I stand at the door, and knock."

15. Lay till six; then writing two or three hours about those primitive martyrs, after the preaching of true Christian religion in this our land; was afterwards troubled at some expressions from a Popish

relation, and Mr. W. a Fleming, of good natural parts, but miserably deluded.

17. Up pretty early, reading and writing about the year 400, concerning Pelagius, whose heresy was well repugned by Germanus.

20. Lay too long, till near seven; but, as a voluntary penance, stirred not out till evening to W. A.'s; then writing again till ten.

24. Up early, about five; uncle Idle called to go to Ardington; was but indifferently furnished with company to follow the dogs; the first time I was a-hunting, and, I think, will be the last, being of Sir Philip Sidney's mind, next to hawking I like hunting worst.

Feb. 9. This morning (Mr. Fairfax) came pretty early and roused me up; stayed with him till noon, then rid, upon earnest entreaty, to Mr. Walker's of Hedingley, but after dinner observing some inclinations to intemperance, embraced the first opportunity of withdrawing. Came home in good time, though a terrible day.

10. Worthy Mr. Henry Fairfax called me up early. At noon at Mr. B. D.'s advising about some Northern business. After dinner had a sad fit of melancholy oppression; I know not how to term it: dreaded somewhat of an epilepsy; but in the evening diverted by some company, and perhaps too much in another extreme.

11. Somewhat disordered in the morning with a Dutch letter of bad debts; and then, to add to the

grief, had too severe a chide from one that was offended with a single expression that I meant no harm by, but I hope it may be a warning to me to be much more cautious. Afternoon writing. Evening sent for by Dr. Stubbs, stayed rather too late.

12. Forenoon writing memoirs. Afternoon at the funeral of two ancient gentlewomen, Mrs. Child and Mr. Myrfield's mother. As for the week past in general, I look upon it as lost.

14. Writing in the morning, then with Dr. Stubbs at Woodhouse-hill, though could scarce get there for the sudden flood, occasioned either by some violent rains in the West, or rather from the sudden melting of the aforesaid snow; but the flood increasing to such a prodigious greatness as has scarce ever been known in these parts, brought large pieces of timber over our garden wall, and carried the largest logs of wood as far as Dow Bridge.

15. With Mr. Garnet to observe the greatness of the flood; most of the day and evening abroad and spent too little time either in reading or writing, not above three or four hours these two days.

20. Die Dom. Mr. Ivison, from Acts iii. 19, had a good discourse of repentance, an honest, sound, serious sermon, as was his prayer; wherein this expression, that God would please to preserve this church from popery in her doctrine, superstition in her ceremonies, and tyranny and oppression in her government; and when praying for the clergy, begging that they may be exemplary for their purity,

holiness and true virtues; that such as are scandalous may be removed and better put in their places.

26. Rid to York to the election of the two lords as Knights of the Shire for the ensuing Parliament.

27. Die Dom. Too much vanity and idle discourse in the morning, and too unsuitable a carriage all the day. Mr. Ward in the forenoon, Psalm cxix. 32. Mr. Bloom in the afternoon, discoursing of perseverance.

28. In the Castle-yard at the election, then making some visits, and after the dispatch of some business returned home.

March 7. Perusing some letters, papers, &c. in order to the collection of Memoirs of the best of fathers. Afternoon at a funeral, and to visit Mr. Robert Hickson. Recover him, O Lord! if it be thy will, and deprive us not of such serviceable persons.

8. Employed about ditto letters. Then abroad about business, had some friends at dinner, received a visit from Mr. Heywood,* who gave me a pleasing account of holy Mr. Angier, his father-in-law.

* Oliver Heywood, who was removed from the chapel of Coley, in the Parish of Halifax, by the operation of the Act of Uniformity, but who continued to reside near the scene of his early ministerial labours during the remainder of his life, which closed in 1702. He was one of the most assiduous and zealous of the Nonconforming ministers: instant in season and out of season, at home and abroad, he emulated the character of an apostle. In his many journeyings he often visited Leeds, and it appears, both by the Diary before us, and by his own Diary, that he rarely visited Leeds without calling on Mr. Thoresby. There was in both a deep feeling of piety, a dissatisfaction with the restraint of the church on the public expression of devotional sentiment, a fondness in both for topographical enquiry, and

14. Up before five, writing letters for Durham, &c., rid eight miles with cousin Walker, of Durham; in return, viewing the monuments in Harwood church, which are indeed extraordinary, especially that for the famous Judge Gascoyne, who so faithfully reproved, and stoutly imprisoned Prince (afterwards King) Henry V.; and a noted warrior, J. Redman, or Redyman, as the King called him, for his quick valour.   Was afterwards, with some company, at the Judges coming to town.

15. Spent all the day vainly, and idly walking or talking, or doing worse, drinking in company, and though not to excess, yet more than was necessary. Evening, at Mr. T. W.'s, in the same humour, &c. *Væ væ mihi peccatori!*

25. Rid to Ledsham, with ditto worthy Mr. Richard Sykes, (the minister of Spawforth's son,) was kindly entertained at Mr. Sykes's, transcribed the epitaph from the Lady Bowles's tomb, whose statue, in her winding-sheet, is well cut in white marble; but that of Sir John Lewys is almost unparalleled—a most delicate stately monument, of

a disposition in both to honour and preserve the memories of men who had been in any respect famous in their generation. These resemblances produced an intimacy and friendship, and it appears by some of the letters of Mr. Heywood, which will appear among the Correspondence, that at a critical period in the life of Thoresby, Mr. Heywood performed the part of an honest and intrepid friend. In 1702, we find Thoresby going to Mr. Heywood's house at Northowram, to attend his remains to the grave in the parish church of Halifax.

curious white marble, with well-cut statues, to the life.

28. Forenoon, writing; after at Woodhouse-hill, with Mr. Wispelaer ; then at the funeral of Lawyer Bathurst's brother, who was interred with the greatest state has been known in this town; near one hundred torches carried in state ; the room hung with black, and escutcheons and tapers ; so was the pulpit ; a velvet pall, hung with escutcheons, and carried by the chief gentry, who had gloves and scarfs ; all the company had gloves, with sack and biscuits.   Mr. Benson preached at nine at night, from Job xix. 26, 27.

April 5. Up in the morning, writing to Mr. T. D. and to Hull, by my best Flemish friend, Mr. Wispelaer, with whom most of the forenoon ; after, rid with him out of town, took leave of him, troubled at the loss of so well-humoured and accomplished a gentleman, whom I scarce expect to see any more. I have sometimes been in hopes that what he has heard disputed and read in England, may, *Deo juvante,* have some good influence upon him.   Lord grant it may !

7. Up in the morning, writing in Diary ; then walked with cousins, &c. to Temple Newsham, observing the structure ; then to Whitchurch, transcribing some monuments of Sir Arthur Ingram, jun. &c. ; returned well home.

8. From morning to evening overlooking the labourer, and filling a glass globe with pictures ; had

this day a serious admonition from old Mrs. Sykes, a noted Quaker, and notable good woman, about the vanity of foolish ornaments and ribbons. I would not (as they) look upon it as unlawful to wear them, but desire to make a good use of such a reproof, and am very thankful for her commendable Christian freedom.

9. Lay till six, then with the labourer, and drawing the picture of Life and Death in one, till noon.

10. Die Dom. Awaked with a sad dejected heart, much troubled within me; went to church, and heard an excellent sermon from Mr. Baines, (son to good old Thomas Baines, of Holbeck, and " his speech bewrayed him,") educated in Scotland, from Luke xiv. 24. He preached excellently; and though many at first looked upon it as too fanatical, yet it pleased God so to order it, that, I think, most were too much scared to mock at the conclusion.

28. Morning, writing from five; forenoon, assisting at Mr. Robert Hickson's, in preparing for the funeral of that good man, whose loss will not easily be made up to this poor congregation, which has but few such eminent and useful members; afterwards advising with uncle Idle about northern affairs, one of the tenants being come over.

29. Forenoon, writing and summing up ditto accounts; then advising with Mr. B. D.; afterwards visited old Mrs. Sykes; towards evening had a visit from Mr. Wilson, a poor nonconformist; at Mr. R. W.'s, about his concerns.

30. At Mr. W.'s, about a collection for ditto Mr. W.; writing to the North; then at the funeral of worthy Mr. Hickson, but not able to refrain from tears. Lord, make me serviceable in my station, that I may live beloved, and die lamented, as my dearest father did, whose example Lord help me to imitate!

May 1. Die Dom. Mr. Sharp made an excellent practical sermon, upon account of Mr. Robert Hickson's funeral, from Eccles. xii. 5.

11. Up at four, writing till near ten, then at Mill-hill. Mr. Sharp, from Hos. vi. 1, showed the happy estate of those that return unto the Lord. After-noon, with aunt, &c., but spent too much time idly in seeing the activity of a rope-dancer, and though many things were admirably done, yet too much time lost.

12. All day writing memoirs of worthy persons, eminent in their generation, about the year 1500, collected chiefly from Fuller's Worthies and Church History, Goodwin, Isaacson, Speed, &c. Sent for to cousin Idle about five; with him till near eleven o'clock.

13. Not up till after five; writing all the day ditto collections, and some worthy martyrs, that suffered not only the mark of Christ in their bodies, but those bodies to be burnt in the fire, rather than yield to that accursed religion, which is established in blood. Lord keep it from ever setting foot again in these nations, for Christ's sake!

25. After dinner, rid to visit honest Mr. Marsden,* a learned and judicious Nonconformist; but, beyond Morley, met the man with the sad tidings of his death; stayed there most of the afternoon with poor Mrs. Marsden, very weak, and dangerously sick.

27. Writing about an hour or two; about as long at the Close; then rid to Tingley, to the funeral of that holy man, Mr. Gamaliel Marsden, whose death was much bewailed, not by relations only, but many good people and godly ministers, as a public loss. After my return, at Mr. Thomas Wilson's.

31. Rid with Mr. E. H. by way of Aberforth to York, only stayed a while at the good Lady Barwick's; spent most of the evening, having first visited my sister, too freely in company.

June 1. At awaking in the morning not very well; gave a piece of a curtain lecture to E. H. and resolved, *Deo juvante*, to be more watchful for the future. Dispatched some business in town, and after dinner, to the displeasure of some, but abundant satisfaction of myself, (especially when afterwards I understood the dreaded effects of delay) came out of town alone, but was overtaken by the company. Stayed with them at the Warrant-house, had the good company of Mr. Fairfax and Mr. Corlas, but

* He was the pastor of a congregation of Nonconformists at Topcliffe, between Wakefield and Bradford, and a brother of the Mr. Ralphson, before-mentioned.

somewhat troubled at the freedom of another party.

2. Up pretty early, writing till after five, then walking with Mr. Bevet, then with John Rookes about business; dined with him, which took up too much time. After, had the Vicar, Mr. Milner's good company at my house, who corrected some mistakes and errata in transcribing epitaphs.

3. Up rather too early; by three o'clock took a walk, and I think paced betwixt seven or eight miles on foot this morning. Was at Holbeck, to visit Cousin Stubbs, very ill of a wound given her in a kind of Bacchanalian fray on Tuesday night.

7. Up at five, walking till six, writing till noon, completing catalogue of my books for our learned and good vicar, Mr. John Milner.

11. Up at four, writing memoirs about the year 1544 till noon; then walked with Dutch cousin to Woodhouse-hill; where, in Cousin Fenton's best chamber, I gathered some of the corn that was rained down the chimney upon the Lord's-day seven-night, when it likewise rained plentifully of the like upon Hedingley-moor, as was confidently reported; but those I gathered with my own hands from the white hearth, which was stained with drops of blue where it had fallen, for it is of a pale red or a kind of sky colour, is pretty, and tastes like common wheat, of which I have one hundred corns. What it may signify, and whether it doth proceed from natural

causes, (of which some may be prescribed) or preter-
natural, such an ignorant creature as I am cannot
aver.

14. Up about four, writing till eight: sent for
abroad to Mr. Hill, of London. About noon, went
with cousins and much company to the Spaws, and,

15, 16, 17. Drank the sulphur water plentifully;
walked much for health and recreation with the
company, but alas! little regarded any good thing,
generally either omitted duty or but slightly performed it.

18. Morning, drank the waters, and afterwards
rode to St. Mungo's Well at Cotgrave, the coldest of
all waters I ever knew.

July 2. Forenoon, viewing the heads cursorily
of Ferdinando Gorge's America; chiefly what was
relating to Mr. Hooker, Shepard, Elliot, Davenport,
&c. worthy ministers who fled thither.

8 and 9. Both days spent at the Spaws, in
drinking the waters at the usual times; and in company, wherewith better furnished than ordinary, with
Sir Ralph Jennyson of Newcastle and his lady, (my
dear father and uncle's friends,) and that accomplished gentlemen, Charles Scrimshaw, Esq. of Staffordshire, from whom I received the pleasing account of some Protestant benefactors in those parts;
Mr. Chetwynd, yet living, who built and endowed
a church, and Mr. Taylor, his father-in-law, who
built some alms-houses at Chesterfield.

10. Die Dom. Forenoon, drinking water, and

afterwards wine, too regardless of discourse, &c.
After, rode with Mr. Scrimshaw to hear Mr. Kirshaw of Ripley.

11 and 12. Spent both days in drinking the
waters and the usual recreations, walking, &c. Went
to Knaresborough, writ the heads of St. Robert's
life from an old manuscript; gathered some remarkably petrified moss, viewed the Castle, &c. with the
ingenious Mr. Scrimshaw, (since Sir Charles) with
whom,

13. In the afternoon, I returned home. Showing
him the collection of Roman coins, medals, &c. till
almost midnight.

14. Rode to Wakefield with ditto worthy gentleman. Transcribed for him Dr. Symson's epitaph.
After, rode to Snidal to visit aunt, and returned
well home.

15. Forenoon, abroad about business. Dined
with some Spaw company at Mr. M.'s; stayed there
till four. Spent the rest of day and evening with
cousin B. Milner of Holland.

18. Most of forenoon consulting Mr. Camden for
the memorables in Derbyshire. Afternoon, spent
mostly in visits.

19. Up about five in order to a journey to Buxton. Rode from Wakefield, after an hour's stay,
to New-Miller's-dam; thence over the forest by
Justice Wentworth's, a worthy gentleman, who is
now erecting an hospital at . . . . .* and designs

* Woolley.

to endow it liberally for poor persons; and by Justice Blythman's, another pretty seat, by the Old Dam, and upper end of Black Barnsley to Wuspar,* where Justice Edmunds has a pretty hall; thence to Sheffield, a large market town, most noted for knives, scissors, and iron-work. Here is a stately hospital, erected by the Earl of Norwich, great grandchild to Gilbert Earl of Shrewsbury who worthily gave 200*l.* per annum for the maintenance of twenty poor people. There is another for eight persons, built by the town stock. The church is a handsome well-built fabric, with some pretty monuments, especially for the numerous family of the Spencers of Attercliffe, inlaid many of them with brass in the stone very artificially; but as the town of the hospital, so the church may chiefly boast of the stately tombs of the Talbots, Earls of Shrewsbury, the inscriptions whereof I was with much difficulty transcribing till eight at night, and

20. Up by four this morning to finish them. From Sheffield we came into a more hilly country, till, by degrees, we were got into most prodigious high mountains as ever my eye beheld, with rocks and stones, of an extreme bigness, one whereof, at the bottom of one of the biggest, is entirely the height and length of a pretty large room, and, with a little addition, serves for the side of a house. Over such vast and prodigious craggy mountains we passed

* Worsborough.

some miles; till, at last, we arrived safely at Hope,
a pretty country-town, seated upon the river Now,
in a valley, and thence to Castleton, at the foot of
the Peak, properly so called, as the learned Camden
observes ; Peakland, from its peaking up into such
high mountains.   Upon the top of the hill is an
ancient ruin, (whence the town, I suppose, had its
denomination,) called the Castle in the Peak, in
Latin *de Alto Pecco,* formerly belonging to the Pe-
verels, and which, together with a manor and an
honour King Edward the Third gave unto his son
John Duke of Lancaster, in lieu of the Earldom
of Richmond, which he surrendered into the King's
hands.   Under which there is a most prodigious
cave within the ground, which, for the vast largeness
of it, is esteemed one of the wonders of England ;
and, indeed, God, who is truly Θαυματουργος, the
only worker of wonders, has more manifested his
might in this than in any other county in England,
such the heaps of wonders therein.   Of a marvellous capacity is the mouth of this Cave, wherein are
five cottages, whence, furnished with candles, we
descended lower and lower, till we were forced to
creep upon our hands and feet till we came at
another large place, called the Belfrey ; then lower
again to a water, which was then so high that it almost touched the lowering rock, that we could not
possibly get farther, else, beyond this, they say is a
narrower and then more spacious place, to a second water ; and after a third interval a third river,

which, *ut vulgo traditur*, never any passed and returned again.   Coming back to the entrance, I left
the company, and with a boy alone, and each a
candle, went into a narrow hole, (commonly called
the Swinehole,) where, creeping upon our hands
and feet, we descended lower and lower; till, at
length, the narrow passage divided itself into four
narrow lanes, or passages, too straight to contain our
bodies to make farther inspection.

Having ascended that vast mountain, the high
castle, which, when we were below, seemed almost
to kiss the sky, could scarce be seen, it was so low
in a seeming vale.   Upon this height we had a full
prospect of Mam Torr.   Torr signifies, in the Derbyshire dialect, a stony, craggy hill; and Maim, either
because it is maimed and broken at the top thereof,
or, to follow the vulgar pronunciation, it is Mam
Torr, or the Mother Hill, because, as the ingenious
Dr. Fuller expresses it, it is always delivered, and
presently with child again; for incredible heaps of
sandy earth constantly fall down from it, yet it
is no way diminished, having, it should seem, as
a constant stream, so a secret spring whence it
is recruited.   The inhabitants positively affirm, it is
neither larger nor less than in their infancy; notwithstanding there is, as I am now, and others in
the company, have been many years eye-witnesses
of a continual flux of sand perpetually descending;
so that it may well pass for the emblem of a liberal
man never impoverished by his well bounded and

grounded charity, his expenses being resupplied by
a secret Providence.   From Castleton, as I said,
having ascended the Peak, and riding some miles
upon the mountains, there is digged up lead, the
best in England, not to say Europe, and the best
in quantity, improving yearly in the increase of it.
Thence by the Chapel in the Forest, through a
hilly country, we came by Fairfield, a country village, to Buxton, such another, only noted for the
warm-bath, the effects whereof are little less than
miraculous in Mr. Hobbes' verses in Dr. Fuller's
Worthies in Derbyshire : the place is also famous
for the abode of Mary Queen of Scots, who found
much benefit by the water thereof, and took her
farewell with this distichon :—

> " Buxtona quæ calidæ celebrabam nomine limphæ,
> Forte mihi post hac non adeunda, vale.*"

21. I went from Buxton to see Poolshole, as marvellous a place in my opinion as any; the entrance
whereto is very straight and narrow, only to be
crept into, but within very spacious : it had its denomination from one Pool, of Pool's Hall, in Staffordshire, a man of great valour, who, being out-

---

* This pleasing anecdote has been often told ; but scarcely any
two persons have given the distich alike. Thoresby's copy must be
erroneous. Here we may, perhaps, best depend upon good old Fuller, who tells us he had the glass in his hand, and read the inscription thus :—

> " Buxtona, quæ calidæ celebraris nomine lymphæ,
> Forte mihi posthâc non adeunda, vale."

Church History, b. ix. p. 181.

lawed, resided here for his own security. There are within many turnings and windings through the rocks, and vast craggs. Going along one steep stony passage, we return by another, both which do at length join in one passage, wherein the active fancy of some hath created many wonders, some of the stones resembling a lion, another a man; a font, into the middle whereof is one particular drop of water continually trickling down from the top of the vaulted rock, which, in this place, is very high. They show you too his chamber, closet, parlour, shelf, (a hanging rock,) whereon he laid his viands, his lurking-hole, for there are many inward recesses, and a pleasant well of water, whereof we all drank; and, after several other remarkables, we came to the Queen of Scots' Pillar, a curious large white rock, a piece whereof I brought along with me. The Pillar is daily increased, notwithstanding the multitudes of pieces broken off, by the waters running down it, which have a petrifying virtue in them, whereof there are long icicles, very white, and curiously wrought, which you must fancy to be his organs; and they will show you too the belfry, *cum multis aliis.* Spent the rest of the day in bathing, and with the good company.

22. Came by Eldenhole, which is indeed of a huge wideness, exceeding steep, and of a marvellous depth, into which I throwing a large stone, it fell from one rock or partition as it were to another, with a great thundering noise for a pretty consider-

able time. Speed saith, that waters trickling down
from the roof of it congeal into stones. Not many
miles off is a well that ebbs and flows three or
four times in an hour, as Camden relates, which I
enquired of, and had the truth of it confirmed, but
not an opportunity of being an eye witness of it.

23. Returned home, but over another part of the
forest, where I observed plenty of lime and mill-
stones digged up; we came by Lady Bower, passing
the river Darwen, a shallow one surrounded with
great hills; and then over vast mountains, &c. to
Bradfield, thence by Barnsley to Wakefield, where
lay all night.

25. Spent much of the day in visits and company,
writing a little after dinner, then went with uncle
Idle to visit cousin Hick, who with Mr. Nevill and
Mr. Banister are for London, with the Address from
this town.

26. Up before four, writing all morning till seven.
Then rid to Mrs. Marsden's to view the library;
bought a few books and returned in time. After
with good aunt, then at Mr. W.'s; and with Junr.,
too late at tavern; can take time for any thing but
what I should.

31. Die Dom. The learned and ingenious Dr.
Sharp,* (Chaplain to the Lord Chancellor) being
come to visit his father at Bradford, preached at the

* Dr. Sharp, the Rector of St. Giles-in-the-Fields, was at this time
in the height of his popularity as a preacher. He was soon advanced
to higher stations in the church, being made first, Dean of Norwich,
then, Dean of Canterbury, and finally, Archbishop of York. His

old church from Ephes. i. 16, showing excellently what it is to redeem time.   Time past, as a traveller that has been stayed upon the road, doubles his haste to get to the end of his journey.   If we have not spent our time so carefully as we ought, we must so redeem it that we may through extraordinary diligence arrive to that height of virtue we could possibly have done by a constant course ; but more particularly we must redeem time present, not spend it either idly in doing nothing, or badly in doing what is worse than nothing, but in the service of God and for the salvation of the soul.   Showing excellently, that it is a duty incumbent upon all persons of what sort soever to redeem the time. ˙ Those that have trades and callings they must indeed observe them, that is a duty to God as well as themselves; but they cannot, at least ought not, to employ all their time in it; they must devote the remainder to God's service ; as for those that are ready to bless God they are not put to those shifts to get their livings, there is the more necessity for them to allot a greater time to the service of God ; greatly lamenting the folly of many

last preferment he owed to King William, having been silenced by King James for preaching warmly against Popery in his church of St. Giles.

Thoresby was afterwards introduced to the acquaintance of Dr. Sharp, and was honoured with many letters from him, both on sub_jects of antiquity, particularly coins, in which both were eminently skilled, and on the more important subject of his opinions and prac_tices in respect of the outward profession of Christianity.   We shall find that the Archbishop had a great share in determining Thoresby to conformity at a later period of his life.

persons that know not how to spend their time—
could wish themselves as in a sound sleep all the
intervals of pleasure,—they know not how to get over
this hour till sweet company come.   Alas, alas ! have
such no souls to save ?   Will not they find them
work enough not only for hours, but all the days of
their life.   But, besides there are no persons of so
mean capacities but they may improve time, though
they can neither read nor write, yet may they medi-
tate and discourse of good things.   Then came to
the reasons.   Redeem the time because the days are
evil.   The days we live in, blessed be God, are not
such days of persecution as those under which the
Apostles lived, wherein it was death to profess Christ;
we live under a gracious Prince, and have the laws
for our security in the true Protestant religion ; and
yet, notwithstanding, the argument holds good, we
should redeem the time because the days are evil.
Our sins justly merit judgments, and God may
bring them upon us as in a moment ; we should therefore redeem the time we have, we should walk cir-
cumspectly, not as fools but as wise.   Came very
accurately to describe the Christian's politics, as he
should carry himself in a time of danger : he should
serve the time ; comply in things that are not unlawful by the law of God, if enjoined by a lawful authority, if he can do it with a safe conscience, as Paul
endeavoured to be all things to all men, and do
all things with discretion and moderation, and swim
down the stream calmly, though that must be under-

stood with caution, when it is not contrary to the law of God, nor the testimony of our own consciences, for then we are of all most inexcusable.   But if it may be, we should submit to the government by law established, submit ourselves to the present state of things, that is, again, if not contrary to God's law ; for the man and his doctrine is to be abhorred that will always be upmost in all things; if the Protestant interest, or Popery, or Mahometanism come up he will be of it.   No, if it be contrary to the word of God we must not comply in the least ; and, if you ask what must then be done ?   1st. A man is not obliged, either by the law of God or man, to discover his opinion and blazon it to his own danger.   But 2d. If he should be persecuted upon it, he is allowed by the scripture, and example of the Apostles, to flee from place to place to secure himself, though both these must be cautiously understood ; for when we are called to give an account of our faith, then either to deny it, or comply in the least contrary to our consciences with Popery, would be to deny God ; in such cases we must commit the whole to God, and beg his strengthening grace.

Aug. 10. Before five, to get the horse in order to a journey to Swaith, to advise with Mr. Wadsworth; found much civility, and returned home well ; was writing Esquire Blythman's Epitaph in Royston church, and an inscription upon an hospital of the virtuous Lady Armine's, at Burton Grange.

22. Up at four, writing till nine ; then took leave of good Mrs. Hickson, senr. the flower of our female flock, a virtuous, good, holy, wise, prudent woman, of vast parts and abilities, and indeed above encomiums: exceedingly troubled we must lose her.   With her brother Mr. Gunter, Mr. Garnet, &c. till noon ; then had Bulmer uncle, and relations, to dinner ; sat till four, but without the least intemperance, or the fruit of it, the least angry word, or falling out; then with them at tavern till evening.

Sept. 4. Die Dom.   Mr. Ivison, from that of the Apostle, " none can come unto me, but whom the Father draweth ;" an excellent discourse, truly showing our impotency, though to the distaste of some, hot zealots for Arminianism ; there seeming to be an opposition betwixt them, as of old time betwixt Hooker and Travers ; and at our town old Mr. Cook and Garbut, all worthy good men, yet at great enmity about general redemption—though in my slender opinion, many were much to blame (as Alderman L. and honest Mr. S.) to leave the Church, especially considering it is the fundamental doctrine of the Church of England, asserted in the very Articles of it; and to oppose the contrary, King James sent over four eminent divines to the Synod of Dort, but now it is almost out of fashion.

6. We rode to Burrowbridge, and thence to Topcliffe, where supposing we should not stay long, left my charged pistols in the bags, which at my mounting again, being gone, caused a great jealousy of some

design against us; and the rather, because Mr. H.
and his debtor had come to high words, and the
landlord took the debtor's part, and denied to send
for the ostler, till upon some brisk compliments, we
were just for riding to depose upon oath before Sir
M. Robinson, and then in the very same straw we
had sought carefully before, they were found, and
one of them where the horse could not get to ; which
more fully manifested the knavery, as also their leaving, for a pretence, the red bags in the holster ; but
we got very well, though late, to Northallerton that
night.

7. Thence by Darlington to Durham; whence,
after a short stay with relations, to Newcastle, but
did little business.

8. Morning, visited some drapers, in order to their
accounts; then went with E. H. down to Shields by
water, but it proved a most terrible stormy day . . .
visited Tinmouth Castle, now almost ruined, and
maintained by a slender garrison; and the new fort
called Clifford's, fortified with thirty culverins, and
ten demi-culverins, under the government of the Earl
of Newcastle; in the evening not daring, without
imminent hazard, as the ship-master said, to return
by water, were forced to hire horses and return by
land to Newcastle.

9. Morning, finishing my business with some drapers; went to Sandgate to enquire of, and receive
some out-rents, and at return, took horse for Nor-

thumberland ; about five miles off, transcribed some verses from a monumental pillar, erected in the highway, by John Pigg, the mathematician ; thence by Captain Edward Widdrington's, at Felton, to Morpeth, and after a short stay there, over the Moors to Alnwick, an ancient town fortified with a curious castle, and an old wall.

10. By Rock ; where I found the old tenants repenting their unkind dealings, and continual murmurings for abatements, which hastened the sale of the estate; and now they would gladly have the same lands at an ordinary advancement ; discoursed Mr. Clavering about the arrears; thence over the Moors to Belford, thence over the Sands, where we had a fair prospect of Holy Island, to Berwick, where we got well, and in time to view the town, which is ancient and ill-built, but stands very commodiously and is well fortified.

11. Die Dom. Being at church too early, was transcribing some monuments, which was the first place I observed the Scotch mode for Aldermen and persons of some rank to be buried in the churchyard. The church was built, 1652, Colonel Fenwick, then Governor, being a chief instrument (in memory of whom there is an inscription in the church, of which, see p. 125, of my Collections,) by procuring monies owing to the town for soldiers' pay ; it has no steeple, the old one in the midst of the town serving : the Minister was on the different sorts of sor-

row, the benefits of the godly, and the disadvantage
of the carnal; was to visit Mr. Windlows, and after
walked round the walls.

12.   Morning, from Berwick over the Moors,
where we found the proverb verified, that a Scotch
mist, for I cannot say it rained, wets the Englishman
to the skin, to Hayton, a country town, seated upon
the river Hay, the mouth whereof is not far distant
from St. Abb's Head; then near Coldingham Abbey,
the nuns whereof cut off their noses to preserve their
chastity from the insulting Danes; leaving on the
right hand Dunglass, the lordship whereof belonged
to the famous soldier, Patrick Ruthen; thence to
Dunbar, seated on the sea, an eminent town, built
after the Scottish manner; most tombs (of which
Stephanides is of most note) of persons of good rank
are without the church, only in an aisle adjoining to
it there is a stately monument for George Hume, (a
numerous family in these parts, most of the castles,
lands, and houses we past by being of that name)
Earl of Dunbar, and Lord High Treasurer of Scotland.   Here I was, with three more, dubbed Knight
of the Bass, a little island near the town, rising up all
on a solid rock, where is a prison, that of late has
been stocked with Nonconformists: here, I must confess, I was too impatient at the Scotch victuals, not
able to eat any thing, though we had the bailiff's (or
alderman's) own dinner; only at last made a shift to
get down some eggs, without bread, butter, or salt,
but spent the time in the church-yard, transcribing

epitaphs, viewing the town, and the way of making and drying red herrings very dexterously. From Dunbar through many small towns, and a pleasant country, we came to Haddington, where we lodged all night.

13. Up pretty early, and transcribing some monuments in the church-yard, amongst which, a curious one for Mr. Cary, a minister of thé Earl of Roxburgh's family; but in an aisle belonging to the church is a most stately one for Duke Lauderdale's father and mother and sister, of curious black, white, and speckled marble, with four statues, and curiously wrought pillars, and a large inscription, *vid.* p. 130, of my Coll. From Haddington, we rode to Mussleborough, where was the great fight betwixt the Scots and English, *An.* 1547, and where we observed a curious engine for draining the fire from the coal mines; thence through a pleasant country to Leith, a pretty town, populous, and well-built, not far from Edinburgh, the metropolis of that ancient kingdom.

14. Morning, standing in the yard of the Parliament House, observing the several members and nobles as they went to the House, and after them, the Duke of York and Albany in great state. Was, after, in the great Church, at the ordination of a minister by the Bishop of Galloway, which was (contrary to all expectation) by the English Common Prayer. After which, he gave him a most serious charge to mind his duty, and live worthy of his high calling; showing very well, how little their

words can prevail, if their lives preach not. After
dinner, viewing several parts of the town; the castle, where the kings of the Picts used to keep their
daughters at needle-work till marriage, thence called
Màiden Castle, built upon a rock, and well fortified;
Goldsmith's Hospital, a most stately structure, but
sadly perverted as to the design of the founder,
many of his vast donations being either lost or mis-
employed; and transcribing several mottoes there,
and monuments in White Friars churchyard, the
only place where the generality of persons are interred.

15. At Holyrood house, observing the state of the
building and attendants, where many judge is as
great a court as at Whitehall. Afterwards, at the
Bibliotheca, transcribing several benefactions, of
which *vid.* p. 139. The library is adorned with
many curious books, and other rarities, a skeleton
very exactly done, a speaking tube, a large leaf of
a tree, a skull of a most prodigious thickness, and a
horn out of a woman's forehead, with an inscription
upon a plate of silver giving an account of it, *vid.*
p. 140 Collection; with the pictures of several great
personages, the famous Lord Napier, Knox, Hender-
son, Buchanan, whose skull is there also, the thinnest
ever seen or known, such indeed as is scarce credible
without the sight of it. There are the pictures also
of the foreign Reformers, Calvin, Beza, Luther, &c.
a thunderstone, &c.

16. Up pretty early, preparing for a further jour-

ney.   Left Mr. Hickson at Edinburgh, but had
Mr. Eleazer Hodshon along with me.   We found a
pleasant country to Kirkliston, thence to Linlithgow,
where is a stately palace, built mostly by King
James VI. which is now much ruined; especially a
curiously wrought conduit in the midst of the court,
of very good workmanship.   The town arms are
the picture of a dog, chained to a tree, growing out
of a lough, which tree is yet to be seen in the great
lough near the town, upon which depends the name,
and an old fabulous story too tedious to relate.
Thence to Falkirk, where, in the churchyard, I found
an ancient monument for John Græme, a famous
warrior, slain by the English anno 1298.   Thence
to Stirling, a very fair town, adorned with a curious
large church, a stately hospital, founded by Cowin,
a strong castle, and many noblemen's houses, the
Earls of Mar and Argyle, &c. being seated near the
Highlands; which shows to be a most formidable
country, full of mountainous crags and terrible high
hills.

17. Up pretty early, and over many a high hill
and barren mountain for nine miles to Kilseth, a
little country town.   Thence nine more, but in a
pleasant country, full of little towns, to Glasgow, the
university; a very pleasant city, far exceeding Edinburgh itself, in the situation and cleanness.   Transcribing some epitaphs from the Cathedral, and other
inscriptions of benefactions from the College, Hutchinson's hospital, &c.   From Glasgow, we returned

the same day to Kilseth, and from thence, with a guide, in a most terrible stormy night, over the hill to . . . . . bridge; and thence, though very late and tempestuous, to Falkirk by twelve o'clock, stretching so far, though to the hazard of all our bodies, that we might the less trespass upon the Lord's-day.

18. Die Dom. Rose very early again, after but a little sleep, and got by Linlithgow to Kirkliston, and thence to Edinburgh; though somewhat wearied with the hasty journey, thinking to return for England the next day. Went to the great church, beside the Parliament-House, where the minister made a very good and seasonable discourse against the sins of the times, particularizing many with the several apologies that are made for them, which he well confuted. Observed the stall of the Provost, many of the Bishops and persons of quality.

19. Not setting forward, as was designed, spent this day more in viewing the town, transcribing some monuments, those especially in the Abbey church, one most stately for the Lord Belhaven, another for Bishop Wishart, Lady Hamilton, and Lady Scot. Evening, taken up with company, and making ready for our journey.

20. Morning, set out pretty early with ditto Mr. Hickson, &c. from Edinburgh; we passed a pleasant country to Lubberton, thence to . . . ., and the Earl of Dalkeith's house over the moors and hills, (not far from Dalkeith, Monmouth's title,) to Bort-

wych castle; thence to Heriot House; then in the dale, with great hills on both hands; we crossed the river of Gallowater sixteen or fifteen times, as I counted it; and then the famous river of Tweed, near Selkirk.

21. Up by twelve o'clock, in order to a journey, and, with a guide, were got over most prodigious high hills and very many of them by daybreak; thence, by Teviotdale, upon the brink of a steep hill for some miles, to Usedale, where, upon the sudden, the precipice grew to that height and steepness, and withal so exceedingly narrow, that we had not one inch of ground to set a foot upon to alight from the horse. Our danger here was most dreadful, and, I think, inconceivable to any that were not present; we were upon the side of a most terrible high hill, in the middle whereof was a track for the horse to go in, which we hoped to find broader, that we might have liberty to turn the horse; but, instead of that, it became so narrow, that there was an impossibility to get further; for now it begun likewise to be a sudden declension, and the narrow way so cumbered with shrubs, that we might be forced to lie down upon the horses' necks, and have our eyes upon a dreadful precipice, such as mine eyes never till then beheld, nor could I have conceived the horror of it by any one's relation. We had above us a hill, so desperately steep, that our aching hearts durst not attempt the scaling of it, it being much steeper than the roofs of many houses;

but the hill below was still more ghastly, as steep
for a long way as the walls of a house; and the
track we had to ride in was now become so narrow,
that my horse's hinder foot slipped off, which Mr.
Hickson, following after, saw, but wisely concealed,
else the fright might possibly have sunk me.   To
add to our torments, there was a river run all along,
(which, added to the dizziness of our heads,) close
to the foot of the precipice, which we expected
every moment to be plunged into, and into eternity.
In this extremity (which now, many years after, in
transcribing this imperfect account from the loose
papers, makes my very hairs stand on end upon my
head,) there was no way but by catching hold of the
boughs of a tree, to throw myself off on the wrong
side the horse, (which I expected to have been dashed in pieces,) and to climb up the hill, which became, in a short space, less steep, that the horses
also escaped.   In the like danger were my fellow-
travellers, and by the like watchful providence preserved.   The river Use brought us to Langham, a
country town; thence we came to the Malees, the
first town upon English ground (in Cumberland);
from whence we got well, and in good time, to
Carlisle.

22. Viewing the castle, an ancient structure, a
seat of the present Earl of Carlisle's; then the
church, but frustrated of my expectations, most of
the monuments of antiquity being defaced, and nothing new worth observing.   After, at a feast at Mr.

Basil Fielding's; then with the mayor and several aldermen of Carlisle, but stayed too long, and drunk too freely. We made it pretty late ere we got to Penrith, where (as at Stirling) constrained to transcribe some monuments in the church, by candlelight.

23. From Penrith, leaving Brougham Castle on the one hand, and Lowther and Strickland, which give their names to two ancient families, on the other, we came by a monumental pillar, erected by Ann, Countess of Pembroke, where she parted with her religious mother, Margaret, Countess Dowager of Cumberland, to Appleby, a well-built pretty town, with a stately castle, rebuilt by the said noted Countess, who, with her mother, the said pious lady, lie entombed under two stately monuments; thence by some country towns, amongst the hills, to Kendal, the chief town in Westmoreland.

24. Viewing the town and church, transcribing some monuments of the Bellinghams, Stricklands, Judge Nichols, &c.; thence by Kirby Lonsdale, so called from the river Lune, that runs by it, over the Moors, &c. to Giggleswick, where viewed the noted well, (below the Scar, which is so high and rocky, that, in my opinion, it mightily resembles the Peak in Derbyshire,) that ebbs and flows daily, though far from sea; where likewise is a pretty church, and noted school, founded by Mr. Bridges, and endowed with about 50*l.* per annum; thence to Settle and Long Preston, a pretty country town, where is

an hospital for twelve poor widows, who have each 40*s*. per annum, by James Knowles, who left the remainder of the interest of 800*l*. to the use of the church; thence over the hills several miles in the dark, to Skipton, a larger town, that lies skulking among the hills, where is a stately castle, adorned with several pictures of the Cliffords, that ancient and eminently noble family, to whom it belonged, and who are buried under stately monuments in the church, which I transcribed.

25. Die Dom.   Got up pretty early, and rid to Ighley, and thence hoped to be in time enough for forenoon sermon, at my Lord Fairfax's, but came too late.   After an exceeding kind entertainment at dinner, we heard his Lordship's chaplain, Mr. Rymer, who made an excellent discourse from Revelations : " Blessed are the dead that die in the Lord, for they rest from all their labour.'   After sermon (though much against his Lordship's kind humour,) returned by Burley and Otley, to Leeds again.

28. Coming up the street with Mr. Hickson, we were sent for by the Earl of Eglinton ;* had some discourse with him concerning Scotland, his motion in that Parliament, &c.   After dinner, writing some epitaphs I had collected in my travels till evening.

Oct. 2. Die Dom.   Mr. Medcalf (to speak modestly, because of his function,) made a very ordinary mean sermon, full of bitter, malicious reflec-

* The Earl of Eglinton resided at Bretton-hall, having married a Lady Wentworth, of that place.

tions upon the Nonconformists, ripping up the wounds of the late unhappy times, exposing the blemishes of that worse than Egyptian thraldom, as he called it; expressly affirming that, but for the goodness of God, and wisdom of our rulers, we had at this day been brought to the same pass again; unworthily reflecting upon the whole Parliament, as though the abatement of a few ceremonies would have been the ruin of both Church and State,—a bad preparation sermon for the Sacrament.

6. Sorting letters, &c. till about eight, then rode with Mr. Jolly and Mrs. and Mr. Jackson to visit our friends at Swaith, who were gone to a sermon at Esquire Rodes', at Houghton-hall, but at evening returned accompanied with Mr. Kirby and his mother, a religious and ingenious young minister, from whom I had some information concerning his good father now with Christ.*

Nov. 2. To visit honest parson Ivison, and to thank him for his good sermons, those especially against Arminianism, whereat many dons were offended, though it was nothing but the doctrine of the true Church of England, as drawn up at Lam-

---

* In the early periods of his life Thoresby was a frequent visitor at Swaith-hall, a house standing in a retired and pleasant situation, about midway between Barnsley and Houghton. It was the residence of a Puritan family named Wordsworth. The Kirbys whom he met there were the widow and son of Joshua Kirby, who was the Lady Cambden Lecturer at Wakefield before the Act of Uniformity. He died under sentence of excommunication in 1676, and was buried in bis own garden. The son, who bore the name of God's-gift (Diodati) died when he was just entering on the ministry among the Nonconformists.

beth itself, and confirmed by Archbishop Abbot and
the Church in his time, by King James and the
whole Synod of Dort, and all the Reformed Churches
abroad.

5. Lay sluggishly too long in the morning. Rode
to Gleaday, being invited as a bearer to Mr. Waddington's funeral. Mr. Medcalf preached from Job
xix. 26. Afterwards went to Holbeck, rest of relations being gone before; stayed till pretty late, yet
after that up street, where upon earnest importunity
I had sent my ship to be discharged with the other
fireworks.

16· To Loftus to have a sight of some manuscripts of Mr. Hopkinson's, late Norroy King-at-
Arms.*

* This entry introduces us to the name of another labourer with
Johnston and Thoresby in retrieving the History of the County of
York. Lofthouse is a member of the Parish of Rothwell, which immediately adjoins to the Parish of Leeds; but though they were thus
neighbours, and both acquaintances of Dr. Johnston, it does not
appear that Thoresby had any intercourse with Hopkinson who lived
till 1680.

The manuscripts which he went to examine must have been those
which now form the forty-two volumes of " Hopkinson's Collections,"
preserved in the valuable library of Miss Currer, of Craven. They
consist of Surveys, Grants, Deeds, Tenures, Inquisitions, Sessions-
Proceedings, Letters, Pedigrees, in short, the whole apparatus of
Topography; but there is nothing arranged. In this he resembled
Dodsworth, in whose immense collections we look in vain for any
thing which can show to what extent he possessed the ability to com-
bine what he had with so much labour collected. The volume of
Hopkinson which is best known and most highly valued is, that
which contains the genealogies of West Riding families. It has been
often transcribed. There is a good copy in the Museum, (Harl.
4630); another, with many additions, in the Public Library at Leeds. -
In the preparation of this volume Hopkinson owed much to the

18. Evening reading the well writ life of that holy and renowned judge, Hale, the honour of England, and pillar of justice, of a christianly moderate temper. Oh, for such another incomparable triumvirate as Hale, Bridgman, and Wilkins, to heal our breaches and compose our differences!

Dec. 1. Evening reading the Earl of Northumberland's funeral sermon (a manuscript borrowed of kind cousin Sykes), and much affected with the seriousness and piety of that great lord.

24. Spent most of the day in writing of Mr. Bilney, martyr, who at the stake repeated the 143 Psalm, but paused upon these words, " Lord, enter not into judgment with thy servant," &c. ; with deep recollections, the sense whereof mightily affected me.

labours of Flower, Glover, and Saint George, the visiting heralds in 1585 and 1612: and still more to Sir William Dugdale's visitation in 1665 and 1666. He has followed too much in the track of the Heralds, and has admitted, without examination, whatever received their sanction. His work cannot be regarded as at all a critical disquisition. He has, however, some pedigrees which are illustrated by reference to charter-authority : he has a few which are not in any of the visitations; and he has some valuable notices of changes in the West Riding families between 1666 and 1680.

Thoresby owed much to this volume. Many of the pedigrees in the *Ducatus* are nothing more than transcripts of Hopkinson.

When Thoresby speaks of Hopkinson as being Norroy King-at-Arms, he means Deputy to Norroy, an office which Le Neve afterwards tendered to himself.

Hopkinson's Abstracts of Inquisitions, Grants, &c. are invaluable. Dr. Whitaker professes, that while engaged in preparing the *Loidis and Elmete*, not a day passed in which he was not indebted to some part of these extensive collections; and other persons engaged in similar researches have owed to them, and their liberal owner, the like obligations.

27. Up in the morning writing till ten; then heard Mr. Kay's Commemoration sermon, for the pious founder of the New Church, Mr. John Harrison, upon St. John's day.

31. Enquiring of Archbishop Margetson, a native of Drighlington, who there built and endowed a free-School, with seventy pounds per annum. After return had some visits. Evening at Mr. E. H's.; was concerned for some sad news of intentions to suppress conventicles, &c.

A.D. 1682.

Jan. 1. In the morning with several friends consulting; several of the Spiritual Court men being come to town : but it pleased God to prevent our fears, &c.

10. Somewhat discouraged in mind, and troubled about concerns in this world, for want of a way of trade; which is so frequently a trouble to me, that I am ready to think it is the hand of God to keep me humble.

13. Morning writing of martyrs about the latter end of Henry the Eighth. Was all day writing, and much satisfied till evening, when sent for to some company, Mr. Vandro, the Dutch painter, &c. though stayed not long, yet not the best employed.

24. With others, of better account than myself, to see a wonderful sight, a native Irishman, Edmund Mallory, (of whom see Dr. Plot's Staffordshire, p. 294,) born about twenty miles from Dublin, about sixteen years old, two yards and a half tall, wanting about two inches, and all parts proportionable, except legs, which were rather too slender for so vast a body. Some friends came home with me, and we sat up rather too late.

February 8. Writing of Heraldry till noon, then at Mrs. Scarborough's till evening, observing the way of casting waxen images.

11. Forenoon casting some medals and figures in plaster, with good success; but afternoon not spent so innocently, being called for by Mr. E. H. and though not in bad company, yet rather too free. Rise in the night to see the noted eclipse of the moon, reminding me of that text wherein the sun's being turned to darkness, and the moon into blood, (and so it seemed to be in the midst of this dark eclipse,) are recorded.

13. Forenoon employed chiefly in cementing the broken pieces of a large, ancient figure of Seneca's head, that worthy philosopher: after, writing of some pedigrees.

23. Up about four, transcribing the Earl of Northumberland's funeral sermon till day, most of which was spent in drawing the pictures of Cardinal Wolsey and Queen Catharine Dowager, from Burnet's History, &c.

25. Having rested badly, lay longer than ordinary; most of the day drawing in Indian ink the effigies of Queen Ann Bullen, Bishop Fisher, and

Dr. Collet; was mightily ashamed of myself, when I perused the pious and incomparable Lord Harrington's life; who, though a courtier, and in the prime of his days, was a most admirable example of true piety.

28. Most of the day spent in company at the marriage of Mrs. Mary Sykes with Mr. Thomas Rayner. Evening, sat up rather too late with young company.

March 1. Morning, when Mr. Sykes had prayed well with the family, the old gentlewoman, a Quaker, made a very seasonable exhortation to rejoice in the Lord,* and that Satan might not get advantage by our carnal mirth; the more proper being in her son's private house, (though a vast company of men and women,) and upon this occasion; else I am taught a woman's duty is rather to learn in silence than teach in public; afterwards, officiated as a servitor, and employed in like affairs not only the day, but too much of the night.

9. Morning reading; then cleansing the Misery of War, and other pictures, and employed about such affairs till five; then worse employed, though not in bad company, till pretty late.

24. Up at five, writing much of that prudent, just, pious, and valorous Prince, Algernon, Earl of

---

* A younger sister of Mrs. Mary Sykes, was afterwards the wife of Thoresby. The " old gentlewoman," who has appeared once before, was Mrs. Grace Sykes, the grandmother of the bride, one of the daughters of Jenkinson, a considerable benefactor to Leeds.

Northumberland; then about pictures, and attending relations till four; then sent for by Mr. I. of Lynn, to the Talbot; stayed too late, and was much troubled to see the besottedness of some persons there before.

25. Lay sluggishly till almost seven; sent for immediately to Mrs. S. to compose some differences betwixt two neighbours; employed there about it not in the morning only, but too late at night, even till twelve; the afternoon was spent with friends, &c.

27. Lay too long, and was then immediately called out to make peace betwixt two neighbours, of different nations, which, with other help, was at last effected; was then at the funeral of honest Mr. Lever, a sound, orthodox, and ingenious man. After dinner attending cousins, mostly at uncle M. I.'s. Alas! how much of the short time I have to remain in this tabernacle of clay am I constrained thus to spend in vanity. Evening also spent in the like offices.

28. So too much of this day, especially the afternoon, (when with them to see the activity of a tumbler on the stage,) spent in the like waste work, which somewhat disordered me; for, alas! what answer can I make for all this lost time!

April 5. Forenoon with cousin Thoresbys, of Sykehouse, who, notwithstanding former unkindnesses, (endeavours to deprive me of the estate in the north) have been very welcome in their present

straits to my house, but have exceedingly straitened me for time about better things, and made me
lose much of that precious commodity in every respect. After their departure, was at Mr. B. D.'s,
and at uncle M. I.'s, which took up most of the
afternoon, as the sight of some baboons, bear, and
wolf did the evening.

6. Was the whole day entirely at the new garden,
by the water, overseeing workfolk, and reading
Sir William Waller's Divine Meditations, which I
thought exceedingly sweet and agreeable, especially
his content in his study, books, and a solitary life.
But, Lord! teach me, as the holy author desires, so
to study other men's works, as not to neglect my
own good: take me off from the curiosity of knowing only to know, from the vanity of knowing only
to be known, and from the folly of pretending to
know more than I do know, and let it be my wisdom to study to know thee, who art life eternal.
Afternoon was much afflicted with what I heard of
the foolish actions and wicked words of a near relation, so near and dear to me that it wounded me
to the very heart.

17. Rode with aunt Idle to Tong, to procure
flowers for the new garden, of the noted florist
there; but was severely wet, and not without danger in passing a small rivulet prodigiously risen with
the thunder-showers, but got well home.

18. Up before four, writing, then setting ditto
roots till about six, then rode to York with sister.

Had company of several relations of Mrs. Hickson, (where left her) that somewhat mitigated the trouble of the rainy journey.

19. Up pretty early, in order to a Hull journey, which was prevented by the wetness of the season. Spent the forenoon in viewing the Minster monuments. After, in visits with ditto company.

20. Forenoon abroad, viewing the Tower with the armoury for about 3000 men, the dungeon, &c. with a large crocodile (about four yards long).

26. Rose not early this morning; till ten collecting for Mr. Sharp, who would not be prevented by the uncomfortableness of the season, nor danger of the floods, but came to do good.*

May 5. Rode to Snidall. Paid Aunt the full of this year's gratuity. Went on to Pontefract; found an unexpected occasion to manifest charity to Uncle Captain Thoresby's widow, now ruined through the extravagance of her son. Oh, how sadly is this once flourishing family now changed, since my grandfather (not to mention former ages, when our ancestors lived at, and were Lords of Thoresby, Sedbar, Dent, &c.†) then chief magistrate, with his

* Mr. Sharp resided at his own house at Horton, some miles from Leeds, while he was pastor of the Presbyterian Nonconformists in that town.

† This was always a favourite topic; and Thoresby seems to have been well satisfied with the pedigree presented to him by the Heralds in 1701; without enquiring too scrupulously for the evidence by which a series of generations is to be established from the days of Canute to those of King Edward I. The reader who feels any curiosity on this subject, may peruse the pedigree in the *Ducatus*, p. 71.

four sons and their wives, were in their meridian splendour. Dr. Johnston being out of town, returned the sooner with Mr. E. H.; but stayed too late at his house.

6. Lay too long in the morning. After, taking leave of Alderman Jackson, of Carlisle, which lost most of the forenoon; as some little accounts and discourse with my good old servant, Judith, who is about altering her condition, did the after. Abroad till after seven; then reading in Mr. Young's Christian Library.

13. Forenoon, with Cousin W. and advising with Mr. B. D.; then writing till noon. Afternoon, visiting Aunt Lucy, but spent most of it in reading the Apology for Nonconformists, in my poor judgment well done; in answer to the High Tories, that are for closing with the Papists, rather than Protestant Dissenters.

June 1. Morning, writing letters; then at the marriage of Nehemiah Cloudesley by old Mr. Armitage. Discoursing him concerning old Mr. Saxton :* except an hour or two in the afternoon, and about as much in the evening, that I was with Mr. Illingworth. Spent the whole day at the wedding house, and most of the night, it being too late ere I could get away.

2. Up again before three, in preparation for a

---

* Peter Saxton, who held the vicarage of Leeds during the Commonwealth. The result of Thoresby's enquiries respecting him may be seen in the *Vicaria*.

journey with ditto Mr. Illingworth. Was much
satisfied with his learned discourses, and many
remarkable stories concerning almost all places we
travelled through, particularly concerning the last of
the family of the Elands, of Eland, slain at Both-
omley Wood, by the children of those knights he
had before barbarously murdered when High Sheriff.*
Upon the height of Blackstone-edge, we left Yorkshire, and had a pleasant prospect of Lancashire in
a fruitful vale below, where stands Littleborrow, a
country town, and, somewhat beyond, Cleghall on
the one hand, and Howard on the other, the ancient
seat of the famous family of that name.†   Not far
from Rochdale, a fair market town, is Hopwood-
hall, the seat of the famous Justice Hopwood, whose
memory I exceedingly honour for the many good
offices he performed to the good old Lancashire Puritans, and the many remarkable passages related of
him by the ingenious Mr. Illingworth, who hath
promised me copies of many of his letters, wherein
he gives very favourable characters of the good old
Nonconformist ministers, Midgeley Sen., Langley,

---

* The historical labours of Mr. Watson and Dr. Whitaker, have
thrown but little light on this feud, which is the subject of two nar-
ratives, one in prose and the other in verse, portions of the popular
literature of Yorkshire. I find also in one of Dodsworth's MSS.,
that the circumstances of this tragical history were represented on a
stage by itinerant performers, in the reign of King James I. Such
performances, rather than the moralities and mysteries, seem to be
the rude beginnings of the English drama.

† This is contrary to what was at that time the received doctrine
on the origin of the house of Howard. Dr. Whitaker has stated
with great clearness the presumptions in favour of this opinion.

&c. to the Bishop.   Thence by Middleton, where the
church has a wooden steeple, built almost like a dove-
coat, but a living of . . . . per ann, and has been in
the name of the Ashtons since long before the Reformation.   Thence within view of the house where
Ralph Brideoak, late Bishop of Chichester, was born,
to the famous town of Manchester, where

3. I was employed from morning to evening, observing the library and college richly endowed for
the maintenance of sixty blue coat boys, by the eminent benefactor, Mr. Humphrey Chetham, sheriff,
eleventh of Charles I. ; was also in Salford, and the
Collegiate church, writing the inscriptions from monuments of Huntingdon, the first, and Heyrick, the
last (and fourteenth) warden, from those of the Radcliffes, Howards, &c., assisted by the ingenious Mr.
James Illingworth, the worthy President of Emanuel
College, Cambridge.

4. Designed for the Morning Sermon but missed
the beginning, which I was more concerned for, because the latter part was so good ; then heard Mr.
Warden.

5. Morning, rose early, by three, or sooner, designing a journey to Chester, though not so well furnished as I should, having consulted neither Camden
nor Fuller, not designing further than Manchester,
near unto which is seated Hulm, the present habitation
of Judge Moseley, and not much distant Ordesal, the
ancient seat of the warlike family of the Radcliffes,
now Colonel Birch's, and thence by the river Mersey

to Trafford, whence a family of great note has their name; thence to Bowden, in Cheshire, where I found in the church a stately monument of the Breretons, (of which family Camden has a remarkable story of some trees floating in Bagmere, only upon the death of the heirs), Warburtons and Booths of Dunham, now deservedly honoured with the title of Lord Delamere; as for the inscriptions, *vid.* my Collection of Epitaphs, p. 171. Upon the hill I had a fair prospect of the country; Baggeleigh, the ancient seat of the Baggeleighs, now Leighs of Baggeleigh; Rawston church, where, as I was informed by Mr. Martindale, chaplain to the Lord Delamere, is an ancient monument of a knight in armour, of the Venables' (patrons of the living) which has been of great reputation ever since the Norman Conquest, and the Leighs of High Leigh, another ancient family: but the most noted in this age is the Booths of Dunham, by reason of that famous knight, Sir George Booth, now Lord Delamere, and not far off Henry Booth, Esq. a learned and pious gentleman.   Thence through a most pleasant vale abounding with wood and fruitful pastures, which produces the famous Cheshire cheese, to Norwiche, a pretty market town, in which pleasant vale Sir Robert Leicester's, a pretty seat, is not to be omitted; thence through a delicate country to the famous forest of Delamere, now honoured by giving honour to that worthy knight, by the Chamber in the Forest, (some houses seated upon the height of the hill and seen far off,) to Tarvin, whereabout we have a prospect of Beeston Castle, about five miles off, seated upon a high towering hill, and seems to me not very unlike Stirling, or Maiden Castle, in Edinburgh for the situation. It was built by the last Ranulph, Earl of Chester, that ancient and famous city where I spent the rest of the day, (except about two or three hours discourse with Dr. Bispham, the ancient sub-dean of Chester and Alderman Floyd, about the antiquities of the town) mostly in the churches of St. Werburgh, St. John Baptist, and St. Mary, but met with a disappointment as to tombs of bishops; this being one of the bishoprics of the royal foundation by King Henry VIII. there can be none of any great antiquity : of the modern bishops, none are buried there but Dr. Hall and Dr. Bridgeman, (brother to the famous Lord Keeper) late Bishop of the Isles, who dying about May, 1682, was interred in St. Werburgh's, but as yet there is no monument or inscription. Evening, I walked round the walls; observed the situation of the city, and had a prospect of Wales towards Flint; the walls are kept in excellent repair by the Muringers.*

6. Up pretty early writing; took a view of the Castle, in which is the Hall for the Judges, inferior to none in England, that I have seen, except Westminster. In St. Peter's church, I found a remarkable tomb for the Offleys, great benefactors ; and in the pentis or town-house, his picture, with Mr. Randall's, and Sir Thomas White's, with an account of their

* See King's *Vale Royal*, p. 18.

pious gifts, and of Broughtons, from which pentis there is a curious prospect into the four best streets, in all which, and indeed, most of the city, we may pass through the rows in a stormy day without the least rain or prejudice; it is a sort of building peculiar to this city, the like they say not being to be seen in Europe again; they are as walks chambered above, and cellared below, with shops mostly on both sides. From this ancient city (though I could find few monuments of antiquity in memory of the famous Earls of Chester) I departed about ten o'clock, and rode through a very pleasant country, and over a remarkable hill called Helsby Tor, (a Derbyshire word I think, for crag, or rock,) to Frodsham, near which we have a most pleasant prospect of Rock Savage, a stately house, formerly belonging to the Savages, and now to the Earl of Rivers, on the one hand, and a delicate new building of Sir Willoughby Aston's, on the other, with delicate gardens, &c.; seven miles further stands Warrington, a pretty market town, upon the Mersey, in Lancashire, whereof the Butlers were lords; in memory of some of which family is an ancient monument of a Knight in armour, and a modern white one for Sir George Butler, slain in the wars, and his lady; thence by Eccles, where is a stately monument for another branch of the numerous family of the Breretons, to Manchester.

7. Employed in observing the Earl of Derby's and Chetham's chapels in Manchester Collegiate Church, walking abroad in the town, and taking

leave of Mr. Newcome, a worthy good man and pious divine.

8. Took leave of the learned and ingenious Mr. Illingworth, and of Manchester, famous for the vast quantity of wares and commodities made there, whereof I was most taken with their inkles, eighteen several pieces whereof they can weave in the same loom.   Got very well home with the other company.

19. At Mr. Scudamore's to see his collections of heraldry, which merit commendation.*

30. After four at Mrs. R's. perusing her brother's, Mr. Lever's choice collection of books.   Thus one month more of my short pilgrimage is slipt away never to be recalled.

July 1. Morning writing at Mr. Rooke's.   After with cousins F. and I. at Ledston-hall, had the opportunity of discoursing with Mr. Bean concerning some memoirs of the famous Sir John Lewys, whose manuscript I have by me.

2. Die Dom.   Mr. Kein had not only a well worded but serious affectionate discourse concerning the last judgment.   Mr. Sharp had a learned discourse from Micah ii. 7.   Doctrine, that the word of God is a means of good to them that walk uprightly; if this word bring not life it brings death.   Evening, disturbed by a message from the Lady Dalston and her sister (since Countess of Wiltshire)† intro-

* Thomas Scudamore, an inhabitant of Leeds, who died in 1693. See *Duc. Leod.* p. 32.

† These ladies were of the family of Ramsden of Byrom.

duced by Madam Dawkrey to see my collection of
rarities and coins, which with reluctance I resisted,
because of the unseasonableness, with proffer of
service to-morrow, whereby I avoided the outward
breach of the command. But, alas! my vain
thoughts, like tinder, are easily enflamed, and any
good motion like a spark quickly extinguished.

4. Morning abroad inquisitive after public concerns.
Forenoon advising with Mr. B. D.; after till near three
with Mr. E. H. expecting but disappointed of his
company at G's., where several were consulting about
our public liberties now in much hazard.

5. Morning at old Mr. Boyse's writing London
letters, and advising with Mr. Sharp; showed the
order of Court for suppressing conventicles, which
with other circumstances (the officers having surprised Brook and got the key of the chapel) prevented our public assembly, but through mercy enjoyed in private an excellent sermon, from Hos. vi. 1.
Doctrine, that God's people in afflictions may promise themselves mercy upon their returning to him.
Showing that mercy is not absolutely ready for them
but only upon their renewed repentance; the stress is
not to be laid upon our first repentance before afflictions, but upon that renewed under them. Old
repentance will not serve for new guilt. Added a
word of caution that temporal deliverances could not
be expected at the very juncture of repentance like
spiritual pardon might, but in God's due time,
which is best: then came to the grounds upon which

mercy may be expected ; viz. upon our returning to
God, as it is a condition of the promise, else our returning in itself, strictly taken, can no more oblige
God to show mercy than a beggar's coming to receive
alms doth the giver, who only is bound by his promise.   1st. Use for doctrine : it teaches 1st. wherein
our security, comfort, and peace doth consist in an
evil day; not in carnal confidence, but in returning
to the Lord, who is both shield and buckler ; the
world and sin are but like eclipsing evils, which
interposing betwixt God and our souls, deprive us of
all light and comfort, as the body of the earth betwixt the sun and moon, which of itself is but a
globe of mere darkness.   2. That the goodness that
is in us cannot merit any thing of God.   3. That
the wicked who are apt to promise themselves most
have least reason to expect mercy. . . . . Dined
with Mr. Sharp at E. H's., then consulting where to
meet on Lord's-day.

6. Morning up writing ; then at cousin Fenton's
christening, and to visit Stittenham friends, stayed
there late in the evening, but avoided even the
tendency to intemperance, notwithstanding solicitations, which I take notice of not for self-applause,
but for the praise of God, who is a God hearing
prayers.

7. Forenoon with the haymakers, and at Mr. R's.;
but after till about four at Mr. B. D's., advising—
then with relations till late in the evening.

9. Die Dom. Much affected in meditation of the

inexpressible loss of our public liberties, which cost
me multitudes of tears and sighs, and yet infinitely
short of the bitterness of heart that might, and
should have seized upon me for those crying sins
that have provoked God to deprive us of a mercy
that certainly is more valuable than all the world
besides.   Lord, help me to forbear murmuring at
man who is only thy instrument, and to take revenge upon my own corruptions, that are the meri-
torious cause of these sad dispensations; and do
thou graciously pour down a double blessing upon
thy word dispensed in private.   After ten, walked
to Holbeck, to late uncle Idle's house (now Mr.
Scur's) where, through mercy, we enjoyed the learned labours of worthy Mr. Sharp, from Micah ii. 7,
which he now concluded, being upon the fourth use
for instruction, how we must do to profit by the
word, and walk uprightly.   1. With a troubled spirit reflect upon the little good thou hast obtained.
2. Renounce the evils that are contrary. 3. Receive
the word for its own ends.   4. Possess yourselves of
it by a particular application.   5. Digest the word
of God.   6. Labour to get the Spirit, whose hand is
not shortened. 7. Labour to find out your defects. 8.
Look unto Jesus Christ, the essential work of God;
it is life above all to know him as thy possession.
There are three sorts of good things that the mind
of man looks upon—what is pleasant, profitable, and
honourable, and the end of God is also these.   1. It
brings with it more true and satisfactory pleasure

than that of the greatest epicure.   2. It is not only transcendant pleasure in itself, but is that which sweetens all else.   3. It is a means to the highest and most refined comfort.   Lastly, profitable both for temporal and eternal salvation.   It brings the highest honours.   Liberty to be God's freemen is no petty honour; but it makes us the sons of the King of Heaven by adoption.   Oh! that I may experience it is good for me to draw nigh unto God, whose name be blessed for protection vouchsafed to us, even when others of his own people are disturbed and broken up, as two meetings at this town to-day have been.

12. Up about three, writing heads, &c. and preparing for the Spas.   Got well thither, and so early as to drink the waters this morning; and was unexpectedly happy in good Mr. Corlass's company, so with Mr. E. H. and T. W.'s.

13. After the morning drinking, had the additional felicity of Mr. Henry Fairfax's company, which was still the more acceptable, because the most of the guests at this house are Papists.   Had the advantage of Mr. Corlass's prayers, morning and evening.

14. *Ut prius*, drank the waters; but lost our good company.   Had some ineffectual discourses, *ut prius et postea*, with the Torycal Papists.

16. Die Dom.   Forenoon, drank of the sweet Spa, but not sulphur water; after, went to Knaresborough, where heard a stranger discourse from that

of the Pharisee: " Lord, I am not as other men, extortioner, &c." whence he spoke well, concerning the advantage of humility, and the plague of a proud, contemptuous spirit.

17. Morning, drunk the waters, and returned by noon ; in return, upon Chapeltown Moor, saw Mr. Sk. and Mr. Sm. ride their own horses for a wager, which was the first, and, for aught I know, may be the last horse-course ever seen by me. Most of the afternoon at Mr. Scarborough's, taking leave, and assisting, in order to a journey. Evening, at uncle Idle's and Mr. S. Ibbetson's.

19. Up about five, writing post letters, and perusing accounts till ten ; then at Mr. B. Dixon's; had the opportunity of hearing an excellent discourse.

23. After dinner, went to Hunslet, to hear Mr. Sharp, at Mr. Thomas Fenton's, but was so crowded with the multitudes, that almost sick and fainted, and altogether displeased at some inconveniences, through the unmannerliness of some of the ruder sort ; which hindered me, in some measure, from profiting by the good word, the excessive crowd, and intolerable disorder of the common people constraining them to begin an hour before the time appointed.

25. Up at four, in order to a York journey; got well thither, double-horsed, pretty timely ; dispatched business with sister and Mrs. Hickson, and visited poor Mr. Tricket, (a nonconformist minister, pri-

soner in York Castle, merely for conscience sake,) and widow Bell. The Lord doth more than reward anything that is done in uprightness of heart for his poor suffering servants.

26. Up about four, to hear Mr. Ward at cousin I. I.'s, from Heb. x. 38.

30. Die Dom. Morning, and much of the fore-noon, walking in the garden, reading or meditating; was sometimes much affected, especially with Dr. Wilkins' incomparable treatise of Prayer. Mr. Sharp, from Isaiah lv. 6, 7, made a most incomparable dis-course, both learned and long, (not tedious) for he preached two hours and a half, by Mr. W.'s, and church clock.

Aug. 4. Lay till about six, then writing; doing some little business before noon; designed for the Spas; we called at Mayor's, and took Bardsey in our way, where Baron Thorp* lived, died, and lies interred; got well thither; had the good, serious company of cousin Ibbetson.

6. Die Dom. After water time in the morning, had the opportunity to hear good Mr. Gunter, but was indisposed with the waters which made me ex-cessively drowsy. Afternoon, he preached from the same, Isaiah xxxviii. 14, being the prayer of Heze-kiah upon his sick (and, as he thought, death) bed, of the plague. Was somewhat disturbed with the sight of an informer, who got cunningly into the

---

* A Baron of the Exchequer, in the time of the Commonwealth.

meeting; but, blessed be God, for restraining him from doing any harm as yet.

8. Morning, spent this also, as the former, in the course of the Spas, but lost cousin I. and Mr. Gunter's company, a greater loss, because good company so scarce.

12. Up before five, writing; rid to Halifax, had the pleasing society of Mr. Brearcliffe, the ingenious antiquary, who kindly lent me his manuscript collection; in return, visited Mr. Sharp, &c.

14. Rose pretty early. Most of the day taken up with visitants, to see Holroyd pass by to his execution, for the horrid murder of Mr. Scurr, his mother, and a maid-servant. After, rode to the moor, where were many thousand spectators; but, alas! frustrated exceedingly in their expectations, he dying in the most resolute manner that ever eye beheld, wishing (upon the top of the ladder) he might never come where God had anything to do if he was guilty, and so threw himself off in an anger as it were, without any recommendation of himself to God that any could observe, which struck tears into my eyes, and terror to my heart, for his poor soul, earnestly imploring, while I saw any signs of life, that God would give him repentance for his crying sins, and be better to him than his desires.

15. Morning, writing; most of the forenoon with Squire Lambert,* (son to the old Lord General,)

* In one of Thoresby's MSS. at the Museum, there is a biographical notice of Mr. Lambert, in which, it is said, that "he was a

showing him my collection of coins, pictures, &c., and with Mr. Lodge, our townsman born, an ingenious traveller and painter; rest of the day abroad, about trivial occasions.

16. Writing to Rotterdam. Lord, succeed my lawful endeavours : this is the first I ever made trial of in this kind.

25. Up at five ; for an hour abroad about business ; then transcribing from a manuscript till noon ; after, taking a catalogue of English pictures till seven ; was then at Mr. T. S. and S. H., who came along with me to see the comet upon our turret. Lord, fit us for whatever changes or alterations it may portend ; for, though I am not ignorant that such meteors proceed from natural causes, yet are frequently also the presages of imminent calamities.

26. Up at five, writing till noon, chiefly for Mr. B. D., Englishing the town's charter, and reading Sir John Lewys' manuscript account of Madagascar and Johanna ; spent the afternoon idly, in visits at uncle M.'s and Mr. Whitaker's,* though in good

most exact limner, and had a choice collection of paintings ; an excellent scholar, man of much reading, great memory, admirable parts ; and in the exercises of bowling, shooting, and the like, excelling all the gentry of Craven." It may be doubted whether, what has been often repeated of General Lambert's attachment to the arts, and skill in painting, does not rather belong to his son.

* Beside the nonconforming community, with which Thoresby was connected, there was at Leeds another body of Nonconformists, whose public services were conducted in a place called The Main Riding House, till 1691, when they built, what Thoresby calls, a stately chapel, in a street named Call Lane. The original pastor of this congregation was Christopher Nesse, who had been the lecturer

company, and not ill-employed, (perusing his library,) yet too little time redeemed for the *unum necessarium.*

29. Morning, up at five, writing; then showing our collection of coins to Dr. Howel, the learned Chancellor of Lincoln,* who professed it was the most curious and complete collection he ever beheld, except one in France, wherein were 15,000*l.* in gold and silver medals.

31. Most of forenoon abroad with strangers, and discharging some messages; after, visited by Mr. Joseph Boyse, spent all the afternoon in his good company, visiting with him several friends.

Sept. 6. Up at five, perusing some part of Mr. Waterhouse's manuscript, which he lent me yesterday, wherein he exactly hits the mark, and avoids both extremes with great caution and prudence. Afternoon, a great part in showing the collections to Squire Ramsden's daughters, till about five.

---

at Leeds, in the time of the Commonwealth.   He left Leeds in 1675, and was succeeded by Mr. Whitaker, son to a physician, at Burnley, in Lancashire.

Mr. Whitaker was the pastor of this congregation from 1675 to 1710, in which year he died.   He was, during this period, the contemporary of Thoresby, at Leeds, and a great degree of intimacy seems to have subsisted between them.   Some account of Mr. Whitaker's useful life, and specimens of his mode of preaching, may be found in a volume, dedicated to his memory, published in 1712.

He was succeeded by Mr. Moult, another friend of Thoresby, and contributor to his museum, on whose death, in 1727, a second Thomas Whitaker, son to the former, became pastor of this society, and continued to be so till his death in 1778.

* Author of *An Institution of General History,* 1661.

7. Morning, up at five; rode to Wakefield, and after to Swaith-hall; and afternoon with cousin Wadsworth to Silkstone, viewed the delicate and noble tomb of Sir Thomas Wentworth, whose widow is since married to the Earl of Eglinton; saw the glass-houses.

8. Forenoon, at Wentworth, to see and transcribe the monuments of that ancient family, but found none erected yet for the Earl, but two curious ones for (his) father and grandfather, and Sir William Rokeby. After dinner returned home; had the company of the good old gentleman to Wakefield. This day, Mr. L. stabbed in the heart Nath. Hoy's man, with his shoemaker's knife, that it is feared he will die of it.

20. Lay till after five; morning writ to London; then at the Moor to see my kind friend Mr. Henry Fairfax, the soldiers trained, and a foot-race, three times round, above six measured miles, which they run in thirty or thirty-three minutes, at the utmost: *cuique sua dos:* afternoon writing, &c.

25. Employed in the upper study writing and reading till four. Evening at W. A.'s, discoursing with his former servant, now Dr. Newton, author of an Herbal, with cuts, in 8vo. to which subscribed 10s. as also did Mr. Samuel Ibbetson.*

---

* That no enquirer into the progress of botanical knowledge may search in vain for this volume, I add from the *Review*, that Newton never finished it, and refused to return the subscription money he had received. The letters W. A. denote William Atkinson, who

October 6. Morning reading a little; after rode with ditto, E. H. to the funeral of the good, religious, Lady Barwick; but could not stay to hear Mr. Corlass preach, which vexed me.

15. Die Dom. Mr. Milner, from Isaiah liv. 13, made a very learned discourse in confutation of our modern enthusiasts, who, upon pretence of being taught of the Lord, do slight all public Ordinances.

16. Evening sent for by lawyer Hilliard, an ingenious antiquary,* and Dr. Robinson, with whom spent some time pleasantly.

17. Most of the day abroad, partly with dear aunt Lucy Idle, condoling her great affliction in her son Thomas; spent rest of day and evening with ditto lawyer Hilliard, brother to the late Sir R. H.

31. Morning received a letter of bad news; imprisonment and persecution of many good ministers in Middlesex, merely for conscience sake; the Lord be their comfort; very much or most of the day abroad, about that and other occasions, with Mr. O. Heywood, Mr. Boyse, &c. with whom evening likewise spent to some satisfaction.

November 1. Morning up very early; writing heads of sermons till near eight; then writing to

---

was a Whitesmith, living in the same street with Thoresby. Newton had been his apprentice, and, at this time, kept a house in London, for the reception of lunatics.

* Christopher Hildyard, Esq. Recorder of Headon and Steward of St. Mary's Court, at York. He published *A Catalogue of the Mayors and Sheriffs of York from* 1273 *to* 1664. Thoresby says that he had a good collection of ancient coins and modern medals.

Newcastle; rest of forenoon abroad, with worthy Mr. Heywood and Mr. Boyse, at Mr. E. H.'s, with whom rode after dinner to honest Mr. Middlebrooke's, steward above twenty years to the Earl of Sussex, to hear some remarkable stories of old Sir John Savile, which took up rest of day.

2. Perusing Camden and Speed, in order to a northern journey, most of day; about three visited by Mr. Mann; after by Madame D. and Mrs. M. N. with whom spent the evening.

3. Employed as yesterday, consulting Fuller; then maps, till after three, when surprised with the sad news of Mr. Sharp's being dangerously sick, went abroad about that and some other occasions, but spent evening not so cautiously.

4. Morning, up pretty early writing; after with Mr. E. H. and T. W. rode to Little Horton, to visit worthy Mr. Sharp; whom, blessed be our gracious and merciful God, we found much better than we expected.

6. Morning up rather too early, about two, writing and perusing some books and papers, in order to a journey; after employed about some friends' concerns, and taking leave of relations till noon; then rode with Mr. Richard Mann by Harwood, where is an ancient castle, that has often changed the owners. In the church are some ancient tombs; the most remarkable is for Judge Gascoyne, of whom *vid.* Fuller's Worthies in Yorkshire; then by Rip-

ley, the seat of the ancient family of the Inglebys,
whereof Sir William died this day at his prayers,
(as informed by worthy Mr. Kirshaw, the minister,)
of an impostume, having been twice at church the
day before, and repeated sermon at night.   We designed to have reached Massam, but being benight-
ed, got well, though in the dark, to Fountains.

7. Husbanded not the morning so well as might
be ; rid by, (and through mistake almost round,) the
famous Abbey of Fountains, built by Thurstan,
Archbishop of York ; formerly a stately Abbey, as
appears by the very ruins, now full of trees, within
the very body of it ; and a stately modern hall, with
Benedicite Fontes, Domine inscribed upon the portal.
Thence we rid to Ripon, which boasts of a stately
Cathedral Church, wherein is St. Winifred's needle
and some tombs ; thence by Stavely, where Justice
Stavely, a great traveller, has a pretty seat, to Tan-
field, which has a pretty tower, belonging to the
Earl of Elgin, and a church, with monuments of the
ancient family of the Fitz Hughs, and a Free-School,
built and endowed by the Lady Diana Cecil, (of the
Earl of Exeter's family,) first married to the Earl of
Oxford, and then to the Earl of Aylesbury, to whose
son she married her niece ; and, having no children
of her own, left them a great estate, and built there
a Free School, which she endowed with 25l. per
annum, as I was informed by Mr. Hutchinson, the
master and hired minister.   Thence by Wells, a

pretty country town, with a handsome church, by
Snape Hall, a stately fabric of the . . . .* now
by marriage of one of his co-heirs, the Earl of Aylesbury's; after, not far from Thorp Hall, now the
Lady Danby's; and near Bedal had a prospect,
at a distance, of Hornby Castle. Bedal is a pretty
market town, which has a handsome church, with
several old monuments, particularly a very stately
one of a knight cross-legged, in armour, and his
lady, curiously cut in stone to their full proportion;
as one in the wall, which I could fancy some Bishop.
There is another knight in armour, with his shield,
a chevron betwixt three roses, but without any inscription; as also is one of the Escues, near Fitz
Alan's; and another nearer the door, of a knight in
armour, with a lion at his feet, but could not be informed of what families. I transcribed only that of
Lambert and Young.

Here is also a Free School, to which some of the
Wrays, either Sir Christopher or Sir John, was a
benefactor; and an hospital of Mr. Young's for
three poor widows, who have each 40s. per annum,
which was lately recovered to their use by Sir Miles
Stapleton; who has the disposal of 100*l.* left by
another Mr. Young, who died about twenty years
since, the interest whereof is yearly disposed of for
the education of youth, or some other charitable
purpose, as informed by ditto clerk. In a mile

* This blank might be filled up either with the words " Lord
Latimer," or " Lord Burghley."

whereof, at Firby, is an hospital built by Mr. Clapham for six poor old men, and a master, who have
each 5*s.* per month, (two-pence per day) beside coats,
caps, gowns, &c. and each a pretty orchard, and the
master more.   He left also to the disposal of Bedal
Church six five-marks, to be lent gratis, for three
years, to six or twelve poor tradesmen.   Thence, by
Catterick, where is a pretty hospital, built and liberally endowed by Mr. Siddall (born at York) their
Vicar.   In the church is an ancient monument of a
knight in armour, for one of the Saltmarsh's, as supposed; and several curious large blue stones, with
statues in brass, and inscriptions as old as 1412, for
the Burghs, of Burgh, hard by; where now inhabits
Sir John Lawson, whose lady, and Lady Braithwait,
are here interred, but without any inscription.

8. From Catterick we rid to Piercebridge, an ancient Roman colony, where have been dug up many
of their coins and inscriptions, particularly that
altar I have at home.   It is now a poor village,
without either church or chapel.   Thence, by Wal-
worth-hall, a delicate seat of the Jenisons, built
archwise with turrets.   Thence, by Highinton and
Elden, to Kirkmarinton, the church whereof is built
upon so high a hill that it is seen many miles off.
There, had a prospect of Durham Abbey, whither
(leaving Branspeth Castle, the delicately pleasant
seat of the ingenious Sir Ralph Cole, on the left
hand) we arrived in time to observe the antiquities
of St. Cuthbert and his Cow (cut in stone upon the

Minster,) and venerable Bede, who lies interred under a stately blue marble, but without inscription save this, handsomely chalked round the edge, *Hâc sunt in fossâ Bedæ venerabilis ossa.* Observed too, the Castle and Bishop's Palace, much built and beautified by the memorable Bishops Tonstal and Cousins, who built also the alms-houses in the Square, and the Library, as appears by the arms fixed upon them in many eminent places. Viewed also the Tolbooth and Cross, built by ditto Tonstal; and spent much of the evening with Cousin Mich. Walker's.

9. Morning, rode to Chester, and stayed with Aunt Thoresby and cousins. Wrote some of the inscriptions of the tombs of the Lords Lumley, from Lyulph the first, who flourished in King William the Conqueror's time, and was a great cherisher of St. Cuthbert; whose ancient monuments scattered in the neighbouring abbeys, and at Durham, were collected and placed there in a curious delicate manner, by John, ninth lord. Thence, got well to Newcastle; spent the evening in business, viewing the town, &c.

10. Up very early, and having dispatched business, rode with ditto Mr. Richard Mann to North Shields. By the way had a sight of a pleasant hall of Mr. Clark's, now Captain Bickerstaff's. Went to view Clifford Fort; copied the inscription. It is fortified with forty cannons. Had a prospect of Tinmouth Castle, and ancient church; and below,

of the Spanish fort, built close by the sea by Queen
Elizabeth.   After having observed their way of boil-
ing salt, ferried over to South Shields.   Thence,
through Weston, and within sight of Whitburn, by
the sea to Hilton, the seat of an ancient family of
that name ; whereof Baronet Hilton (as the report
is, from some private dissatisfaction because of his
marriage with an inferior woman, which put him
upon a resolution that none from her should heir
above 100*l.* per annum) gave the ancient estate
(being about 3000*l.* per annum) to charitable uses,
making the Lord Mayor of London and Aldermen
trustees, for the term of one hundred or else one
thousand years, wanting one.   Thence, by Cle-
den and Fulwell, to Monck-Wearmouth, where Sir
Thomas Williamson has a pleasant house and gardens.   Thence ferried over to Sunderland, where we
lodged.

11. Having overnight observed what was remarkable in Sunderland, which is of late grown to
a considerable repute and resource for coals and
salt, rode through Bishops-Wearmouth ; which was,
saith Camden, much beautified with chapels by Be-
nedict Bischop, who first procured masons and gla-
ziers in England.   Thence, through some country
towns, Easington, &c. to Hartinpoole, where transcribed some things from the ancient church, now
much ruined, as all the town, which has been of
great repute and circumference, as appears by the
large walls, &c. and two very old monuments, to the

full proportion of a knight and his lady, in the
church-yard, and a large marble over the ancient
vault for the . . . . . . It now consists mostly of
shippers, fishers, &c. to the poor whereof ditto Hilton,
Baronet, left 24*l.* per annum (though now it amounts
not to above 16*l.*).   Thence over the sands to Cre-
tham, where is a very old hospital, built by Robert, Bishop of Durham, for thirteen poor men,
who have 40s. per annum, and have an old chapel
for Beadsmen's prayers.   Thence to Billingham,
the ale whereof is noted in Northumberland, Durham, &c.; through Norton to Stockton, which has
a pretty Town-house and handsome buildings, but
of no antiquity, but very prettily covered with
Dutch tiles.

· 12. Die Dom.   The vicar (this being only a chapel of ease) preached from Psm. xxxiv. 9, " Fear the
Lord;" showed prettily how apt we are to fear such
things as are seldom observed, or that appear in an
extraordinary manner, as eclipses, lightnings, thun-
ders, &c. which proceed even from natural causes,
and yet how few make them arguments to fear the
Lord, who made the heavens and earth; and then
for comets, apparitions, whales, what strange effects
they have upon vulgar apprehensions ; and then gave
a lash or two at the poor Dissenters, if not at serious
piety, under the odious name of Presbyterians, full
of fears and needless jealousies, and tumultuary peti-
tions; but, saith he, " if we did but aright fear the
Lord, we should not need to fear Pope, or French,

or Presbyterians." After dinner, I thought to have rode some miles to a sermon, but could not hear of one in the whole country; so went to hear the town minister, after prayers, catechise children, and expound, which I was glad to observe, in a plain, profitable manner, for instructing the vulgar; he was upon the eighth Command, and having before insisted upon the several sorts of stealth, theft, robbery, oppression, sacrilege; and showed well the reason of all this to be from want of content with the state and condition wherein God has set us, and advised very honestly to that great duty, from the dauger of the contrary error, which without repentance would ruin the soul, which was more worth than the whole world.

13. Morning up pretty early; ferried over the river at Stockton, thence to Acklam, where Sir William Hustler has a pretty seat, thence through a blind cross-road, to Marton, a church-town, and thence over the bad moors to Gisborough, famous for a stately abbey, built Anno Dom. 1119, by Robert Lord Brus, and the ruins whereof discover it to have been a spacious and stately fabric: in the church is a delicate altar made of an old marble, about three yards long, which some say was a tomb-stone in the quire, the sides whereof are yet to be seen in the church, upon each whereof I counted five statues with escutcheons, and most of the ten figures were in armour, but could receive no account of what family, but could fancy it the founder's. In the church-yard is an

old hospital, built by one of the abbots, (but by what particular one I find not) for six poor men, and as many women, each whereof have fourteen pence per week ; and under the same roof a free school with twelve pounds per ann. salary for a master ; thence over the rotten Moors for many miles without anything observable ; the sea at a small distance upon the left ; and upon the right hand, hills, whereof a round one, called Roseberry Topping, is a mark for sailors ; within a few miles of Whitby, we passed not far from Runswick, the place where, near by the sea-side, stood a little village of six or ten houses the last spring, of which I find from credible persons, the report we had of its being swallowed up of the earth, too true, though blessed be God, all the inhabitants were saved, they happening to be at a kind of wake (as the old manner is) at the house of a person immediately deceased, where observing the earth to crack and gape, made all their escape ; shortly after which, the chinks grew suddenly wide, and the houses fell into the gulf. On the right hand we left Moulgrave Castle, that ancient fabric, and passed through Lith, a pretty country town ; thence over the Sands to Whitby.

14. Morning walking and observing the town, especially the famous old abbey, built by St. Hilda, to whose sanctity they impute the falling down dead of the wild geese when they fly over the adjoining fields. Of which inquiring, could only be thus far satisfied, that such fowls flying in shoals, do seldom

alight there, in the Strand, as they call their lordship, but fly to the inland where is plenty of corn,
the want whereof they look upon as the main [cause.]
But I was informed of another odd but ancient
custom, upon this account : some of the neighbouring
gentry, particularly the Allensons, were hunting the
wild boar, which being hotly pursued took shelter in
a little chapel about three miles off, where a devout
friar was at prayer, who being unwilling to have
the holy place polluted with blood, shut the doors to
prevent the dogs and hunters, one of which in the
height of his fury ran him through at one of the
chinks of the door, whereupon all their lands were
confiscated, only afterwards mitigated by the Abbot
upon this penance, that every Holy Thursday eve
they should make a hedge with a penny whittle, about
three or four yards within the river, and all the
while a horn sounding upon the shore ; which said
penalty was enjoined them till it should happen to
be high water that eve, which ever since, you must
believe to be miraculously prevented, (*vid.* old writings of Sir Hugh Cholmley's, being the Records of
the Abbey.)   Whatever the former part of the story
has of truth, I know not, but most true it is, that to
this year (for I was credibly informed by several
worthy persons that were eye-witnesses of it the
last Holy Thursday's eve) the heirs of that family do hold their estate upon that tenure to this
very day, and do yearly make a hedge there : but
the miracle is taken away when we consider that

the festival is always upon such a day of the moon,
which by a natural cause produces the said effect;
viz. that it is always low water upon that eve.
Adjoining to the Abbey, Sir Hugh Cholmley has a
most delicate and stately hall, supposed to be ex-
ceeded by few in England for the bigness of it.
The hall is of freestone, with large courts and walks
with iron grates and a curious statue in solid brass
as large as the life in the midst of the square, with a
delicate bowling-green, gardens, &c. which are extremely pleasant. Upon the hill is an old cross,
and in the churchyard are several ancient tomb-
stones, some with plain, others wrought crosses upon
them, removed, I presume, from the abbey. In the
church is a pretty monument for Sir Richard Cholmley; it stands very high; I counted about one hundred and ninety steps as I came down the hill. At
the foot of the cliffs and rocks are found the stony
wreathed serpents Camden mentions, which are likewise ascribed to the sanctity of ditto Hilda, who
converted all the snakes wherewith the country was
then mightily annoyed, into these stones, several of
which, and one especially of an extraordinary bigness, I brought along with me. I gathered some
out of the hard black rock, cutting them out with a
knife, but look upon them merely as the sport of
nature, as variety of instances may sufficiently demonstrate.

Whitby has a secure harbour for vessels, which
by a drawbridge, after the Dutch manner, are let

into the town, which is of good esteem for trade.
Thence four miles to Robin Hood's Bay, so named
from that famous outlaw, who was born in Notting-
hamshire, and flourished temp. Ricardi I.   Thence
over the sands to the moors, where was only observable his Butts, two little hills a quarter of a mile
asunder.   Thence by Cloughton to Scarborough, famous for the medicinal waters.   Viewed the ancient
and strong castle built by William Le Gros, and
after by King Henry II., upon so high a rock and so
naturally defensible that the very ruins are almost
impregnable.   It contains within its circuit so much
pasture ground as will summer about twenty cows.
The town boasts of her piers as they call them,
which are in the nature of a quay, which both se-
cures the town, preserves the haven, and limits the
insulting sea and prevents its encroachment, which
is. of such importance to sailors that they unanimously petitioned for its preservation, and obtained
to that end an imposition of four-pence per vessel
(or eight-pence if above one hundred chaldrons) of
all that shipped with coals from Sunderland and
Newcastle.   But to preserve the haven, because
there is none but Hull, betwixt this and Yarmouth,
that in stress of weather can preserve life and goods,
the mariners too have been so noble as by contribution to build an Hospital, (for the very ground
whereof they gave 100*l*.,) for poor seamen's widows,
to whose maintenance every master gives four-pence,
vessel four-pence, and every man that receives above

fifteen shillings wages two-pence a piece, the whole
whereof amounts to a considerable subsistence, and
is given them every Christmas.

15. Morning, observing some other parts of the
town, and the noted Spa well; then rode by country
villages to Bridlington, in good time; there observing the town, now well paved, through the benefaction of Mr. William Hustler, draper, (grandfather to
Sir William, near Stockton,) who from a mean fortune attained a vast estate, partly by diligence and
industry, partly by the kindness of a rich old widow,
who, looking upon him as a careful young man,
encouraged him by lending him money to buy his
cloth at Wakefield, which he made sure to pay
again within the time prefixed. She told him he
need not have brought it again; she had a great
many more bags at his service, which hint (*verbum
sat sapienti*) he improved in courtship, and married
her; and now having a considerable stock, in a
gainful trade, he grew so exceedingly in estate and
esteem, that after her death, Mr. Sympson, of . . . .,
gave him his daughter, and a vast fortune, whereby
his family was raised to a worshipful degree. His
son married one of the Saviles, and his grandson, Sir
William Hustler, enjoys a plentiful estate, and pleasant seat at Acklam, and, in gratitude, became a
singular benefactor to Bridlington, and at his own
proper cost and charges, (except, as some say, the
townsmen found their own stones,) he caused the
whole town to be paved, which before was trouble-

some to pass for dirt: he made also a Free School, and left forty marks per annum to the master, and twenty to the usher, where now is taught his great-grandchild, Sir William's son. This town had the happiness of another noted benefactor, Mr. William Bower, who was born of ordinary parentage, and served as a sailor to one Peacock, of the quay; but, by God's blessing on his lawful endeavours, raised himself and numerous family to a very plentiful estate. He erected, at his own charges, a school-house, and gave to it 20*l.* per annum for ever, for maintaining and educating of poor children, in carding, spinning, and knitting of wool: he died 23d March, 1671, ætat. 74. I walked down to the lower town, and observed the quay; and the tide being in, saw a porpoise sporting within some yards of the piers, which some of the seamen looked upon as ominous, portending a storm.

16. Morning, up pretty early upon the journey; we rode about three miles upon the sands; then by Barmston, where Sir Francis Boynton has a pretty seat; then through Burton, Leven, Sutton, &c. to Kingston-upon-Hull; spent much of the afternoon in viewing the town, hospital, north and south ends.

17. Morning, viewing several other parts of the town, and transcribing several monuments in the church, Mr. Wincop, Listers, Skinners; and several benefactions, with inscriptions upon some hospitals Mesendieus (Maison dieus); and afternoon, performing several visits to Alderman Field's, Mr. C., cousin

Th., and much of the day with Alderman Richard-son's son, to whom engaged for a sight of the long parchment scroll, with the list of the Mayors; but towards even drunk too freely (though not to ebriety); with him Mr. G. Brooks and T. Sche-man, the two masters with whom I went and re-turned from Holland.

18. Morning, up pretty early, in order to a journey from Hull by Newland (rightly so called, for, I think, by the Dutch-like dykes and plenty of water in the marshes, it has but lately been reco-vered from the waters,) to Beverly, most noted for the ancient Minster, which has been of famous ac-count; witness the sepulture of St. John of Beverly, Archbishop of York, for whose sake King Athel-stane endowed it with a sanctuary and many privi-leges, both whose pictures are there, with these old words: "Als free make I thee, as hert may thynk, or eyh may see." Here is also a stately tomb for the famous warrior Piercy, Earl of Northumberland, and one for his Countess, with an arch of exquisite work-manship. Of late years, Sir Michael Wharton's is the neatest, having his figure as large as the life, in armour, in a kneeling posture, with a book before him, and pillars, all in white marble. There are, too, some ancient large blue marbles, but without inscription, the brass being torn off; may be sup-posed of great antiquity, as that near Earl Piercy's tomb, which, of late being digged under, there was found an ancient stone trough-like coffin, (which I saw there yet remaining,) with a silver lamp, but

cannot yet be informed for whom.   The town is nothing so famous or populous as I presume it has formerly been ; only the Merchants'-row, St. Mary's Church, and a house of the Wharton's, are most observable.   Thence we came by Bishops Burton, (where Mr. Gee and Mr. Hodshon have each a pretty seat,) to Weeton-ou-the-Wolds, a market and church town ; and thence by . . . . to York.

Dec. 26. At four o'clock rode with Mr. R. Bevot to Pontefract.

27. Forenoon spent with relations ; afternoon mostly with Dr. Johnston, viewing his curious collection of rarities, which for some parts cannot be paralleled, and admiring his indefatigable industry in the multitude of his manuscript volumes in folio.

A. D. 1683.

Jan. 11. Morning, as once before, much disordered about the imprudent carriage of . . ., which, good Lord reform, which made my journey with sister to Helaugh more uncomfortable, though the extremity of the weather was enough to make it unpleasant ; but, blessed be God, we got well thither, though Mr. C. Morris,* whom we overtook upon the road, by a sudden and dangerous fall with his horse, had like to have been killed.

12. All forenoon employed with Mr. Gunter† in

---

* Castilion Morris, town-clerk of Leeds, son of Colonel John Morris, famous for his surprise of Pontefract Castle.

† John Gunter, L.L.B. ejected at Bedal, 1662. He acted as steward to Philip Lord Wharton, residing on his estates at Helaugh, in the Ainstie. He died in 1688, and was buried in the vault of the

his library, noting his manuscripts, lives, funeral sermons, &c. ; afterwards returned well home.

13. Forenoon, writing ; after, with Mr. W., at Mr. I. F.'s, of W., which took up rest of day. Even, perusing and marking books in two catalogues, sent me by worthy Mr. Stretton.

20. Forenoon, perusing and comparing ancient Saxon coins with those in King Alfred's Life, to send them to Oxford, to be inserted, if different, in the next edition.* Afternoon, abroad at stationer's ; rest reading.

23. Too much disturbed—by a message from Mr. H. which I feared might stir up the magistrates against us ; abroad about that, and other affairs, all the forenoon ; after with Dr. Johnston, of Pontefract, perusing some books and coins. Evening, at Mr. Hill's with Mr. Kay, Mr. Br. Dixon, &c. till eight.

25. Morning, rode to Wakefield, thence with Mr. R. Beavot, to Ackworth, where kindly entertained by honest Parson Bolton, whose library kept me company some hours ; rest of time and much of the next day,

Lords Wharton, at that place.   He was brother to the Mrs. Hickson, of whom Thoresby has before spoken in such high terms.

* Thoresby complains, with some show of reason, of the conduct of Dr. Johnston in respect of his contributions to this work. " Dr. Johnston was long an acquaintance of both my father and myself ; but though he called me his adopted son, and so procured some quires of my notes, promised me transcripts of some of his, I never got one sheet from him, and he got the thanks in the printed edition of King Alfred's Life for the Saxon coins that I transmitted by him ; and neither my father's name nor mine are so much as once named, though the proprietor of many therein engraved."

26. Spent there in society of friends and relations ; part of forenoon taking several inscriptions relating to Dr. Bradley, the last rector, who married the Lord Savile's daughter, very memorable for constantly wearing a veil day and night, having made a vow no Englishman should see her face, and which according to the strictest account I can procure, she observed till within six weeks of her death ;* after dinner called at cousins, at Preston, and thence returned well home.

27. Forenoon, mostly abroad ; afternoon had some special friends at our house, consulting how to order our meetings inoffensively, that we may enjoy them in private.

Feb. 2. Morning writing, and perusing several authors concerning the British affairs under the Roman Conquests, till three ; then at Mr. B. D.'s, consulting about a necessary work of charity, but spent not the evening so well when at dancing-school with Md. D., Mr. T., &c.

10. Forenoon abroad ; consulting about to-morrow's meeting: afternoon, employed in upper study till evening, which was spent till eight, at Mr. T. W's. Rest, till rather too late, in perusing the fourth part of the Conformists' plea for the Nonconformists, containing several passages in the north, the truth

---

* For this lady there still remains in the church of Ackworth, a monument, with a long inscription, in which much is said in her praise. Her husband, Dr. Bradley, was one of the Chaplains to King Charles the First.

whereof we practically know.   Lord, do thou restrain
the fury of the oppressor, and give us a sanctified use
of all thy dispensations to thy afflicted servants for
Christ's sake.

17. Morning up at five, writing a bond, and dispatching the remainder of my small concerns; then
rode to York, got well thither and in good time.
Spent the afternoon there in visits and trivial business.   Evening in discourse with good Mrs. Hickson.

19. Up pretty timely preparing for a journey, and
somewhat concerned about company, fearful of being
confined to a coach for so many days with unsuitable
persons, and not one I know of.   At Streethouse,
took up a gentleman and his man, who proved very
good company, (not so hot as I feared, being the
Archbishop's son,) Richard Sterne, Esq. Parliament-
man for Ripon; thence passed by Tadcaster, where
took leave of uncle and cousin Idle, then through
Sherburn and Milford, to Ferrybridge, and thence
after dinner, to Doncaster, where we lodged, and
there took in Mr. H. and daughter.

20. Morning viewing the church; then in journey
passed by the noted eel-pie house, and left Tuxford
(where is a famous benefaction) on the right-hand.   To
Newark very timely; transcribing some monumental inscriptions in the church.   Evening, with our
company.

21. Left Newark, which chiefly boasts of a delicate market-place, (quadrangular, and built upon pillars and arches) a curious church and steeple, and an

ancient castle, whose walls yield a pretty prospect on the north side the town. Thence to Grantham, whose fair steeple is so high as to occasion the proverb, it's height makes Grantham steeple stand awry. This place is famous, in my esteem, for Bishop Fox's benefactions, but is chiefly noted of travellers, for a peculiar sort of thin cake, called Grantham Whetstones. Thence to Stamford, where spent the evening in transcribing the monument of the famous and deservedly honourable Lord Burghley, that great, pious, and moderate statesman, in Queen Elizabeth's reign, with the inscriptions upon the stone and leaden coffins in the vault.

22. Left Stamford; which glories in four handsome churches, and two hospitals. We had the prospect of two most delicate and stately houses, Burghley and Exeter house, most princely seats of the noble family of the Cecils; thence by several country towns and villages to Bugden, where the Bishop of Lincoln has a very commodious, curious, pleasant house, moated about. In the church lie interred Bishop Barlow, whose monument is most inhumanly defaced; and the famous Bishop Sanderson, who lies under a flat plain marble, with a modest inscription.

23. From Bugden to Bicklethwait (Biggleswade), where we baited; and thence through country towns, and had a pleasant prospect of St. Neots, a large church town, to Stephenage, where we lodged.

24. Forenoon, passed by the noble kingly palace, at Hatfield, the seat of the Earl of Salisbury, (whose

Countess is lately deceased) than which, a more
stately, pleasant fabric can scarce be imagined.
Thence to Barnet; thence through a continued town,
as it were (excepting some pleasant fields and Enfield
Chase intermixed) by Highgate, where there is a most
delicate hospital and free-school, to London.   Spent
the evening at my good cousin Dickenson's, where I
find undeserved favours still continued to me.

25. Die Dom.   Morning heard Mr. Slater.   After,
heard Mr. Kidder, afterwards, Bishop of Bath and
Wells, who made an excellent discourse from Joshua's
resolution, " I and my house will serve the Lord."
Evening, went to hear worthy Mr. Stretton, in his
own family, where he preached well from this doctrine, that God's greatest gift next to his giving
Christ to suffer for our sake, is to give us grace
to suffer for his sake.

28. Morning, at Mr. Stretton's; then at St. Clement's Dane, accounted the most delicate church in
London for workmanship.

March 1.   Morning writing, and then at Blackwell Hall, and with cousin R. Idle; after dinner, at
Mr. Wright's; employed in his shop amongst books
till about four, when called upon by cousin Milner;
spent most of the evening with him, at Mr. Hill's;
by-the-bye, observing his comely and virtuous daughters, concerning whom I have had some letters from
the north.   Then at Mr. Stretton's.

3. Forenoon much abroad, buying the effigies of

many noted persons; after, at Mr. Wright's shop till pretty late.

4. Die Dom. Morning heard Mr. Slater; afterwards, I went with cousin Idle, designing to hear Dr. Burnet, at the Rolls, but he not preaching, heard the worthy Dr. Tillotson, after Archbishop of Canterbury, who was discoursing very judiciously and charitably concerning rash censure; that because God chastises some in an extraordinary way, that therefore they must needs be greater sinners : showing, that though we may sometimes see the clear hand of God in the punishment, when the sin is accompanied with diseases, that are a natural consequence of it, yet we ought to be very modest and charitable in our observations ; and, therefore, justly blamed the Papists for attributing all the calamities that have befallen this nation to our forsaking of their idolatries. Then dined with cousin at Mr. H.'s, in Leicester Fields, where was importuned to go to Westminster Abbey and St. Margaret's, which I was the rather inclined to, because it was supposed Dr. Sprat and the Bishop of Rochester would preach ; but was disappointed in both, and had not my expectations answered in either sermon, both being too full of severity, and censuring those that dissent from the Church. Oh, good Lord ! heal our breaches, compose our differences, and grant those that profess the same faith may live in brotherly love and kindness, without these animosities : and

be graciously pleased, O Lord! to influence the
hearts of all men, especially those in authority, to
favour thy righteous cause; and grant that those
who profess thy name may demean themselves with
purity, piety, and blamelessness, that none may have
just cause of reproach.

5. Morning, at Mr. Str.'s and with cousin D. to
visit honest Captain Wilkinson, under confinement for
debt, which, was it a hundred times more, deserved
to be paid out of the common treasury, for the public service he did for the whole nation and the Protestant interest.*   Evening at funeral, and a bearer,
of young Mr. Cholmley,† who yesterday sevennight,
when I was first with him at Mr. Stretton's, was, I
thought, much likelier for life than myself.

6. Forenoon writing, and with cousin Idle; then
dined at Mr. Hill's; was after that at Mr. Wright's,
with cousin Milner, and bride, Dr. Bright, &c. with
whose company in Paradise, (an ingenious and innocent show,) were entertained till pretty late; much
concerned in my mind with what Mr. Str. was discoursing of, a matter of great moment as to me.‡

12. Morning writing; spent most of the day in

---

* In the *Review*, Thoresby speaks of him thus :—" Honest Captain Wilkinson, formerly of Leeds, a great royalist, but in straits,
yet had the honesty to refuse a considerable pension, 500*l.* per annum, tendered him if he would swear High Treason against the Earl
of Shaftsbury, of which see the Captain's printed narrative, and the
Life of the said Earl."

† The son and heir of Richard Cholmley, Esq. of Sprustey, in the
Wapentake of Claro.   He was supposed to have died of the plague.

‡ This was a projected marriage with a daughter of Mr. Hill,
mentioned above, who was a considerable merchant.

visits, particularly at Mr. Hill's, till pretty late in the evening, endeavouring to observe, &c. ; after, discoursing cousin D. very seriously, about what I am solicited to by some that wish me well. Lord! direct me therein.

13. Most of the forenoon advising with Mr. Str. and D. about ditto matter, of consequence as to my particular . . . . dined at Mr. Goodenough's, and spent the afternoon with cousin Milner there, and at the west end of the town, and too much of the evening, made it past eight ere we returned.

14. Forenoon, till almost eleven, writing and reading ; after, walked in Moorfields, picking up some old pieces; afternoon in visits, till evening.

15. Morning pretty early with honest Mr. Elkanah Hickson, (returned from Flanders,) with whom at Stepney, at Mr. Rooksby's, which took up forenoon; after, till three, at Mr. Wright's ; after, variously employed till night.

16. Morning up pretty early, at Mr. Str.'s ; after, at the Temple, to see cousin Idles, which took up too much time; heard only the latter end of a discourse from Dr. Sharp, (since Archbishop of York,) on the joys of heaven : dined at Mr. Wright's ; had Dr. Bright's company till three ; then went to Dr. Martin, and to Mr. Str. with whom went to visit Mr. Steel, author of that excellent and profitable tract against Distractions ; and after, advising with Mr. Str. on a matter which occasioned a visit with my good cousin D. to Mr. D.'s, &c.

17. Former part of the day spent in Mr. Wright's

shop, amongst books; dined at Mr. H.'s, with Mr.
E. H.; with them till near four; then discoursing
with Mr. Denham on a matter of moment as to me.
. . . . went home with him to visit his lovely
daughter, &c.*

22. Morning at Blackwell Hall, but most of the
forenoon at St. Clement's, where Dr. Burnet, since
Bishop of Sarum, made an excellent sermon from
Rom. vi. 22, on the service of God. Exceedingly
surprised with an unexpected, and, I had almost
said, an unconscionable demur of Mr. Denham's,
without any show of reason, about which spent the
evening till pretty late, with Mr. Stretton and cousin Dickenson.

23. Spent forenoon at Blackwell Hall, with cousin
D. now and then discoursing the business. I was
under great anxieties and disquiets; afternoon
mostly spent with cousin Milner, dispatching some
business at the west end of the town; evening discoursing with Mr. Str. about ditto concern.

26. Forenoon reading a small treatise and writing
till noon; spent afternoon at Mr. D.'s, discoursing
his lovely daughter; perceived several invincible
difficulties from some foolish relations.

27. Morning writing: forenoon abroad, mostly
at Mr. Wright's looking out books. After exchange
consulting with cousin D., then at Mr. D.'s, and had

* Another negotiation, commenced during this visit to London,
which, like the former, was not conducted to a successful issue. Mr.
Denham was a Blackwell Hall factor.

a full account of some disingenuous (to say no worse) transactions not becoming Christians, much less those that profess a greater exactness than the vulgar.

28. Forenoon at Westminster Hall and Abbey, transcribing some monuments. Spent the afternoon in buying odd things for self and friends.

29. Morning within, but most of the day spent amongst booksellers, Mr. Wright, Alsop, and Parkhurst, and in Holborn.

30. Forenoon packing up, &c. After with cousin D. at Mr. Foster's, Clerk to the College of Physicians, a civil, obliging person, by whose interest viewed the College and pictures; whence transcribing a memorable account of Dr. Harvey, took up most of the day.

31. Morning in the Strand, taking leave of poor cousin Stubbs : Lord remember her in mercy! which, with some trifling business at that end of the town, took up the forenoon.

April 4. Morning up pretty early, making preparations for a journey home. About six or seven took place in the stage coach, passed with good company to Highgate, five miles, where is the Lady's famous Charity School, and where likewise our countryman, Sir Roger Cholmley, Knt. Lord Chief Baron, built and endowed a Free-school, to which the famous Bishop Sands added a chapel, with maintenance, which appears by the inscription over the gate ; but, alas, had not time to transcribe both.

From Highgate, over Enfield Chase, to Barnet five miles ; thence to Hatfield seven, where the Earl of Salisbury has a spacious park and a noble house, one of the most curious prospects I have seen : thence to Welwyn (where we dined) four. Here is Dr. Gabriel Towerson, whose printed works are said to be much esteemed, the minister of a poor ruinated church, upon the outside of which, where has been a breach made, is an inscription, of which *vid.* p. 241 of my Collections. Thence to Stephenage, five, and through the bad lanes to Baldock, four. As we passed I espied a pretty hospital, but could not be permitted to stay for inquiry. To Bigglesworth, where is nothing observable but a delicate new Inn, with a curious bowling-green as can easily be met with ; here we lodged the first night.

5. Thence to Thameford, four, where is the Lady St. John's house. Thence passed through Eaton, and after had a pretty prospect of St. Neot's, to Bugden, five, where is the Bishop of Lincoln's house, &c. to Bransford (which has a pretty charity) three, near which the Earl of Sandwich has a noble house and park ; thence to Huntingdon, three, at which county town we dined, but found not many things observable, save the three churches, in which are several ancient marbles, but the brass torn off. As for Protestant benefactions I could hear of none, save an imperfect relation of one Mr. Fitzburne, who (his mother travelling this road) was born here, (about an hundred years ago) and who after coming

to a great estate, left to the Mercers' Company at London 100l. per annum ; viz. 60l. to a Lecturer, and 40l. to the poor of this town of his nativity. Here is an ancient seat of the Cromwells, but I find no monuments, (except " R. Cromwell and Turpin Bailiffs, anno 1609," in a church wall), but here was the late usurper or Protector born. Thence in the way to Stilton, passed the place where Sir Ralph Wharton slew the highwayman, and had a prospect of Peterborough Minster, and a very pretty house of Sir Hugh Cholmley's; thence to Stamford, near which had a prospect of Burghley and Exeter houses, the Lords of which are interred in the Great Church of Stamford, which boasts of five churches and four hospitals; one founded by the famous Cecil, in Queen Elizabeth's time, for twelve poor aged men and a master, who have each seven groats a week, besides convenient lodging and firing. The other by William Brown, anno 1495, for ten men and two women, who have each seven groats per week. Here we lodged the second night, so had a sight of the town and hospitals.

6. We came from Stamford to Bridge Casterton, two, and Castleford, eight ; thence to Grantham, six, (where we lost the company of Mr. Felton, an ingenious gentleman,) chiefly famous for its high steeple; thence to Gunnerby, two, which stands upon a high hill, where is a pleasant prospect of many country towns ; had also a prospect of the famous Belvoir Castle : through Long Billington to

Newark, five, where we dined.   Newark, chiefly
famous for the castle and market-place, as curious
a one as any upon the road; thence on the back
of Tuxford, over Sherwood Forest to Barnby-on-the-
Moor, where we lodged the third night.

7. Thence through Scrooby to Bawtree (famous for
millstones and pigs of lead, hence transported beyond
seas) which parts three if not four counties, Nottingham, (if not Derby,) Lincoln, and Yorkshire.   Thence
to Doncaster: thence over the high hills, where we
may have a prospect of Bilborough Spring and York
Minster, to Wentbridge; thence to Ferrybridge,
where we dined, and thence (not finding a horse according to expectation) through Sherburn to Tadcaster, where left the coach and company and rode
to Healey for my sister, with whom returned safe,
though very late, to Leeds.

8. Die Dom.   Morning waited of cousin Jos.
Milner and his bride to hear Mr. Kay, who made a
serious affectionate discourse, as always, of the power
of Christ's resurrection to the mortification of sin.
Dined at cousin Milner's, and after heard Mr. Benson, in reference to the day, much upon the same
subject.

13. Morning taking leave of Durham and Chester
friends.   Then employed till near noon within, and
thought to have stolen an opportunity to hear a
good sermon, but was prevailed with, by the importunity of several messengers, to spend this day,

as too many, with ditto relations, in mirth and
jollity at Kirkstal Abbey.

15. Die Dom.   Forenoon, had an opportunity for
riding three or four miles to hear Mr. Sharp.   Afternoon, Mr. Cyprian Hunter preached at the old
church ; but made a sermon more suitable to his
stature than his pedigree, descended from so excellent a father, and which became him worse, because
reflecting upon the Nonconformists as praying non-
sense, in not being tied up to their forms.   But, alas!
it is no new thing for this sinful compliant generation to trample upon the precious ashes of their religious ancestors.   Evening, after repetition, reading
Bishop Reynolds's Meditation upon Peter's fall.

18. Morning, writing to Pontefract to Dr. Johnston, and sending the Saxon coins to University College in Oxford, whence, after a full perusal, and inscriptions taken to be inserted in King Alfred's Life,
they are promised to be faithfully returned me by
Mr. Walker.

26. At York. Morning, writing the inscriptions, and
afterwards, with cousins, dined at Alderman Elcock's.
Spent the rest of the day in perusing his collections
of Roman coins and modern medals; and through
him had the happiness of a little discourse with Dr.
Comber, a great antiquary, as well as eminent divine.*   After, with cousins and young ladies, at

---

* This was Dr. Thomas Comber, afterwards Dean of Durham.
In the course of this year, he was made Precentor to the Church of
York.

dancing school; and at the exercise, though at a private house, till pretty late in the evening.

27. Morning, writing. After, abroad with Mr. Boldero and the most ingenious Dr. Lister; but spent most of the day in less understanding (though thereby more fit for my) company. After dinner, returned for Leeds, where I safely arrived at my own private home.

May 6. Die Dom. Morning, sent for by Dr. Johnston of Pontefract, to Squire A.'s, which took up too much of this holy day.

7. Morning, with Mr. Sharp, about subscriptions to a new impression of the Martyr books and Dr. Manton's works. Then reading Charnock's incomparable Discourse upon Practical Atheism.

10. Sent for by Dr. Johnston of Pontefract, my adoptive father; employed in procuring for him writings, charters, inscriptions, benefactions, and antiquities, relating to this town and parish, to insert in his History of Yorkshire.

11. All day reading or writing; chiefly perusing authors concerning Cæsar's conquest of Britain.

12. Employed mostly as yesterday, consulting Roman historians about his after conquests.

28. Forenoon, abroad, chiefly at cousin Milner's. After, rode with Mr. B. to Howley-hall, to see the place and pictures of the late Earl of Sussex and family.

31. Spent less time than I designed in Charnock's works, and went to Mr. E. H.'s; stayed there writ-

ing. After, at good aunt Lucy Idle's, which took up most of the evening. But, alas! how little of my time is spent in the business for which it was chiefly granted, that for which I was created. Alas! it is not enough to keep from being ill employed, or to be employed in things that, in some respects, are necessary, and perhaps commendable in their season, if I do not spend more of my time about the main thing, the *unum necessarium*, which I fear is too much slighted. How are the most necessary duties frequently omitted, postponed, or performed in a too transitory carnal manner—too little time devoted to them, too little life or vigour exeicised therein! Lord, help me to improve my time better for the future ; more to the glory of thy name, the good of others, my own soul, and those orphans by thy Providence under my tuition! Help me so to discharge my duty in every respect, that when thou shalt give me a summons to appear before thy tribunal, I may be able, through the merits of my blessed Redeemer, to give up my accounts with joy for Christ's sake.

———

[Here ends the First Volume of the Diary. The second has not been preserved. The period contained in it was from the beginning of June 1683 to April 1691. For the occurrences in the life of Thoresby during this interval, we must be indebted to the *Review.*]

A. D. 1683.

My second Diary begins with a melancholy account of the sickness and death of the excellent Mr. Kay, minister of the New Church, (whom my dear father had been very instrumental in fixing at Leeds). He was an excellent preacher, and of moderate principles, and was buried with universal lamentation, 20th June, 1683. He was succeeded by Mr. Robinson, who is also a good preacher; but censured by some for giving us his father's sermons.* Be whose they will, they are indisputably admirable good ones, and such as we have great cause to bless God for. This may be argued in his defence, that at least some occasional passages relate to later transactions.

Such learned, pious, and practical sermons as have been, and yet are preached in public, occasioned my frequent attendance upon them, which some hot heads censured me too severely for; and when I could not get in such time to the private meetings,

* The father had been in early life Chaplain to the Earl of Southampton; was elected Vicar of Leeds, the appointment being in the inhabitants represented by a body of trustees, in 1632; and though, in Thoresby's opinion, to be reckoned among the Puritan divines of his day, removed by the Parliament. He died Rector of Swillington in 1663.

Leeds has many obligations to this family. Harrison, the founder of St. John's Church, was uncle to the elder Robinson; and the younger Robinson, who succeeded Kay as Minister of St. John's, endowed a third church at Leeds, erected in 1721.

The younger Robinson was contemporary with Thoresby many years. He survived him, and died in 1736, in the 90th year of his age.

as those who came not at church, some confident young fellows would usurp the best places that were most convenient for hearing and writing, excluding several others as well as myself, who are chiefly concerned in supporting the ministry, which at other times they too much slighted (belonging to another congregation); but now in times of restraint flock in multitudes to the great inconvenience of others, which moved my indignation, and, though not vented in passionate expressions, yet was inwardly too much resented, for which I was afterwards troubled, and hope repented sincerely. One day, indeed, we had an opportunity of meeting more securely, though in greater numbers, when the race was at Chapel Town Moor, to which many came from London, Chester, Newcastle; the Leeds butcher, Edward Preston, being esteemed one, at least, of the best footmen in England. Three thousand pounds were said to be won by him this day.

Oct. 6. We had an unusual memento for repentance, viz. an earthquake; very uncommon in this island, which reached this town about midnight.

I cannot wholly omit my concern for some poor deluded Quakers, who were hurried down this street to York castle, in greater numbers than was ever known in these parts. The Lord open the eyes of the one party, and tender the hearts of the other!

Not many days after I was partly in the same predicament, being prosecuted for being present at what was called a factious and seditious conventicle

at Hunslet, where Mr. Sharp was preaching most
admirably and practically, from Hebrews xiii. 9.
" It is a good thing that the heart be established
with grace." In the application, he recited that of
the pious martyr, Mr. Bradford, that he would not
rise up from prayer till he had received somewhat
from God, exciting his love and affections; but,
alas ! do not we, on the contrary, though we sometimes come with strong resolutions and affections
into the presence of God, rise up halting and half
dead, as if we came into his presence to put out
our candles ? how can we expect that the prayer,
which warms not our own hearts, should move God,
—which very sentence I was writing, (and not without some ardency of affection,) when notice was
given us that the officers were coming to break us
up ; but we had so much time as to disperse. Notwithstanding which, I was indicted at the next Sessions (3d Dec. 1683.) That morning I rose about
five, and spent an hour in secret, not unprofitably, I
hope, especially begging wisdom and guidance of his
Holy Spirit, that I might not dishonour his name,
when I should be called before rulers for his sake.
I received comfort from that of the Psalmist (before
family prayer) : " Our fathers trusted in thee, and
thou didst deliver them."

I appeared at the sessions with more courage than
my naturally so bashful temper made me expect.
The adverse party were enraged, when I appeared
with two counsel, lawyers Witton and Atkinson,

who pleaded it was no riot, or conventicle, &c. ; so that they missed of their hoped-for prize, 20*l.* for the house, and as much for the minister ; but it pleased God to preserve him.   He was in a neighbour's house, whither the informers pursued him, and searched two rooms; the key of the third (where he sat alone,) being in the door, one of them providentially locked it by turning the key the contrary way, and then lifting up the sneck, said, he could not be there, for the door was locked, and the key on the outside.

As to my own case, all the magistrates (except Mr. Headley, the prosecutor,) carried themselves very civilly to me, and our zealous Recorder, Mr. Whyte, for my dear father's sake, of whom he used to say, that he never thought there was an honest Presbyterian in England, till he was acquainted with that learned and ingenious gentleman.

A. D. 1684.

My usual course after this was, to hear our learned and pious vicar, Mr. Milner, in the forenoon, and in the afternoon, Mr. Skargil, of Holbeck, or Mr. Moor, of Hunslet, both plain practical preachers ; and when we had not the conveniency of Mr. Sharp's excellent sermons in secret, to prevail with Mr. Elk. Hickson, to repeat one of them in private.   He had a peculiar talent of taking in characters those admirable sermons with more accuracy than any other person, and was on that and other accounts very dear to me, but in some respects not so circumspect as was to be wished.

I rode with most of the gentry in the neighbourhood, to meet Archbishop Dolben, who was much honoured as a preaching bishop. May 1, 1684, he gave us an excellent sermon at the parish church; see his remarkable preliminary discourse concerning holy-days, their institution, and abuse in the Romish Church, which makes many good people (his own expression,) averse to them, even as celebrated in the Church of England, though without superstition. In the whole he showed great temper and moderation.

The 4th instant I rode to Rawden, where his Grace preached excellently at the consecration of that chapel, built by Esquire Layton.

The 12th instant, I began a London journey with Mr. Fenton, of Hunslet : besides other inscriptions and epitaphs, I took a particular account of Mr. Read's noble benefactions at Tuxford. We made Peterborough our road, and were kindly received by the Bishop's chaplain, brother to my friend, Dr. Johnston, of Pontefract, who showed me a manuscript relating to the antiquities and monuments in that cathedral. I transcribed others that yet remain.

At London, I took my freedom of the Hamborough Company, and that of the Eastland, but, born under some unhappy, at least some unsuitable constellation, I never made a merchant worth a

farthing, or got so much in those parts, as my freedom cost me.

I went with cousin Fenton, to see the copperas
works at Redriffe: in my short stay at London, I
heard some eminent divines of both denominations,
Dr. Stillingfleet, Kidder, with Mr. Gunter, &c.   I
walked with good cousin Dickenson and his nephew
Collins, of Queenborough, to Newington-green, and
thence to a little hill, surrounded with a moat, where
cousin told me had stood Jack Straw's Castle.   Called at the new burying-place* on my return, and
stayed alone till about ten, transcribing epitaphs of
Dr. Goodwin and others.

The 24th. I took leave of good cousin Dickenson
and rode with Mr. Fenton to Windsor, a most noble
royal palace; was mightily pleased with the exquisite paintings in the castle, and St. George's Chapel
for the Knights of the Garter, but had time to
transcribe no epitaphs, but one on a stately monument
lately erected for a north country Bishop, Brideoak,
but unhappily missed that of Sir [Richard] Wortley;
and that night to Maidenhead, and next day to
Oxford, where we viewed the fronts of many colleges,
chapels, and halls, but was best pleased with an
evening Catechetical Lecture, by the famous Dr.
Wallis.   We had our townsman's, Mr. Nathaniel
Boyse's company next morning, to show us the
most remarkable of the public structures, as New

* The great cemetery of the Nonconformists in Bunhill-fields.

College Chapel, the Hall at Christ Church, but was most surprised by the noble Theatre (Archbishop Sheldon's benefaction) seventy feet one way and eighty the other, without any pillar to support it.

. The ancient altars and other inscriptions in the area were very agreeable, with the pictures of the learned men and founders of the colleges; but, above all, the famous Bodleian library. The skeletons and stuffed human skins in the Anatomy School suited my melancholy temper. Nor ought the Museum Ashmoleanum to be forgotten, being adorned with a very curious collection of natural and artificial curiosities, from most parts of the habitable world; the Scrinium Listerianum, was the more pleasing, because of a Yorkshire benefactor, my father's friend, the learned Dr. Lister,* afterwards my correspondent. These were shown us by the famous Dr. Plott, who was very obliging, and his company made Mr. Boyse's treat at University College more acceptable. Our said learned townsman was Proctor this year, and his kindness kept us too long, that we rode unreasonably fast to recover our journey's end.

At Banbury I was very inquisitive for an epitaph of the pious Mr. Whateley, the once famous minister of the town, but found none; which I told them was a reproach to the place, and in my journey some years after, I found what was called a second edition

---

* Dr. Martin Lister, the naturalist, an early Fellow of the Royal Society.

of his tomb, erected a few months after this ; as also that for the memorable Mr. Heyrick and wife at Leicester, and the Duke of Lancaster's benefaction there.

Thence eighteen tedious miles to Nottingham, where I transcribed those of the two Earls of Clare of the religious family of the Hollises, and that upon Hanley's Hospital ; the next day (through the merciful Providence of God) I reached Leeds, though fifty miles, as I had from Huntingdon to London in one day also, this very journey. I was entertained with the melancholy news of the deaths of Alderman Samuel Sykes and his brother Mr. Kirshaw, Rector of Ripley, two excellent persons, and very useful in their several capacities.

June 1. Bishop Lake, formerly Vicar of Leeds,* preached learnedly at our parish church. I had some little business of trade, buying cloth at the new market, now by general consent (afterwards confirmed in the new charter) removed from the bridge where it was formerly, to the Broad-street.

---

* Dr. Lake had the vicarage of Leeds for above two years, soon after the return of King Charles II. He was at this time Bishop of Sodor and Man; but, in the August of this year he was translated to the See of Bristol ; from whence in 1685, he was removed to Chichester. He was one of the seven bishops committed to the Tower by King James; but on the Revolution he refused to subscribe the oaths to the new Government, and like his friend and brother-in-law, Mr. Milner, retired from his station in the Church. He died on August 30, 1689, having on his death-bed signed a solemn protestation against the Oaths of Allegiance and Supremacy to the new King. See more respecting him in Thoresby's *Vicaria*.

The Honourable Henry Fairfax giving me a visit, would oblige me to return with him to Denton, where I was most kindly received by my Lord. I was mightily pleased with the religious order of the family. Rode to Skipton, where, for near eight hours, I was thoroughly employed in copying the inscriptions in the folding pictures of the famous Earls of Cumberland, and others in that ancient pedigree, in the castle there, and returned that night to Leeds.

Having dispatched some cloth for Holland, I went with Mr. Ibbetson to Manchester, where I found my dear sister, Abigail, more indisposed at the boarding-school than I expected, but satisfied with Madam Frankland's prudence and care. I was pleased with the agreeable conversation of Mr. Newcome, and Mr. Tildsley, from whom I received several remarks concerning Bishop Wilkins, and Lord Keeper Bridgeman, their temper and moderation, &c. Took leave of sister. Her physician, the ingenious Dr. Carte, lent me his transcript of Mr. Hollingsworth's MS. History of Manchester;* of which see my *Excerpta*.

Being now twenty-six years of age, I was solicited to change my condition, and was peculiarly recommended to Mrs. Mary Cholmley, eldest daughter of Richard Cholmley, of Sprustey, Esq. to whom I made

---

* A Copy of this History is in the College Library at Manchester; and another in the Library of the Heralds' College. Hollingsworth was a Puritan Divine, and Dr. Carte, the son of the puritan rector of Hansworth, on the southern boundary of the county of York.

my application, finding the young lady lovely, pious, and prudent, and withal a considerable fortune; being not only co-heir to her father, but an additional portion given her by the Lady Morgan, her aunt. I was courteously entertained by the whole family, and after some time all matters were agreed upon, and the very day of the marriage appointed; yet all came to nothing, by the interposition of a Member of Parliament, whose estate preponderated mine, to whom afterwards she was married, in pure obedience to her parents, who in this matter, acted not agreeably to the great profession of religion the family had been noted for. The pretence was, that her present fortune and my estate could not maintain us genteelly till the parents' death; yet afterwards very solicitously endeavoured to fix me to the second daughter, a beautiful and pious young gentlewoman; but I told them the objection (if of any weight) was much more in this case. She was afterwards married to an alderman of Hull.

This unexpected disappointment was to the mutual grief and sorrow of myself and the lady of my affections, and we parted, not without many tears on both sides. The poor lady had no great comfort in her advanced state, and survived not long; the kind Providence of God which foresaw this, and how unfit I was for such a trial, prevented it in mercy. I was supported in the perusal of Charnock of Divine Providence, which I found most suitable in my present condition. I was often most deeply affected in me-

ditation, and had reason to ascribe all disappointments and afflictions to my own sins, which though
not many visible to carnal eyes, are all open to the
All-seeing.

> When o'er my sins I seek to draw the curtains of the night,
> All's clear to thee, and what we call darkness, to thee is light!

The death of my dear father was now (though some
years ago) so fresh in my mind, and my hearty
sorrow so great, that I could not read the funeral
sermon for tears; and I was concerned that, being
deprived of the most desirable society that earth
could afford, I do not look up more to what is infinitely more valuable in Heaven.

To divert so strong a torrent of grief, I accompanied Alderman Idle, and my dearest aunt Lucy,
to visit relations beyond York, and was surprised,
when, on the Lord's-day, we rode from church to
church, and found four towns without sermon or
prayers.

A. D. 1685.

As effects stand related to second causes, they are
many times contingent; but as to the first cause,
they are acts of His council, and directed by His
wisdom.   God can choose better for us than we for
ourselves, when he grants not our prayers in what is
most agreeable to our present desires; yet he really
grants them, not only by way of equivalence, (to use
Dr. Hammond's expression in another case,) but of
running over, denies us what is good, and gives

what is much better for us, as I found in my next attempt of this nature.

Mr. Thomas Wilson, who accompanied me when I took leave at Sprustey, recommended his wife's sister, Anna, the comely and virtuous daughter of Mr. Richard Sykes, senior lord of the manor of Leeds, &c. I was very solicitous for divine directions, and prayed fervently for guidance in a matter of so great concern to me, both in respect of this world and a future. And it pleased God to hear and answer, so that we were joined together in holy matrimony, in the parish church of Ledsham, by Mr. Hammond, the vicar, my father Sykes living then at Ledsham Hall, (now the estate of the pious and Right Honourable Lady, the Lady Elizabeth Hastings,) Feb. 25, 1684, a day of mercy never to be forgotten by me or mine, having since that happy moment enjoyed her endeared society thirty-five years, (in which space it has pleased God to give us six sons and four daughters,) and I have by experience found her to be the greatest blessing, she being eminent for piety and devotion, meekness, modesty, and submission, though there has rarely been occasion to try this, except in matter of the baptizing and education of our children, (after I changed my sentiments as to conformity, of which in the sequel,) and singular prudence in a provident management of the family concerns. Notwithstanding our designed privacy, we were met at our return to Leeds by about 300 horse.

But our joy was presently turned into mourning, for the death of the King, which was bewailed with many tears, for the gloomy prospect of popery. The license was taken out in King Charles the Second's time, and we were married the very next week, yet King James II. was then upon the throne; the hectoring of some Romanists in the neighbourhood, and their Popish servants abusing the town's watch, increased my fears.

Upon the landing of the Duke of Monmouth, not only such as had been engaged in the late wars were committed prisoners to Hull, but many good old ministers, and such private gentlemen, as were obnoxious to the censure of the Court, or their correspondents in the country: among the rest, my father Sykes, though he had carried very kindly to the Royalists, when he was a justice of the peace.

I accompanied him to the Lord Down's, who was very respectful, entertained us genteelly, and, which was more, permitted him to return home for some time. We were also at another justice's and deputy lieutenant's, Sir John Boynton's, whose lady was nearly related;* but a person of that eminency in the late times, and who had married a most notorious republican's daughter,† could not long be kept

---

* Sir John Boynton, of Rawcliffe, was married to Frances, daughter of John Bernard, an Alderman of Hull, by Mary Sykes, his wife, aunt to Mr. Sykes, of Ledsham.

† This was Thomas Scot, Esq. of West Thorpe, county Bucks, Member in the Long Parliament for Aylesbury, and Member of all Cromwell's Parliaments. He sat on the trial of the King, and affixed

from durance, though not long detained in it, for upon dispersing Monmouth's forces in the West, they were released.

In the mean time, the High Sheriff, Captain Tankred, and the Deputy Lieutenants, came to Leeds, and summoned me, with many other Protestant Dissenters, to appear before them; but nothing, save Nonconformity, being objected against me, I was immediately dismissed, and returned to dine with relations, many of whom had been invited before we knew of this little remora.

One of the first hardships put upon us in these parts was, quartering soldiers in gentlemen's houses and private families: I had two for my share, and afterwards an officer of a good family in the neighbourhood, (Sir Henry Goodrick's kinsman,) but himself no saint. The danger that our holy religion was now in, from the common enemy, made me more sensible of, and I hope penitent for, a practice I had unwarily (since my marriage into a family, which, though very pious, was more averse to the public establishment than ours had ever been,) and insensibly slipped into, viz.: reading some piece of practical divinity at home to my family, when I should have been joining with the congregation in public. For this, though good at other times, has neither so good success, nor promises made to it in

his signature to the death-warrant. On the return of Charles II. he was brought to trial, convicted, and suffered death on October 17, 1660. Thoresby, with all his fondness for biographical anecdote, scarcely ever alludes to this person.

Scripture; I therefore more constantly, as heretofore, joined in the public prayers and worship, as judging the Church of England the strongest bulwark against Popery, and a union of Protestants absolutely necessary.

Upon a surmise that the chapel at Mill Hill, whereof I was, in my father's right, one of the proprietors, might, by a mandamus, be converted into a mass-house, we had a private consultation, and resolved to convert it into an hospital, or sell it, and appropriate the monies to the use of the poor, so that, what was designed for the increase of piety, might terminate in charity. My curiosity, when at Pontefract, had tempted me to step into the mass-house there, where the gaiety of the altar, and gesticulations of that worship, presently satiated me. Father Norris, the Jesuit, after he had taken his text, and a little opened it, kneeled down to invocate the Virgin Mary, or, to judge more charitably, the Divine assistance, and all the people in a moment were upon their knees, I standing, like a foolish may-pole, in the midst of them ; whereupon I hasted to the door, but one of the priests was got thither before me, and held the door in his hand. I told him, with anger enough, that I would not fall down, or be imposed upon as to my gesture ; he said I should not, and by this time all were on their feet again, so I stayed a little to hear him preach, (for if the mass had been celebrating, I should have thought it idolatry, and durst not have been under

the same roof ;) and to give him his due, he made a
good moral discourse against keeping bad company,
which was seasonable to me, who was never in the
like before or since. To this, may not unfitly be
added, that though I was never fond of cards, yet
was once tempted with relations upon a Christmas-
day, (after I had been at church in the forenoon,) to
spend too much of the afternoon (it being a week
day,) in that wicked diversion, which caused me
much sorrow upon reflection ; for, though being
educated a Dissenter, I had no great veneration for
the festivals, yet was sensible that so eminent an
instance of the Divine benignity should have been
commemorated in a quite different manner, and
have ever since, for more than thirty-five years, and
I hope for ever, wholly thrown them aside.

A. D. 1686.

This summer I accompanied Father Sykes to
visit relations in Derbyshire. The first night we
lodged at cousin Rodes's, at Great Houghton ; was
pleased with the pictures of some eminent statesmen in Queen Elizabeth's time, and family pieces,
originals, of the Earl of Strafford, Sir Edward
Rodes, and was glad of some letters from that nobleman to the Countess* (Sir Edward's sister, daughter of Sir Godfrey). Visited Dr. Ellis, another relation, who has built two or three alms-houses at
Brampton, but by will bequeathed to ten viilages in

* These letters are printed in the *Biographia.*

that neighbourhood, each 10l. per annum·to pious
uses.

The next night we lodged at uncle Storr's, at
Chesterfield, where, as at Rotherham, I took an
account of the benefactors, of whom the Foljambes
have been chief here. The next morning, I left my
relations, and rode through many country towns in
Scarsdale, (which gives the title of an earldom to
the family of Leke,) to Derby ; where, at All-hal-
lows, I transcribed the epitaph of the celebrated memorable Countess of Shrewsbury, who built the two
great houses at Chatsworth and Hardwick, of which
I had a distant prospect on the road ; and returned
at night to Chesterfield.

The next day we returned to cousin Rodes's ;
only calling to visit Dr. Eaton at Darfield, and Squire
Wombwell of Wombwell, in whose ancient house one
of the kings, during the Heptarchy, is said to have
been imprisoned.

Yet could not all this so far divert me, but that
upon the annual return of the day of my dearest father's death, I was, as usual, overwhelmed with sorrow;
but got my cousin, Richard Idle, (then part of my
family) to read the sermon preached upon the mournful occasion. I was troubled also to consider how
many years I have *spent*, and how few I have *lived*.
The resolutions taken then how to spend my time
for the future are registered in my Diary upon New-
Year's-day 1686-7; but upon review, I am apt to think
them such as are not easy to be kept strictly by one

that has commerce in the world, but in general I hope
that I was more cautious in the expense of time.

A. D. 1687.

I begun also to be sensible of the pressure of the
world, great charges and small incomes; but was
sustained by Matthew vi. 30, which fell providentially
in my usual course of reading before secret prayer;
my dear wife also sustained me with suitable advice
and comfort.

Though I can by no means quit my father-in-law,
who gave over house-keeping, and came with wife,
daughter, and servant, to live upon his children, and,
though he sometimes went to brother W.'s and R.'s,
[Wilson's and Rayner's] yet I think he was half, if
not two-thirds, of his time at my house.; and, being
of a generous spirit, was too liberal of my liquor to
visitants, that I saw it absolutely necessary to give
over wine.

I was also much concerned for the incautious carriage of a near relation, and mourned in secret; but
my poor sister having buried her little daughter, got
a new husband, my cousin Richard Idle, Vicar first
of Rothwell, and after of South Dalton, capable of
taking care both of soul and body.   Though alas!
too much alike unfortunate in living above their
incomes, so that not only I suffer in loss of monies,
but, which I more lament, their poor children to
this day.   My chief comfort was in my library,
reading, and writing the memoirs of learned and

pious men in former ages, *optimi consultores mortui.*
This kept me more retired, and thereby less obnoxious to company-keeping and drinking, the uncomfortable misfortune of some relations.   Blessed be
my Preserver, from whom alone is this advantage!

As to religion in general, Mr. Milner, the Vicar,
preached excellently and lived answerably. I cannot
say so much of the Lecturer ; but as the Vicar and
Mr. Robinson in public, so Mr. Sharp in private,
as we could get opportunity, for which we went several miles.

King James II.'s Declaration of Indulgence gave
us ease in this case, and though we dreaded a snake
in the grass, we accepted it with due thankfulness.
3rd of April, 1687, Mr. Sharp preached the first
sermon in public, from Psalm lxviii. 28 ; that whoever be the instruments, yet the supreme author of
all good to his people, is God himself. We were infinitely happy in his ministry, he being a person of
great piety and learning, judgment and moderation.

A. D. 1688.

1688 was a memorable year. My first concern
in it was for fear of the loss of my beloved privacy,
there being, it seems, a project for new modelling
the corporation. The places of such as were to be
ejected were filled up with the most rigid Dissenters,
who had put my name in the fag end of their reformed list, there being but one (a smith by trade)
after me, as I was told by Mr. S. J., who put my

name among the Aldermen, for which I was far
from thanking him.

I can scarce forbear reciting a passage in a sermon
of the incomparable Mr. Sharp, which he told them
plainly, was the country's observation, concerning
the generality of those of a middle sort in and about
Leeds, that in a time of trade and plenty they carry it
out in such an extravagant manner, as leaves nothing
against a time of dearth and scarcity, wherein they
find as little pity as formerly they paid respect to
others. I would not be partial or too particular in
my application of this to some good people. Only
'tis plain from hence, that when they thought their
interest strong enough in the government, they were
not content with their private stations, but were for
ejecting others and making new models in their *addle
noddles;* but the public concussions that presently
followed, put a happy period to their projects.

April 16th. I was at the funeral of the Right
Honourable Henry Lord Fairfax, the fourth Baron
of that ancient and religious family, where was the
greatest appearance of the nobility and gentry that
ever I had seen: the poor wept abundantly,--a
good evidence of his charity. I waited upon the
Lord Thomas, his son, and his uncle, Bryan Fairfax, Esq. a gentleman of great accomplishments and
reading. His compliment of me to his nephew
pleased me the best of any that I ever received;
" He speaks like his father;" to be like whom is
the height of my ambition.

Amongst others that came to see the Museum about this time were the Earl of Eglinton and Captain Montgomery, but I was most pleased with Mr. Hugh Brown, of Irwin, a gentleman who well understood the ancient coins and manuscripts.

Sept. 30th. After forenoon sermon, I rode with Mr. Dixon, Ibbetson, to Tadcaster, to wait of Sir John Kay, where the freeholders from several other parts of the West-Riding joining us, we were computed to be 3000 in number, but no writs for election of Parliament-men being produced, we returned home next day. A strange face of affairs presents itself. We were told of an invasion from Holland, and that a Dutch fleet was seen off Scarborough and Hull, but it proved to be at Torbay, where the Prince of Orange landed the 5th November 1688. We underlings knew not what to make of these affairs, nor is it my design to intermix public with my private memoirs, otherwise than as they were merciful or afflictive to me and my family with the neighbourhood: therefore shall take no notice of King James's abdication, the seizing of York by the Earl of Danby, (afterwards Duke of Leeds) Lord Fairfax, &c. or the reading in the Moot-hall, at Leeds, the Prince of Orange's declaration, by Jasper Blythman, Esq. afterwards Recorder.

Only I cannot omit the dreadful alarm of the flying army of Irish, and massacring Papists, who with unheard-of cruelty burnt and killed all be-

fore them. Nottingham was by express said to
be so treated, insomuch that all artificers, even
the most precise, spent the next, though the Lord's-
day (16th December) in mending the fire-arms of
such as had any, and fixing scythes, &c. in
shafts (desperate weapons) for such as had none.
The Mayor's account of them, with original letters,
sent express to this town from divers places, are
in my Collection of Autographs. Watch and
ward were kept every night by the principal inhabitants in their own persons, and despatches
sent to bring intelligence, so that on Monday there
were assembled at Leeds, about seven thousand
horse and foot, in defence of their lives and liberties, religion and property, against those barbarous
and inhuman wretches.

These were digested into several troops and companies, under Sir John Kay, colonel; Sir William
Wentworth, lieutenant-colonel; Mr. Nevile of Chevet,
major: it would be endless to enter into a detail of
the captains and subalterns. Our fears were now
somewhat abated, when all upon the sudden at night
they were raised to the height upon a most dreadful alarm, " Horse and arms, horse and arms! the
enemy are upon us—Beeston is actually burnt, and
only some escaped to bring the doleful tidings!"
The drums beat, the bells rang backward, the women shrieked, and such dreadful consternation seized
upon all persons; some men with their wives and

children left all behind them (even monies and plate upon the tables) and ran for shelter to the barns and haystacks in the fields.

Their horror was so great and universal, that the aged people who remembered the Civil Wars, said they never knew any thing like it. Thousands of lighted candles were placed in the windows, and persons of any courage and consideration (if such a thing was to be found) ran with their arms to the bridge, and so marched towards Beeston; so that in a very small time some thousands appeared, and I among the rest, with horse and arms; and, blessed be God! the terror disappeared, it being a false alarm, taken from some drunken people, who cried out horribly, murder! murder!

I had left a cabinet with some of the most valuable moveables for my dear to cast into the well; but she had that presence of mind, after I was mounted and gone, to go up to the turret, and told the females Beeston was safe: for if but one house was on fire, it might be discovered there.

The town being pretty well satisfied, were generally gone to bed; but about midnight was a more dreadful alarm than the former — a knocking at every door, "Fire! Fire!" "Horse and arms! for God's sake!" It was a piteous sight to observe the terror and confusion that all sorts of persons were now in. I was most concerned for my dear wife, who was in the family way; and when I was mounted again, I could see nothing but paleness and horror in the

countenances of all men. Our scouts had brought
word that Halifax beacon was burning as a general
warning to the country, and that Halifax and Hud-
dersfield were burnt. The first part was really true,
though from a mistaken panic and fear, that had
seized them as well as us.

But no enemy appearing near, and watch being
set at several passes, I lay me down again, but with
my clothes on; and when I awoke, rejoiced to see
the light of another day, when my Lord Fairfax
came to town with three or four troops of horse,
completely armed, and we slept more securely, the
expresses bringing pretended advice that the Irish
were broke into parties and dispersed.

Upon the whole, this matter of the alarm, which
was general, and spread over most parts of England,
was managed so artfully, that even when all was
over, I could never learn who was concerned, even
in this neighbourhood.

A. D. 1689.

Jan. 13. I rode with many others to York, where,
next morning, my Lord Fairfax and Sir John Kay,
were unanimously elected Members of the Convention appointed by the Prince of Orange.

Feb. 14. Was a day of public thanksgiving for a
national deliverance in the late wonderful Revolution; and the 19th, King William and Queen Mary
were proclaimed at Leeds, with such a general satisfaction and joy as seldom has been known.

And here I cannot but take notice and lament that persons are generally more sensibly affected with private deliverances than public ones, and must particularly blame myself, who, though I was sincerely thankful for both, yet was more sensibly touched with what more immediately concerned myself and family, who were all asleep, when a fire suddenly broke out in the house, very nigh the stairs, which were of fir and very dry; yet it pleased God it was extinguished without any human help, and little harm done, save the burning of the children's coats upon the lines close by the stairs. And at another time part of the oak ceiling in the hall, under my library: I preserve the bit of wood, as a grateful memorial of so great a deliverance.

I concluded Mr. Pool's Annotations upon the Bible, which my old friend, Mr. Illingworth, recommends as the best family book that ever was printed in the world; because containing the sacred text in a good character, together with pious and learned annotations upon it. The second volume being the Continuation, is by various hands, of which I have there inserted a list, (somewhat different both from the Oxford historian's, and Dr. Calamy's,) from Mr. Stretton's Letters to Mr. Sharp, wherein he owned (in order to draw in that too modest man) that himself did Peter, and, if I mistake not, Galatians too. The next day, I began Diodati's Annotations upon the Bible.

I was frequently attempting to draw up some Me-

moirs of my honoured and dear father, which though
never perfected, yet were not, I hope, without some
good to my own soul ; and I found more real satisfaction and pleasure in reflections upon the days
thus spent, than in the merriest company I could
meet with.   But I was unhappily deprived of these
pleasant enjoyments of my papers, by an unhappy
engagement at Mr. Samuel Ibbetson's request, to
make rape-oil.*   The inducement was my father
Sykes's estate at Sheepscar, where there had been a
mill formerly: and when I pleaded my ignorance in
the affair, he argued I need not be concerned for
that, he had a right notion of it, and could manage
the stock and accounts, and my industry would be
serviceable in overseeing the servants, in making the
oil, receiving seed, delivering oil, and keeping those
accounts: the reputation he had of a religious and
substantial man : and the prospect of an advanced
rent upon that part of the estate that was designed
for my wife: and both his brother and mine deal-
ing in that commodity, there was no question but
we might with ease dispose of all the oil we could
make.

These arguments induced me to engage in the unfortunate enterprise, which was in many respects a
vast loss to me : the first I was immediately sensible

---

* This was a very unfortunate affair, and embittered many years
of Thoresby's life.   Mr. Ibbetson was a Leeds merchant, grandfather to Henry Ibbetson, Esq. who was created a Baronet by King
George II.

of was loss of time, which was necessarily consumed
in supervising and directing workmen and servants;
another was expenses in company, that I was unavoidably engaged in.   Of others, more in the sequel.

A. D. 1690.

The Revolution had deprived us of our learned
and pious Vicar, Mr. Milner, but a kind Providence
furnished us with a worthy successor, anno 1690,
the excellent Mr. Killingbeck, a public blessing to
this parish, whose preaching was with so peculiar an
energy and fervency of spirit, as was very affecting;
and his life was answerable to his preaching, truly
excellent.   I will give an instance of the conclusion
of a sermon, which suited well with my constitution.
" I will," says he, " conclude with a familiar instance,
like to be all our cases ere long.   Suppose thy chamber darkened, thyself laid speechless upon a dying-
bed,—a profound silence,—nothing heard but sighs
and groans and inarticulate sound of mourners, and
thy poor trembling soul ready to take its flight into
an unseen world, now just gone, and then for a few
moments recalled by the strugglings and gaspings of
nature :—suppose thou hadst then the liberty of
speech—oh! how pathetically wouldst thou bemoan
thy loss of time, and delays of repentance and reformation, never sufficiently bewailed, though in an
ocean of tears, to all eternity."

This year also, 1690, the no less pious than Right

Honourable Philip, Lord Wharton, began his noble charity, in sending Bibles to be distributed to the poor. Some of a warm spirit were displeased at the conditions required of the poor children, not only to repeat seven Psalms *memoriter*, but the Assembly's Catechism, which wanted the stamp of public authority, and was above their capacities. But this did not hinder their repeating the Church Catechism in public; nor was it above their capacities when more adult, and it comprehends an excellent summary of the Christian religion.

Upon these conditions, fourscore Bibles were sent to Leeds, and the like number to York, &c. ; a most excellent spiritual charity, whereby many poor families, not otherwise provided, became acquainted with the Holy Scriptures, which are able to make them wise unto salvation. My Lord was pleased to continue this number to the time of his death, and condescended to acquaint me that they should be for my time too, and perhaps for ever.

I could say much concerning the good effects of this most excellent charity upon thirty years' experience: that whereas at first there came many young men and women in hopes of the Bibles, that, at sixteen or seventeen years of age, could not say (though perhaps the Lord's Prayer) the Commandments, and much less the Creed, there are now numbers that can, both these and the entire Catechism, at six or seven years of age, as appears by my book containing a list of their names, &c. ; and many other people's children have been taught to read, in hopes of getting Bibles.*

I had the honour of several kind letters from his Lordship; and this year also began my correspondence with the Rev. Mr. Nicholson, then Archdeacon, and since Bishop of Carlisle,† a most learned and ingenious antiquary, from whom I have received many instructive letters upon those subjects, and in return communicated some matters that were not unacceptable to his Lordship. About the same time, I had the happiness to become acquainted with the pious and learned Richard Thornton, Esq. (afterwards our worthy Recorder). He had a good library, and curious collection of manuscripts; his conversation was most pleasing and agreeable. He condescended to admit me into his intimate friendship, which was continued, to my great comfort, to the time of his never-enough-lamented death.‡

---

* Lord Wharton made ample provision for the perpetuity of this excellent charity. Leeds, and many other large towns in the North, still receive the Bibles each year. The whole number to be distributed annually was to be 1050.

† Bishop Nicholson was a very zealous and successful investigator of English antiquities. His account of what had been done to illustrate the history of England, Scotland, and Ireland, is full of valuable information. He was acquainted with all the eminent antiquarians of his time, many of whose letters are printed in two volumes of Bishop Nicholson's Correspondence, published by Mr. Nichols in 1809.

Many of the Bishop's letters to Thoresby will be found in the Correspondence.

From his English bishoprick he was translated to the see of Derry in 1718; and on the 9th of February, 1727, he was made Archbishop of Cashel, but died suddenly on the 14th of that month.

‡ An entire and perfect friendship appears to have subsisted be-

A. D. 1691.

The weekly fasts were revived by the King; when I had the opportunity of hearing two sermons, at the church and chapel, which revived my spirits under the fatigues at Sheepscar, which so oppressed me, that sometimes I could scarce get half an hour at home all the day, especially when seed was brought in.   I was also, during my brother's London journey, obliged to attend his shops at Armley and Leeds in the afternoons; and the forenoons, during the time of my drinking the Spa waters at Quarry Hill, were almost entirely lost, that though for my health, I could scarce forbear repining at it.

[We now resume the Diary.]

April. 1. Morning, read Diodati's Annotations upon 1st Thessalonians before family prayer, and wrote before secret; then attended the lecture.   Mr. Sharp preached excellently from Psalm xix. 13, whence he raised many doctrines.   1st. Restraining, preventing, assisting grace is needful and desirable to all. 2d. Though all sins ought to be avoided yet more especially presumptuous sins. 3rd. Secret sins un [corrected]

tween Thoresby and Mr. Thornton, the Recorder, of whom he never speaks but with some epithet expressive of the high esteem and even reverence in which he held him. Mr. Thornton is indebted for being now remembered, chiefly, if not entirely, to his acquaintance with Thoresby.· We cannot, however, doubt that he was a good man, who well deserved to be remembered, and that he might have been able to leave permanent and public evidence of those high intellectual endowments which Thoresby attributes to him.

may grow into presumptuous. 4th. It should be our great desire and prayer that sin may not gain dominion over us. 5th. Presumptuous sins not avoided will usurp dominion. 6th. Only Divine grace can preserve from presumptuous sins and their dominion. 7th. Uprightness is a qualification very fit and meet for a servant of God. 8th. Uprightness preserves from presumption. 9th. No man can be a servant both to God and sin. 10th. It not only concerns us to renounce the service of sin, but to profess the service of God. 11th. Presumptuous reigning sins make dreadful approaches towards the great transgressions. Lastly, No man can have any so strong security against that great offence, as by shrouding himself by prayer, and care against presumptuous sins and their dominion. He insisted excellently upon the second, and mainly designed doctrine from the text, We ought with a more special care to beware of presumptuous sins : which he proved—1st. Because David doth not expressly pray against the being of other sins of daily incursion, but against these he doth. And that 2nd. under the notion of God's servant, implying that presumptuous sins are more unbecoming a child of God than any other person ; and 3rd, of dominion ; because presumptuous sins, of all others, give power and dominion to sin ; 4th. of the great transgression (supposed to be the sin against the Holy Ghost) implying that presumptuous sins do lead to that unpardonable sin. But the marrow of the doctrine consisted in a showing what these presumptuous sins are; he discoursed learnedly and excellently thereupon. The Hebrew word properly signifies proud men and prides; but to confine to the translation it imports a boldness to do a thing, and is taken sometimes materially, sometimes formally. 1st. Taken materially, it is one particular kind of sin opposed to despair, when the thing wherein we sin is a thing unwarrantable by the word of God, and the cause hereof is misbelief; and by this we may condemn for presumers, 1st. All you who go on in a continual wicked course all your days, yet hope for salvation. 2nd. You who cast yourselves into extraordinary dangers, either spiritual or civil, as to travel in dangerous ways without a guide, to thrust oneself into a knot of drunkards where must either drink or quarrel. 3rd. Such as promise themselves the end but neglect the means, as parents that would have comfort in their children without pains in their education. 4th. All you that place any confidence in any thing of your own or others devising, which is not instituted by God; as the silly Papists in holy water, signing with the cross; and others in lucky or unlucky days, spilling salt, holding children over the smith's anvils for rickets, meeting hares, with other devilish inventions (to give them the right names.) 2d. Other times presumption is taken formally for a disposition that may adhere to all other sins; murder, adultery, &c. are distinct sins, yet may agree in being presump-

tuous sins, which he discoursed learnedly and largely
upon in several particulars, &c.   Lord, help me to
profit by these extraordinary means of salvation!
Afternoon at Mill-hill about business, father's and
my own, till four ; then writing heads of excellent
sermon in Diary, before secret prayer, and read
Diodati in family.

7. Morning pretty early writing of last sacrament :
much melted in spirit, blessed be God!   Concluded
Diodati's on 2d Thessalonians, in family.   Most of
the day abroad about business, receiving a 100*l.* of
brother W.'s, with workmen, &c.   Evening at Mr.
B. D.'s, with good Mr. Corlass, lamenting the death
of the pious and learned Mr. Hough, late Vicar of
Halifax.   Begun Annotations upon 1 Timothy, and
cannot but observe that the Analysis to each book in
this English Translation of Diodati in 4to. is done
by a different author, if not of different sentiments :
as *inter alia* appears, p. 319.

9. At Mr. B. D.'s, perusing some manuscript
papers, relating to benefactions, corporation, &c.
with some proceeds of the late untoward Alderman
Martin Headly, containing his methods for the extirpation of Fanaticism, &c. out of this populous
parish, with his Petition to the King to that end,
and for *Quo Warranto* against Corporation ; which
unhappy man, notwithstanding, at his death could
find none he durst trust with his concerns but one
of those, *viz.* ditto Mr. Bryan Dixon, whose name,
together with my own and many others, were found

under his own hand writing, *inter Puritanos*, devoted to destruction : and I can scarce forbear another passage wherein that cruel persecutor seems to be under divine infatuation : he would have made no will (being childless) but purposely to prevent Jo. Hornby, of London, succeeding him in all his labours, wherefore he bequested them to Martin Hornby, a little knave who picked several guineas out of the Lord Dumblane and Latimer's pockets when at his uncle Headley's house at Leeds, whereby he had so far incurred his displeasure that he had sent him a far voyage into some of the plantations, but now in as great trouble how to dispose, as formerly how to get, an estate, he makes him his heir, to prevent this Jos. of London ; who, notwithstanding all his endeavours (the said Martin being dead before the date of the will), now enjoys whatever remains of the wretched man's labours, whose name he has erased and set his own upon his house. Eccles. iv. 7, 8. Was after with workmen at Sheepscar. Evening abroad, somewhat surprised with the surrender of Mons to the French tyrant :—Lord, put a hook into his nostrils and draw him back ! Read Annotations.

10. Morning read ; then heard the vicar, who preached very well and suitably to the preparation of the sacrament : but being after abroad collecting for worthy Mr. Sharp, was prevented of noting the heads till too much out of mind. Lord pity, &c. Evening read Annotations.

15. Morning read Diodati before family prayer, but prevented not only of writing but of secret prayer itself. Lord, pardon all sinful omissions! The whole day and part of evening with cousin Rodes and other relations and friends, but had a good event and accommodation of those differences betwixt the two brothers, that has involved them in Chancery suits and was too likely to have proceeded. Read Diodati in family.

17. Morning read Annotations, &c., then at Sheepscar with workfolk. Afternoon walked to Armly; attended brother's shop there; in the intervals of business had good Mr. Wilkinson (Mr. Corlass's nephew) the minister's company. Returned late enough, weary and wet, so read only Annotations.

18. Morning read Diodati, but wrote not. Part of forenoon at brother's shop, rest with Mr. S. Ibbetson at Mr. H.'s about mill. Afternoon, writing some memoranda for Mr. Thomas Jackson upon his journey for St. Andrew's in Scotland, where he is to be educated under Mr. Monro, the Regent, for the Ministry.

22. Morning, read Annotations upon last of Titus before family prayer, and wrote. Forenoon visited by cousin Rodes and uncle Pool; then writing till about three, when sent for by ditto Esquire Rodes; found more difficulty than was expected in the accommodation of differences, yet left it in a hopeful way, but stayed at Mill-hill with ditto com-

pany and others concerned, till late enough. Read only Annotations on some verses in Paul to Philemon.

24. Morning wrote, and read in family. Most of forenoon within, rest at Sheepscar. After had Mr. S. Ibbetson's company perusing Headley's papers, wherein we found our own names, and with many others devoted to ruin and confiscation. After walked with him to cousin F.'s of Hunslet, which took up evening, that read only Annotations, but wrote not.

25. Wrote pretty much, and read Diodati in family. All day perusing papers, &c. and in library. Evening wrote, and read Baxter's Dying Thoughts, &c. in family.

29. Morning wrote remaining heads of sermon: Lord write them upon my heart! Read Diodati before family prayer; then attended the Fast sermon, (revived by the King's special command.) Mr. Sharp prayed affectionately, and preached excellently from Jonah iii. 5. A mixture of mercy and judgment in preaching, works most powerfully on people's hearts. God's institutions are mostly composed of mercy and judgment; earthquakes and tempests to break rocks, remove mountains, every thing that opposes: and still small rain to melt, &c. What God has joined together let no man put asunder . . . Never approved the humour of those, though eminent in their times, who were constantly flashing fire and brimstone; but a more dangerous

extreme prevails of late, of decrying duties as Old
Testament dispensations . . . nothing but the open
arms of Christ, &c.   I afterwards repeated it in
family.

May 4. Morning, wrote and read but little, being
all day abroad about business, assisting father Sykes
in affairs of the manor, and at Mr. Sharp's, paying
the small pittance collected for him, infinitely short
of his merits.

11. Morning, read in family.   Forenoon at Sheepscar, taking leave of cousins for London.   Afternoon
walked with the Vicar, Alderman Ibbetson, and Mr.
S. Ibbetson, to Northall-wood, the pleasant seat of
the late Mr. B.: in return had their company at my
house.

23. Morning, read Diodati; forenoon, with father
advising; then abroad at Bridge and Mill-hill;
after, abroad also at M. Hutton's and Sheepscar;
then waited for post till nine, but, blessed be God!
had the acceptable news of the retaking of the ships
designed from Hull to Holland, wherein these northern parts, (and especially this town,) were deeply
concerned : read only Annotations.

26. Morning, read Diodati; walked to Sheepscar
about an hour; rest of day in library, consulting
authors about Archbishop Thoresby, in Edward the
Third's time.   Evening, concluded Annotations on
Peter.

29. Morning, prevented of reading and writing
before prayer; rid with Mr. S. Ib. to Thorp Arch,

to view the lately erected rape-mill; visited our quondam neighbour (W. A.'s daughter,) Mrs. Loft, where kindly received; in return, stayed awhile at Clifford with L. S. but returned well, and in good time; read only Diodati.

June 4. Forenoon reading Sheringham's de Anglorum Gentis Origine; after, with workmen; then visiting poor cousin Tim. Idle. Lord sanctify every indisposition!

6. Morning, writing per post to St. Andrew's, in Scotland, and Dublin, in Ireland, to two of good old Mr. Boyse's posterity, so remote from each other and the place of their nativity.

12. Morning, read Wilkins and Diodati; after, walk to Sheepscar; most of day writing and consulting old authors on the antiquities of Leeds; till six abroad, to inquire the issue of the commission betwixt cousin Rodes, complainant, and brother Wilson, defendant, which it was endeavoured to bring to a final determination of the business, but prevented by the obstinacy of Mr. W. R. about charges, that they must now to Chancery again. Evening, with Mr. B. D.; after, had Mr. S. Ib. another of the Commissioners; read only Diodati.

July 1. Morning, read Dr. Hall in family, walked to Sheepscar; after, walked to Armly, attended brother's concerns there; in return, with Parson Wilkinson, took a particular view of the high mount, nigh the river, called Giant's-hill, which I cannot tell what to make of, except it has been a Danish fortification; the smallness of its circuit is the most discouraging argument to the contrary, but yet the situation of the place, and the moat round, seem to intimate as much : read only Paraphrase in family.

8. Morning, began to drink the Spa-water at Quarry-hill.

16. Morning, read Hall and Wilkins before prayer; forenoon in library, collecting notes and the antiquities of Leeds, till about three; then at Sheepscar.

18. Morning, read Bishop Hall's Paraphrase, Exodus, 1 ; forenoon in study, about the antiquities of Leeds, till near three.

20. Morning, read Hall; from ten to four was happy in the pleasing society of the Rev. Mr. Sharp and Mr. Whitaker ; after, with workmen. Evening at Mayor's; read only Hall.

21. Morning, read Wilkins and Hall ; then walked to Sheepscar to workmen; after, with Mr. S. Ibbetson, to view the new chapel at Mill-hill, and agree with several workmen, in order to a new erection for the like service in Call-lane. Evening, walked again to Sheepscar; read only Paraphrase.

22. Morning, read Hall, but omitted Wilkins ; walked to N. H.'s and Sheepscar ; after, walked with poor E. H. to Mr. B. D.'s ; then with Mr. S. Ib. at Sheepscar, and drawing for him a model of their designed chapel ; read only Hall in family.

23. Morning, read Wilkins and Hall ; then with

workmen at designed chapel and mill till noon ; had
relations at dinner.   Evening, at pasture ; read only
Hall.

24. Morning, read only Hall ; with Mr. S. Ib.
setting out the plot of ground for new chapel ; then
directing workmen at Sheepscar and home ; twenty
men at one place or other ; read only Hall.

25. Morning, read Wilkins and Hall ; then rode
with my dear and . . . . relations to Dewsburgh ;
was very inquisitive for the stone Camden mentions,
inscribed *Paulinus hic predicavit et celebravit*, but
could not so much as hear of any that had seen it.
Mr. Pierson, an ancient minister, a native here,
whose father was the minister here for thirty years,
told me that neither of them could find any thing of
it ; but I transcribed Bishop Tilson's epitaph ; and
some inscriptions upon several places at the noble
and stately fabric of Howley Hall, founded by Sir
Robert Savile, augmented by Sir John, and finished
by Sir Thomas, Earl of Sussex, in three generations,
though enjoyed but by one more, his son dying sans
issue ;* returned late enough, but, blessed be God!
very well ; read Bishop Hall.

Aug. 8. Morning, concluded Spa-course ; fore-

---

* In a note, added in 1717, it is said, "Now pulled down, and the
materials sold." Little is known of the two Earls of Sussex, of the
family of Savile. There is a portrait of one of them, at the hall at
Sharlston, a few miles from Wakefield, one of the few remaining
Elizabethian houses. The heiress of the Earl of Sussex married
Lord Brudenel, and carried Howley Hall, and their other great
estates, to the Cardigan family.

noon, receiving rape seed; after, at the funeral of
honest Obadiah Woodroofe, a serious good Christian, (the fifth husband of the same woman,) then at
mill, &c. Evening, too greedy of news, had time
only to read Hall.

10. Morning, concluded Paraphrase on Exodus;
then at Mr. Sharp's, taking leave of Mr. John,* for
Mr. Frankland's academy.

18. Morning, read Hall and Wilkins; then at
mill, &c.; afternoon, with Mr. B. D. advising with
Mr. Sharp, about uncle †Wilson's legacy to chapel;
then with the High Sheriff (the Hon. Henry Fairfax, Esq. my very kind friend,) father Sykes, &c.
Evening, at mill, and after at Mr. S. Ib.'s, with
good Mr. Heywood; read only Hall.

23. Die Dom. Read Hall's Paraphrase before
family prayer, and Wilkins's Gift before secret. Mr.
Sharp preached from Matthew x. 15; raised this
doctrine, that those who will not receive Christ's
ministers, nor hear their message, are judged by him
unworthy of that peace which the Gospel brings,
improved in the words of Habakkuk i. 5; you
that God gives so full a character of, Ezekiel
xxxiii. 31, that come unto me as my people cometh,
sit before me as my people, and hear my words,

* The only son of Thomas Sharp, the minister. He was a physician, but died early in life, January 13, 1704.

† As illustrative of the language of the time, we may notice the
loose manner in which Thoresby uses the word *uncle*. Mr. Wilson
was father to Mr. Thomas Wilson, who married the eldest sister of
Thoresby's wife.

&c. it was an aggravation of Julian's wickedness, he had been a Christian, and Judas's being an Apostle; and, therefore, deeplier punished, according to the German proverb, that hell is paved with priests' skulls, gentlemen's breasts, bishops' mitres, kings' sceptres, popes' triple crowns, &c. It is now almost 140 years since the Reformation, and almost as long that we have been declining: we fail in hearing, obeying, maintaining, and adorning the Gospel; and those who have held closest in the land to the interest of the Gospel, are most despised. Consider these things, and you will sigh, as I do, and say there is reason to read the text thus; "It will be more tolerable for Sodom in the day of judgment than for *this* nation."—1. Dost not thou grow indifferent? 2. Grudge the Gospel its maintenance? 3. Will not an ill morning keep thee from church, that would not from the market? 4. Hast thou not said, as those wretches, Mal. iii. 14, "It is vain to serve God, and what profit?"

28. Morning, read *ut prius*. With Mrs. S. of Y. about brasses; after, rid with Mr. S. I. to Mr. C.'s about business; after, had a visit from Mr. A. of G. with recommendation from Rev. Mr. Frankland; with commissioners of pious uses about ditto school concern till four; then walked with Mr. Ib. to Bank, and evening to Sheepscar.

29. Up early, writing to the Archdeacon of Carlisle about antiquities, per parson W. of A. by whom sent some coins and inscriptions; had ditto

parson W.'s and Mr. A. of G.'s company till near noon.

September 2. Morning at worthy Mr. Sharp's, with whom, and Mr. Whitaker, and Mr. S. Ib. rode to Wakefield; heard the lecture sermon; Mr. Heywood preached well, and suitably to the Convention from Zach. xiv. 9, " In that day there shall be one Lord, and his name one." Afterwards, that good man (itinerant preacher, or apostle of these parts) read each of the Heads of the Agreement of the United Ministers in and about London. Most were unanimously assented unto by the brethren of both per-suasions; others modestly discussed and explained; and, which I rejoiced to observe, without the least passionate expression. The truly Rev. Mr. Frankland and Mr. Sharp in their arguments showed abundance of learning as well as piety, and were unanswered, even in what was not readily assented to by some juniors about synods and re-ordination; had the pleasing society of many excellent ministers from all parts of the West Riding.* I afterwards performed a visit to our Recorder, Mr. Whyte; was acceptably entertained with the sight of some rare pieces in Saxon and Gothic; took some notes as to Leeds, &c. was much pleased with many of his

---

* This was the first of a series of periodical meetings of the Presbyterian ministers of the West Riding, in which, for a time, something of the appearance of Presbyterian discipline was maintained. In the manuscript remains of Mr. Heywood is a very particular account of what was done in this Assembly: where are also briefer notices of what was done at nine subsequent meetings.

learned observations upon several authors, which he courteously communicated; but stayed full late in a dark night, but our good God preserved us from dangers; blessed be his name! Read only Hall in family.

4. Morning, up early; receiving rape till noon; after, paying money on ditto account, and with workmen at Sheepscar, till about five; then at the sad funeral of Mrs. Whitaker,* who, having borne her first child a fortnight ago, died very suddenly last night. I was much affected, and heartily sympathized with the good man in this affliction, having had sad experience almost of the like dispensation.

14. Morning read Hall; rode with Mr. S. Ib. to Mr. C.'s; had workmen; afternoon rode to brother's shop at Armly; there, per Parson Wilkinson, received a letter, with remarks upon coins, the Idol Thor, &c. from the admirably learned Archdeacon Nicholson; after, had the Vicar and four other parsons; evening, read *ut prius*.

26. Morning, as once before this week, had a memento of mortality, perhaps of sudden dissolution, in violent pain in the back parts of head;† forenoon writing; after, abroad, partly about business; read little.

---

* The second wife of Mr. Whitaker, minister of the congregation for whom the chapel in Call Lane was then building.

† Thoresby often speaks of the recurrence of these pains, which he regarded as apoplectic symptoms, an apprehension which the event seemed to justify.

Oct. 5. Morning, read only Hall. All day with Lords of Manor, constituting the constables for the succeeding year, and other affairs of the manor, till towards evening ; sent for to cousin Milner's, where the Providence of God has made a breach this day, the good old man dying suddenly of a palsy fit.*

6. Morning, read Hall ; then at cousin Milner's advising as to funeral. After, writing heads of sermon, till visited by Parson Hammond of Ledsham. Then with Lords of Manor. Dined with our learned Recorder at uncle Idle's.

7. Morning, read Hall. After, at Court, to hear the learned Recorder's ingenious charge. Then at brother W.'s. Again dined at the Mayor's, but hasted away to the funeral of old cousin Milner. Mr. Sharp preached from 1 Cor. iii. 21, 22. Doctrine, that temporal death is a true Christian's patrimony. Had a visit from my good friend, the truly reverend and pious Mr. Corlass, and his virtuous consort.†

8. Morning, read Hall; then preparing for a jour-

---

* William Milner, an eminent merchant of Leeds, father of Mr. Joseph Milner, of Rotterdam, who is mentioned in the earlier years of this Diary. The first Sir William Milner, of Nun-Appleton, Bart. was grandson to the Mr. Milner whose death is here noticed.

† The name of Mr. Corlass has been often mentioned, and few persons appear to have enjoyed more of the respect of Thoresby. He had been Chaplain to Lady Barwick, and was at this time Rector of Marston, near York. His wife was a daughter of Thoresby's early friend, Mr. Bryan Dixon, and was remarked among her acquaintance for the strength of her memory, of which there is a particular notice in the *Ducatus,* p. 612.

ney.   Rode with my dear to Father Sykes's at
Ledsham, and thence, with Mr. S. Ibbetson, *et filius*,
by Selby to Howden, where lodged.

9. Morning, viewing the town and ancient church,
now in part ruinous, but has been adorned with very
delicate stonework, the remains of several curious
statues and stories yet testifying its ancient glory,
vide Camden and Speed, as to the nominal shire, &c.
but found no inscriptions, save two moderns for Mr.
Arlush and Mr. Roots, eminently holy and serviceable ministers.   Then we rode by Cave and Kirk-
ella (which I could fancy so denominated from a
Saxon king of the name) to Kingston upon Hull.
Blessed be God for protection !

10. Forenoon, with several friends and acquaintance.   After, with Captain Idle, viewing the garrison side, the new fortifications, and storehouses.
Then performed a visit to cousin Hilliard (Sir Robert's mother,) and others.   Evening, ditto company.

11. Die Dom.   Morning, (as indeed all along)
Mr. S. Ibbetson prayed very well; then heard Mr.
Astley from 2 Tim. ii: 19.   Doctrine, that such are
built upon a sure foundation that profess the Lord
Jesus, and depart from iniquity.   Afternoon, we
heard Mr. Charles at the other place, (where they
were reading the strict orders made by their magistrates, as at York, Beverley, &c. for the better observation of the Lord's day); he preached well from
2 Peter, iii. 14. " Be diligent that you may be found

of him in peace." Evening, not so strictly employed, being engaged in a visit at Mr. Thornton's.

12. Morning, took leave of Mr. S. Ibbetson's son; the Lord send him a prosperous voyage! &c. Afterwards, rode per Beverley, (where transcribed monument) to Weeton upon the Wolds (Deirwald), where lodged.

13. Morning, rode thence to York, where at the Minster, enquiring for the Lady's Chapel (now ruinated) where Archbishop Thoresby was interred: was acquainted by Dr. James, Master of Queen's College, Cambridge, that in Sir Thomas Hardress's family in Kent, they still gratefully retain the name in memory of this family, and there is yet living Mr. Thoresby Hardress, (vide monument in Hackney). After, rode with ditto to Tadcaster, and thence to Ledsham.

20. Morning, read Hall on Ruth; then abroad about business, om gelt te ontfangen, &c. Afternoon, at the funeral of Dr. Neal, an aged, eminent, and very able physician of this town. After, at the mill, seeing them now first make oil there; then with father Sykes and Mr. S. Ib. Read only Hall.

28. At mill, fretting at reiterated disappointments. There most of day.

Nov. 2. Morning, read Hall; then hasted to Sheepscar. Afternoon, had a kind visit from Mr. Sharp; then, at the request of the Mayor, Vicar, &c. consulting about setting up a linen manufactory to employ the poor, &c.

18. Morning, *ut prius.* Forenoon, taking leave of relations for Ledsham. Afternoon, received a kind visit from the High Sheriff, my honoured friend —— Fairfax, Esq. with whom perusing manuscripts about his ancient and honourable family till four. Then at Mr. Sharp's.

21. Morning, read Hall. Writing to Bryan Fairfax, Esq. (Secretary to the Archbishop of Canterbury,) advising with Mr. B. D. about disposal of Bibles. Afternoon, at Sheepscar.

22. Die Dom. Morning, read Hall Mr. Sharp preached excellently from former text and doctrine, that Jesus Christ and the Spirit of Grace are the gift of God. Afternoon, Mr. Whitaker (whose congregation has now a second day been with us, till their new meeting-place be fit for their reception,) preached very well from Matthew xi. 28.

Dec. 9. Morning, read, &c. Then distributing the eighty Bibles, and as many Catechisms, to the probationers for the ensuing year, with eight of Lye's Catechisms, and eight Allen's Sure Guide to Heaven, to the eight best proficients of the former year, with 12*d.* for each parent; the noble and pious charity of Philip Lord Wharton. Mr. Sharp preached from John v. 39; doctrine, that those Scriptures wherein we think to have eternal life, and which testify of Christ, are to be diligently searched by us all. Afternoon, at Mill-hill, enjoyed ministers' and relations' company.

11. Evening, at the Free School, with much good

company, to hear the boys act a Latin *vendu* of books.

15. Morning, read two last chapters of 1 Chron. Rest of day abroad, *om gelt te ontfangen ende beta-eten.* Sending money from ditto religious lord to the Rev. Mr. Prime, of Sheffield, Mr. Heywood, of Halifax, Mr. Waterhouse, of Bradford.* Paid also Mr. Sharp his, with whom, and Mr. B. D. at chapel, upon the advising as to repairs, &c. Evening, read but little.

16. Morning, read, &c.; then abroad, *om gelt, ut prius,* about Father S.'s concerns. After, transcribing dates of the deaths of eminent persons from Wood's Athenæ Oxonienses. Then at Sheepscar. Evening, reading from ditto partial author.

23. Morning, read, &c.; then at mill. Afterwards, about domestic affairs till noon : enjoyed the good company of Vicar, Mr. Whitaker, with many friends and relations at dinner, and till evening, when with some of them at H.'s till late.

25. Morning, read . . . . . The Vicar preached excellently from John i. 14, " And the word was made flesh ;" whence he very learnedly refuted the Socinian errors.

27. Die Dom. Morning ; *ut prius.* Then attended in public ; Mr. Robinson, at the New Church, preached the Commemoration sermon, from that of

---

* These were all Nonconformist ministers, who had left the Church in 1662, and to whom it appears that Lord Wharton made an annual allowance of money.

the Evangelist, " He loved our nation and built us a synagogue;" wherein he earnestly recommended charity, to show our faith by our works ; and especially to make our own hands our executors, and our eyes our supervisors. Afternoon, at Mill-hill; Mr. Wright preached very well from Rom. viii. 9, doctrine, that none but such as have the Spirit of Christ, are members of Christ. Evening, repeated in family, and read in Mr. Heywood's Heart's Treasure.

31. Morning, read ; then at mill; but most of the day transcribing manuscript of ejected ministers, &c. Evening, &c. ; but, alas ! too little of my time spent about the *unum necessarium,* though another year of my short pilgrimage irrecoverably past.

A. D. 1692.

Jan. 1. Morning, began Bishop Hall upon Nehemiah ; forenoon, transcribing manuscript account of ejected ministers courteously communicated to me by the author, the reverend and useful Mr. Oliver Heywood.

3. Die Dom. Morning, read Dr. Hall, &c. Mr. Bovil, jun. preached at Old Church from Matt. ii. 16, whence he discoursed eloquently of Herod's cruelty in the actual murder of fourteen thousand infants, and the intentional murder of our blessed Redeemer. Afternoon, Mr. Dawson, jun. preached well from Psm. cxix. 67, doctrine, that prosperity often occasions a backsliding from God. Evening, read Mr. T. Rogers's Persuasion to a friendly Corres-

pondence between the Conformists and Non-confor-
mists, preached at the funeral of Mr. Anthony Dun-
well (our neighbour's brother); was much pleased
and affected therewith.   Lord, succeed all such pious
and peaceable endeavours ! having a peculiar anti-
pathy in my spirit against the extravagant heats of
indiscreet persons of all hands.   Read Hall.

11. Morning, rise pretty early; read Hall; walked to mill; and afterwards to Mill-hill.   Forenoon, `
enjoyed the ingenious Mr. Priestley's* company in
library.

12. So this morning.   Then rode with Mr. Ihhet-
son to Knaresborough; found the ways not so ill as
dreaded; was preserved from dangers, though many
others were for several hours lost in the terrible mist,
upon the forest.   After, walked to the petrifying well,
and St. Robert's (of whom, *vide* Fuller's History of
Abbeys, Lord Fairfax's Pedigree, &c.) Chapel, hewn
out of an entire rock; the altar yet remains, with three
heads over the hollow upon the right hand, which I
had not light enough to distinguish whether designed
for the blessed Trinity, according to the ignorance of
those bemisted days.   Evening, transcribing an old
legend of his life and death . .. but very imperfect.

13. Morning . . . for some hours in the fair, but to
no purpose, goods being dear; bought none.   Walking to Mr. Petty's rape and hemp mills.   After, to the
ruins of the Castle, which has stood very pleasantly

* Nathaniel Priestley, a young man just entering the Ministry
among the Nonconformists.   He settled at Halifax.

upon a steep precipice to the water. Afternoon, returned home.

30. Evening, reading Dr. Bates' excellent sermon upon the funeral of the incomparable Mr. Baxter.

Feb. 10. Evening, reading Archdeacon Nicholson's Letter to Sir William Dugdale, concerning Runic Inscriptions.

21. Die Dom. Read Bishop Hall. Mr. Sharp preached ; after repetition, read Heywood's Heart's Treasure, and Bishop Burnet's sermon at the funeral of the Hon. Robert Boyle, with the extraordinary characters deservedly bestowed upon that excellent person and his virtuous sister, the Countess of Ranelagh, which rejoiced my heart, &c.

March 7. Morn. read Hall and Alsop. Forenoon, consulting the two oldest registers of Leeds parish, for the two famous Cooks, whom at length I found ; Robert baptized July 23, 1550, and Alexander, Sept. 3, 1564, both under the name of Gayle :* *anno* 1570, being the first time I found the name Cook, without *alias* Gayle, or Gaile *alias* Cook, as both the two families at Beiston, and that of Hunslet, were denominated. Afternoon, with Lords of Manor. Evening, read manuscripts, Hall, &c.

11. Morning, read Hall and Alsop; then walked to Sheepscar ; most of day examining old registers of Leeds Church. One generation goes and another comes, &c.

---

* These were early Vicars of Leeds. A full account of them and of their writings may be found in the *Vicaria*.

21. Morning, read Hall and Alsop; then walked to Sheepscar, to view another miserable breach made by a storm and sudden flood last night. Perusing registers. After with relations, &c. to Moortown, to the funeral of Aldress Hick;* the vicar preached from that of the wise man; "But the righteous hath hope in his death."

23. Afternoon, perusing Inquisition of Pious Uses.

25. Morning, read; at Sheepscar, collecting Fee-farm rents. Evening, reading Mr. Fairfax's (formerly of Kirk-gate) learned and ingenious manuscript of Witchcraft, and Hall, *ut prius.*

29. Attending the commissioners at Moothall, where in an arbitrary unreasonable manner, again appointed assessor for this third Poll Bill (having been upon both the former.)

30. Concluded Mr. Fairfax's manuscript of Dæmonology, wherein he learnedly disputes the point, and judiciously relates the manner of his children's trances, with ingenious remarks.

31. Morning, hastened to workmen, read only Gouge; in return visited Mr. Sharp, then with Mr. T. collecting for him; with Mr. D. about society affairs. Afternoon wholly at Sheepscar, where are renewed disappointments daily, sometimes hourly. Evening, had Mr. S. Ibbetson's company, which somewhat mitigated; read, &c.

April 12. Morning, read; then at Sheepscar, after

* The wife or widow of an alderman.

at Mill-hill and with arbitrators, endeavouring accommodation of differences amongst relations.

29. Morning, *ut prius*, directing workmen. Evening, with the arbitrators, who now determined the controversies betwixt mother and son.

30. Morning, read Hall. Forenoon at brother W.'s, with Esquire Rodes, about their concerns; then with brother J. Th. about his; after with Mr. Ibbetson and the Guild of Salters. Read only Hall's Paraphrase.

May 16. Apprehensions of a French invasion.

22. Die Dom. Morning, read Bishop Hall. Mr. Sharp preached excellently from former text and doctrine, that if children do not turn to the wisdom and religiousness of their parents, the Lord will smite the earth with a curse. Was upon the last reason to prove, that those that do not turn unto the holiness of their ancestors are more likely to introduce the curse than others, because though committed in common with others, are greater and more highly aggravated than the sins of others. 1st. They are committed against more noble and excellent privileges; and 2nd. against better means. As 1st. against the words of their gracious parents, against all methods used for their reformation. 2nd. Against their works, pious examples, &c. 3rd. Against the blessings which they are instrumental to convey unto thee. God's blessing runs in the blood till they degenerate; it is absolute to their seed before they

are capacitated to act for themselves, and condi-
tional to those that can.   4th. Against correction,
which if used by godly parents as an ordinance of
God, has a blessing upon it.   Lastly, Against their
faithful prayers : if thy spiritual diseases be grown
so inveterate thy case is lamentable, if this fails, all
fails, and thou hast sinned thyself beyond the force
of means, and beyond the ordinary power that God
usually exerts to reform sinners.   If thou sin thy
praying parents into their graves before they have
prayed thee out of thy sins, it is a sad sign that God
will have no more prayers put up for thee, but has
devoted thee to that dreadful destruction that shall
devour the adversary.   3rd. Thy sin is greater than
others, and consequently more likely to introduce
the curse, because thou sinnest against more patience
in God than any ; and 4th. Against greater love,
against covenant love, which is a higher degree.
5th. Thou art a more dangerous contributor to the
introduction of the curse, because thou sinnest
against more full and home convictions than others ;
and lastly, Because thou not only frustratest the
prayers of thy parents and others, but thou turnest
thy own prayers into curses ; the provocations of
sons and daughters is most heinous.   Then entered
upon the application by way of doctrine : if when by
the means of grace the spirit and disposition of holy
parents be not wrought into their children, the Lord
will smite the earth with a curse ; it doth certainly
suppose that children do not naturally walk in the

ways of their pious parents; the best do propagate
original corruption. Again it follows, that though sin
be, yet grace is not entailed; again, that birth-privi-
leges are not sufficient to make a man a sound real
true Christian ; again, that it is vain for children to
think to fare better at God's hands if they live in
contradiction to their holy examples; the sins of
those who are best born, will be worst borne by
God : again, that it is the greatest folly and presumption for such to continue in sin, and bear up
themselves upon the covenant of their ancestors;
again, that none are laden with a greater burden
of wrath on earth than those that go down to hell
in the brightest robes. That it shall be eternally
worse for a man to be better born than another, if
he be no better; nothing profits that brings not
nearer to God. That God is no respecter of persons; were it possible thou shouldst be born of an
archangel, of a cherubim or seraphim, yet if thou
livest like a devil, thou shouldest fare no better.
After repetition, read Hall.

26. Morning read Hall; with workmen at home,
and Sheepscar; evening received the confirmation
of that wonderful national deliverance in the utter
extirpation of the French fleet.

June 19. Die Dom. Morning read Hall's Paraphrase; Mr. Sharp, in prosecution of his former
doctrine, proceeded to three heads more that relate
to parents. You may be the cause of their not
turning by setting an ugly face upon religion, by

sourness, moroseness, fanaticalness; when they see you always melancholy, both seed-time and harvest in tears, they are tempted to think, that if they turn to your ways, they shall never enjoy a good day in the world, and their sprightliness must be drowned in sorrow. Lastly, too soon giving them up as irreclaimable, which, I fear, is no less a sin in parents, than a judgment upon children. 2. The causes in children are many; particularly 1, heedlessness; 2, sloth and laziness; 3, pride, or a high fancy for the fooleries or fineries of the world, which many parents instead of reclaiming, teach their children: children at school are often fatally coupled, living and dead bodies together, and the dead too often corrupt the living; 4, desire to be out of control, unaccountable for what they do or enjoy. Evening, repeated and read Hall in family, wherein had father Sykes's assistance.

July 4. Morning, busy about Poll Bill, taking an account of the inhabitants of this division; then had a sight of the best of bishops that have honoured this town with their presence in my time, Dr. John Sharp, Archbishop of York, a most excellent preacher, universally beloved.

11. Most of the day busied in preparation for a trial at the Assizes, sending witnesses to York.*

12. Morning up pretty early; read Hall; forenoon about ditto employ; after, rode with Mr. S. Ib-

---

* It was a question respecting encroachment at Sheepscar.

betson to York, about ditto concern. Lord! give
me wisdom, and direction, and success, in all lawful
enterprizes, so far as agreeable to thy holy pleasure.
Mr. Ibbetson prayed well.

13. Morning, hasted abroad to consult Serjeant,
formerly Judge, Lutwich, about ditto suit; advised
also with Mr. Blythman and Mr. Hatfield; attending
the plaintiff's motion, except from ten till twelve,
that the judges adjourned the court to hear the fast
sermon at the Minster.

14. Morning spent the whole day in a wearisome
attendance with the witnesses upon the opposites,
who would neither desist nor adventure to bring on
the trial, which wearied us.

15. Morning; forenoon at court; at length prevailed for the bringing on the trial; but, upon the
opening of our cause by the Serjeant, the plaintiffs
immediately (before so much as one of our witnesses
were examined,) moved for a View, to delay what
their hearts seemed to faint in the trial of.

16. Morning up pretty early; visited relations
without the Bar, and afterwards, the ingenious and
industrious antiquary, Mr. Torre ; who, from the records of the Cathedral, and other original writings,
has composed a large folio manuscript, which he
honoured me with the sight of, and allowed me
thence to transcribe an account of Archbishop
Thoresby's benefactions; and presented me with
his seal, whereby it appears that he was Cardinal
Presbyter, by the title of St. Peter *ad vincula*; but

had too small time to peruse so pleasing rarities and
consult so obliging a gentleman, who, by his courteous demeanour and importunate requests, has laid
an obligation upon me to wait on him the first
opportunity I can obtain;* afterwards, returned

---

* It might be expected that in some of his many visits to York,
Thoresby would seek and obtain an introduction to Mr. Torre.

While Thoresby was cherishing a native fondness for antiquarian
research, Torre was busily engaged in forming those antiquarian collections, which still remain decisive evidences of the most laborious
application.

The story of his life is soon told.　He was the son of Gregory
Turre, or Torre, of the Isle of Axholme, where he inherited a competent estate.　He was baptized April 13, 1649.　His father died in
1660, leaving him to the care of Thomas Levet and Robert Mirfin, a
clergyman, to the latter of whom he seems to have owed in part his
predilection to antiquarian pursuits.　He spent two years and a half
in Magdalene College, Cambridge, and was afterwards admitted into
the Society of the Students of the Inner Temple.　He was not called
to the Bar; but went to live quietly at York, where he spent his
whole time in historical researches.　His lands in Lincolnshire he
sold, and with the money bought the estate of Snydal, near Pontefract, with the intention of residing there.　He took possession of
the house on the 13th of June, 1699, and died on the last day of the
following month of July.　He has a monument in the church of
Normanton.

In his choice of York for a residence, he seems to have been
guided by the opportunities which would thus be afforded of access to
the records belonging to the see.　Those records commence at a very
early period, and the accumulation of papers, of greater or less importance, is and was then immense.　The information which they contain respecting the parochial history of the county of York is of course
great indeed; but there is also much respecting the gentilitial history, and indeed there is scarcely a point in the topography of Yorkshire, which does not admit of some illustration from those records.

I do not find that much recourse had been made to them for topographical purposes before the time of Torre.　Dodsworth contented
himself with abstracting the registers of the early Archbishops, and such
of the Wills as appeared to him of most importance.　His abstracts
are valuable to those who cannot easily have access to the originals.

with my good friend Mr. Ibbetson, whose assistance
and attendance at York upon account of this suit,
has been very obliging.   Blessed be God for comfortable converse, and for all merciful providences, protection from danger, and that we found all well at
home; but weary and heavy, and prevented of reading.

28. Morning. at the Poor's Assessment making;
was troubled to observe the inequality and passions
of some concerned.   Lord, give me wisdom!   Then
at mill, read not till noon ; then at funeral of cousin
William's eldest and only son.   Lord, sanctify all
monits of mortality!   Then had Mr. S. Ibbetson
and the Guild of Salter's Company at my house till
pretty late.

Aug. 25. Forenoon, *ut prius.*   After rode with

But Torre went far beyond Dodsworth. To him the topography of
Yorkshire owes the digested series of incumbents throughout the
whole see ; with the dates of their institutions, and the names of the
patrons ; abstracts of the ordinations of vicarages, and catalogues of
persons who have directed in their wills that their remains shall be
interred in particular churches. These, all transcribed in a fair and
legible hand, form the chief and most valuable part of his collections.
These volumes are now in possession of the Dean and Chapter of
York ; but it is contended by the family of the Collector, that they
never formally resigned their right to them.

Many other volumes of topographical and genealogical collections
are still in possession of the family, which, when looked at in relation to the history and topography of Yorkshire, derive their chief
value from the many new facts collected by him in his perusal of the
records of the See of York, and preserved only in those records, and
in his manuscripts.

Thoresby often visited Torre after this introduction, and has
availed himself of Torre's admirable labours both in the *Ducatus* and
Vicaria.

brother Thoresby to Bramhope; was very obligingly
entertained at Esquire Dineley's by his ingenious
lady.   Had a pleasant prospect of Wharfdale.
Evening returned safe, &c.

26. Forenoon as before, despatched the Spa and
Sheepscar business together; was rest of the day
putting library, &c. into a little order, in expectation
of the Archdeacon's promised visit.   Evening had
ditto relations (three generations of female Papists);*
read.

Sept. 9. Morning, at mill, then at the Vicar's,
then had a visit from Mr. Lamb, the quondam
operator to the famous Mr. Boyle.

10. Read Hall.   Morning, abroad about business.
Forenoon at Sheepscar, &c.   Afternoon had a letter
recommendatory from the Lord Wharton for the
eminent Mr. Howe of London, whose excellent
company, with the Rev. Mr. Todd's, I enjoyed rest
of day, and evening his assistance in family duty.

12. Morning, enjoyed Mr. Howe's assistance in
family prayer, then accompanied him to Pontefract.
Lord, preserve him from the danger of his journey,
and convey him safe to his own habitation, that he
may be continued as a blessing to this nation.

19. Morning, early at Sheepscar, directing in
laying foundation for a horse mill.   After sent for
by Mr. Jonas Waterhouse, who presented me with
his Discourse of God and Religion, newly printed,

* The family of his uncle Joseph Thoresby, of Sike-house in the
parish of Fishlake.

advised to the publication of the manuscript. Eujoyed his and Mr. Sharp's good company; towards evening again at Sheepscar.

22. Much concerned at the terrible earthquakes in these parts of the world.

26. Morning, rose pretty early, rode to Healey (with brother) to wait upon that excellent pattern of true nobility and piety, Philip Lord Wharton, who received us with abundant respects and kindness.   Dined with his honour and several persons of quality; had afterwards particular orders in private about the Bibles, &c., and after rode to York with Dr. Nicholson, Alderman Tomson, (Parliamentmen,) &c. where made a visit to the ingenious Mr. Torre.   Evening, had cousin Addison's company. Then sat up till past midnight transcribing from Mr. Torre's manuscript a catalogue of the Abbots of Kirkstal and Vicars of Leeds.

29. Directing at setting up the new iron balcony.

Oct. 1. Writing about business to Dr. J. at mill. Afternoon, had some visitants, Mr. G. and Mr. A. of Cambridge, to see collections, &c.   Evening endeavouring, in a faint measure, to prepare this unprepared heart for the solemn ordinance of the Lord's Supper.

2. Die Dom.   Mr. Sharp preached from Cant. v. 16. Doctrine, that Jesus Christ is altogether lovely in his nature, person, offices.   The succeeding ordinance was this day first celebrated publicly in the

New Chapel (having formerly been at brother Wilson's.) Afternoon he proceeded to the beauty of holiness. Evening repeated and read Hall.

Nov. 28. Morning, at mill; read Hall; most of the day about the chapel concerns, agreeing with workmen about repairs, &c.; so part of evening with the other wardens at R. G.'s : read little, save Hall.

30. Morning, at mill; and after at Mill-hill Chapel with workmen, till noon; read Hall; after received a kind visit from good cousin Whitaker's; then with Mr. Ib. Evening, read little.

Dec. 12. Evening, at the Free School, seeing the boys act an ingenious comedy.

27. Morning, at mill; then at New Church, where Mr. Bright Dixon made an excellent and suitable discourse to the occasion, Mr. Harrison's commemoration sermon; very well recommending charity in its different kinds and degrees; but being rest of day busied, was prevented of entering the heads till too much forgot.

29. Morning, *ut prius;* then transcribing poll-bill, and presenting it to commissioners; afternoon, with many others at the auction,* (the first that ever was at this town,) by Mr. Simmons, which took up rest of day and evening.

30. Afternoon, at the auction.

---

* A book auction. Mr. Simmons, the salesman, was a bookseller at Sheffield. The auction was held at a great stone house in Briggate, where Dr. Skelton afterwards lived. At this auction, Thoresby bought the *Scala Mundi,* an historical manuscript, which he highly valued,—No. 13, of the folio MSS. in his library.

A. D. 1693.

Jan. 4. In return, had Mr. Simmons' company, the ingenious auctioneer.

7. Morning, read Hall; was at mill; rest of day at the auction, where in the evening had like to have been a dismal conclusion, but for the watchful providence of a merciful Saviour. The large chamber, being overcrowded with the press of people, in an instant sunk down about a foot at one end; the main beam breaking, gave so terrible a thunder-like crack, and the floor yielding below their feet, the people set up such a hideous noise, apprehending the fall of the whole house, at least the sinking of the room, (which, in all probability, had been the death of most present,) as was most doleful and astonishing, though I, sitting upon the long table by the books, was not at first apprehensive of the danger; but being informed by a friend of the imminent danger, I hasted out with what expedition I could, so as to take good Mr. Wright (whose lameness and weakness prevented his haste in the crowd) with me; and perceiving how much it had sunk immediately below my seat, which had fallen the first part of the room, if the Almighty had not put under his omnipotent arm to sustain it, and how much of the plaster-work in the hall below was fallen down, my heart was overcharged with admiration, and I hope, I may truly say, thankfulness, for so signal a deliverance was above expression. Evening, con-

cluded Hall upon Ephesians before family prayer,
wherein had good Mr. Wright's assistance, who very
well blessed God for so remarkable a deliverance.

9. At the auction of the Latin books.

18. Was at the Mayor's (Mr. Calverly's) feast;
stayed there with suitable company till about five.

25. Transcribing list of eighty poor children of
this town and parish, who have each a Bible and
Catechism, the gift of the religious Lord Wharton.

Feb. 24. Read Hall in family, then at mill; most
of day writing to Dr. Johnston, Mr. Stretton, and
Mr. Ness, about bookish business. Evening, about
two hours at Mr. H.'s; then within, reading, concluded that of the most excellent Bishop Usher's
life, and letters from many pious and learned divines, and others now, I think, all at rest.

March 1. Morning, writing to Mr. Str.* about
books; then at mill, but hasted to church, where
the Vicar preached excellently and suitably to the
season, from James iv. 9, 10 : " Be afflicted, and
mourn and weep;" exhorting earnestly to repentance, mortification, newness of life, &c., and yet
having done all to disclaim merit, and own ourselves
unprofitable servants; spent most of the afternoon
and evening with neighbours at Dr. Jacque's banquet : read only Hall.

8. Was much of the afternoon at the new library,
at the free school, transcribing benefactors. Some
of the chief, with the founder, came presently after;

* Mr. Stretton.

stayed with them some time, and after, had Mr. Robinson's (who gave the Polyglot Bible,) company at my house, which, with other visits, took up rest of day and evening : read only Annotations.

14. Morning, at mill; then at Mill-hill, advising with father. Most of day writing the deeds for Dr. Stubbs's and cousin R. Idle's sixth part of chapel. Evening, had them executed, which stayed me too long : read little.

May 3. Morning, writing to the Archdeacon, and W. J. at St. Andrew's, and sending manuscript to ditto ingenious Mr. Nicholson. With Mr. Ib. upon a sad occasion, being upon an inquest, for the murder of George Doddel, a poor man, slain by two Dutch troopers ; the evidence was full, that it was found murder *nemine contradicente;* the same evening, a child was slain by the fall of a piece of wood ; and the day before, the master of the Spring Garden drowned.

June 11. Morning, read Annotations; rode with Mr. Ib. to Harewood, upon rape-seed account, with William Bolton, a cant old man, who walked from that town to London five times, off and on, in half a year's time, (the winter terms,) yet never lay more than three nights upon the road betwixt London and Harewood, and so, *e contra,* in the ten times, whereof one was strictly at Christmas ; and he told us some remarkable passages of the late Sir John Cutler's charity to his tenants, which I purposely record, because of the unworthy reflections of cove-

tousness cast upon so worthy a benefactor, (as his
noble foundation of the College of Physicians ; and a
Lecture, founded and endowed by him, of which,
vid. Dr. Sprat's History of Royal Society, do clearly
evince him to have been,) particularly, in a dear year,
(in the great drought, ann. 168–,) he not only forbore
their rents, saying, they should not make an ill bar-
gain, (by sale of their goods at an underworth,) for
his sake, but gave express orders to his steward to
send them monies to retrieve some that had done so,
and prevent it in others ; and now at his death, his
tenants there are, through his lenity and forbear-
ance, 5000*l.* in arrears, viz. two years and a half rent.

16. Morning, up pretty early ; rid with brother to
Esquire Dineley's, of Bramhope, about tenantship ;
returned at noon, (though poor brother dismounted
in a bog.) In return, with the young Esquire D.
and Mr. Walker, (the Governor and Bishop of Lon-
donderry's son,) viewed the ingeniously contrived
walks in Mr. Kirk's wood, being the most curious of
that nature that ever I beheld.*

Jùly 7. Rode to the Spas.

8. Morning, rose pretty early, drank of the sulphur Spa ; afternoon, rode with Mr. Ib. to St.
Mungo's well, bathed there, &c.

11. Forenoon, drank the waters ; afternoon, rode
with Mr. Ib. to ditto well at Copgrave, and he with

---

* A plan of these walks is given in the *Ducatus*. Of Mr. Kirk we
shall hear much more as we proceed.

me two miles further, to see Sir Edward Blacket's stately house, which is indeed a most noble fabric, to which are adjoined very curious gardens, with delicate statues, and pleasant walks, &c.

28. Morning, sent for by Mr. Ardern (Sir John Ardern's nephew) an ingenious Cheshire gentleman, who returned to see collection of curiosities, and stayed dinner.

Aug. 12. Writing to Undertakers for Camden.

15. Morning, taking account of the ancient coins and medals (above one hundred British, Roman, Runic, Saxon, &c.) sent to the editors of Camden.

16. Rode with Mr. Ibbetson to Parlington. Paid to John Gascoigne, Esq. 100l. upon rape account; he showed me a very curious pedigree of that ancient family, whence I transcribed what relates to Judge Gascoigne, ob. 17 Dec. 1412. I was very obligingly entertained and respected by two R. C. knights, Sir Thomas Gascoigne and Sir Miles Stapleton. Oh, that they were enlightened with the truth as it is in Jesus!

19. Morning, writing to Mr. Obadiah Walker about coins for Camden. Much of day with Mr. Waterhouse, and to visit Mr. Sharp. Oh, that he may be restored as a public blessing!

21. With Mr. Waterhouse and Mr. Whitaker to visit Mr. Sharp; they both prayed excellently; I was much affected, yet betwixt hope and fear.

24. Morning, sent for by the excellent Mr. Sharp

(which deferred family prayers till noon) to consult
about the disposal of his concerns ; being very apprehensive of his danger.   Advised with Mr. B. D.
also, and acted, at his request, the melancholy part
of a clerk, &c. with a sad heart and dejected spirit.
All forenoon there.

25. Morning, read Annotations.   Directing workmen till past ten.   At a meeting, when several prayed well and earnestly for worthy Mr. Sharp's recovery.   Oh! that the Father of mercy, fountain of
all goodness, would extend mercy to his afflicted
servants, who are much oppressed by this severe
threatening.   He was afterwards somewhat better,
that hopes of his restoration refreshed us abun-
dautly.

26. Morning, read Annotations.   Forenoon, with
workmen.   At noon, sent for again by Mr. Sharp.
I hasted thither with all speed, but he told me he
feared I was too late ; his strength would scarce
permit him to arise.   I made particular enquiry concerning the estate at . . . . . whether liberty to dispose of it to . . . . ., which he answered distinctly
to, and called for the writings.   But, perceiving
there was no time to demur, (as we had done upon
Thursday in hopes of recovery and for ditto scru-
ple's sake) I entered upon the sad employ, put the
Will into form, (the first I ever attempted) transcribed it, which he subscribed and declared to be
his last Will and Testament, and returned thanks to
us by name, for kind assistance and former respects.

When others pressing in, he began a most excellent,
affecting, astonishing exhortation, which, in vain, I
wished some present to take in writing, but all were
too much affected: tears would have rendered the
paper incapable of impression. I observed especially, that the graces of faith and humility were
predominant. He was noted for this latter, by all
that knew him, through the whole course of his life,
and it increased to the very last. He was nothing
in his own eyes; had the most self-debasing expressions that could proceed from any mortal—a
poor creature, sinful worm, vile wretch, self-con-
demned, that had intruded into the high calling of
the ministry, and had no gifts, no graces, no abilities, to discharge so great a trust; loathed himself
for it; and if the great God should spurn him out
of his presence, he could not but justify him. "Oh,
woe, woe, woe is me, that I have sinned! I even
tremble to appear before the dreadful tribunal of
God, who will come with flaming fire to take ven-
geance upon those that know not God, and obey
not the gospel of the Lord Jesus Christ. Remember what I preached to you from that text, "I have
endeavoured to discharge a good conscience," though
with a multitude, multitude, multitude (thrice repeated) of imperfections, and "have not shunned to
declare unto you all the counsel of God;" and then
fell into an holy ecstasy of joy, for hopes of salvation
through the blessed Mediator. Oh, the infinite riches
of free grace!—" And I bless God for the sweet com-

munion I have enjoyed with you in his ordinances, and humbly beseech him to supply the breach that is shortly to be made; and to send you a man of judgment filled with his Spirit, that may better discharge his duty than I have done, who deserve to be made a spectacle of misery to angels and men," &c. To his wife, who feared he spent too much his faint spirits (for he spoke with hesitancy and pain), he replied, " My conscience is open, and I must speak. Thou hast been a good wife to me, but hast hindered me too much from coming to Leeds to preach : let it be a warning to others, that they dare not to hinder their husbands from preaching. There is no comfort at death like a faithful discharge of duty;" and calling his daughters, gave excellent advice, to improve time, before we launch into the vast ocean of eternity. Oh, eternity! eternity! eternity! what shallow conceptions have we of it! As to his son (John) who was at Mr. Frankland's Academy, he prayed that God would incline his heart to the ministry, and desired he might be continued at Mr. Frankland's, who is an excellent person, and very serviceable to the Church of God. And (when I was hasted down to send for Dr. S.) speaking of good old Mr. Wales, he said he was a humble holy man of God, and himself should think it an honour to be buried near his sepulchre. He spoke much and excellently; but what through the extremity of my sorrow, infirmity of my memory, inability to word them in his most apt expressions,

I find myself altogether incapable of doing what I both earnestly exhorted others unto, and fully designed to attempt according to my poor ability myself. To which, in my excuse, I may justly add the hurry of the funeral preparations which lay much upon me, with almost a constant attendance upon his disconsolate widow while she abode in town, which both his and her requests laid me under an indispensable obligation to. I sat up a sorrowful mourner all night, endeavouring to support her under so pressing an affliction; through mercy was much affected in prayer, (for which her importunity prevailed) broken for those sins that I have cause to fear have had too great a hand in hastening so dismal a calamity. He was very patient even to admiration under the pangs of death; for all night long, he breathed so faintly and with difficulty, that we despaired of his continuance an hour longer. But he spoke little after seven, when he discoursed about his library, &c. The Polyglot Bible, Pool's Synopsis, and English Annotations, with Cambridge and Symson's Concordance, he particularly mentioned as serviceable to his son. Was so distinct in his memory, that he told me the particular shelf where my dear father's Manuscript Diary, &c. were laid; except some cases of conscience, which were in his studying desk, which he desired to be carefully returned. When once in the night we expressed fear he should catch cold (for he would needs have had all clean linen about him,) he replied, with a gene-

rous disdain, "What fear of cold, when so shortly
to be dissolved, and, as a cold lump of clay, depo-
sited in the silent grave?" &c.   But continuing till
past five in the morning, we thought he might possibly do so till the time he begun; whereupon I
hasted home, hoping for an hour or two's refresh-
ment to prevent drowsiness.   But when I awaked
about seven, I found little of it; *e contra*, surprised
with a bitter agony of weeping, to that excess as
to prevent the putting on the remainder of my apparel for a considerable time, at which instant he
died, (having again called his dear wife and two
daughters, and taken a solemn leave of them; and,
with great faith and cheerfulness, recommended his
precious soul into the hands of his dear Redeemer,
which last moments my unworthiness prevented my
particular presence at,) for as soon as it was in any
measure abated, I hasted up, and met our maid at
the Bar with the sad tidings of his decease.   O
Lord! O Lord! what a bitter and heavy burden is
sin, that has deprived us of the choicest mercy under heaven; such a minister of Jesus Christ as very
few have equalled in this or former centuries—an
irreparable loss.   Oh black and dismal day! a darkness like that of the Egyptians, which may even be
felt, has overspread us.   How have my sins found
me out! how bitter are the fruits of them! the
whole world is nothing—every thing is a burden to
me,—I even envy the dead! . . . . Attended Mr.
Dawson's ministry both ends of the day, but I fear

with little profit.   Was extremely dejected in spirit; had many bitter pangs of grief; and when any friend, as brother, and cousin F. came in the interval to condole, we were dumb with sorrow, not able to express our mutual sorrow and overwhelming passion for some time, further than by the silent but expressive language of tears.   After latter sermon, went up with some friends to endeavour to support his dejected widow.   Read not, much less sung; had father's assistance in prayer.

28. Morning, hasted up to assist his sorrowful widow, and was there melancholily employed the whole day.

29. Morning, hasted up to the house of mourning, assisting in the disposal of gloves to ministers, &c. at the sad funeral; he was interred betwixt two eminently holy ministers, Mr. Wales and Mr. Todd, in the New Church, which, upon this occasion, might justly be called Bochim, being full of weepers; his death being as generally lamented as his life was loved and desired.

30. Morning; all day with poor dejected Mrs. Sharp, discharging funeral expenses, securing sermon notes, and other papers of the incomparable Mr. S. with a sad and dejected heart.

September 3. Die Dom.   Morning read Annotations.   Mr. Waterhouse preached well from Genesis xlviii. 21, and concluded with some affectionate expressions relating to the sad providence, &c.   Evening, heard the ten orphans (to whom the Lord

Wharton's former year's Bibles were distributed)
their catechism and psalms; most repeated very
well.

5. Morning, read Annotations; with workmen
most of day; rest, with poor disconsolate Mrs. Sharp,
and with good Mr. Heywood, whose assistance we
had in family prayer.

6. So this morning; then sent for by ditto sorrowful widow, whom I accompanied to the chapel;
which, upon this solemn occasion, was so extremely
crowded, that we could scarce get in pretty early,
and afterwards, multitudes turned back, that could
not get so nigh the walls and windows as to hear;
it was the greatest and saddest assembly that ever I
beheld. I was even dissolved in tears, and scarce
able to bear up under the afflicting dispensation.
My cousin Whitaker prayed most affectionately and
excellently, and so he preached from Acts xx. last
verse; doctrine, that when God takes away his
eminent and faithful ministers from this lower world,
it is just matter of deep lamentation to the places
and people from which they are removed. Mr.
Heywood immediately succeeded in this solemn
work, praying also affectionately and suitably, as he
preached from 1 Kings xiii. 30, " Ah, my brother!"
the different significations of the word brother,
natural, political, ecclesiastical, and spiritual : doctrine, that Ah, or alas my brother! is the proper
elegy of a people, and of all men, in reference to a
godly deceased brother, which is a memorial of eu-

dearing relation. 1. We that are ministers must say, Alas, my brother! under this Providence especially, wherein the Lord has taken away from us, 1. a brother, trained up in the schools of the prophets, Master of Arts of Clare Hall, under the most excellent Mr. David Clarkson, (whose works praise him in the gates,) and he might have added, upon Mr. Clarkson's removal, under the famous Dr. Tillotson, the present Archbishop of Canterbury; 2. of capacious natural parts, fit for any learning. 3. orthodox, sound against the errors of the times, Pelagianism, Socinianism, and Arminianism; some manuscripts of his testify his great abilities in defeating them; 4. an excellent preacher, accurate, fit for an academic order; 5. of a peaceable temper, never wrangling either about spiritual or temporal concerns: but that which indeed recommended him beyond any of his brethren, was his humility and self-denial. God has greatly weakened our strength in the way; let me tell you my sad observation, that since that black Bartholomew, that silenced all, he was one of the most eminent of fourscore ministers that have been taken away in these thirty-one years. 2. You of his congregation especially, and others that heard him occasionally, have also great cause of lamentation. Consider, 1. what has sin done? Sin has made all the funerals that have been in the world; 2. alas! what has my sin done? my sin has worm-eaten the finest flower; 3. his death is a sign of God's displeasure; a black cloud overspreads this assembly; 4. his place is vacant, and who is able to fill it up? 5. alas, for poor England! did he not stand in the gap to stop the wrath of God? Alas! that a Baxter, Flavel, Steel, and Sharp, should be taken away in so few weeks or months; 6. this seems a presage of more judgments; and 7. doth not the present state of things aggravate the loss? God takes the better, and leaves the worse, &c. Was afterwards with several ministers, entreating their assistance in officiating weekly for us; enjoyed Mr. Manlove's company in library; evening had Mr. Heywood's help in prayer.

7. This morning also enjoyed his good assistance in prayer; was after, to take leave of the mournful widow; (the Lord comfort her;) and afterwards, of Mr. Heywood; had Mr. Manlove's company much of day, and cousin Whitaker's.

8. Morning, at Mill-hill, taking leave of Mr. Manlove, who prayed well; had bitter reflections upon our sad loss.

9. Morning, read Annotations; with workmen most of day; received a visit from Parson Robinson, of the New Church, who courteously communicated his intentions of being a considerable benefactor.

12. Morning, rode with many relations to York.

13. Being fast day, I went to the Minster, in the forenoon, where I heard a most excellent sermon, and suitable to the occasion, full of candour and moderation. After, walked with my dear to the new meeting, where I was as much disappointed and dis-

gusted at some expressions of an old minister—a good man in the main, but to me seeming too rigid and uncharitable; though afterwards Dr. Colton, (the late Mr. Ward, senr's. son-in-law,) made a very serious, affecting, and suitable discourse to the occasion. Even, with Mr. Torre, transcribing manuscript, &c.

14. Morning, at shops with my dear, and amongst books. Afternoon, rode with relations to the Lady Tomson's (my father's cousin) at Middle Thorp, whence I walked to Bishop Thorp, where I was most courteously entertained by the worthy Bishop* in his library, where he also showed me his curious collection of coins : laid an obligation on me to see him at Bishop Thorp, and dine there when on that side; designed to see mine at Leeds. Mr. Pearson,† his chaplain, was also very desirable company, and of obliging deportment.

15. Morning, visited Dr. Nicholson (another of my dear's relations,) and afterwards returned to Ledsham. Blessed be God for protection to all! those especially in the coach, which escaped a considerable danger.

16. Spent forenoon at Ledsham; and afterwards returned with Mr. Manlove, and found all things well at home.

17. Die Dom. Morning, read Annotations; Mr. Manlove prayed well in family and public; and

---

* Archbishop Sharp.

† This was Dr. William Pearson, Archdeacon of Notts, Chancellor of York, and Rector of Bolton Percy : a Divine possessed of much curious learning in ecclesiastical antiquities. He died in 1716.

preached excellently and affectingly from Luke
xvi. 8.

18. Morning, rode with Mr. Ibbetson to Pool, to
view the mill there.   At noon, had many relations
and acquaintance at a venison feast ; enjoyed their
company rest of day.   Evening, read Annotations
before family prayer, wherein Mr. M. assisted.

19. So this morning, in presence of some others
of our society, who made application to Mr. Manlove,* &c.

25. Evening, with Mr. B. D. consulting about a
minister ; after, received a discouraging account of
Mr. Manlove from Cousin W.

Oct. 2. Morning, with Lords of Manor, choosing

---

* To succeed Mr. Sharp, as pastor of the Mill-hill congregation.
We have the following general account of the proceedings in this
affair, and of Thoresby's concern in it, in the *Review*. The particulars
are in the Diary.   " We had several meetings to consult, in order to
the choice of a successor.   I had the usual hap of Moderators, to dis-
please both the extremes.   In the interim I wrote to several ministers
to supply his place.   We rode to Ovenden, and made our first application to Mr. Priestley, a person of moderate principles, learned, ingenious, and pious : but the people about Halifax and Horton could not
be prevailed upon to resign their interest in him, without which, he
was not willing to desert them.   I afterwards rode with some of the
people to Pontefract, to solicit Mr. Manlove, who was at first very
compliant, yet after relapsed, but in the conclusion accepted the call,
and removed to Leeds."   The settlement of Dr. Manlove at Leeds,
was, in the event, of great importance in the history of Thoresby. He
was nearly related to Manlove, the writer on the Mineral Customs of
Derbyshire ; had been educated for the Dissenting ministry in the
great northern academy under Frankland; and had taken a degree
in medicine.   There is an engraved portrait of him prefixed to his
treatise on the Immortality of the Soul.   He was not many years at
Leeds, from which town he removed to Newcastle-upon-Tyne, where
he died in the prime of life.

constables, and at great court with lawyer Thornton, the Vicar, and Mr. Brook about Camden,
being solicited by the editors to take care of the
West-riding, which I am as unwilling as unfit for,
yet urged by friends to do what I can, lest wholly
omitted.*

5. Morning, at the meeting at Mr. B. D's. to im-
plore Divine assistance, in the choice of a minister;
had discourse with several in consultation; had the
hap of most moderators, by some thought too hot, by
others deemed too cold, in the business of Mr. M.

6. Morning, rode with Mr. B. D. Mr. F. and brother T., to Pontefract, to solicit Mr. Manlove's assistance, who seemed very inclinable; but had some
hot bickerings with some of the people, who thought
themselves injured thereby. I desired a fair hearing
and understanding, that there might be no future
animosities betwixt the two societies.

---

* This was the edition of which Dr. Gibson was the Editor. For
some time after this period, most of the time of the Leeds antiquary
was devoted to this work. The additions to the West-riding were
chiefly by him. He had been led to expect assistance from Dr Gale,
but the Doctor's many engagements prevented him from rendering it.
What Thoresby did for this edition of Camden was very satisfactory to Dr. Gibson, and to other learned persons of the time. In the
Review, Thoresby speaks of this work being " the happy occasion of
making him known to many learned and great men, which has since
been of use to me and my poor family, particularly Dr. Gibson, (now
Bishop of London,) Dr. Nicholson, Bishop of Carlisle, Dean Gale, of
York, and Dr. Hickes, the non-juring Bishop-Suffragan of Thetford."
Of the hundred coins sent for the use of this work, many were
never returned. Some were exchanged; others lost, owing to the
age and infirmities of Obadiah Walker, the learned and unfortunate
scholar, to whom this department of the work was committed.

10. Morning, with Mr. S. H. about his father's concern. Afternoon, with Mr. J. Sharp, and uncle Abraham,* approving goods, &c.

15. Die Dom. Communicating a letter from Mr. Manlove to the society, quite contrary to their expectations, which he sadly frustrated.

16. Morning, with Mr. B. D. and W. W. about chapel concerns, and soliciting for worthy Mr. Priestley; after, collecting for Mrs. Sharp.

19. Forenoon, with workfolk directing. Afternoon, had Mr. Whitaker's company till evening; when received the sad tidings of Mr. Lister's fall from his horse, and thereby breaking both his thighs, which I was much afflicted for, the rather, because it happened in his return from preaching to us.

22. Die Dom. Morning, heard Cousin Whitaker who preached from Mark ix. 24.; repeated, and begun though with a sad heart (being intermitted ever since the death of Mr. Sharp) the duty of singing. Read Annotations.

Nov. 3. Spent much of day in adding to Camden's Brit. in West-riding.

7. Morning, at funeral of Mr. Scudamore, an ingenious gentleman; at Mrs. F's., and another funeral; yet spent evening in company, not suitable to such providences.

9. Morning, forenoon with workmen. Dined with relations at brother W's. : after, had the meeting at

---

* Abraham Sharp, F.R.S. eminent for his mathematical attainments and his laborious calculations. He was brother to Sharp, the minister.

my house, endeavouring to re-establish it (which since Mr. Sharp's death has been intermitted): R. G. prayed well and I endeavoured to repeat the fast sermon, which was the last he preached, but could scarce read the text for sorrow. After, consulted with several of the society about a call to Mr. Priestley.

10. Morning, rode with several friends by Horton, (where visited Mrs. Sharp) to Ovenden, to Mr. Priestley's, where we were kindly entertained, and contrary to our resolutions stayed all night, but I hope for the better, having (after the return of some Hortoners, who vehemently opposed our design) greater opportunity of discourse. He prayed well in family.

Dec. 7. Morning, read Annotations; with workmen, and at mill, till noon. After, at meeting, S. W. prayed well. I endeavoured to repeat a sermon of Mr. Sharpe's.

27. The Vicar preached an excellent anniversary sermon from 2 Cor. ix. 12, very suitably in commemoration of so noble a benefactor, earnestly pressing charity. Afternoon, wholly spent with the ingenious Lawyer Thornton about the West-riding.

29. All day, writing memoirs in the interleaved Britannia.

31. Die Dom. Mr. Elston preached well, from Heb. xiii. 7, doctrine, that it is the duty of the faithful, or faithful Christian people, to remember their spiritual guides and rulers, so as to imitate them in their faith and conversation: for example named Sharp, Wales, Todd, Armitage, Ward, Mars-

den, Nailor, Marshall. Evening, catechised, repeated, &c.

A. D. 1694.

Jan. 9. Much of day abroad about chapel concerns, under discouragements for Mr. Priestley's
negative determination. Lord, pity us, that have
sinned away the best means, and provoke thee justly
to deprive us of hoped-for supplies !

15. Morning, up pretty early ; rode with Mr. Ib.
to Aberford ; dined at Mr. M. Hickeringhill's, (brother to the noted* writer of Colchester,) with whom
bargaining about rape and black wares rest of day
and evening too late.

17. Morning, dispatching away additions to Camden's Brit. ; afternoon, with Esquire Lambert, (son
to the General,) an ingenious painter, inquiring of
cousin Lodge's† works, but spent too much time.
Evening, read.

---

* Thoresby's extreme good-nature leads him to bestow his lauda-
tory epithets a little too indiscriminately. This noted writer is probably known to few who will peruse this Diary, but he was held in
estimation by others of his contemporaries; for thus writes John
Dunton:—" Mr. Hickeringhill, Rector of All Saints, in Colchester.
His wit is excellent, of which he has given the world an undeniable
specimen, in his *Character of the Ceremony-Monger.* His humour is
good and pleasant. He is his own lawyer, the treasury of knowledge,
the oracle of counsel, and his talent that way has been very serviceable to many. He is a man of a bold spirit. He wrote for me *The
Divine Captain,* and often did me the honour to invite me down to
his noble seat in Essex."—*Life and Errors.* New edit. p. 161. One
of the most curious letters in Thoresby's Correspondence is, one
from Mr. Hickeringhill, containing an account of his life and
writings.

† We have before had the name of Mr. Lodge, in connection with
that of Lambert. He, as well as his friend, was an amateur drafts-

18. Morning at mill; much of forenoon with Esquire Hatfield, of Hatfield; the more welcome to him, (as he to me, for his concern for the supposed loss of me,) hearing at Rotherham that I was suddenly dead. Oh, that I may improve this false rumour of death to a real preparation for it! Afternoon, at the meeting at old cousin M.'s.

19. Morning, read Annotations; all day writing to Mr. Nicholson and editors of Camden, except a little at mill.

20. Morning, writing per post; afternoon, at Mr. Scudamore's study, and with Mr. Fenton and others about chapel affairs.

22. Writing to Mr. Stretton about a supply for our desolate society.

25. All day in library, according to yearly custom about this time, to examine its condition. Evening, read Saxon, &c.

27. Morning, writing post, then abroad, to receive and pay money; afternoon, heard the Vicar preach well at a funeral, from Coloss. iii. 3. Evening, read two of old Mr. Todd's excellent sermons, from Isaiah xxxviii. 1, (concerning Hezekiah's sickness of the boil, which some conclude the pestilence,) preached at Leeds during the plague, 1645.

Feb. 2. Morning, read Annotations; directing workmen till about ten; then rode with Alderman

man and engraver. Several of his works were in Thoresby's museum, and the best plate in the *Ducatus* was from his hand. There is some notice of him in Walpole and Granger. He was related to the wife of Thoresby, through his mother, who was a Sykes.

Sawyer to view a controverted estate at Hunslet, where the rest of day endeavouring to compose the differences betwixt two near relations, engaged three years in suits.

3. So this morning with Alderman S. about ditto controversies, which we happily put an end to.

6. Morning, most of forenoon consulting with several of the society about Mr. Manlove; after all, rode pretty late with cousin Fenton to Pontefract; enjoyed Mr. Manlove's company some hours, and received an absolute promise of his assistance at Leeds, and resolution to continue with us till death.

10. Morning, writing to the ingenious Mr. Gibson, (publisher of the Saxon Chronicle,) in answer to his letter and present. Afternoon, with the chief of the society, subscribing a paper in reference to Mr. Manlove. Before we had well finished, an unexpected message informed me, that Mr. Fern, of Chesterfield, (the Derbyshire minister recommended by Mr. St., who, in three weeks, had not writ word whether he ever received mine of the 21st past, or had made any proceeds in that affair,) was arrived at my house, which startled me. Evening, enjoyed his good company, and assistance in family prayer.

11. Die Dom. Forenoon, Mr. Thorp preached well from Psalm cxliv.; doctrine, that a people, whose God is the Lord, are happy and blessed. Afternoon, Mr. Fern preached excellently. After sermons, discoursing with brother R. and cousin W. of Pontefract, about Mr. Manlove, &c.; it

was warmly enough argued on both hands. I afterwards penned a letter, which was immediately subscribed by eight, and sent away per a special messenger.

12. Morning, prevented of reading, by Mr. Fern's haste, who prayed well; walked with him to Mr. B. D.'s, and after to cousin F.'s, of Hunslet, where had Mr. Thorp's company an hour, but spent the greatest part of the day with cousin F.; walking to a great number of places to discourse with them about Mr. M.'s coming, found an unanimous desire of him testified by voluntary subscriptions. Evening, while solacing our wearied selves, surprised with Mr. Manlove himself, and seven or eight Pontefracters, with whom the case was again agitated; we sat up too late, or rather early, yet to small purpose; prevented of reading, but Mr. Manlove prayed excellently.

13. After so few (as could scarce be called) hours' rest, was prevented by the unseasonable visit of the rest of the company, of a better employ. We afterwards had a solemn debate betwixt the two societies, which was managed without that heat, and those passionate resentments, I dreaded; the result whereof was, that though we desire to be very tender of the concerns at Pontefract, yet think it reasonable to stand firm to the voluntary promise which Mr. Manlove gave us, being then a free agent, and which has a prospect of a more general service to the church, as well as to the society.

14. Morning, writing to Mr. Str. a tedious account of the whole; in library, cleansing books from moths. Afternoon, heard the Vicar preach an excellent sermon at a funeral, from Matt. xi. 28.

15. Morning, early abroad about business, *om gelt te ontfangen.* Afternoon, had Esquire Gascoigne and the Lady Stapleton, with her Priest, &c. to view collections.

19. Surprised with another retrograde motion of Mr. M.; solicited by friends, I wrote to Newcastle, to have Dr. Gilpin's opinion of the business.

21. Morning, read Annotations; heard the Vicar, who made a learned discourse, suited to the occasion, concerning the discipline of the ancient church, from 2 Cor. vii. 11, showing that public devotion ought to be preferred before private: 1. as more honourable and acceptable to God: 2. as more agreeable to the discipline of the ancient church: 3. more edifying to others. Afternoon, in library.

March 7. Evening, received Dr. Williams, (Dr. Nicholson being prevented by his mother, the Lady Boynton's illness,) from York; Dr. Russel and he had a consultation about father.

8. Morning, read; forenoon, with the doctors at the consultation about father; after, at a meeting at honest W. W.'s. I was especially affected, when R. G. and B. C. prayed for direction in our choice, and a blessing upon our endeavours for a minister for our poor desolate congregation.

9. Morning, received an encouraging letter from Dr. Gilpin, in reference to Mr. Manlove's remove hither.

10. Morning, writing to the no less religious than Honourable Lord Wharton ; at mill, with father after, and then with cousin F. about chapel affairs ; was better, yet did not walk suitably to renewed mercy.

24. Morning, called up again after about an hour's sleep to witness the dying moments of my dear father-in-law, who slept sweetly in Jesus about two this morning.

26. Prevented this morning of reading, &c. by preparation for the funeral, which was solemnized this afternoon about five, when he (father-in-law) was interred in the grave of my great grandfather, the old Alderman Sykes.*

29. Rode with cousin F. and brother Th. to Pontefract, to Mr. Manlove, who upon the sight of Dr. Gilpin's excellent letter confirmed his promise to us, and advised those of Pontefract immediately to apply themselves for probationers.   Left my friends at Pontefract, and returned late enough, &c.

April 3. The night past begun a lamentable fire

---

* The alderman of Leeds was the common ancestor of a very numerous family ; many of whom have been in different departments truly useful, honourable, and conspicuous characters.

Of his father-in-law, Thoresby says, that " he was a good man and a pious, and of admirable natural parts ; was a good justice in bad times, and favourable to the royalists, that were then under a cloud, as I have heard some of them acknowledge."

in a flaxman's house in Ouse-gate, York, which consumed about thirty houses before day.

4. Morning, walked to mill; read. Mr. A. of H. preached from Matth. viii. 4. whence, as from a pantheon, he brought forth arguments for the observation of Lent, for absolution, tithes, the priestly function, &c.; and the title of "the mightily learned Calvin" was not so grateful, as a reflection upon the excellent Mr. Perkins was unpleasant. Afternoon with brother R. receiving rents of tenants, the intemperance of some of whom was odious.

12. Morning, omitted Annotations, hastening for a journey upon chapel accounts. Rode with cousin F. to Bradford, engaged Mr. W. for Lord's day; visited Mrs. Sharp and family, and accounted for collections. After, rode to Halifax, where we met with several ministers (whom we engaged for their respective days) at the auctions, where I squandered away some money in books. Evening, visited the Vicar of Halifax.

13. Morning, we rode to Mr. Priestley's, and in return to Mr. Heywood's, at Northowram, was pleased with the chapel himself lately built there for his people, into which he told us the late Vicar of Halifax (my good friend Mr. Hough) entering with him, put off his hat, and with fervency uttered these words, "The good Lord bless the word preached in this place." After visited Mr. Dawson, at Morley, that have procured supplies till June.

15. Die Dom. Morning, Mr. Waterhouse preach-

ed excellently from, Jude, verse 4. Doctrine, that there have been, there are, and there will be, persons in all ages that turn the grace of God into lasciviousness.

20. Rode with a few friends to meet Mr. Manlove, who considerably damped our spirits by his hesitancy after renewed promises.

22. Die Dom. Morning, Mr. Manlove preached excellently from 2 Cor. vi. 1.; and before afternoon sermon spoke excellently to the institution of baptism: then baptized my daughter Grace, and as many more as made a dozen, amongst which the only son of the Rev. Mr. Corlass, late parson of Marston. Lord, confirm in heaven what is done in thy name upon earth.

23. Morning, received a visit from Mr. Manlove, as he from so many others, as prevented family prayer. After with him to visit cousin Fenton indisposed; after return from Hunslet, with Mr. Whitaker.

24. With Mr. B. D. at the Vicar's about registering our children.

May 7. Morning, perusing letters and accounts about the estate in Ireland. Afternoon appraising and dividing books.

10. About executorship. After rode with Brother R. to view the estate at Rodwel and Ouselwell-green (if not Oswald's-green.)

18. Perusing a curious survey of the manor of Leeds, taken 9 Jac. I.

June 1. Read Annotations, and began Math. in manuscript Bible, collating it with the common Latin Version and the Saxon Gospels. After reading Dr. Hicks's Saxon Grammar, Saxon Chronicle, &c.

6. Received a kind visit from Mr. Bright Dixon (the Duke of Leeds his chaplain) who brought my coins from the Editors of Camden's Britannia, the examining of which, and concern for the loss and exchange of several, took up forenoon.

20. Morning, perusing papers and writings concerning estate at Wexford. Proved father Sykes's will ; was solicited to take a voyage for Ireland ; had some inclinations.

22. Morning, extremely solicited to forbear the journey for fear of pirates : renewed solicitations from friends, relations and acquaintance in abundance, but above all my dear, whose silent language of sighs and tears altered my sentiments.

30. Morning, read ; at mill ; sent for by mother Sykes, to consult about a Cumberland gentleman (Mr. Salkeild), that would court sister D. S. ; discoursed him seriously and plainly. Evening had good Mr. Eleazar Heywood's* company, &c.

July 12. Morning, read Annotations in family, and Peiriscius in walks to and from Gypton ; afterwards sent for by Mr. Mayor, Mr. Recorder, and Mr. Sorocold, about waterworks.

25. Morning, writing to Dublin, read, then at Mill-hill till noon ; after at Mr. Thrisk's, an inge-

---

* Son to the Mr. Heywood so often mentioned.

nious artist, making a mould of my hand and W. H.'s face, and casting each till four.   Then with Mr. Ibbetson to visit the Alderman at his Montpelier.

Aug. 1. Busied about Pontefract journey, it being past noon ere I returned from Hunslet. After at mill, then in library exposing the collections to Sir G. Hatton's son, and cousin A. of York, with whom evening.

2. Morning, rose early, read Annotations, then rode with my dear wife, and several relations and friends with their wives to Pontefract, but missed Mr. Manlove's good company; viewed the ruins of the stately castle, and returned safe in evening.

5. Die Dom.   Morning, read Annotations.   The Vicar preached excellently from Matth. xiii. 16, 17, whence he showed the obligations that the Christian religion lays upon us more than the Mosaical law to the Jews of old, and improved it excellently against the Deists and Socinians of the age.   Evening, cate-chised thirty poor children.

8. Morning, writing per post, read Annotations. Forenoon, employed in Saxon authors.   After walked with Mr. Ibbetson to Hunslet, stayed late enough.

10. Morning, read Annotations in family, and Saxon in study till noon ; after had visitants, rela-tions and Esquire Salkeild, with recommendation from the Archdeacon of Carlisle, as to courtship.

12. Die Dom.   Morning read Annotations ; then heard the Vicar, who preached excellently from Matth. xiii. 16, 17, and was deservedly sharp upon

the too common vices of lying and injustice, especially when it gets upon the bench.

13. Morning, read Annotations in family, and Saxon, &c. in study. Was all day (except a walk to the mill) in library, perusing an ancient manuscript communicated to me by Justice Stanhope, of Eccleshill, and thence transcribing a charter of Maur. Painell (9th King John) to his burgesses of Leeds, &c. Evening, began to peruse Mr. Somner's Antiquities of Canterbury.

14. Morning, read Annotations; abroad about business. After received visits from Mr. Heywood, sen., Mrs. Noble and Edwards. Evening, rode with cousin Fenton to Pontefract, where enjoyed Mr. Manlove's company, consulting, &c. till very late, or rather early.

15. Morning, returned well; then writing till noon; then at Lawyer Thornton's about ditto old charter; and evening, with Parson Robinson, (the Archdeacon's neighbour and friend,) about Mr. Salkeild's courtship.

16. So this morning: received a visit from ditto Cumberland parson and Mr. Salkeild; after sight of collections, discoursed of ditto affair; then, with brother Rayner about ditto concern; and after, with the Vicar and neighbourhood at Mr. Ib.'s banquet; evening, again at Mill Hill, about ditto weighty affair, seriously discoursing sister D. S. about it. By these affairs much straitened in time, and much more

in affections, that I little thought upon the mispence of so much precious time as I have unprofitably consumed, being this day thirty-six years of age.

17. Morning, early at Mill-hill, about ditto concern, having received a somewhat discouraging letter; arguing the case seriously with the young gentleman, and all others concerned.

22. Was several times with Mr. Sorocold's workmen, who this day first began in Kirk Gate to lay the lead pipes to convey the water to each family; rest of day writing, till towards evening, &c.

24. Morning, most of day writing; rest, taking leave of Mr. Salkeild.

31. Morning, prevented of reading in family : rode with Mr. Ib. through Pontefract Lane, by Temple-Newsham, (near the place where, of old, the Temple stood,) over Castleford Bridge to Pontefract, where enjoyed Mr. Manlove's company; thence, through Darrington, (where Captain Mason was rescued,*) Stapleton, a pretty village, where the Dutch tiles are much used, Smeaton, and Campsal, where I transcribed some monuments of the Yarboroughs, through Bawn, "*forsooth*," to Bramwith, where passed

---

* Captain Mason was a State prisoner. He was on his way, with others, to the Castle, at York, under a warrant of Lord Arlington, when the persons under whose care they were placed, were attacked by five men, well mounted and armed. A stout resistance was made, but it ended in the escape of Mason. It is mentioned as an event which had recently occurred, in a letter from Sir John Reresby to Lord Arlingtou, dated August 22, 1666, in a manuscript at the Bodleian : Rawlinson Misc. 204.

the river Don, at Sir Thomas Hodgson's pretty
seat, and thence to Hatfield, where kindly entertained at John Hatfield's, Esq.

September 1. Morning, Mr. Ib. prayed; we after
rode over part of the Chace, where the cast up works
do, to this day, testify the entrenchments of that vast
army, A. D. 633, when Edwin, the first Christian
King of Northumberland. was slain, his army defeat-
ed, and his palace at Cambodunum burnt down,
whereupon, the succeeding kings built them a
cininȝaɼ boʈle, at Leeds. We rode by Hatfield Woodhouse, upon the banks, in the watery levels,to Wroot,
in the Isle of Axholme, all along seeing pieces of those
trees digged out of the ground, and frequently espy-
ing the ends of them within the ground, in the
trenches: we had the like banks to Stockwith, where
we ferried over the famous river of Trent, where we
saw near twenty of the thirty sail of ships belonging
thereunto; thence, we rode to Gainsborough, where,
after dinner, we viewed the rape mills; was much
pleased with the workmanship and contrivance of
the new horse mill, which was the main design of
our journey; was after at the Mart Yard, by Sir
Willoughby Hickman's, and to visit cousin Whitaker,
at Mr. Coates's; evening, again at the mill, and to
visit Mr. Bedford.

2. Die Dom. Morning, enjoyed Mr. Ib.'s happy
help in prayer; after, a little at the church, viewing
the monuments of the dead; heard cousin Whitaker
both parts of the day.

3. Morning, Mr. Ibbetson prayed ; we after walked to the mill, and viewed the town ; after, returned with cousin Whitaker, by Stockwith and Wroot, through the Isle of Axholme and the Levels, where admired the cheapness of the ground, &c. (though, none, I confess, like the cottage and appurtenances we rode by, which Captain Hatfield, our Gaius, lets a poor man for 12s. upon which he feeds ten head of cattle,) and goodness of the crops this year, worth the value of the land in some places, to Hatfield, where we were most obligingly entertained by the good family ; where also we enjoyed Mr. Westby's pleasing company ; I made also a visit to Cornet Lee's,* who showed me his collection of rarities, pictures, and armoury ; Mr. Whitaker prayed well in family ; Mr. Ib. in secret.

4. So this morning ; we after returned through Baun, &c. to Pontefract, where stayed so long with Mr. Manlove, that put us too late in the night ; but we returned safe, and found our families so.

17. Preparing for a journey into Cumberland, about sister D. S.'s concern, taking leave of relations; set forwards about ten ; rode by Mr. Kirk's, (the virtuoso) of Cookridge, to Otley, seven miles ; walked down the Chevin, but had not time enough to view the church, wherein is the monument for the first Lord Fairfax ; thence, through Burley ; had the prospect of Newhall, Mr. Vavasour's seat, and Denton Hall, the Lord Fairfax's to Ilkley, three ;

* At Hatfield Woodhouse.

the Roman Olicana, as Camden thinks; but it was
the first cohort of the Lingones that resided here,
for I strictly transcribed the altar, VERBEIE
SACRVM; and the last line is P LINCON, as is the
original, which my father saw and transcribed at
Stubham Lodge; thence, by the side of the river
Wherfe, (Verbeia,) which seems, indeed, to have
been cruel enough, by the breaches it has made;
(whence, more probably, the occasion of that altar,
to pacify so angry a nymph, which has taken down
the stone bridge several times); to Long Addingham,
a church town also, where we entered upon Craven, two miles; thence, over Rumblesmoor, where we
had a very severe storm, and the way, as well as
weather, not very desirable, four miles to Skipton,
where left the church and castle unviewed, (not so
much as baiting in the town;) thence, over the
river Are, eight times in three miles, to Gargrave;
thence, one to Cunniston, where the young man
lived that was of late years so remarkably converted
by reading some pages (dropped from Madam Lambert, of Cowton, as she was reading in the book in
her way to the meeting) of Mr. Baxter's Call to the
Unconverted, strangely brought into the house by a
little dog; thence to Hellyfield two miles, and Long
Preston, severely wet, and very weary with travelling so many miles in a dark, rainy night, yet received little or no prejudice; was most of the evening transcribing heads of Mr. Knowles's benefaction
to this his native soil.

18. Rose early, to write remainder of ditto Will, &c. Had sat up too late for same purpose; had a morning as severe as yester-night, and worse, in respect of the waters being out with the rains. Saw the place where Mr. Lambert, (the General's younger son) was lately drowned. Left the Settle road, and rode by Cowbridge to Wigglesworth-hall, Mr. Sherburn's seat, where saw the finest barn possibly in England, measured by our servant twenty-two yards wide and forty-six long, of stone, &c. Thence to Rathmel (three miles from Preston), where most obligingly entertained by the learned and reverend Mr. Frankland, (who directed us as to the main occasion of our journey); admired the number and hopefulness of his pupils, amongst which Mr. Sharp and my nephew Wilson; had much pleasing discourse with reference to his son's memoirs and other memorable transactions, he promised me an account of; and we rode thence through Giggleswick, and at the foot of that very remarkable scar, alighted to observe the famous well, which in a few minutes we saw several times ebb and flow eleven inches or a foot perpendicular, and continually agitated, either increasing or declining visibly. Then mounted our horses, and the scar too, clambering up a rock, steep enough, for the prospect's sake. By Austwick, to Clapham, four miles, and thence over part of that exceeding high mountain, Ingleboro', the highest of our English Apennines, which had enveloped his head in the clouds, so that we could not distinctly discern

the height of that other hill, which is, as it were,
set upon the head of it, as the learned Camden observed with wonder, p. 749.   To Ingleton, three,
and thence, five, to Kirkby Lonsdale, a very pretty
well-built market-town, with a church, &c. which
the shortness of the days and length of the miles
prevented our observance of, more than the bare
view as we rode through the town, where we passed
the river Lean, or Lune ; thence over several high
hills, where yet we had the prospect of much higher,
to Kendal, eight miles, where we lodged.

19. Morning, rose pretty early ; went to church
before well light, transcribed some monuments erected since those I formerly noted ; that, especially, of
Mr. Sands, a benefactor to this town, where A. D.
1659, he erected an hospital for eight poor widows,
who have each 12*d*. per week, besides a salary to a
Reader or Schoolmaster, &c. ; which fabric (wherein
we saw one widow weaving their woollen manufacture,) I believe he first designed as a workhouse,
by the tazels, &c. cut in stone upon the front.   And
this town, which is the chief in Westmorland, is yet
a place of trade, Kendal cottons being famous all
England over.   It is a handsome well-built town,
but cannot pretend to any great antiquity ; and the
Castle is ruinous, formerly the prime seat of the
Parrs, where the Lady Catherine Parr, (the last of
King Henry VIII.'s wives, and a great favourer
of the Gospel,) was born.   From Kendal, we rode by
Stavely, four miles, to Ambleside, six (at the end of

Winandermere, *prægrande stagnum,* the most spacious lake in all England, saith Speed,) now a country vill, but of old, as appears by the many heaps of
rubbish and ruins of walls, as well as by the paved
highways leading thereto, a noted Roman station—
Amboglana, as Camden conjectures: Thence, over
Eyn-bridge, and many high hills, amongst which the
said melancholy river runs, upon which a remarkable
catadupa, cataract, or waterfall, which falling from a
great height, and breaking upon the rugged rocks,
affected both the eyes and ears with somewhat of
horror, especially us that were riding upon the steep
and slippery side of the hill ; to Fellfoot, four
miles ; and then ascended a dreadful fell indeed,
terrible rocks, and seemingly inaccessible ; much more
likely for the goats to scramble over, than horses or
men ; especially those two more notorious of Wren-
nose and Hard-knot, which were really mighty dangerous, terrible, and tedious, and had nothing to
comfort us but the certainty of being in the right
way, for the prodigious rocks on the right hand,
upon that ugly Wrynose were absolutely inaccessible,
and on the left nothing but a ghastly precipice to
the Fell-foot, which I think may as well be called
Hell-foot, as those riverets (which Camden mentions
p. 727) Hell-becks, because creeping in waste, solitary, and unsightly places, amongst the mountains
upon the borders of Lancashire ; which, not distinctly remembering, I mistook several little becks
for, which came rumbling down these high moun-

tains into valleys, hideous enough in places. Upon
the height of Wrynose, we found the three shire-
stones reared up, which bound as many counties,
upon two whereof a man may set either foot, and
sitting upon the third, may be at the same time part
in Lancashire, Westmorland, and Cumberland, which
we here entered upon, and walked down the hill.
After which, we rode over several high hills, but
accounted little because of Hard-knot, whose rugged head surmounted them, upon the top of which
(when not without difficulty we had scaled it) I was
surprised to find the ruins of some castle or fortifications where I thought the Romans had never
come.   Having at length surmounted the difficulties
of these eight miles' tedious march from Fell-foot to
Dale-garth, (which was rendered still more uncomfortable by the loss of a shoe from the servant's
horse, which much retarded our journey,) we came
into a pleasanter country by the river Esk ; and being recommended by Mr. Frankland, visited Justice
Stanley at Dalegarth, to enquire after Mr. S.   Thence
seven miles good way in a habitable part of the
earth, by Gosforth, the pleasant seat of Mr. Copley,
to Cauder-bridge, where we arrived safe, though
late, in a dark night and strange country, but ne-
cessitated thereto for want of conveniences nigher,
and here found them very slender ; jannock bread
and clap-cakes the best that gold could purchase ;
but we made ourselves merry with the music of our
clog-slippers, and complimented them to entertain

us at Bernard Swaneson's, whose family, he saith has been there 380 years, as Mr. Patrickson, an ingenious gentleman of Cauder Abbey adjoining, tells him.

20. Morning, enjoyed Esquire Curwen's, of Sellay Park, good company, and serious advice (upon Mr. Frankland's recommendation) to decline a Cumberland match, &c.; in our road from Cauderbridge we had a fair prospect of the Irish sea, to Egremont, three miles, where we saw the vestigia of an ancient castle. Thence by the iron mines, where we saw them working and got some ore, (which is transported to Ireland where it is smelted) and . . . where worthy Bishop Grindall was born; to Whitehaven five miles, where we spent the rest of the day in pursuing directions in quest of Mr. S's. estate; and in viewing the town, which is absolutely the most growing thriving town in these parts; much encouraged by Sir John Lowther, the lord thereof, who gave them four hundred pounds towards building the pier, and two hundred pounds towards the building of a church, which is one of the prettiest I have seen, (after the London mode of their new churches) with the ground that it stands upon; and he is now building a very stately school-house, to which he designs the addition of two wings, one for teaching the mathematics, and the other writing. We walked thence along the designed Lowther-street, for it is grown from a village of six houses, as Major Christian, a native of the Isle of Man, (which

we had the prospect of upon the hills,) and many others can remember, to a large town, full as big as Pontefract (even in brother Rayner's judgment), to Sir John Lowther's stately house at the Flat, where we were most obligingly entertained by William Gilpin, Esq. (the doctor's son, of Newcastle,) a most ingenious gentleman, who showed us the pictures and curiosities of the house and gardens, wherein is placed the original famous altar, GENIO LOCI, (mentioned by Camden, p. 770,) for which Sir John gave twenty pounds. This ingenious gentleman, who is an accurate historian and virtuoso, presented me out of his store of natural curiosities, with a very fair piece of Marchesites, and obliged me extremely with his pleasing converse, till pretty late at night with Dr. Jaques and Mr. Anderton, (one of Mr. Frankland's pupils, and the Nonconformist minister there) with much good company, amongst which, honest Mr. Atkinson, the ship-master, who wrote an obliging letter, to recommend us to Mr. Larkham, for further instructions about Mr. Salkeild, though little expectations of success.

21. Morning, rose pretty early; yet prevented of too hasty a journey by the most obliging Mr. Gilpin, who afforded us his acceptable company till we left the town. We rode very pleasantly upon the shore, and had a fair prospect of the Isle of Man, (which peaks up with mountains in the midst) and part of Scotland, which appears also vastly mountainous; eastward also, we had the noted Skiddaw hill on our right hand, which with its high-forked head, Parnas-

sus-like, seems to emulate Scruffel-hill, in Annandalè, in Scotland. The Cumberlanders have a proverb:—

> " If Skiddaw hath a cap,
>   Scruffel wots full well of that,"

applied to such who must expect to sympathize in their neighbour's sufferings by reason of the vicinity of their habitations; *Tum tua res agitur paries cum proximus ardet.* We rode by the ruins of an old building, which seemed to have been some religious house, and through a silly boor's mistake, prevented of the sight of Workington, a noted market town by the sea, and turned a worse road over the Moors, and some slender country vills, Clifton, &c. to Cockermouth ; a well built market town, with a church and castle upon two hills, almost surrounded with Darwent and Cocker ; it enjoys, also, a good school, endowed with about thirty pounds per annum, by the Lord Wharton, &c. ; but we saw little, save the town-house we rode by, designing, though prevented, to return and lodge there. Having passed Darwent, I called at Bride Kirk, or St. Bridget's Church, to see that noble monument of antiquity, the font, with a Runic inscription, which, even the learned Camden understood not; but is since accurately described by my honoured friend, the reverend and learned Mr. William Nicholson, Archdeacon of Carlisle, in a letter to Sir William Dugdale, Nov. 23, 1685 ; printed in the Philosophical Transactions of that year ; and in another to me, of Sept. 9, 1691, wherein he obliged me with the curious drafts of several Roman monuments found in Cumberland since Mr. Camden's time, and that famous cross at Beaucastle, with the Runic inscription, explained in a letter to Mr. Walker, then Master of University College, in Oxford, 2d November, 1685, printed also in the said Transactions, p. 1287, &c. though in this to me he has added a delicate inscription of nine lines upon the west side of that stately monument, found out, I presume, not only since that communicated by the Lord William Howard to Sir Henry Spelman, and mentioned by Wormius Mon. dan. p. 161; but since that to Mr. Walker, being not exemplified in the said Transactions, as the shorter inscriptions upon the north and south sides are. My said worthy friend, was pleased at the same time to favour me with his notes of my embrio manuscript account of Leeds, and very learned and accurate remarks upon some coins I had transmitted to him, especially upon that Amulet of the old idol Thor, with the Runic inscription, of which, *inter alia,* he writes me; " I never yet saw any Runic inscription so plain and intelligible, which I hope to find exemplified in the new edition of Camden's Britannia, being engraven (though badly enough, Table II.) with many more that the importunity of the gentlemen concerned prevailed with me to communicate, most of which are returned, with very kind expressions of gratitude, from the said poor (but ingenious) Mr. Ob. Walker and Mr. Edmund Gibson, who published the Saxon Chronicle, my very obliging

and kind friends, though yet never seen by me,
no more than the glory of my correspondents
about antiquity, Mr. Archdeacon, till this journey
from Bridkirk, where the honest parson was very
obliging in showing us the said famous font and
the register, where one of his predecessors had
writ a small account of it, but without any knowledge of the letters; we rode to Talentire to
consult Mr. Larkham, the Nonconformist minister,
to whom Mr. Atkinson recommended us, (son to a
good old Puritan, some of whose works are in print,)
about Mr. S. but received the strongest reasons
imaginable against it, and not fit to be communicated but to very choice friends concerned; he
walked with us to Mr. Fletcher's, Copper Grove,
where they are beginning to mine for the mineral
ore, which abounds in this county; thence, after a
consultation, we rode over the Moors, directly to
Threepland, to Esquire Salkeild's, who, being all
abroad at Bothal, &c. about the harvest, we were
under a necessity to comply with them, and thankfully accept a night's lodging, though against my
inclination, because foreseeing a rupture, &c.

22. Morning, discoursed the old gentleman about
the terms; and after, walked to view part of the
land; and, by their excessive importunity and pretence of business in giving particulars of estate, prevailed with to stay till Monday; spent part of the
day in coursing with the young gentleman, while
the old Esquire was preparing a rental, and in visit-

ing honest Parson Robinson, of Plumland; after, had Mr. Orphir's company; evening, discoursed Mr. Salkeild, sen. again about ditto concern.

23. Die Dom, it should be; though, alas! some part little like it, no prayers of any sort in family; we walked to Plumland, where worthy Mr. Robinson prayed and preached very affectionately and well from Luke x. 42. Doctrine, that nothing is needful comparatively to the salvation of the soul; many gentlemen invited to dinner, so that rest of day and evening was spent very unsuitably to the duties of the day, though we enjoyed the modest parson's good company, and Esquire Dyke's; evening, sat too late, or early rather, with the young gentleman, and was foolishly cheerful, and vain in my expressions; too compliant, &c.

24. Morning, taking leave of ditto family, who have very obligingly entertained us; of honest Mr. Robinson, Parson Holms, &c.; then rode by Bold, or Bothal, where viewed the land and mill, which gave little content; thence, to Torpenna two miles, their parish church, where Mr. Archdeacon preacheth; thence, to Ireby, a market town, three miles, which Camden supposes to have been that Arbœia, where the Barcarii Tigrienses kept their standing guard; thence, by Caudbec to Park Gate, three miles; thence, to Heskit two miles, Newgate one mile, and to Hutton, four miles, where we viewed Sir George Fletcher's very stately hall, which is by far the most delicate noble structure we saw in these

parts, (not having time to see Lowther, where Sir
John Lowther is building such a palace-like fabric,
as bears the bell away from all): thence five miles
to Salkeld, the pleasant habitation of my honoured
and kind friend, Mr. Archdeacon Nicholson, whose
long-desired society I now enjoyed with great delight. We presently retired from the company to
his museum, where he showed me his delicate collection of natural curiosities, (and very kindly bestowed several of them upon me,) some coins and
medals, but the earth in those parts, where most
have been found, being of a very corroding nature,
many of them are extremely eaten; many choice
authors in print, but, above all, I was most pleased
with his own most excellent manuscripts, especially
his manuscript history of the ancient kingdom of
Northumberland, in two volumes, in Latin folio,
which yet put me to the blush; looking in the Vil-
lare for what remarks he had procured concerning
Leeds, I, altogether unexpectedly, found my name
inserted with titles far above me, for the etymology
of the name, &c. We after walked to see the town,
and river Eden, which rumbles not as most in Cumberland, whose courses are much obstructed with
rocks and stones, but runs sweetly by the town,
which is, without compare, absolutely the pleasantest country town we have seen in these parts of
England; but we had not time to visit Long Meg
and her daughters at the less Salkeld, longing to be
again in that little paradise, his study, &c. After

supper, he showed us several remarkable sea-plants, and obliged us with most excellent converse, that I almost grudged my sleeping time.

25. Morning, rose early, to enjoy Mr. Archdeacon's most acceptable converse and papers, which were the most pleasing and instructive that I could tell how to wish for ; after, took leave of his modest good lady and family, but enjoyed his excellent company ten miles to Appleby, in the way whither, he showed us an old Roman camp, and the ruins of Gallatum, of which, *vide* Camden, p. 761. At Appleby, (the Roman Abbalaba, where the Aurelian Maures kept a station,) we were very nobly entertained with much good company at a venison feast, at the Rev. Mr. Banks', the head schoolmaster there, whose learned company, with that of the nonesuch Mr. Nicholson, was extremely obliging ; he showed us the school and library, and a most curious collection of Roman inscriptions on the walls of an adjoining garden-house, placed there by the learned Mr. Reginald Bainbridge, whom Mr. Camden and Sir Robert Cotton celebrate, as the excellent master of the school, when they made their survey of these parts ; the late learned Bishop Barlow, of Lincoln, and this present Bishop Smith, of Carlisle, (who is now building a public edifice upon pillars and arches, for the use and ornament of the town,) have been considerable benefactors, &c. The late worthy Bishop Rainbow's life is writ, and published by the said ingenious Mr. Banks, who has also printed

other things.   After much pleasing converse, (wherein I had abundant reason to admire, as the ingenuity, so the candour also, of these learned persons,
in taking notice of so insignificant a being, &c.) I
left this ancient and pleasant town, and most excellent company, which I was so enamoured with, that
I would not spare time to view the church, castle, or
hospital, of which, *vide* my former journey into these
parts, thirteen years since this very month, &c., and
rode by Warcup, four miles off, to Brough, for distinc-
tion called Market Brough, where lodged, but walked
to the Castle Burgh, to see the church, which had a
good ring of bells, but no monuments, except we
reckon the old-fashioned stone pulpit one, and the
painted glass in the windows, which remain the most
entire of any I have seen, having the entire pictures
of many saints, &c. with inscriptions, *ave gratiâ
plena ;* but I was sorry to find the castle so ruinous,
as is also that at Brougham, yet dare hardly entertain so much as a harsh thought of the Earl of
Thanet, because I hear so great a character of his
charity to the poor, in sending both books, apparel,
and considerable sums of money to the poor, and
less able inhabitants of many towns, and that with
so becoming a privacy, that they scarce know their
benefactor, and know not what inducements he
might have totally to demolish Pendragon Castle,
which the late memorable Countess of Pembroke
had so lately built from the ground, three hundred
and twenty years after the invading Scots had wasted

it, &c., being one of the six castles, which, with seven churches or chapels, and two hospitals, that noble Countess either built from the ground, or considerably repaired, for the good of the country, and the praise of her well-deserving name.

26. Morning, rose early, (having rested badly,) and left this ancient town, the Roman Verteræ, where, in the declining state of the Empire, a captain made his abode with a band of the Directores, and before daylight entered upon the noted Stane-(or stony) more, but got so severe a cold as much indisposed me, with pain and numbness upon the right side of my head, which rendered my journey very uncomfortable. We rode for many miles upon the famous Roman highway, (as also yesterday,) which was here well-paved, by the notorious Spittle on Stanemore, which, though an ordinary inn, yet often most welcome to the weary traveller in this solitary country, which, for twelve miles, has but one other house (Baitings) for the reception of distressed wayfaring persons. About a mile thence, we passed by the noted Rerecross, or Reicross, as the Scots call it, (Roi-cross rather, or the King's-cross,) which their Hector Boetius would have a mere-stone, confining England and Scotland, erected when the Norman William granted Cumberland to the Scots, to hold it as his tenants. It is yet indeed a bounder, but of two counties, Westmoreland and Yorkshire, which we here entered upon ; and about six miles thence, came to Bowes, a small country town, where we saw the

ruins of a small castle, formerly belonging to the
Earls of Richmond, who had here a thorough toll
and furcas, or power to hang : it was a place of eminency in the Roman time, the first cohort of the
Thracians lying here in garrison in Severus's time;
and in the declining state of the Empire, the band
of Exploratores kept their station at the same La-
vatræ, (or Levatræ ; for so its ancient name, in the
Itinerary,) which being burnt, the succeeding vill was
named Bowes by the Britains, with whom, at this
day, a burnt thing is called *boath*, *vid.* Camden's
Brit. p. 732.　　From Bowes, four miles to Greta
Bridge; in the road, we had a very fair prospect of
Barnard Castle, built, and so called by Bernard
Baliol, great-grandfather's father of John Baliol,
King of Scots, now chiefly famous for bridles there
made : at Greta, we baited to inquire of Roman
coins, but found none worth the notice, though of
late years there was dug up a stately piece of Roman
gold, which, by the description, seems to have been
in the declining state of the Empire, in the midst of
the moat (as they call it,) behind the house, which
has been a fair Roman camp, double trenched.
Upon the bridge was the coat of arms of the warlike
family of the Bowes', as I suppose, being three bows,
&c. ; but had not time to wait of Mr. Johnson, at
Brignal, recommended by Mr. Archdeacon, as a person of the greatest curiosity in botany, ornithology,
antiquities, &c. : we travelled thence over Gaterley-
moor, where had a prospect of Kirkby-hill, and

several country vills, to Hartforth, where kindly
entertained at worthy Mr. Smith's, my brother's
uncle, and a feoffee for Sir Thomas Wharton's benefaction, viz. a very delicate school-house, (which,
on the Lord's-day, they use as a meeting-place,) and
a very fine convenient house for the master, which
he endowed with 40l. per annum, viz. 20l. per annum to the master, and the rest for repairs, and putting forth poor boys apprentices to trades, (to whom
5l. each) ; but the sight thereof, though very delightful, and did for a little somewhat mitigate the
violence of the pain in my teeth, yet it returned with
greater force, and made the time tedious enough to
myself, and, I fear others, brother Rayner especially,
being not able to lie in bed till midnight ; but, having got on my clothes, longed for the daylight.   Mr.
Dawson, jun. prayed very well, both evening and,

27. this morning, but it being a severe morning,
and my teeth and head so badly, we made it nine
ere we began our journey, and forbore our designed
progress by Richmond or Midlam to Thoresby, three
miles thence, the ancient seat of our family, whence
my great grandfather's father first removed into a
more trading part of the country, &c. and returned
by Gaterley Moor to Catterick, in the way having
a prospect of the ruins of Ravensworth Castle,
which, of old, belonged to the Barons Fitzhugh; of
Gilling, a pleasant seat of the Whartons ; and Aske,
a noble seat of the Baron of that ancient and
honourable name, where Sir Thomas Wharton, a

most religious knight, and father to the truly pious, as well as noble Peer, Philip Lord Wharton, now living, died before his father, the old Lord, A.D. 1627, whose deserved praises Mr. Wales exemplifies in his Totum Hominis. We passed the river Swale, (which our predecessors reputed sacred, for Paulinus's baptizing therein ten thousand men in one day, when the English-Saxons first embraced Christianity,) at *Catterick*, so called from the *catadupa*, a little above this small town, now chiefly worthy of note for Mr. Siddal's benefaction, and the monuments in the church for the ancient family of the Burghs, of Burgh ; and the later alms-houses (for four poor persons) erected by Sir Strafford Braithwait (who was slain at sea, latter end of Charles II. or beginning of James II.) but a famous city in the Roman times, being their Cataractonium, and eminent amongst the Saxons, King Ethelred solemnizing here his marriage with King Offa's daughter; but it was burnt, A.D. 769, by Eanred, one of whose brass coins I have, found nigh the Roman highway upon Peckfield. From Catterick we passed through Leeming-town and part of the noted Long lane, and then by several country towns, of which Burniston must not be omitted, for worthy Dr. Robinson's sake, once their vicar, (yet living retiredly and piously with his kinsman, at Ripley,) who has built, and amply endowed, a very curious hospital for six poor persons, who have each 4*l*. 10*s*. per annum, and a school, whose head-master has 16*l*. per annum, and the usher 7*l*. in all 50*l*. per annum; whose lively character is extant, in A Treatise of Faith, by a Dying Divine, 8vo. To Ripon, where we stayed not to make any observations, pressing forwards in hopes of what surmounted our morning expectations of reaching home, which, blessed be God, I did, though some hours within night, but we experienced much of the goodness of God, in the protection of us in our journeys and our families at home, where I found all well, though the small-pox round about us, of which my poor brother Jeremiah Thoresby's daughter, Ruth, died last fast-day, the 19th inst. Evening, read Assembly's Annotations in family.

28. Morning, lay too long, but was much better, though scarcely able to swallow either meat or drink: read Annotations; then to visit dear brother Jeremiah and sister; after with brother Rayner, making known to Mother Sykes the circumstances of the estate and family in the North: after at cousin Whitaker's; then walked with my dear to Kirkstall, to see my daughter Betty; returned late enough.

29. Morning, read Annotations: then with relations and Dr. M. at Mill-hill, farther discoursing ditto concern, and writing to Esquire S. to prevent any farther proceeds: after with Mr. Ibbetson, cousin F. and brother Th.; so part of the evening, &c.

30. Die Dom. Morning. Dr. Manlove preached

excellently from Rom. i. 16, was upon the second doctrine, that the Gospel of Jesus Christ is the instrument or means God makes use of for the salvation of poor sinners. Evening, discoursing Dr. Manlove about the young man, who again solicitously applied himself, with tears, &c. to be a minister.

Oct. 1. Morning, with the rest of the lords of the manor, constituting constables for the year ensuing; had Mr. Mayor's company, old cousin Hick, now this fourth time, chief magistrate of this borough: after walked to Sheepscar; read Annotations; dined with the lords, and with them subscribed Mr. Sorocold's lease for the new water-works; afterwards assisting several widows in their fee-farm rents, from father's papers, to rectify mistakes; then with Dr. Manlove, &c.

6. Morning, read Annotations; then at Sheepscar: afternoon, at funeral of my honoured and dear friend, Mr. Thornton's lovely child, heartily sympathized with him : enjoyed the ingenious Dr. Richardson's company upon that occasion.

17. Morning, consulting Camden, and writing Journal : about three, at the new water-works; a most ingenious contrivance.

15. Paying fee-farm rent for the park to the Duke of Leeds's receiver.

17. Morning, writing to Mr. Frankland, &c.; read Annotations; writing till noon. After, rode with some friends to Rodwell, to meet Dr. Manlove, and conduct his modest wife to town; but stayed at

cousin F.'s at H.; and áfter with ditto good company at brother W.'s till pretty late.

26. Morning, read Annotations. Forenoon, with Esquire Rodes and cousin Whitaker. Then at funeral of young Esquire Atkinson, dead in the prime of his days. The Vicar preached excellently from 1 Cor. v. 32, concerning the resurrection of the dead.

: 31. Morning, read Annotations; then with Mr. Ibbetson to see the statutes, now first time kept at Leeds, wherein servants stand to be hired in the open market-place, in great numbers, of both sexes. Had Dr. Manlove, cousin Whitaker, and many friends to dinner. Evening, received a visit from Esquire Liddall, (Sir John Bright's son-in-law,) to view curiosities.

Nov. 5. Reading; wrote to the Archdeacon; then attended in public. Dr. Manlove preached well and suitably to this memorable anniversary, from Rom. xii. 1. Was after with him, and Mr. Whitaker, at Mr. Ibbetson's; but fell into an ungrateful discourse, which much discomposed my spirits. Lord! pity this poor divided land, and heal the breaches thereof; for thy mercy's sake moderate the spirit of all parties, and make all concur in serious endeavours to promote the power of religion, without bitter reflections upon each other; which were so afflictive to me, as to disturb me both awake and asleep.

7. Morning, reading. Forenoon, writing. Dined with Dr. M. and Mr. W. and other good friends, at cousin F.'s, at Hunslet; where enjoyed good com-

pany till evening. But then the spirit revived, which, in my poor judgment, is too bitter and uncharitable. Lord, pity, pardon, and heal us!

20. Morning, read Annotations. Much of forenoon, about cousin F.'s concern with Lords of Manor. After, at Mill-hill. Evening, with Dr. Manlove, Mr. Ibbetson, cousin F. and brother, yet much dejected for the alteration in a friend's countenance, occasioned, I presume, through his mistake of the grounds of my attendance upon the public, which is not dislike of the private ministry, but to promote a brotherly love amongst all good Christians of whatever denomination, which censorious accusation of one another doth destroy; and because I apprehend it my duty to go as far as I can, possibly, in a national concord in religion, as the most excellent Mr. Baxter judiciously states it in his Catholic Communion. The apprehension of a growing prevalency of a contrary temper in some of my dearly-beloved acquaintance, has several times of late much dejected me, and somewhat of godly sorrow (I hope) for the divisions of this poor afflicted church and sinful nation, has kept me waking some part of the solitary night, wherein I desired to humble myself before the Lord for my particular provocations, which have had too great a share, &c. The Vicar preached excellently this evening, at the funeral of Aldress Iveson. I was much affected, I hope I may say edified; but upon my return, sent for my ditto good friends, some of whose zeal, in different sentiments, I could

well enough digest, might I but enjoy my own with-out censure, &c. which much afflicts me.

21. Morning, read Annotations; after, to dis-course Dr. Manlove alone, about ditto concerns, which were a continued affliction to me ; and, bless-ed be God! we better understood one another, and my mind was much more easy. Was after employ-ed collecting, &c. about chapel affairs. Evening, with Dr. M. friends, &c.

24. Wrote per post, read Annotations. Then, with Mr. B. D. to visit Mr. Elkana Hickson, whom we found weak beyond expectation, somewhat paralytic, yet very sensible: called me per name, and desired me to pray for him, which, upon my return home, I endeavoured in secret. And then walked with my dear to visit Betty at Kirkstall ; and, upon return, surprised with the death of my said dear friend, who was thought might have continued several days. Visited his pious widow and afflicted family, with whom I cordially sympathized ; and walked, with a heavy heart, from one house of mourning to ano-ther, being sent for per the poor disconsolate sisters, to the orphans of poor Mrs. Smith, who died last night. Was much affected with this double breach.

26. Morning, read Annotations in family; writ-ing to Mr. Stretton, concerning this mournful pro-vidence. After, at both the houses of mourning, and thence about the graves at New Church. Stayed awhile ruminating upon the dispossessed bones cast out at the grave's mouth ; and was after at the

piteous funeral of my dear friend Mr. Elkana
Hickson, and his own sister Smith, whose corpses
were carried together to their graves, attended by
the joint cries of the poor orphans and afflicted
relations of both families.

Dec. 7. Morning read; with workmen till eleven;
then at private meeting at W. W.'s: after, had a
branch from the main pipe fixed into the kitchen, to
directing which, made me lose the beginning of an
excellent sermon of Dr. Manlove's, the first preparatory for the Sacrament that was publicly preached
at the chapel, the former being always at private
houses.

16. Die Dom.   My dear's indisposition continuing, sent for Dr. Manlove, who prescribed *inter alia*
the Jesuits' bark, which seemed to do her much
good.   Was confined forenoon, but after, at New
chapel, where Dr. Manlove preached well for cousin
Whitaker, who began of an illness yesterday, not
much unlike my dear's.

27. Morning read; received a visit from Mr.
Henry Thoresby of Newcastle; then heard the commemoration sermon at the New-church, and recital
of Mr. Harrison's noble benefactions, Mr. Artinstall
of Hunslet preached from, " the greatest of these is
charity." Afternoon, to visit lawyer Thornton, with
whom discoursing of antiquities.

29. Morning, writing per post; forenoon within,
after to gratify the Londoner's importunity, walked
to show him Kirkstall Abbey; found a door open

which I had never seen before, clambered up seventy-seven steps to a pinnacle; there are seven pillars on each side from those upon which the steeple stands to the west end; at the east, three chapels for the several altars on either side the high altar; in viewing the ruins of the lodgings and the out apartments near the river, was pleased to find some of the British or Roman bricks.

A. D. 1695.

Jan. 1. Morning, read Assembly's Annotations; somewhat affected with sorrow for so many years I have unprofitably spent; was much afflicted with the news of the Queen's death, a public loss to the nation and the Protestant interest in general.

8. Morning, read Annotations before family prayer, wherein more affected than my hard heart usually is, because of the loss of a near relation, my dear brother Wilson,* who died this morning; was with relations there most of the day consulting about funeral.

10. Morning, read Annotations; assisting at the funeral of dear brother Wilson, who was interred in the choir of the New Church, by his father.

13. Die Dom. Afternoon, Dr. Manlove preached

---

* Mr. Wilson married a Sykes, sister to the wife of Thoresby. His eldest son was Recorder of Leeds, father to Dr. Christopher Wilson, Bishop of Bristol. Richard Fountayne Wilson, Esq. one of the representatives in Parliament of the county of York, the grandson of the Bishop, has lately been a munificent benefactor to the town of Leeds.

from ii. Cor. v. 5, 8, doctrine that the souls of believers when they are absent from the body, are present with the Lord, which he explained, proved, and applied well; gave an ample and just (though brief) character of my dear brother Wilson; prevented of writing per the crowd of hearers.

17. Morning, friends parted for Beverley and Hunslet; and Mr. Ibn. and I, for Hatfield; found the way and weather better than expected, so that we ventured through Baln, and were the first that passed the river Don at Bramwith upon the ice.

18. Morning, Mr. Ibn. prayed; forenoon, in the fields with Esq. Hatfield, and Bro. Ibn. after, to visit my cousin Mr. Cornelius Lee, and view his collection of curiosities,* he presented me with his grandfather's pickadilly.

20. Die Dom. Morning, rode to the meeting at Doncaster; Mr. H. and I attended the public in the forenoon; Mr. Erat preached from Titus ii. 12. Mr. H. having called in his numerous family, spent the afternoon very commendably in reading the word, singing, and repeating a sermon of Mr. W's.

22. We took leave of kind friends and returned

---

* Thoresby has before visited Mr. Lee, who had been a cornet of horse in the Royal Army. He lived till the beginning of the next century, and in his old age was fond of speaking of the civil wars and the great men whom he had then known. De la Pryme, who was born in the neighbourhood of Mr. Lee's house, was in his youth an attentive listener to the lore of this old officer, and has preserved in his Diary many of the stories related by him. The collection of curiosities of which Thoresby speaks, consisted for the most part of pieces of armour which had been used in the civil wars. A piccadilly was a ruff.

over the river at Bramwith, through Baln, by
Campsall and Smeaton, to Stapleton; but could expect no epitaphs in the chapel, Mr. Greenwood having converted it into a barn for corn, which affected
me.   Thence by Castleford-bridge, to Ledston-hall;
and thence home.

24. Forenoon, writing, and in library with Mr.
John Sharp, and nephew W.; after, at funeral of
my dear cousin, Mr. James Moxon : the Vicar
preached well from John xvi. 33, and concluded
with a short, though deserving character of the gentleman deceased, because he would not offer violence
to that privacy he so studiously affected all his life.

28. Much of the day collating an old manuscript,
de Privilegiis Ordinis Cisterciensis,* with Henriquez.   So Evening.

30. Read Annotations.   Heard Mr. Emison from
Gen. xlix. 6, which he applied to the occasion of the
day. After, at the funeral of cousin John Kirkshaw's
wife; the Vicar preached from Num. xxiii. 10,
whence showed that there is something in the death
of the righteous, and something in the very nature of
man, that makes even the wicked to wish that their
end may be like theirs.

31. Evening, reading ditto manuscript of Fountains Abbey.

Feb. 1. All day collating ditto manuscript with
the printed Henriquez.

---

* This manuscript had been part of the library of the Monks of
Fountains.

March 16. Morning, read, &c. Forenoon, writing. After, paying Dr. M. the collections ; had some unpleasant converse with, &c.* which pretty much discomposed my spirits.

April 6. Consulting with Mr. Simmons about printing Memoirs.† Read Gouge of the Lord's Supper.

8. Morning, read Annotations. All day, consulting authors about the ancient Kings of Northumberland, in reference to the History of Leeds, in Manuscript Memoirs.

14. Die Dom. Morning, Dr. Manlove preached excellently. Some discussion with an ingenious stranger (Dr. C.) about those studies, or vanities rather, that have too great a share of my affections, and makes me suspect myself too much of the temper of those poor wretches, who when their duty is over, carry it as though religion was over with them too. Evening, catechised.

15. Morning, read Annotations ; then had Dr. Cay's, of Newcastle, company, viewing collections, &c. with several other friends at dinner; with whom

---

* This is more fully explained in the *Review*. " No little time was spent in collecting, and receiving what others also had collected, and paying it to Dr. Manlove ; yet, instead of thanks for my pains and charge, was frowned upon, and downright told, except a greater stipend was advanced (which I and a few more were constrained to advance besides our usual quantum) else he threatened to leave the town. He also expressed a particular disgust at my practice in going to hear the Vicar and Mr. Robinson, two excellent preachers, in public, which was a further uneasiness to my spirits."

† Probably, the Historical Memoirs of Leeds. Mr. Simmons was again at Leeds selling books by auction.

spent most of the afternoon amongst the coins;* rest with them abroad.

19. Morning, read Annotations. All day, transscribing Historical Memoirs of Leeds. So evening, reading Camden.

May 9. Rode with relations to Ledsham, to the funeral of my brother Rayner's father, an excellent person.

13. Morning, walked to cousin F.'s of Hunslet; rode with him and my other dear friends, Mr. Samuel Ibbetson and brother Thoresby, to Rodwell, where took leave of relations, thence through Medley, Pontefract, and Wentbridge (upon the famous Roman highway, and by the noted Robin Hood's well) to Doncaster, where we dined; thence by Bawtry, Scruby, Ranskall, to Barnby-on-the-Moor.

14. After a weary night rose pretty early; rode over Shirewood Forest, by the noted Eel-pie-house,

---

* Thoresby often complains of the loss of time occasioned by showing his collection of coins and other rarities to strangers, who were often persons unable to appreciate them, or to benefit by the sight of them. The publication of Camden had made him known, and his curious museum talked of, so that scarcely a week passed in which he was not visited by persons for the express purpose of inspecting it. This was a means, however, of increasing his collection, for many returned the favour by making additions to the museum.

There is a very complete view of the contents of his museum, and of the more curious articles of his library, which was rich in manuscripts and early printed books, as they stood in 1714, in the *Ducatus*, with the names of the donors of many of the articles. Little was added either to the museum or library after that date, but it was a collection, which, made by a private person in a provincial town, and with but a very limited income, was truly extraordinary; and, if a few articles had been rejected, as creditable to his taste and skill, as to his industry and zeal.

Who shall presume to say what his coins, medals, prints, manuscripts, books, and autographs would bring on a sale by auction at the present day? Would 5000*l*. be too large a sum?

through Tuxford to Carlton, where baited; thence by Cromwell and Muskam-bridge, where we had a pretty prospect of the Lord Lexington's house, to Newark, where we dined, and found a considerable fair for sheep and beasts; thence by Long Billington and Gunnerby-on-the-Hill, to Grantham, where baited, and thence to Coltsforth, where we lodged, and after a better night's rest was much refreshed.

15. Thence by the long Hedge and five mile Cross, where Sir Ralph Wharton slew the highwayman, upon the noted Roman highway, to Bridge-Casterton, the name and situation whereof plainly import it a Roman station, and very probably the old Gausenæ; thence to Stamford, where we baited, and I transcribed a monument, which was all the slender addition I made to my former notes. Thence we rode by Wansford " in England," and Water Newton to Stilton, whence we wrote to our dear wives. Thence by Sautry Chapel, Stonegate-hole, (a noted place for robberies) and Stuckly to Huntingdon, where we lodged.

16. Morning, rose early, rode with the good company, per Godmanchester, to the deservedly famous University of Cambridge, where we enjoyed our late Vicar, the learned and obliging Mr. Milner's, good company, who showed us the delicate walks, &c. of St. John's College; but was yet more pleased with the curious library, where are some valuable manuscript Hebrew Bibles, delicately writ, and other old gilt ones, a book in the Chinese character, the Greek Testament used by King Charles I. and

a serious book, richly embroidered by Queen Elizabeth; the pictures of the excellent Archbishops
Grindal and Williams, Sir Robert Hare, noted benefactors, and Mr. Bendlows, who bestowed several
curiosities; variety of natural marbles so delicately
placed- and inlaid as make curious prospects; we
saw there also a little chameleon, &c. After dinner
we viewed the Public Schools and Library, where I
took chief notice of the manuscripts, Beza's Greek
Testament, a Turkish Herbal, and the Autographs
of King James I., and Sir Robert Naunton's, before
his works when presented to the University, and
the Lord Bacon's before his. There was also an
imperfect collection of Greek and Roman coins,
some very choice, others as mean, and all hand-
over-head: observed also the Egyptian bark, with
the Coptic characters, (of which I have some). We
had not time to view the Library at King's College
Chapel, but admired the fabric, which would have
been, perhaps, one of the most noble things in the
world if the designed college had been proportionable; then it might well have been *Stupor mundi*,
as a foreign ambassador styled Trinity College,
which we also viewed, with the delicate fountain
lately erected, and the stately library, which is the
noblest *case* of any, but not yet furnished. We were
straitened in time, but enjoyed also the ingenious
Dr. Archer's company, till we took horse, for we
after rode by Fulmire and Barlow to Barkway,
where we lodged at old Pharaoh's.

17. Morning, rode by Puckeridge to Ware, where we baited, and had some showers, which raised the washes upon the road to that height that passengers from London that were upon the road swam, and a poor higgler was drowned, which prevented our travelling for many hours, yet towards evening adventured with some country people, who conducted us (after we had passed Hogsden, which has a fountain in the midst of the town and several very good houses) over the meadows, whereby we missed the deepest of the Wash at Cheshunt, though we rode to the saddle-skirts for a considerable way, but got safe to Waltham Cross, where we lodged.

18. Morning, rode by Edmunton (where we had our horses led about a mile over the deepest of the Wash) to Highgate, and thence to London. I have the greatest cause of thankfulness, for the goodness of my heavenly protector, that being exposed to greater dangers by my horse's boggling at every coach and waggon we met, I received no damage, though the ways were very bad, the ruts deep, and the roads extremely full of water, which rendered my circumstances (often meeting the loaded waggons in very inconvenient places) not only melancholy, but really very dangerous. Afternoon, I visited the excellent Mr. Stretton, and condoled the loss of his dear wife: after visited good cousin Dickenson and her ingenious sister Madox; then enjoyed friends' company at our *pro tempore* home.

19. Die Dom. Morning, heard the famous Mr.

Howe, both before and afternoon, who preached incomparably.

20. Morning, writ in Diary, accounted, &c.; after visited the obliging Mr. Churchill (an undertaker of the late edition of Camden) and the learned Dr. Gale, chief master of St. Paul's school.* Afternoon, with worthy Mr. Stretton, Mr. Carrington, (discoursing of the Demoniac he is about printing the account of,)† Dr. Grier and Mr. Bays; and after visited the excellent Dr. Sampson, who also obliged me very much by his courteous demeanour.‡

21. Morning, rose pretty early; walked with Mr. Churchill to Westminster, there visited the industrious antiquary, and ingenious poet, Mr. Rymer,§

* Afterwards Dean of York, a station in the Church which he held for only five years. Thoresby must have delighted in an introduction to this his learned countryman, to whom English History and English Antiquities have many obligations. He is too well known to render any further notice of him necessary in this place.

† A wretched impostor, named Dugdale, living in the wildest parts of Lancashire, whose artifice falling in with the opinions of too many of the Puritans, respecting possession, many were deceived, and especially some of the most influential among their ministers. A catalogue of the tracts relating to this affair, may be seen in Gough's *British Topography*, i. 506. Mr. Carrington, who published the first account of this person, was a young minister, then lately settled at Lancaster.

‡ Dr. Sampson when prevented from exercising his ministry, by the provisions of the Act of Uniformity, betook himself to medicine. He was recommended to Thoresby by a similar taste for biographical and historical knowledge. Thoresby has left transcripts of some part of Dr. Sampson's collections.

§ Mr. Rymer, to whom we owe the *Fœdera*. He was a native of Yorkshire, being born either at Hinderside or Yafforth, near Northallerton. This fact we learn from the biographical Adversaria of Thoresby, where we also find, what there can now be no reason for concealing, that " his father, Mr. Ralph Rymer, had been unhappily

whom we found amongst the musty records supervising, his Amanuensis transcribing, but missed of my honoured friend Bryan Fairfax, Esq. and Dr. Lister, both being in the country, and also of the sight of Sir Robert Cotton's famous manuscripts, &c.; in our return we visited poor old Mr. Obadiah Walker, an ingenious and obliging person, whose misfortune, or mistake rather, that occasioned it, I am sorry for ;* after dinner, at Mr. Churchill's, then at cousin D.'s and Mrs. M.'s, and at the Exchange, throwing away money. Evening, with the obliging Mr. Johnson, since knighted, who kindly presented me with a curious copy of a most noble medal of Constantine the Great, the original whereof, in gold, was worth above 100*l.* ; rest of evening with friends at the inn ; sat up late, as too usually.

22. Morning, walked with brother Thoresby to Covent Garden, whence the courteous old gentleman, Mr. Walker (*alias* Williams†) walked with us

engaged in sequestrations in the late times, for which he fared no better after the Restoration ; being trepanned into the Yorkshire Plot, 1663, and, upon very slender evidence it is said, executed. But though he was cut short, his children lived long. Thomas, who was made Historiographer Royal, by King William, is seventy-two years of age, yet is the youngest of four now living, in health and perfect memory, whose ages amount to 316: as I noted from his brother's son, the 18th July, 1710."

* He became a Roman Catholic, and so lost the Mastership of University College, Oxford, at the Revolution.

† This was Obadiah Walker, mentioned in the preceding note. It has been very completely proved that the name of Charlton was one assumed, in the place of that which he had inherited from his ancestors, by the gentleman, whose collection of coins they went together to see. See Dr. Kippis's Edition of the *Biographia Britannica,* art. *Courteen,* for the museum of Mr. Charlton.

to the Temple, and introduced us to the ingenious Mr. Charlton's museum, who showed us a noble collection of Roman coins; he has very choice of the Emperors, but the vast number of the Family, or Consular, was most surprising to me.   I after visited Mr. Nicholson, the Archdeacon's brother, and dined at Dr. Gale's, who, after, conducted me to Gresham College, where, by his means (being himself a Member of the Royal Society, and benefactor to their museum,) I had the privilege to hear Sir John Hoskins, President, and several learned gentlemen, manage several ingenious arguments, &c.   We after viewed the curiosities in their repository, which are well described by Dr. Neh. Grew ; but I was especially in love with the noble collection of the Arundelian manuscripts, which the late Earl Marshal of England bestowed upon them, of which I had as particular a view, as I could wish for, by the courtesy of the Rev. Mr. Perry, Music Lecturer.   When the members were risen, we took a more particular view of the pictures of many learned persons in that apartment, Bishop Wilkins, Dr. Harvey, Mr. Boyle, &c., Malpighius, &c.   Evening, with several of the Salters, and our fellow-travellers at tavern ; spent too much time.

23. Morning, at Mr. Stretton's ; walked thence over Lincoln's Inn Fields to Westminster, and viewed the monuments of the Kings of England, and the noble mausoleum for the late most excellent Queen, but again prevented of the enjoyment of Dr.

Lister and Mr. Fairfax ; transcribed only a few monuments.   Afternoon, with the learned Dr. Plot, at
the Heralds' Office, to whose kindness when I first
saw Oxford, I was exceedingly engaged ; after
amongst the books till towards evening, when enjoyed the Rev. and learned Mr. Joseph Hill's, of
Rotterdam, excellent company, and writ from him
Mr. Styles's dying charge.

24. Morning . . . . ; forenoon, with Mr. Ib. in
Southwark, weighing eleven packs of wool ; at Justice Lewyn's and Mr. Weyman's till noon ; dined at
Mr. Hardcastle's, where very courteously entertained ; after walked to Mr. Charlton's chambers,
at the Temple, who very courteously showed me
his museum, which is perhaps the most noble collection of natural and artificial curiosities, of
ancient and modern coins and medals, that any
private person in the world enjoys ; it is said to
have cost him 7,000*l.* or 8,000*l.* sterling ; there
is, I think, the greatest variety of insects and
animals, corals, shells, petrifactions, &c. that ever I
beheld.   But I spent the greatest part of my time
amongst the coins, for though the British and
Saxon be not very extraordinary, yet his silver series
of the Emperors and Consuls is very noble.   He has
also a costly collection of medals, of eminent persons
in church and state, domestic and foreign reformers.   But before I was half satisfied an unfortunate visit from the Countess of Pembroke, and
other ladies from court, prevented further queries,

&c. Afterwards, discoursed Mr. Ross about Judge Craig's manuscript de Hominio, which I lent him, the English version whereof is now in the press. Then walked to St. Giles's, to wait upon the pious and noble Lord Wharton, who entertained me most obligingly, gave me a dispensation to dispose of his Bibles to such as perform the conditions, though not resident within the parish of Leeds, and at the parting condescended to desire an interest in my prayers. Was much affected with his piety and charity.

25. Morning, busied about wool concerns; then at Mr. Churchill's and Parkhurst's amongst books; opportunely met there with worthy Mr. Taylor, my Lord Wharton's Chaplain, that had missed of. Then at the Exchange, busied about bills and other business. After at the shops, buying tippet, black silk, &c. and other things for the country.

26. Die Dom. Rose pretty early; then heard Mr. Smithyes (at St. Michael's, Cornhill, to the building whereof Sir John Langham gave 500*l*. Sir John Cutler 20*l*.), he made an excellent sermon from that of Agur Prov. xxx. 9., and very well showed the danger and inconveniencies that frequently attend high estate, that a medium is quit from. Then breakfasted at Mr. Moore's; in our way saw the Lord Mayor of London, Sir Thomas Lane, with most of the Judges and Aldermen in their robes: though found the excellent judge Rokeby at Haberdashers-hall, where Mr. Stretton preached excellently from that of the apostle, " he

hath not left himself without a witness, in doing them good and giving them rain." After dinner took coach for Westminster with Mr. W. B., was again frustrated in my expectations of seeing Dr. Lister, but happily met with my honoured friend Bryan Fairfax, Esq. ; thence I went to Mr. Alsop's meeting, where Mr. Kentish, from . . . . made an excellent discourse against the Socinians, but, alas! I was as of the rest, prevented of noting the heads till too imperfectly remembered. Evening to visit Mrs. Thwaits (Mr. B. D.'s daughter.)

27. Morning, walked to the Savoy ; visited poor Dr. Johnston, who by his unhappy circumstances is little better than buried alive, and I fear his vast collections, which with prodigous industry he has made, will be in great danger of perishing ; then took leave of Mr. Ob. Walker, and Mr. Nath. Boyes, under like piteous circumstances, persons of learning and ingenuity, but alas, unhappy in their mistaken notions of antiquity and Primitive Christianity : the Lord illuminate them ! In return bought many books, (cheap I thought, which made me throw away too much money,) near Gray's Inn ; called at Dr. Horsman's, and Mr. Stretton's, but found neither at home ; after exchange dined with Mr. Hill, and Mr. Str. at a cook's-shop ; enjoyed their company, then took leave of the courteous Dr. Gale, but missed of Dr. Sampson and Mr. Howe.

28. Morning, rose pretty early ; walked with brother Jer. Thoresby to Westminster ; viewed West-

minster-hall, where saw the Lord Keeper, the excellent as well as honourable Sir John Somers; viewed the Parliament Houses, Westminster-abbey, and the monuments, &c., returned by water, but came full late to the Salter's (formerly Pinner's) Hall lecture; heard only the latter end of Mr. Alsop's excellent sermon, which was serious and affecting.

29. Morning, took leave of Mr. Hill, bought some valuable pamphlets of his kinsman, and at Parkhurst's putting up books, &c.; then set forward with the former company; had a prospect of the King's-palace at Kensington, then rid by Hammersmith, Brentford, and Hunsloe, *Canum Collis*, where we dined; by Colebrook and Slowe, to Windsor, where we viewed St. George's Chapel, in which the knights of that noble order are installed, and the monuments there; had time only to transcribe that of the famous Junius: then viewed the royal castle, which I suppose is one of the most noble palaces in the world; admired the very delicate painting in several apartments, that in the chapel especially, of the famous Mr. Antonius Verrio, and the admirable wood-work carving of our countryman * Mr. Grinlin Gibbons, the famous statuary who made also that exquisite statue of King Charles II. in the Royal Exchange at London, which is of white marble; here is a very stately one of the same king in brass,

---

* By " our countryman," Thoresby, who never forgot to what county he belonged, means Yorkshire. In his *Review* he describes Gibbons as " late of York."

on horseback ; here is also the finest prospect that
ever I saw : in the evening we rid thence to Maidenhead, where we lodged.

30. Morning, rose early ; rode by Henley, where
are abundance of faggots, a church of flint, with
monuments in the yard of wood.   Thence by Net-
tlebed, Benson, and Dorchester, to Oxford, which
we had a very delicate view of upon the road, where
the churches and colleges afford a most delightful
prospect, but nothing to what the inside, I mean the
libraries afford, which we viewed, especially the
famous Bodleian with great delight, and wished in
vain for more time to take a particular view of the
Saxon manuscripts, &c.   I was pleased with the
sight of the pictures (in the adjoining gallery) of so
many noble benefactors and learned and pious members of this famous university; we admired the
stately theatre within and without, in the area
whereof is the noblest collection of ancient inscriptions, Greek and Latin marbles, &c. that I ever saw.
We were much taken with the famous Mr. Ash-
mole's museum, but much at a loss for the excellent
Mr. Llhydd that Mr. Nicholson had recommended.
We saw several colleges, halls, and chapels, of which
that stately new one at Trinity is the most remarkable.   And were very kindly entertained by Mr.
Sizer, at University College, whose good company
we enjoyed in the evening, with Mr. Dockray of
Bennet, but above all the most excellent and courteous Mr. Gibson, of Queen's, editor of the new

Britannia, whom I know not whether more to love
or admire, both passions are so extravagant; that
when I could scarce hold open my eyes, I yet grudged nature her due rest.   Lord, direct the force of
my love to that fountain, whence whatever is really
lovely doth proceed, and which I can never love too
much, as I am apt to do all sublunary enjoyments!

31. Morning, rose early.   Was twice at the Museum, and at the very last, had the scanty happiness
(when mounted, and my friends before on the road)
to see the learned Mr. Llhydd, and present him with
the Archdeacon's recommendations, but was prevented of all further converse.   Then rode with my
former friends, and Mr. . . . . . of Wakefield, over
the delicate plains (though thereby we missed the
towns, and had only a prospect of Woodstock at a
distance,) to Banbury where we dined; and thence
rode by Byfield and Daventree, a considerable market
town, to Lutterworth, famous for the excellent
Wickliff's sake, where we lodged.

June 1. Morning, rode over the Moors to Leicester; but had no time allowed to make any remarks, being foolishly guided on the backside of the
town.   Thence to Nottingham, where the like humour put more of the company than myself into a
fret.   I walked to the Church, but found nothing
further memorable; so to Mr. Hanley's hospital,
collated the copy I had formerly taken with the original inscription, transcribed another upon the school,
and, after dinner, rode over the noted and spacious

Shirewood forest to Mansfield.   Took. account of an hospital founded by a Quaker, E. Heath, which I was much pleased at.

2. Die Dom.   Rode with the company from Mansfield to Rotherham, but were too late for the forenoon sermon.   Afternoon, heard the Vicar, Mr. Bovill (whose father was for some time minister of Bramley, in our parish); made a very ingenious and serious discourse, concerning the woman's being deceived by Satan in the form of a serpent.   Spent the evening there, but unsuitably enough to the day.

3. Morning, rode with friends through Brampton and Wombwell, to Stairfoot, where baited.   Thence by Burton Grange (where is the pious Lady Armine's benefaction) and Chevet to Wakefield, where we dined, and I transcribed a monument.   Thence home, where found all well.   Blessed be our good God for all mercies !   Oh, that I may so visit my habitation as not to sin against thee !

10. Preparing a catalogue of manuscripts for Mr. Gibson.

12. Morning, read ; then taking account of manuscripts till ten ; when with brother Rayner engaged in a treaty with Esquire Copley, of Doncaster, and Mr. Stansfield (a memorable old gentleman, whose seventh son has a seventh son living) on behalf of Mr. Hough, whose reverend father's will and other writings we perused, and concluded upon articles in respect of an intended marriage betwixt the said Mr. H. and sister D. S.

15. Forenoon, writing list of manuscripts; then with workmen; after, with Dr. M. and his Derbyshire friends; to whom showed collections. Had a promise of some curiosities from Mr. Sanders.

17. Morning, writing to Mr. Gibson with catalogue of my manuscripts; then read. All day writing and accounting, and poring upon some old Saxon coins lately found at Ripon.

20. Poring on the Saxon coins sent me by the Archbishop to unriddle.

21. Forenoon, writing to our learned and ingenious Dr. Sharp, about the coins he sent me.

27. Morning, rose pretty early; rode with mother to the Spas, and after a few hours' diversion, my dear and I returned well, without so much as fear of the coach overturning, though some hills steep enough.

July 3. Morning, read; then abroad upon business, and after with Major Fairfax, and to see the trained bands exercised.

25. Morning, read Annotations; then rode to Rodwell, where sister Deborah Sykes was married, (by my brother Idle) to Mr. John Hough, eldest son to the late Reverend and very pious Mr. Edmund Hough, late Vicar of Halifax. Had the company of new relations to my house; enjoyed their company rest of day and evening, till midnight.

31. Morning, read Annotations; then rode to York; dined at Bishopthorp in the way; was most obligingly entertained by the learned and excellent

Archbishop in his library, and by his ingenious chaplain, Mr. Archdeacon Pearson ; as after at York by the industrious antiquary, Mr. Torre, with whom at an auction ; was with the poor old Dean Wickham, who, being superannuated, I could learn nothing from him, but that he had parted with the manuscript I desired, though it happened well he had presented it to the Bishop, who very willingly lent me it, viz., Archbishop Tob. Matthew's Diary ; as also, Spanhemius *De Raris Numismatibus,* to transcribe, and bestowed upon me two rare coins.

August 1, Morning, rose pretty early, reading ditto Bishop's serious Diary ; then rode almost to Bulmer, but meeting cousin Jeremiah Idle, returned ; found also Parson Pratt, an antiquary,* and had much of his company.

7. Morning, read Annotations ; preparing for a journey ; we made it full noon, through repeated disappointments about the coach, ere we set forward ; then rode through Wibsey, by Revva Beacon, down the easiest, (if any at all be so) of the steep banks, by Ovenden to Halifax, yet had like to have been twice overturned ; even, enjoyed relations at good Aunt Hough's ; cousin Heald prayed well in family.

8. Forenoon, perusing the excellent Mr. Hough's library ; after, enjoyed relations and others, good Mr. Priestley particularly, who prayed well in family.

9. Morning, took leave of good old aunt and rela-

---

* Mr. Pratt, a clergyman, who had a small collection of antiquities. —*Review.*

tions ; returned by Ovenden to Little Horton, to visit good Mrs. Sharp and family, thence through Bradford home, and found all well.

13. Morning, read Annotations. Forenoon, drinking our Leeds Spa water, which has a good effect. Afternoon, with Mr. H. paying Lady Armine's gift.* Then sent for to Salters, which spent rest of day.

16. Forenoon, in course of the waters : read Annotations. Afterward, with good Mr. Priestley, of Ovenden, and then collecting for Dr. ; but much dejected in my spirits, in consideration that I have this day filled up the iniquities of thirty-six [seven] years, which sat heavy upon me.

17. Forenoon, writing to Mr. Stretton ; after, as all this week at spare hours, transcribing the diary or journal of the excellent Archbishop, and indefatigable preacher, Tob. Matthew. After, with the Dr. &c.

.Sept. 5. Finished the transcript of Archbishop Matthew's Diary.

6. Morning, read ; at mill ; transcribing Spanhemius *De Raris Numismatibus.*

18. Rode with cousin Whitaker to Cawood, and thence by Wistow to Selby. Evening, returned to cousin S. Sykes's.

---

* The alms-houses at Monk-Bretton before mentioned, were founded by this lady. The money which Thoresby was employed in distributing, was probably part of a rent-charge of 40*l.* for 99 years, which she directed to be appropriated to charitable purposes. There is an engraved portrait and memoir of this charitable lady in one of the collections of lives by Dr. Samuel Clarke. She was of very illustrious birth, being a daughter of Henry Talbot, a younger son of George the sixth Earl of Shrewsbury.

19. Morning, walked to view the ruins of the Bishop's palace and the Church. Wrote Bishop Mountain's monument. Then rode by Stillingfleet, Naburn, and Foulforth, to York : in the road, had a pleasant prospect of Nun Appleton, and Bell-hall. Dined with Mr. Suttall ; visited Dr. Nicholson ; and after rode to Bishop Thorp, where obligingly entertained by the Archbishop, at whose condescending entreaty I stayed all night there, and spent the evening extremely to my satisfaction; and cannot but admire the learning, piety, moderation, and ingenuity, of his Grace, and his chaplain, Mr. Pearson ; and evening and morning, cordially joined in the family devotions.

20. After, rode by Tadcaster to Tolston, where obligingly entertained by Major Fairfax, who showed me many Roman antiquities about Newton Kyme, &c. After, returned home safe, and found all well.

22. Die Dom. Morning, read Annotations. The Vicar, Mr. Killingbeck, preached incomparably and suitably to the occasion (a thanksgiving for national mercies) from Psalm ciii. 2. Afternoon, Dr. Manlove also preached excellently from Psalm ii. 11. Evening, catechised, &c.

30. Morning, read Annotations ; with workmen till noon. Then at the funeral of cousin Moxon (being invited, as at her late husband's, to bear the pall). The Vicar preached excellently from that of the Psalmist, " To him that ordereth his conversation aright, will I show the salvation of the Lord ;"

whence he showed very well what it is to have a
well-ordered conversation ; not to circumvent our
less knowing neighbour, but to deal uprightly and
justly.   He gave a deserved character of the virtuous gentlewoman.

[This Volume of the Diary closes at September
30, 1695.   The next Volume, which contained from
that date to September, 1701, is lost.   For those
six years, we have therefore recourse to the *Review.*]

A. D. 1695.

My dear friend, Dr. Sampson, of London, sent me
the manuscript memoirs of the learned and pious
Mr. Rayner, of Lincoln,* who was born in this
neighbourhood, to collate with the originals, that I
might attest the truth of them.   I was also much
affected with Mr. Baxter, of the Insufficiency of
Human Friendship, which is included in a small
book of Converse with God in Solitude.

About this time, Mr. Ibbetson's son, James, came
from beyond sea, and began to do somewhat for
himself; and though his father had a considerable
estate in land, yet was apparently straitened for
stock, and now having to supply both their occasions,
our joint stock in the oil trade was exhausted, and

* One of the Nonconforming clergy.   There is a good account of
him in Calamy.

I forced to advance more, which, in the conclusion, was all lost, by the survivor's faithlessness.

A. D. 1696.

To divert myself a little at leisure hours, I pored upon the old registers of the Church, to make a computation of the growth or the declension of the parish; of the health or sickliness of the several years, &c. from Henry VIII.'s reign to the present. By them also I was enabled to make considerable additions to the pedigrees of the gentry in these parts, since serviceable to me in the Ducatus Leod. This also put me upon viewing their ancient seats at Farnley Hall, Armley.

A. D. 1697.

In the registers also, I met with the mention of several places upon the Moors, as Street Lane, Street Houses, Haw-caster-rig, &c. which gave occasion to search for the remains of some Roman antiquities; and so intent was my mind upon those discoveries, that I could scarce rest till I had surveyed the several places as I met with the names of them. These I communicated to the late Dean of York, the learned Dr. Gale, and to Dr. Lister, for information; but without my knowledge, the letters were printed in the Philosophical Transactions, which I was so surprised with, that my dear wife was solicitous to know what was contained in that letter that made me blush, when Dr. Lister wrote that he had commu-

nicated my letter to the Royal Society, where it
had the unexpected hap to meet with approbation.
Upon other discoveries afterwards, Dean Gale, without giving me the least notice of it, proposed me to
the Royal Society, who, upon his recommendation,
(who had entertained too great and favourable an
opinion of me,) admitted me Fellow; at which time
were also admitted, Dr. Bentley, Dr. Hutton, (the
King's physician,) Mr. Stepney, and others, (with
whom I ought not to be named the same day,) of
which, see Sir Godfrey Copley's letter to Mr. Kirk,
and the Dean's to me (St. Andrew's Day, 1697),
wherein he gives me notice of the printing of some
of my letters, and wishes me joy of the respects
due to my ————*

This unexpected honour and the new correspondence that attended it with Sir Hans Sloane, the
secretary, the famous Mr. Evelyn, Mr. Chamber-
layne, &c. supported me under Dr. Manlove's
frowns.

It may not be amiss to insert here a passage
relating to the excellent Archbishop Sharp, who
coming to confirm, preached incomparably ; we were
forced to go a full hour before the bells ceased, to
secure places in our own pews, the church being so
crowded as was never known in the memory of any
person living ; and his Grace owned afterwards,
that though he had preached before vast auditories
both at London and in the country, yet he had

* See these letters amongst the Correspondence.

never seen the like. At the conclusion he spoke most affectingly as to the office of confirmation, concerning which the Vicar had preached the preceding Sunday, when was also read a most excellent and moving exhortation, (which my Lord after told me was that agreed upon at the Jerusalem-chamber.) The day after, his Grace was pleased to honour me with a visit, attended by my dear friend, Mr. Thornton, and most of the clergy, to whom I heard he spoke very honourably of me; but he knows me not to be so very defective (to use the best word I can) as I know myself to be.

But as his excellent sermons did more endear our most pious Vicar to me, so my attendance upon them disobliged Dr. M. exceedingly; whose expressions I thought too warm, and his resentment too passionate, for what in my opinion admitted of a much better construction, especially when he knew that I with Mr. Bryan Dixon, and two or three more of far greater estates than myself, had each advanced thirty shillings above our usual quantum to make him more easy. Good Mr. Tallents,* author of the Chronological Tables, was of a more moderate spirit, from whom I now received, in manuscript, his sermon at the funeral of Mr. Henry, senr., who (as appears by his life since published by his son, my dear friend) was of a like Catholic spirit with our

* Francis Tallents, of Magdalen College, Cambridge, M.A., one of the ministers removed from the church by the Act of Uniformity. He died in 1708. There is a memoir of him by the younger of the two Henrys named in this paragraph.

good Vicar Mr. Killingbeck. I received from both
these some valuable books, manuscripts, and autographs, which I valued as tokens of their respects.
Much of the comfort of this life consists in acquaintance, friendship, and correspondence with those that
are pious, prudent, and virtuous.

What time I could spare from business was spent
in transcribing a large manuscript fol. of Mr. Hopkinson's, containing the pedigrees of the nobility and
gentry, to which dear Mr. Thornton made some
valuable additions from the writings of the families
he was concerned for as counsellor, and other notices
from the registers of many parish churches, that
upon the whole, it was very useful to me in the
Ducatus Leodiensis, and was my employment in the
morning till day-light, and the evening; after, what
hours I could spare in the daytime, were spent at the
request of Mr. Archdeacon Nicholson, in revising the
first part of his Historical Library, consulting what
authors I was master of, to discover lapses and
make additions, for which I received the acknowledgments of the learned and ingenious author.
The little skill I had in historical antiquities, procured me the respect of several eminent dignitaries,
and frequent letters from Lambeth and Bishopthorp.

But I was called off from these more agreeable
diversions, by the sickness and death of relations
and others: that of cousin Hicks was more easily
borne, he being very aged and having served his
generation, being the only person who was four

times chief magistrate of this corporation. The sickness of Mr. Samuel Ibbetson was very piercing, not only as having an extraordinary share in my affections as a Christian friend and neighbour, but as my estate was too deeply and unhappily involved in his concerns; and though he recovered that illness, and I used all the means I could devise to perfect the accounts betwixt us, yet could never prevail to have them proceeded in, after I had once told him that the method we were in was certainly wrong; and so it appeared afterwards, not only to other merchants, but even by the concession of his son, as cunning as he is. This lay me under a temptation almost to suspect the probity of the deceased, though covered with the greatest pretensions to religion, and was a sad requital for all the kindness in advancing monies, and not to mention my acting about this time as a commissioner for his brother Hatfield (without the least gratuity) in a Chancery suit; and the good opinion that my friend, Dr. Nicholson of York, had of me, was very serviceable in procuring a wife with a considerable fortune for his son, which was a good foundation for his present greatness. Besides letters written in favour of the matter, I was obliged to meet both the fathers at Tadcaster, where the terms were agreed upon, and after to go with the younker to York, where the writings were no sooner sealed, than we were surprised with the most dismal news of the sudden death of his father, Mr. Samuel Ibbetson, who riding

out with his brother Hatfield to Hunslet, was brought
dead to his mournful habitation.

I returned post haste with the son, who seemed
not near so much concerned (by his outward appearance) as myself, nor, indeed, as to secular affairs,
had that reason, for the annual payment to the father
ceased; whereas, my concerns were more intricate
and dangerous, and, I have great reason to bless
God, that the melancholy it brought me to, and the
ill state both of body and mind, attended by cold
clammy sweat, and insuperable dejection of spirits,
did not for ever incapacitate me for this world and
another.

This sad accident deferred the marriage for a
month; and then I was (much against my inclination,)
obliged by their importunity to go to cousin Nicholson's at York, to the solemnization thereof, which
was the more suitable, because without the usual
vanities. Upon our return to his house at Leeds,
though I stifled my sorrow all that I possibly could,
yet the repeated sight of my late dear friend's picture, which I could not keep my eye from an earnest
view of, so affected me, that an unusual quantity of
blood violently gushed out of my nose in an astonishing manner, so as I never had in my life before.

The death also of Alderman Idle, my mother's
only surviving brother, was a great loss to me, he
being a person of good natural parts and authority,
(the only magistrate appointed a commissioner by
act of parliament,) might have been a support to me
after the hardships I met with from Mr. Ibbetson's

family; but instead of that the affairs of his pious relict were perplexing enough, especially that of Mr. Shipley and the tolls, which took up much of my time, but I thought I could never do enough for my dear aunt, who had supplied the place of a mother to us in our childhood, and I am particularly thankful that I was of real use to her and the public. When Ripon demanded tolls of the inhabitants of Leeds, she sent her tenant, W. P., of W., to see if I could find any thing in my manuscript collections to that purpose, and I happily found the copy of King Henry VIII.'s charter, and a reference where the original was lodged, which being borrowed of the Vicar, was produced at the assizes and got the victory, theirs being only granted by Queen Mary.

But the multiplicity of affairs, my own upon the unhappy mill account, and others for relations and other friends, that I could not deny, occasioned a great consumption of time, and, not having any reference to eternity, occasioned great perplexity in self-examination preparatory to the sacrament, when I found abundant cause of sorrow. I had now so far lost the favour of my quondam pastor, and was not yet so intimately acquainted with our good Vicar, as to make my moan to either of them; but a kind and merciful God provided me a dear friend and counsellor, Richard Thornton, Esq. a person learned in the law, yet a man of peace and piety, who was very useful to me both for this world and a better, and to him, being my intimate friend, I could unbosom myself, and we had now as

frequent and more endearing conferences about
spirituals, as formerly about temporals; for he was
not only learned and ingenious as a lawyer, historian, and antiquary, but very pious and religious,
his deportment and affections in prayer very move-
ing, and being easy of access, we discoursed with
freedom about the sacrament, and particularly about
communicating at the church.   At length being convinced it was my duty to comply, I resolved upon it,
but having some fears of unsuitable communicants
that might divert my thoughts, my dear friend
readily condescended to leave his usual place with
the magistracy, and retired with me into a more
private corner of the quire, where our good vicar,
Mr. Killingbeck, administered to us both, and
blessed be God, it was a comfortable ordinance.
But this put the Doctor into such a fret that he
sent three of the chief of the society to acquaint me
with his resentment, and refusal, for my supposed
fault, to administer the sacrament to others who had
made none.   I argued that what I was charged with
was at worst but inexpedient by their own concessions, but in my judgment, after the strictest
scrutiny, not only lawful but my duty.   His resolution and doom were very grievous, and so perplexed
me that I was scarce able to manage my secular
affairs; and observing not only his, but the strange-
ness of near relations, and those tradesmen whom he
could influence, it cost me much sorrow.   This my
compliance with the Established Church had a con-

trary effect upon others, who caressed me too much
upon it : and this had also its inconvenient con-
comitants and consequents, for it seems some of
the principal aldermen, upon a consultation, resolved to bring me into the corporation, the notice
whereof was both a surprise and uneasiness to
me.   Other arguments were of no weight with me,
but the plea of being more useful in my generation
at length prevailed with me to accept the place of an
assistant, or common-council-man, wherein my vote
was of equal authority with those of the superior
order, so that at the Vicar's request, and other
friends, I appeared at the court, and took the usual
oaths of Allegiance and Supremacy, but boggled at
the declaration relating to the covenant, which I
argued could have no influence upon me who was
then unborn.   This occasioned a demur, and the
roll of former subscribers lodged in my hand till a
resolution was made, I prevailed with a friend at
London to consult the famous judge Rokeby, who
said it was *casus omissus* that it was not repealed
in the Act of William and Mary that relates to cor-
porations, but that the general practice since makes
it void, and that it is neither used, nor offered to
any at London, Exeter, Bristol, Coventry, Liver-
pool, &c. whereupon I privately burnt the roll, and
it has never been tendered since.   After this I was a
little more easy, when I had got it under the hands
of a great majority of the corporation, that they
would never give their votes to remove me into a

station that I was as averse to, as unfit for; though
cousin Milner and others of my best friends could
never be prevailed with to subscribe it : but I feared
no real damage from that quarter, and he being
mayor, matters went on successfully in public and
private.

The peace was proclaimed with great solemnity;
the assistants appeared first that day in new gowns,
and a new seat was also prepared for them at church,
next to that of the aldermen.

Proposals were now first made for making the
rivers Aire and Calder navigable. I accompanied
the Mayor and Mr. Hadley, the hydrographer, to
view the river; Justice Kirk and I followed the
windings of the river, and measured it with his
surveying wheel, till wearied : left the rest to the
servants and others. We lodged at Ferry-bridge,
ten miles by land and twenty by water. Mr. Hadley
affirmed it was the noblest river he had ever seen,
that was not already navigable.

The next day we went to Weland; this journey
brought me to a greater intimacy with the ingenious
Mr. Kirk, who lent me his observations upon the
registers at Adle, and other curious papers to transcribe, and presented to me a small book, but a great
curiosity, the Manual of Prayers, by Mr. Harrison,
our great benefactor, who had presented it to Mr.
Layton, Mr. Kirk's grandfather, which I had in
vain enquired after for many years past.

August 16. I sadly lament that I have misspent

so much precious time, and blush to think that this day I enter upon the fortieth year of my age.

My aunt Thoresby (relict of Alderman Paul Thoresby) told me a remarkable circumstance concerning my good uncle, Mr. George Thoresby, of Newcastle, whom she visited in his last sickness, and hearing his sighs and groans into her lodging, went early into his chamber to condole his bad night. "No aunt," said he, "it has been a good night, for I hope I have got a step nearer Heaven. It is better for me to have such weary nights, to disengage me the more from this transitory world." A dear friend of his and my father's was the holy and mortified Mr. Elkana Wales, of Pudsey, whose Memoirs I drew up about this time, from original papers in this repository, and transmitted to my friend, Dr. Sampson, of London, in return for those he sent me of Mr. Rayner, of Morley.

On a Lord's-day evening, there being severe thunder and lightning, I endeavoured to improve it on the children to serve and fear God, and avoid breaking the Sabbath-day, from the sad instance of some children that were playing at Holbeck on a Lord's-day, one of whom was downright slain, and others wounded.

A.D. 1698.

In the beginning of February, Mr. Fenton (who had bought Mr. Ibbetson's concerns in the oil trade) and I took a journey into Lancashire, but found no

prospect of business answerable to the trouble and
hazard in passing Blackstone-edge, where we had a
sore storm of snow on the height of it, when it was
fair sunshine on both sides, but we found the snow
so drifted, that in some of the lanes it was as high
as man and horse.   In other places so thin spread
that it served barely to cover the ice, so that upon
the slanting side of a hill, my horse in a moment's
time lost all his feet and fell upon my left leg, in which
I had severe pain all night, and more or less for a
long time after, but, blessed be God! no bone was
broken.

We lodged at Rochdale, where after we had
reckoned with one we dealt with, I enquired after
the memorable old clerk, who in his time buried
1,100 persons.   At Manchester I was much concerned for the death of all my old friends, Mr. Newcome, Mr. Tildsley, Mr. Martindale, and Mr. Illingworth, (all now entered upon the joy of their Lord.)
I enquired for his valuable MSS. but fear they are
all lost.   There was not a face that I knew, but
good old Mrs. Frankland, (with whom I had boarded
my sister Idle,) who continues useful in her station.

Mr. Richard Idle, vicar of Rodwell, who married
my only sister, being under the like melancholy circumstances with my brother Jeremiah Thoresby,
and his creditors more severe than the former, it was
said he had to pay for part of his education at Cambridge, though it must be confessed that both families
lived at too high a rate, and could not be content

with such food and raiment as my wife and I. The younger brother was by them always styled brother Thoresby, and the elder only Ralph, but if our frugality had not in some measure equalled their too great generosity, we might have been in danger of being utterly ruined altogether.

I was now in a most piteous condition, both my brothers forced to abscond, and I left alone to take care of their wives and children; my own sister in child-bed, and sister-in-law at the pit's brink, and twelve children, including my own, to provide for, and I in the poorest condition that ever I was, to sustain them, being 600*l.* deep in my poor brother's concern, and above 1000*l.* in Mr. Ibbetson's, of which I never got one farthing (though his ungrateful son is so grand in his coach) besides I was perpetually dunned by some of their creditors, and once actually arrested, (the first, and I hope it will be the last time, that ever I was in the bailiff's hands.)

This was at the suit of Mrs. F., the most unconscionable woman, I think, that ever pretended to so much religion, ordering me to be arrested, not only without demanding the debt, but contrary to her faith and promise when I offered to pay it her, and when I sent for my sister Wilson, (who was then indebted to me double the sum) to be bail for me, she was likewise arrested for another debt that she might have had for asking. I would not reflect upon the innocent, or blame others for her barbarousness, which might have ruined my family, yet cannot but think strange of this Presbyterian revenge, not upon me only, but one of the same society.

She was, I confess, ashamed of this; and sorry after she saw the monies immediately advanced and paid, but her daughter, (a Nonconformist minister's wife) most impudently argued in defence of the practice, and received the full amount of the interest. I went immediately to Alderman Potter, to whom I was engaged for another hundred pounds, on poor brother Jerry's account, and acquainted him with the whole matter, offering to give further security (the bond being in effect, single) till I could get in my own monies: he took the tender unkindly, and offered to lend me as many hundred pounds as I pleased, upon my single bond. This was a comfort and respect, though blessed be God, I needed not to make use of his kind offer.

But these afflictions, together with that of Mr. Ibbetson's, had so shattered my constitution, that my spirits were sank within me, and sleep departed from my eyes; so that mostly the nights from twelve to five were spent in fruitless tossings, many faint qualms and cold clammy sweats, that looked like the languid efforts of struggling nature to overcome an insuperable difficulty.

Under these difficulties, I had not one relation to direct and assist: my uncle Idle was dead a little before, and my nephew, Wilson, not yet grown up; none but widows and orphans there, and in other families, those under more pitiful circumstances, from whose husbands I received most doleful letters, one or two almost every day, to solicit one person or another in this or the other melancholy affair, which, as they wrote, half distracted them, and I am sure so fatigued me with walking mile after mile, by day and by night, (sometimes till past two before I could reach home,) their affairs requiring secrecy and speed, that now upon a serious review many years after, I wonder how I was sustained.

The concerns of my brother-in-law, Mr. Idle, Vicar of Rodwell, were also yet very much perplexed. I rode to Bishopthorp on his account ; his Grace was pre-engaged in that affair, of the living I went to solicit for, but was very courteous, presented me with some curiosities, and received me most courteously, as did also the learned Dr. Gale at York, and stayed me full late at the Deanery. Their civilities helped to revive my drooping spirits, and the antiquities I met with there, and at Brotherton, Castleford, Pontefract, and Almanbury, (where I rode at the Mayor's request with him and the Vicar, to pay our respects to Sir John Kaye,) diverted me, and I think did somewhat influence Dr. Manlove ; who, upon a designed alteration at the chapel, would have had me his Deacon, which I rejected : but to evidence my Christian charity, I willingly at his request perused his manuscript designed for the press, which was really ingenious and pious. But I was now, blessed be God ! more fully satisfied in communicating with

the public.   Archbishop Sharp had recommended
my case to a very eminent divine, Mr. John Humfrey,*
noted as well for his moderation as piety, who to
use his own expression, was though a Nonconformist
minister, a Conformist parishioner.

    Sept. 4, 1698. Die Dom. I received the blessed

---

   * Mr. Humfrey, whose assistance was called in at this critical
period of the life of Thoresby, had withdrawn from the Church at
the settlement of it on its present basis in 1662; and yet he seems
never to have concurred with the Nonconformists, in establishing
separate communities. He wished for union and peace, and perhaps
was not averse from making some sacrifice of opinion, or even of what
may be called principle, to obtain them. Those were what he aimed
at in a multitude of works, which he published. He was always for
the *Middle Way*, or what he called the *Mediocria*. Archbishop
Sharp showed his judgment in referring Thoresby to such a casuist.
His letter of advice will be found hereafter.

  Mr. Humfrey was living when Dr. Calamy published his Account
of the Ejected and Silenced Ministers, more than fifty years after
they had left the church. It appears by what is said of him, that he
experienced what is usually the fate of moderate men in times of
violence, that he was neglected by men on both sides, while some of
all parties held him in respect. When Dr. Calamy made application
to him for a list of his writings, that it might be transmitted to posterity, he sent it, but with some reluctance, " desiring," as he said,
" no more than to go to his grave with a sprig of rosemary."

  It is to be regretted that we have not the Diary for the time when
this change took place in the mind and religious practice of Thoresby.
Beside what is to be found in the passages extracted from the *Review*,
it appears that he read, with a view to this change, Archbishop
Sharp's *Treatise of Conscience* and all the *London Cases*, and that
the whole question became at last reduced to this: Whether matters
indifferent in their own nature become not necessary as to our obedience to them, when commanded by lawful authority? Mr. John
Howe, a very eminent Nonconformist minister, wrote much at length
on the subject to Mr. Boyse, of Dublin, who happened to be at
Leeds at the time, a letter which seems to have been intended for
Thoresby's perusal; and Mr. Boyse, who was his early and intimate
friend, pressed all the arguments against Conformity which could be
urged to a man of Thoresby's principles.

sacrament of the Lord's Supper, at the hands of our good Vicar, Mr. Killingbeck.

About this time, a distemper began in the night: I burnt vehemently, but by a blessing upon the physician's advice, the fever proved as moderate as could reasonably be expected, though its preying upon the spirits brought me so weak, that many despaired of my life, and therefore I made my will; and as my perplexed affairs (which were my greatest trouble, because of my dear wife and poor children) would permit, endeavoured to settle my concerns, &c. In the midst of all which I was, through the goodness of my God, much supported by the taste of his love. O Lord, if a faint glimpse to a poor frail creature here below be so ravishing, what, oh what, will the beatific vision be!

Nov. 1, 1698, was the first time I put a coat on for nine weeks; I then ventured abroad for monies to defray charges: and now to divert myself a little, till I recovered strength to go about business, I spent much of my time amongst my books and coins, for several of which I now made pasteboard tables to place them in, or nests, as Mr. Evelyn calls them in his *Numismata*, from which learned and obliging author, I received a kind (but too complimentive) letter during my sickness.

That week, the Lord Fairfax, Justice Kirk, and Mr. Bryan Fairfax of London, coming to town, sent for me to congratulate my recovery, and came to see the museum; but I hastened away as soon as I

could possibly do with any tolerable decency, to what
I thought a more suitable employment under my
present circumstances, to hear Mr. Johnson, senior,
and another aged minister, preach thanksgiving sermons upon the recovery of his son from a fit of sickness, wherein I heartily joined.

This month I bought the house, late brother Jerry
Thoresby's, of Mr. J. B. now Alderman, whom I
thought too severe in exacting interest for the interest due from my poor brother, though he knew that
I lost even the principal itself.

A. D. 1699.

I now renewed my correspondence with my kind
and learned friends, Dr. Nicholson (Bishop of Carlisle), Dr. Gibson of Lincoln, Mr. Evelyn, Dr. Lister,
Dr. Cay, &c.; and on the 16th, wrote to the Archbishop of York, in return to a kind letter and agreeable present of autographs, received last night, together with a most valuable manuscript containing his
Grace's curious and critical remarks upon the English coins, which is indisputably the best that ever
was written upon that subject.   At his request, I
made some additionals.

The learned Mr. Boyse, being come from Dublin,
to this his native place, lodged at my house till his
marriage with Mrs. Rachel Ibbetson.   The sermon
he preached relating to the sufferings of the French
Protestants, was very moving, there being once about
eight hundred churches, in which the true worship

of God was constantly celebrated, which are now demolished, one thousand five hundred pastors banished, their flocks scattered, and many thousand families forced into exile, &c. for whose relief public collections are being made. The Vicar also preached excellently upon that occasion.

The Judge (Sir Littleton Powis) being invited by the Corporation, the Mayor, &c. waited on his lordship to see the museum ; but it was a greater happiness to me that not long after, John Boulter, Esq. (Lord of Harwood) favoured me with a visit, and has ever since, for above twenty years, been a kind friend and noble benefactor to me and mine, having sent me more and more valuable curiosities than any one person living.

I received a most comfortable letter from my Lord Archbishop of York, answering many objections against my conformity, and gave me great satisfaction.

My dear aunt Idle's business calling me to York not long after, I took Bishop Thorpe in my return, and after much discourse upon the subject, I showed his Grace, Mr. Howe's letter, whereupon he most kindly offered that if Mr. Howe, or any other, would make particular objections, he would answer them for my sake, and justify my deserting their communion for that of the Church : but I being now satisfied in my own judgment would not give his Lordship the trouble. His Grace also brought me acquainted with the famous Dr. Burnet, Bishop of Sarum, from whom

I received some kind letters about MS. Bibles, and
also a specimen of the writing of the blind gentlewoman at Geneva, mentioned in his letters to Mr.
Boyle, that are in print.   My correspondence with
persons of learning and curiosity increased much : I
find a memorandum, that by the same post, I wrote
to two at Cambridge, two at Oxford, and three at
Gresham College.   Dr. Bentley, being now in his
native country, was obliged by the famous Mr. Evelyn to give me a visit at Leeds.

I particularly lamented the death of my friend,
Mr. Torre, a famous antiquary, who died of a conta-
gious disorder then prevalent, in the prime of his
days, a comely proper gentleman, and more likely to
have wrestled through it than my poor weak wife.
Dr. Manlove also died of it at Newcastle, enjoying
his quadruple salary but a little time.*   My sister,
Thoresby also died of it ; but she caught the distemper at Cowton, where in two months and two days
time, it cut off three generations of adult persons, my
cousin Johnson and her daughter Betty, and my
aunt Savage,† (relict of Charles Savage, Esq. seventh
son of Thomas, the first Earl Rivers ;) also my brother's only son, John Thoresby, which name reminds
me of a passage I heard at another funeral ; viz. that
of Capt. Pickering, of Tingley, where were several old

---

* Dr. Manlove had removed a little before from Leeds to Newcastle-upon-Tyne, where he died on the 4th of August, 1699, at the
age of 36.

† This lady was *Aunt* to Thoresby only, as being mother to his
brother's wife.

soldiers, particularly Mr. Robert Gledhill, (whose son
the Colonel, John Gledhill, is now Governor for
the King in Newfoundland) which Robert, was of
Oliver's life guard, and told me, that at the famous
battle at Marston Moor, he saw thirty thousand of
the Parliament forces beat out of the field, and run
away ; he would gladly have persuaded my father to
do so with him, but could not, for he was one of the
few that rallied and stayed upon the field till the victory turned to their own side.

Dr. Manlove's harshness did not so far alienate
my affections from that poor afflicted people, but that
I endeavoured to do them all the kindness I could:
and since few could be prevailed with to be of my
sentiment as to conformity, I did what was possible
for me to procure a moderate as well as a pious man
to supply the famous Mr. Sharp's place, and accordingly writ by their messengers to Mr. Henry, of
Chester, to have procured Mr. John Owen, a noted
divine, and good antiquary, on which account we had
a correspondence, but it succeeded not : his knowledge in the British tongue making him dou-
bly serviceable in those parts where he preached
to the Welsh as well as English.   Amongst all
the ministers that preached in the vacancy, many
of whom coming from distant parts, procured some
or other to introduce them to see the museum, none
was more acceptable than Mr. Rastrick, which many
wondered at, because he had been once a conforming
clergyman, and I on the other hand, was now
come off from them entirely to the Church, but

when any thing of that nature was started in company, it was managed with that temper that gave no offence to either, both laying the stress upon the essentials of religion, wherein all are agreed; and we after maintained a friendly correspondence about antiquities found in Lincolnshire, and some natural observations, inserted in the Philosophical Transactions.

In the choice of a minister there was great heat, and many angry disputes betwixt the two parties. Mr. Fenton moved to have the matter decided by lot, but the neighbouring ministers opposed that, as not lawful but in extraordinary cases, where it could no otherwise be determined, and not barely to avoid heats. I proposed to give their votes by balloting, whereby both passion might be avoided, and persons might vote with the greater freedom : and this method was embraced.

A. D. 1700.

The discoveries I made about this time, relating to the memorable battle betwixt the primitive Christians in these parts and the Pagans, (mentioned by Bede) and the stations of both their armies, place of battle and sepulture, with many other circumstances discovered by the remains of the Saxon names and views of the places may be found in my Diary, and in the new Camden. What more immediately relates to these papers, is the further affliction of my poor family by the small-pox.

This distemper was now epidemical and very fatal: since the former visitation, which left me childless, it had pleased God to give me four children, who were all sick at the same time, of the same distemper. We were now deprived of two of them, Elizabeth and Ruth ; the elder, my dear daughter Betty, had not only a peculiar loveliness in her countenance, but what is infinitely preferable, was pious above her years.

But I ought also to record the tender mercies of the Lord, who spared the lives of my son, Ralph, and daughter Grace, who yet survive, and I hope may be useful in their respective generations.

I was somewhat diverted from musing too much on my own affairs, by the visits of several persons of quality, (members of both Houses of Parliament) to see the curiosities, the Earl of Abington's brother, (nephew to the Duke of Leeds) Sir Willoughby Hickman, Sir John Kaye, &c. ; but these again were abated by notice of the deaths of my honoured and dear friends, as Dr. Sampson, of London, a pious, learned, ingenious and obliging person, and Dr. Nicholson, of York, another worthy good man. The former left me a valuable manuscript as a legacy, with an affecting letter ; the relict of the other sent me his curious collection of dried plants, in a large folio.

A.D. 1701.

A threatened trial at the Assizes about the Mill,

obliged me to go to York, where I spent several days
in a fruitless attendance, for they durst not try the
cause.   The uncertainty of my stay there made me
walk it, and I took great pleasure in tracing the
Roman way upon Bramham Moor, and inquiring for
urns and other antiquities, sometimes found in their
burying-place, near Bontham-bar, at York.   Neither
the Archbishop nor Dean were in the country, both
being to preach before the King ; but I met with
other good friends that made my time easy, Chancellor Watkinson and Dr. Ashingdon, both natives of
Leeds, Dr. Fall, the Precentor, and Dr. Pearson, dear
Mr. Thornton and Justice Kirk, Major Fairfax and
Mr. Hodgson, chaplain to the Lady Hewley, who
has new built a stately hospital for ten widows, the
building whereof, and the purchase of the ground,
cost above a thousand pounds.

The perplexed affairs of my poor brother, Jerry
Thoresby, and my brother-in-law, Idle, obliged me
to undertake a longer and more expensive journey,
to prevent their utter ruin.   I began my journey to
London on that account, 9th June, 1701.

Dr. Gibson, (now Bishop of Lincoln) was particularly obliging in showing me the library and palace
at Lambeth; also Dr. Burnet, Bishop of Sarum,
who gave me original letters of the Princess Sophia
and Duke of Gloucester, with two MSS. of his own,
and showed me the original Magna Charta, and the
seal of King John.

Dr. Moor, Bishop of Norwich, showed me some

very great curiosities in his invaluable library, both
manuscript (as prayers written by Queen Elizabeth's
own hand, a volume of Letters of Lord Burleigh)
and printed, with the emendations of the noted
authors, written propriâ manu, as Jos. Scaliger
Dan. Heinsius, Junius, Casaubon, Bishop Pearson.

Amongst the entirely printed books, I was surprised to find one Liber Catholicon, Anno MCCCCLX.
almâ in urbe Moguntinâ, which is five or six years
before Tully's Offices, hitherto reputed the first
printed book.

His lordship introduced me to his grace, the Duke
of Leeds, who was at his noble seat at Wimbledon :
the way thither was the pleasantest that ever I travelled, his lordship having keys to pass through the
King's gates, that we had gardens on both hands.
His Grace entertained us most courteously, and told
us some remarkable passages concerning the Czar of
Muscovy, there and at Lambeth ; but what more
concerned me is the Bishop's kind advice to me, as
to the dizziness in my head, to drink our Leeds Spa
water for a considerable time, and to use a flesh
brush to help the circulation of the blood, &c. But
of all the nobility, none was so agreeable to me as
the truly noble Earl of Pembroke, whose incomparable museum of medals, entertained me several days.
I shall recite some of his lordship's instructive observations, for the benefit of my dear son. I was
most surprised with the Roman As, of a pound
weight, and one of eight ounces, which even their

own historians are silent in. They were afterwards
gradually reduced to one ounce, and half an ounce.
The entire As, of whatever weight, has Janus's head
upon it: the Semissis, or half As, is marked with S.:
the Triens, with . . . ; points; the Quadrans, with
. . .; the Sextans, with . .; and their Stips unci-
alis, with .; as originally containing so many several
ounces.   They had also their three sextulæ piece
(or semiuncia) and sextula.

His Lordship also showed me great variety of the
silver denarii, which, when worth ten asses, was
marked X: when the value was advanced to sixteen
of the copper asses, then with XVI: the quina-
rium is marked with V or half X.   His Lordship has
also several double denarii, and the double of them
again, or silver medallions, originally of the worth
and weight of four denarii, such indeed as I had
never seen before.   His Lordship's humanity and
condescension were extraordinary; for, not thinking
this kindness enough, he desired me to make him
another visit, and he would show me other views,
which I, modestly declining, (considering his Lordship's public station, being President of his Majesty's
Privy Council, and one of the Lords Justices,) but
my Lord would have me promise to dine with him
the next day at three, when the Council would be
over, desiring, in the mean time, the perusal of my
manuscript catalogue of my coins.

The day after, was courteously entertained, and
had excellent company at dinner, Dr. Wake, (now

Archbishop of Canterbury,) Dr. Lock, Mr. Secretary Southwell, and Dr. Woodward. Afterwards, my Lord took me into his incomparable museum, where the variety and number made me forget some that were perhaps most remarkable; Roman coins, with *capita jugata;* others, with a head on each side; others, rare for the metal, as a genuine Otho in copper, found at Smyrna, a Constantine the Great in silver; others rare in any metal, as Diadumenianus and Annius Verus, which is an unique, neither the Emperor or King of France having one.

His Lordship also showed me a view of coins of several languages; besides those of Greek and Latin, were Hebrew, Arabic, Syriac, Punic, Palmyran, and Runic: and in another view, these various metals, viz. gold, silver, copper, brass, electrum gold and silver mixed, gold and copper mixed, silver and copper in circular plates, or rings, unmixed, in the same coins; monies of iron and lead, both consular and imperial; leather, that of Leyden; and horn, Queen Christina of Sweden: in another view, a strange variety of counterfeits, in some the metal genuine, but inscription false; in others, one side of the medal genuine, the other counterfeit; in others, one part of the metal right, the other side soldered to it wrong; with a medal of the two famous Paduan brothers, whose counterfeits are not only hard to be distinguished from the originals, but preferred to bad ones, though genuine.

The 5th instant I again waited on this noble

Lord, (at his own appointment,) who most courteously showed me those of the British and Saxon
coins, and took notice, with pleasure, of my Runic
piece of Thor; then his views of the Danish and
Norman. I chiefly took notice of such as I was
doubtful to whom to ascribe them, but being since
inserted in the printed catalogue, need not be here
recited, nor the fourteen distinct denominations of
English silver money, from a farthing to a twenty
shilling piece, which, when I was going to note, his
Lordship most courteously wrote them for me, which
I treasure up as a valuable autograph.

His Excellency also acquainted me with the perfect history of milled money, from the first of Queen
Elizabeth upon the side, to those upon the edge in
Oliver's, or Commonwealth's time : the first that are
lettered upon the edge were indisputably English,
for though his Lordship has of the French before
that time, they are manifestly hooped on, not as
Simon's, upon the money itself. His Lordship also
asked for my Album, wherein he wrote that of
Plautus, (so suitable to every good Christian as well
as virtuoso.) " Illud satius est quod satis est."

My Lord's kindness kept me full late, but though
I returned alone some miles in the dark, yet well
contented ; and to conclude my notes upon this invaluable museum, this truly noble Earl appointed
the 14th to show me other views, particularly the
Greek; all the famous states and cities in Magna
Grecia, and the successors of Alexander the Great in

the four great kingdoms; and because he said it was not to be got here, but he had correspondents to procure one from beyond sea, he presented me with De Wild's *Selecta Numismata,* and gave me a quarter shekel of Agrippa, in memory of the two great feasts of the Jews, viz. the Tabernacle and the First Fruits, mentioned in the Ducatus Leod. and referred to by De Wild, &c.

I have been more particular in relating what this truly noble lord instructed me in, because not to . be met with in any printed author or manuscript that is likely to come to the notice of my dear sons, for whose information this is written. I shall be more brief in what follows.

That noble Lord, Baron Spanhemius, Envoy from the King of Prussia, and author of that learned book, De præstantiâ et usu Numismat. Antiq. desired to borrow the manuscript catalogue of my coins, and told me upon perusal, that he wondered how a private gentleman could attain such a treasure. Disuse had made me very unfit to hold a continued discourse in Latin, so that when Dean Gale was not with us, we had a sad broken mixture of Latin, Dutch, and English.

This being the first time I was at London since my admission into the Royal Society, I subscribed my name in the book; the formality of the Vice-President's taking me by the hand and publicly pronouncing me (in the name of the Society) a Fellow of the Royal Society, and the great humanity of Sir

James Hoskyns, who then filled the chair, Sir Hans
Sloane, the secretary, Abraham Hill, Esq. the treasurer, &c. may be seen in my Diary.

After the meeting was over, I had the opportunity of taking a more particular view of the curiosities in the public museum, to which were added
some Roman plasticks I had brought from York, and
had duplicates of for myself. I was invited by many
eminent persons to see theirs in particular, of which
Dr. Woodward's was most curious in natural curiosities of fossils, gems, minerals, ores, shells, stones, &c.
of which he made me a noble present, since inserted
in the printed Catalogue. He has also, besides a
good library, a curious collection of Roman antiquities, not only of urns, but gems, signets, rings, keys,
stylus Scriptorius, res turpiculæ, ivory pins, brass
fibulæ, &c. The famous Mr. Evelyn, who has
published a great number of very rare books, was
above measure civil and courteous, in showing me
many drawings and paintings of his own and his
lady's doing; one especially of enamel was sur-
prisingly fine, and this ingenious lady told me the
manner how she wrought it, but I was uneasy at
his too great civility in leaving an untold heap of
gold medals before me, &c.

He afterwards carried me in his coach to his son
Draper's at the Temple, and showed me many
curious pieces of his ingenious daughter's perform-
ance, both very small in minature and as large as
the life in oil colours, equal it is thought, to the

greatest masters of the age.   He gave me a specimen
of some prospects he took in Italy, and etched upon
copper by his own hand.   Dr. Hook also, aged and
infirm as he was (being one of the virtuosos that
met in Bishop Wilkins' lodgings at Oxford before
the formal constitution of the Society), was very
courteous, and gave me the description of his new
invented Marine Barometer.

But above all, the Secretary, Dr. Sloane (now Sir
Hans) in whose inestimable museum I was most
courteously entertained many a pleasant hour : he
has a noble library, too large rooms well stocked
with valuable manuscripts and printed authors, an
admirable collection of dried plants from Jamaica,
the natural history of which place he has in hand,
and according to the engraved specimens will be a
noble book.   He gave me the printed catalogue and
some Indian seeds : he has other curiosities without
number, and above value ; Bishop Nicholson (who is
a competent judge, having been in those parts) says,
it vastly exceeds those of many foreign potentates,
which are so celebrated in history.

At Whitehall also I was courteously received by
Sir Christopher Wren, the King's architect, who has
built more churches since the fire of London, than,
perhaps, any one person in the world ever did.   His
ingenious son showed me his valuable collection of
Grecian medals ; of their several states and colonies,
and gave me the printed catalogue, though he has
too modestly concealed his name.

These and others (too numerous to be inserted)
were all of them Fellows of the Royal Society, and
so more particularly obliging to me as a younger
brother; but I had also the opportunity of seeing
whatever else was curious; and in the first place I
ought to mention the famous Cottonian library at
Westminster, where I was surprised to find so vast
a number of valuable manuscripts crowded up in so
small a cell.

I spent what time I had to spare in viewing three
of them. 1stly. Original Charters of Saxon and
Norman kings, to note the different characters of
the several centuries; 2dly. Original letters of sove-
reign princes, ancient and modern; 3rdly. A volume
of those of learned authors, at home and abroad: and
what success I have had therein, may in part be
seen in the Ducatus Leod.

I was frequently at the immense library of my
kind friend, the Bishop of Norwich, where I always
found fresh entertainment; as with Wickliff's MS.
English version of the Bible, shown me by his son,
Mr. Chancellor Tanner, whose Notitia Monastica
sells now at a great rate. Amongst the civilities of
my friends, I ought particularly to remember that
of Dr. Fairfax, brother to the late lord, and uncle
to the present, who has lately published the Memo-
rials of the Lord Thomas Fairfax, the General, which
he presented me with.

I visited also good old Mr. Humfrey, a noted
author: he gave me his Vindication of Bishop Stil-

lingfleet and Mr. Baxter, just now published, with autographs of noted persons. The celebrated Dr. Hicks also, was very civil in showing me several original charters in Saxon and Latin, communicated to him by the Lord Somers, a true patron of learning in men of all denominations, who got him a quietus from some inconveniences he was under as a nonjuror, and sent it under seal, as a present to the Dr., without his knowledge, and without fees.

The very courteous Parson Stonestreet has a good collection of Roman coins, and a most surprising one of shells, a thousand several sorts from all parts of the world, curious for their form, size, colour, &c. I cannot conclude better than with two of my countrymen, Yorkshire authors, William Petyt, Esq. of the Temple, who with his brother, Silvester, are also considerable benefactors, and Robert Dale, Esq. of the Herald's Office, whose civilities rendered a letter to the King-at-Arms needless ; for he readily showed me the MSS. in that College, and particularly the pedigree of my family, which is attested by the King-at-Arms, and carries it up to the reign of King Edward the Confessor, whereby it also appears that Archbishop John Thoresby was a younger brother of this family.

Having brought my poor brother's affairs to a better period than I expected, I returned home, and was mercifully protected from many dangers that others suffered at the same time ; and when being arrived at Leeds, 19th July, where I found my dear and children well, I had uncomfortable wrangling with the country creditors.

After my return, I was agreeably occupied in writing to my correspondents of the Royal Society, (many of which letters are inserted in the Philosophical Transactions,) and others, particularly Mr. Milner, of Cambridge, our late learned Vicar, who desired an account of such coins of Claudius and Agrippa, as might illustrate that passage of the famine mentioned Acts xi., also in disposing of Lord Wharton's Bibles, procured for the poor children, orphans, and servants, who, hearing that they were come, came in such great crowds, that I was almost suffocated with the heat.

[Diary resumed.]

A. D. 1701.

Sept. 17. Read Bishop Hall before secret prayer, but was constrained to put off family prayer and reading till noon, by an uncomfortable business with Mr. Hatfield, of Hatfield, to whom, and upon Mr. Ibbetson's account, paid about 30*l.* that I fear I shall never recover a penny of. Lord, sanctify all afflicting dispensations to this poor family! Afterwards, endeavoured to divert myself amongst Mr. Hillary's papers, at widow P.'s, who gave me several of his, and a yet greater benefactor's autographs, viz. Mr. Harrison, who built the new church.

20. With Mr. Kirk, of Cookridge, of whom glad

to hear of the successful attempt for a public register of lands in the West Riding, which will be of
use in future ages as well as the present.

22. With parson Dixon, a native of this town,
now Vicar of Mask, making an end of the accounts
and mortgage betwixt him and cousin Atkinson of
Burmantofts, to the mutual satisfaction of both parties. Concerning this good honest Vicar (who served
an apprenticeship here before he went to the University) who is a peaceable and pious man, I have
from good hands heard a doleful story concerning
his grandfather, who, either from age or other infirmity, being in a melancholy dotage, one day wandered till he got to Pontefract, and being weary
went into a house, (where the maid, being gone out
with her sweetheart, had left the door open,) and
sat him down in a chair by the fire-side. The maid,
returning in a fright, cries out " Thieves !" Her
master, rising hastily out of bed, brings his faulchion
and cuts him in pieces; the poor creature only crying, " So, so, enough, enough!" but died of the
wounds immediately, which brought the master of
the house into almost as melancholy a state the rest
of his life.

30. All day at Mr. L.'s, assisting Alderman Dixon
in receiving fee-farm rents of manor, and my own
arrears. Discoursed with him about Bailiwick, which
reminds me of what was omitted yesterday, that at
the Court, (where we elected the Mayor and two
assistants, Mr. J. Ibb. and Mr. S. Iles,) Mr. Blyth-

man produced a copy of an old account said to be
Mr. Hillary's, relating to the bailiwick, which seemed
to make against us, but was a cancelled paper, and,
as I apprehend, ten or fifteen years before the real
purchase of the five parts that they indisputably
have a right to.   Now, my argument is, that if the
Corporation really purchased and paid monies for
the nine parts of the Bailiwick in the year 1639,
what need they purchase the five parts (part of the
said nine) in 1665 ?

Oct. 12. Deferred family prayer and reading till
noon, being to wait upon the new Mayor in his formalities.   In the way called to wait upon my Lord
Fairfax, from whom lately received a very kind letter ; had also Sir William Lowther, and other country justices, in the cavalcade.

Nov. 3. With Alderman Dixon, and other lords
of the manor, and in the evening received a kind
visit from the excellent Mr. Archdeacon Nicholson,
of Carlisle, (who has been near ten years in performing it,) and his cousin Mr. Archdeacon Pearson, to
whom, after supper, showed part of library, &c.
Had the ingenious Mr. Thornton's company.

4. Was to show the two Archdeacons our remarkable cloth-market : treated all three after the old
manner at a *bridge and shot* for 6*d.*   Then showing
Mr. Nicholson some of the Roman coins, taking
particular notice of such as relate to Britain.   Dined
with them at Mr. Thornton's : afterwards visited
the Vicar, and in the evening at a treat at Alder-

man Preston's; stayed late with ditto good company, that again prevented of reading before secret
prayer.

22. Walked with Mr. Pawson, &c. by Coning-
shaw (near Nevill Hill and Priestcliffe, &c.) to Os-
winthorp, to the funeral of Alderman Skelton, aged
83 years.

28. Received a very kind letter, with a transcript of an ancient pedigree of our family, from the
time of Canute the Dane to the year 1665, attested
by my kind friend Mr. Dale, of the Herald's Office;
diverted therewith.

Dec. 3. Within, consulting MSS. and Mon. An-
glic. &c. concerning the vicarage, &c. designing an
account of the church and chapels, &c. at the Archbishop's request.

5. Transcribing letter to my Lord Archbishop,
and writing to Dr. Sloane, Secretary R. S.; a little
with the ingenious Mr. Thornton, and after with
Mr. Mayor.

6. Writing letters to the Dean of York, Dr. Woodward, and Mr. Dale, in return of their kind letters.

12. In my walk towards the garden, finished the
second Letter concerning the Archbishop's right to
continue or prorogue the whole Convocation, sent
me from an unknown hand by the London carrier,
but suppose either from Mr. Gibson, (the Archbishop
of Canterbury's chaplain,) or my Lord Bishop of
Norwich, who gave me the former letter, which letters seem to me not only modest and judicious, but

to be absolutely in the right as to the controversy
betwixt the Upper and Lower House, &c.   Lord,
grant a spirit of love and union !   My Lord Archbishop told me since, Mr. Gibson is the author.

14. Took a hasty view of a very noble monument, (said to have cost 700*l.*) lately erected for the
second Lord Viscount Irwin, (son to the first, and
brother to the present Lord.)

15. With the Mayor and several of the corporation ; sent for the treasurer, who was directed not
to pay any of the public stock upon private notes,
(as has been too common of late,) of any of the
aldermen, but by order of the Court of Mayor, Aldermen, and Assistants.

17. Collating the edition of the Prayer-book in
Queen Elizabeth, with the present and the Scotch
Liturgy, &c.   Afternoon, assisting poor cousin Atkinson, of Burmantofts, and Parson Dixon, Vicar of
Mask, from whom received a kind present of what
the sea-shore in those parts affords of natural curiosities.

18. Then being a delicate frost, took a walk to
Bishopthorp; had my dear's company and daughter
Grace's two miles; then the company of a book
over the moors, &c.   Stayed not the least, (because
of the shortness of the days,) till I came at the Ly-
bian Hercules at the Street houses, and there only
the heating of one mug of ale, but, blessed be my
gracious Preserver, got very well to my journey's
end ; was most kindly received by my Lord Arch-

bishop and his whole family, Dr. Deering, Mr. Richardson, &c. ; had also the additional happiness of
the excellent Mr. Thornton and Mr. Archdeacon
Pearson's good company ; passed the evening most
agreeably in discourse.

19. After family prayers (as last night) went with
my Lord Archbishop, Mr. Thornton, and Mr. Pearson, in his Grace's coach, to York, it being the public fast.   Afterwards made a visit to the learned
Dean, but could have little discourse, being sent for
to the Chancellor's, good old Dr. Watkinson, where
had also the precentor, Dr. Fall's, company, &c.
Afterwards returned with my Lord Archbishop, who,
when we were got out of the bar, came out of the
coach, and we all walked to Bishopthorp, a pleasant
and short walk.   After the excellent and serious
prayers appointed upon this occasion, we supped,
and, after family prayers, had instructive converse
with my Lord and the rest of the good company.
Sat up late ; yet still longer kept my dear bedfellow
(good Mr. Thornton) awake, by a melancholy relation of my losses, and the piteous circumstances of
my poor family, which discourse was accidental or
providential, (for I designed it not,) but had thereby
the happiness of his prudent and affectionate advice
and wishes.   Lord, direct me in my concerns!

20. Having retired and stayed family prayers,
took leave of my Lord Archbishop, and ditto excellent company, and returned on foot, (though my
Lord Archbishop several times most kindly offered

me his own saddle-horse,) had a pleasant walk, and got home in good time.

24. Afternoon, writing to my Lord Archbishop, consulting the commissions of pious uses for what has been given to the several chapels within this parish, by his Grace's special order, who has begun a noble and useful manuscript of the endowments, &c. of the churches and chapels in the whole province, that nothing once devoted to pious uses may be lost. Finished the Museum Tradescantianum, (save his plants,) now Ashmoleanum at Oxford, wherein many valuable curiosities.

A. D. 1702.

Jan. 6. Sadly concerned for my most useful and excellent friend, Mr. Thornton's, indisposition. I heard also that my kind friend, Dr. Cay, of New-castle, is very weak, if alive. The Vicar also told me that our learned Dean of York having got cold, after he had heated himself in preaching upon Christmas-day, was very badly, and a fever was dreaded; and, to complete all, my Lord Archbishop himself was much indisposed, and not only dreaded such a fit of the stone as he had at London last Parliament, but seemed apprehensive that it might take him off, but with this Christian expression, the will of the Lord be done! All these things go sore with me, and I went with a sad heart about the concerns of the day.

30. In my walks in the garden, ended Mr. White's

(our late Recorder's) Majestas Intemerata, writ upon this very sad occasion, wherein abundance of reading, as well as zeal appears, but a crabbed style: he was the grandfather of Bishop White.

Feb. 7. Writing letters to the Secretary of the R. S., Dr. Woodward, &c. by my honoured and dear friend, Mr. Kirk, of whom took leave; but there being my Lord Fairfax's sister, and other relations likewise, for a London journey, was more expensive than could have wished, considering losses, &c.

10. Collated the several editions of the prayer-books; then transcribing Mr. Bowles's Memoirs, altering some more rigid expressions, and making additions from MSS. &c. in my own possession.

13. About poor ministers' pensions; afternoon, received a kind visit from Mr. Thornton and his brother Fenay, to see the collection of prints, Vandyke's heads, &c., which took up the rest of the day.

14. Writing per post to Mr. Evelyn, Mr. Kirk, Mr. Petyt, and Mr. Rymer, all in one to save postage.

15. Evening, finished in family Bedel's Diary of a Thankful Christian, a serious and useful piece, wherein also are many historical passages, handsomely applied, and to good purpose; he seems to have been a moderate as well as pious divine, rightly observing the peculiar sin of that age to be enmity against the kingly government of Christ in his Church, justly declaiming against the sectaries, fairly owning that what had been generally loathed, be-

cause the broachers were prelatical, were then greedily
swallowed under a name of sanctity, and what was
insufferable in a prince, was commendable in a
captain.

17. Invited by the courteous Sir Abstrupus Danby to dine with him ; went with him and his only
son to view the old church, to see for the burying-
place of that ancient family, and afterwards to see
the new church.

19. Attending the magistrates and proper officers
about the assessments, which took up the whole day
except usual walks to church, and a little taking
notes from the Saxon Heptateuch.

20. Evening with brother, &c. at Garraway's
Coffee-house ; was surprised to see his sickly child
of three years old fill its pipe of tobacco, and smoke
it as *audfarandly* as a man of threescore ; after
that, a second and third pipe without the least concern, as it is said to have done above a year ago.

24. In walks backward ; ended Davies's Rites of
Durham Abbey, a most superstitious book, yet useful in its place, not only to know the distinct apartments of the old religious fabrics (which was my
main design, in respect of Kirstal Abbey) but to
discover the wondrous superstition of the poor ignorant Papists, in picturing God the Father, as well as
Son and Holy Ghost. Afternoon, showing collections to a traveller, the late Bishop Huntington's
(of Rapho) nephew, (who died at Dublin, 10th
September last.)

28. Writing Memoirs of good old Mr. Todd.*

March 4. Writing Memoirs for Mr. Calamy, till four: at church ; the vicar preached the funeral sermon for old Mrs. Pullain, mother of the late High Sheriff, who was born here, where his father, Mr. Pullain, is yet living, and can read without spectacles (which he formerly used), though ninety-two years of age. *Poulain,* in French, signifies a colt. And his son, Thomas Pullain, Esq. Stud-master to his Majesty, rose from a small beginning to a great estate by horses.

10. Sadly surprised with the news of the King's dangerous illness.

11. Was immediately and sadly surprised by an aged minister, who coming from Bishopthorp, met an express going to my Lord Archbishop, and after to the Lord Mayor of York, with the doleful tidings of the King's death. The vicar afterwards showed me a letter from my Lord Archbishop, wherein he writes, "we are here even at our wit's end because of the King's dangerous illness." What shall we now do that so great a judgment has actually befallen us ! My poor wife was even overwhelmed with grief. Lord help us to put our trust in thee, who art the same God that hast preserved us in former dangers, and thy hand, oh Lord ! is not shortened ; were our sins less, our hopes might be greater. Lord help thy poor servants in this distress also ! Till four at prayers. Lord help me to improve these happy op-

* A divine of Leeds, silenced by the Act of Uniformity.

portunities while they are continued. What an invaluable mercy it is, that we have the liberty of address to the throne of grace at all times, and in all exigencies; but it was melancholy to want both the prayers (in public) for the King and Royal Family.

13. At the Court, where it was resolved by the Mayor, &c. to proclaim Queen Anne the next market-day. The Lord direct her in difficulties, and make her reign prosperous and pious.

16. Walked with cousin C. Sykes to his uncle Elston's; was got to Hunby-ꝑleꞇ (the *canum area vel domus,* when the cẏnꞮnꝜaꝛ boꞇl was at Leeds) when it chimed four, and to Bell-hill before we could have any benefit of its beautiful prospect. At Lofthouse, we saw a smith working with two hammers, one of which, by a pretty contrivance (the first I have seen in these parts,) he moved with his foot, that he had the use of his left hand to hold the iron, while he struck with his right; and this engine supplied the place of a labourer to strike with the great hammer. Thence over the Outwood, (though now scarce a tree to be seen,) and by Newton to Wakefield, where visited uncle and aunt Pool, of the same family with the famous Mr. Matthew Pool, author of the Synopsis Criticorum, who was born at York, where his father, Francis Pool, Esq. (an eminent lawyer) married Alderman Toppin's daughter, near the lower church, in Micklegate, (query, register for date of his birth). His father, also, sometimes lived at Hull; my uncle Pool's father was his

clerk. At the end of Westgate we saw the new erected meeting-place, where his son-in-law, my cousin Sagar, preacheth; and upon the little common beyond had a prospect of Low Hill, of which see Mr. Whyte's notes, and Dugdale on the Sepulture of the Ancients, in his History of Warwickshire. Query, whether Lupset may have any relation to it, or any customs then in use, upon such solemn occasions; hlýp or hlip, signifying *Saltus*, a leaping; and ᛒᛁᚧ *iter*, a journey, or way.* After family prayer and reading, got cousin Elston to let me have the perusal of uncle Pickering's old papers and commissions relating to the late times; found original letters subscribed by the persons in five or six several governments in one year, viz. 1659. Afterwards viewed the house formerly the seat of Sir John Savile, Bart. but found no arms, &c. in the windows; only in the hall is Sir John's and his lady's in plaster; the gardens and orchards are curious, kept in the new order of dwarf trees, &c. except a remarkable yew-tree, and the wall-fruits that are forward to a wonder, the apricots set, and some pretty large; but such a season was never known for hot and fair weather so soon in the year. After dinner, cousin Elston kindly accompanied us to cousin Sagar's, at Flanshill, where disappointed of his company, being from home, that stayed less time there. Flanshill, seems to me to be so denominated from some noted tilting, or the exer-

---

* The terminal *et* is in this instance, and probably in others, a contract form of *heved, head:* Lupset often occurring in the early Rolls of the Manor of Wakefield, and uniformly written *Lupsheved.*

cise of some warlike weapons ; but whether from flan, or flæ, an arrow, or flæne, a sword, spear, or lance, I know not ; or whether from some extraordinary action there performed, or perhaps the customary place of exercise, &c.   Then by Allerthorp, (so called from Aleɲ, or Aloɲ, *Alnus*, the alder-trees,) and Silk-house, to the Pott-ovens, (Little London in the dialect of the poor people,) where I stayed a little to observe, not only the manner of forming their earthenware, (which brought to mind that of the Prophet, " As clay in the hands of the potter, so are we in the Lord's," &c.) but to observe the manner of building the furnaces; their size and materials, which are small, and upon the surface of the ground, &c. ; which confirms me in my former apprehensions, that those remains at Haw-caster-rigg are really the ruins of a Roman pottery. Vide Phil. Trans. No. 222.   Thence, over the skirts of the Outwood, by Lingwell-gate, to Thorp-on-the-Hill, near which were found those clay impressions, or moulds for counterfeiting the Roman coins, mentioned in the Philosophic Transactions, No. 234, which made me very apprehensive of some Roman station, or camp, in these parts ; and there is a long ridge that seems to have been one of their Viæ Vicinales, that passeth over a considerable part of the Outwood, directly to Lingwell-gate, as it is called to this day, in memory, I presume, of the Lingones, some of the Roman auxiliaries brought from Gaul, which Camden places in this West Riding of Yorkshire, viz. the second, or rather the first cohort, at Ilkley, which they rebuilt in Severus's time. Another cohort seems to have been placed here, as the very name Lingorum Vallum testifies, for the Latins pronounced the *u* as we do the *w*, (for which, Vide Somner and Casaubon de Linguâ Ang. Vet.) who particularly instances in Vallum, a wall, (for *well* there is none, nor indeed any need, because a running water at the foot of the hill,) besides, the Roman coining moulds were all of emperors and empresses, about the time of Severus, the Antonines, and Julius. Thence we walked up-hill to Thorpe, *super montem*, as it is writ in the Rowell Registers, now the seat of Mr. Ingram, who courteously procured me some of the Roman impressions found there. Thence by Newhall, once the seat of the most celebrated mathematician, not only in these parts, but I believe in the world, viz. Mr. William Gascoigne, eldest son of Henry Gascoigne, Esq. who so long ago as the time of King Charles the First, (in whose service he was slain,) discovered and made constant use of a curious instrument, that Monsieur Azout, the French astronomer in this age, prides himself as the first inventor of. (Vide Mr. Townley, of Townley's letters, both in the Phil. Trans. and Dr. Leigh's Natural History of Lancashire.) Thence in our way to Woodhouse Hill, we called to see an ingenious engine, &c. lately erected by Mr. Brandling, to drain his coal-mines, &c. but missing of himself, received little satisfaction. After a visit to poor cousin Fenton, (Lord, sanctify afflictions to us all!) returned somewhat wearied, but well, and found all well at home : Blessed be the God of our mercies!

17. Queen Anne was proclaimed by the Mayor and Corporation in their formalities, and by several country gentlemen, Sir Walter Hawksworth, &c. but I was best pleased that my honoured and dear friend, Mr. Thornton complied; heard the like also of the Earls of Clarendon, Lichfield, Rutland, &c. that it may please God to prevent those judgments of a Popish successor, that our sins have merited. Lord bless and direct her Majesty, Council, and Parliament, that all things may be so ordered and settled by their endeavours, upon the best and surest foundations, that peace and happiness, truth and justice, religion and piety, may be established amongst us, and transmitted to succeeding generations, for Jesus Christ's sake.

21. Hasting with my dear and children to visit relations at Newsom Green; in return made some remarks upon the Roman highway, which I traced a considerable way at the lower end of Newsom Green, whence it tends to Thorp Hall, where it is very visible, and thence to Skelton Grange, a little beyond which (over against the mill) it is yet very plain, but, since I can remember, extended much further (towards Knostrop), but was ploughed up by Mr. Clark.

23. With my dear and daughter cleaning the books from dust and moths, and comparing the cata-

logue for such as are lent and not returned, &c. Finished Sir William Dugdale's Catalogue of the nobility of the three kingdoms, with baronets, &c. a useful tract, yet, as to the nobility of England, far outdone by that of my ingenious and industrious friend Mr. Dale.

24. At Town-End, where stayed too late, and had too much occasion to bewail what Dr. Manton calls dry drunkenness, when indisposed for duty.

25. Ended my pious and ingenious friend Mr. Gibson's (now Bishop of Lincoln) Reflections upon a Pretended Expedient; much concerned for fear the opposite party of Hyperconformists should now, upon the King's death, prevail against the Bishops themselves and moderate party, who, in my poor apprehension, seem wholly in the right in this controversy.

April 1. To visit my dear friend Mr. Thornton, per whom my Lord Archbishop had sent me a very curious manuscript almanack (which his Grace had bought for me); the cost was great (ten shillings), but respects greater.

7. Went to see poor brother; in the way met with the sad news that Alderman Lasonby, of this town, and many other passengers and soldiers, were cast away near the Dutch coast; the case of that poor family (a poor melancholy widow, and many orphans, and intricate accounts, &c.) very much affected me. This, in a few minutes, was succeeded with another sad relation of the civil death of cousin

B. M. the Alderman's brother.   Lord, sanctify all
providences.   Afterwards received a kind visit from
Mr. Boulter, of Gawthrop-hall, with whom dined at
Mr. Thornton's.

11. At church, where the Vicar told me the sad
news of the death of my kind friend, the Dean of
York (Dr. Gale), which is a public loss, both as he
was a very religious and truly pious divine, and as
he was one of the most learned men in the Christian
world ;   myself can abundantly testify the former, to
whom he most affectionately bewailed the growing
prophaneness of the nation, &c.; and the great
applause the learned part of the world has given to
his works, is an undeniable testimony of the latter.

14. Received two invitations to the funeral of the
Dean of York ; prepared for a journey ;   and, after
dinner, walked to the warren-house on Bramham
Moor, and Major Fairfax being from home, then to
the Street-houses ; lodged at the Libyan Hercules
(Mr. Corlass's niece).

15. Walked to York, visited Mr. Gyles, then at
prayers at the minster ; afterwards visited Dr. Colton,
Mr. Hodgson, &c.   Afternoon, at the funeral of
my excellent and dear friend, Dr. Thomas Gale,
Dean of York, who was interred with great solemnity ; lay in state, 200 rings (besides scarfs for
bearers, and gloves to all) given in the room where
I was, which yet would not contain the company ;
yet was the lamentation greater for the loss of so
learned, pious, and useful a person, whose death was

deservedly lamented by persons of all denominations. Thought to have returned part of the way, but was invited to sup at the deanery; was kindly received by both the sons; was somewhat revived to see so much of the Dean in Mr. Gale, &c.

25. Writ Memoirs of Mr. Cartwright and Mr. Gunter, &c. to Mr. Calamy, which deferred family prayer till noon (there being a necessity of hastening the Memoirs, the press staying for them). Afternoon, unhappily sent for by Alderman Dixon and Mr. Barker, under colour of business, but indeed to engage my vote for the next election of an alderman. Lord, make them as solicitous to discharge the duties of that station! This, unhappily, prevented my attendance at the prayers, which troubled me. This has been a sad week; I cannot reflect upon it without shame and grief; the Lord pity and pardon.

29. Rode to Halifax, and after the dispatch of brother Hough's concerns, and attestation of the writings, went to the Vicarage to visit Mr. Wilkinson; took some extracts from the registers, &c. Was to see the church and new library, which he has exceedingly beautified.

30. Taking extracts of the chantries at Leeds, &c. from Mr. Nalson's MS. collections, lent me by Mr. Wilkinson. After, became bound (with brother Rayner) for brother Hough's payment of 20l. per annum to good old aunt, during her natural life.

May 5. Heard of the death of my good old friend,

and my father's, Mr. Oliver Heywood; invited to
the funeral: and presently after had news of the
promotion of my ingenious friend, Mr. William
Nicholson, to the bishopric of Carlisle. What various providences are we exercised with! Lord,
help me to make a good improvement of all!

7. Rode with Mr. Peters* to Northowram, to the
funeral of good old Mr. O. Heywood. He was afterwards interred with great lamentations in the parish
church at Halifax: was surprised at the following
Arvill, or treat of cold possets, stewed prunes, cake
and cheese, prepared for the company, where had
several Con. and Noncon. ministers and old acquaintance. The word is derived from the Saxon Aꞃe,
alimentum, sustenance, nourishment, &c. Afterwards
had Mr. Waterhouse and Mr. Brearcliffe's company
at good old aunt Hough's; then, with Mr. Peters,
visited the pious and ingenious Mr. Priestley and
family. Sat up late enough with so good company.

29. Took the measuring-wheel, and having surveyed to the extent of the parish at Wikebridge,
continued it by Secroft, *prælii prædiolum,* or Battle-
croft, over that moor, (leaving Penwell Dale on the
right hand,) and Grimesdike, or Morrickfur, to Winmoor; thence by Scoles Outwood (which an old
man told me himself can remember a thick wood,
though now there is not a tree upon it,) over Cock-
beck; thence over Rakehill, which, whether it have
any historical relation to the memorable battle (·pace

---

* Mr. Peters succeeded Dr. Manlove in his congregation at Leeds.

signifying *historia, narratio,* &c.) I cannot tell; crossed the yet little beck of Cock again; thence over the Car and up Windlehill, (which, whether it have any reference to pınbel, *sportella,* or pınlıc, *latus gratus,* I know not,) to Berwick, seven miles by measure, (from Leeds church to that at Berwick) though but five by computation. Was disappointed of my expectations in the church, there being no monuments for the ancient family of the Gascoignes or Ellis's, save only fragments of their arms, &c. in the painted glass, but most of the windows defaced, &c. But was mightily pleased with a very remarkable mount, which I surveyed strictly, *(vide* the dimensions elsewhere,) which is to this day called the Hall-tower-hill, which confirms my former notion, that when the Saxon kings had their cynınȝaſ boⱦl at Leeds, this was a manor grange farm, country seat, appendant thereunto, one of the Berwicks *(cum suis Berwicis, vide* my MS. notes from Spelman, Somner, &c.) Healle signifies *aula, palatium,* &c. Besides, there is a universal tradition of a king's residence there, &c. The old parsonage house is demolished, and now re-edifying by Mr. Tankard, the Duke of Leeds' chaplain; but I found little remarkable there, save the King's arms in painted glass, which yet must be after Edward III., because the flowers-de-lis are limited to three: King Henry V. first stinted them to three. Returned by Scoles over another part of Winmoor, &c. Observed the toll-gatherer's booth, where the agents of Sir

Thomas Gascoigne are ready to .receive toll of the carriages, which, at a penny a pair of wheels, amounts to a considerable sum. But what I am more concerned for, it seems to me a confirmation of my sentiments, that the old (Roman) road from York over Bramham to Leeds, (the ancient Legeolium) was by Berwick over Whitkirk Moor, where the ridge is visible to this day, quite over the moor, till we come at the enclosures, &c. by Newsom, Thorphall, to Leeds: for the modern way by Kiddal Hall, where Mr. Ellis also receives an acknowledgment, and over Winmoor, that belongs to the Gascoignes, seems to be of late ages, &c.

June 4. Rode to York, but took Bishopthorp in the way; got in time enough to wait of my Lord Archbishop in his library before prayers, &c. Then had the Bishop of Ely's (good old Dr. Patrick's) company, and after a little my special friend, Bishop Nicholson, of Carlisle, (whose election was yesterday confirmed at York.) There was the vastest concourse of the clergy and gentry that ever I saw at once, that, besides the three tables in the dining-room, several were obliged to go into another room, &c. So tempting company made me stay the longer, yet business forced me to York, though my affectionate desires complied with Mr. Archdeacon Pearson's kind invitation to lodge at Bolton Percy with the Bishop, who is for London in the morning. Consulted the Chancellor and Mr. Empson about ditto administration. Evening, at the manor with the ingenious Mr. Place,* with whom, and Mr. Empson, at Montague Gyles's, to enquire after antiquities found in the Roman burying-place.   Received a remarkable account of a lead coffin, surrounded with one of oak planks two inches thick, found nine feet deep, the bones entire, (of which I have the lower jaw and a thigh bone,) though possibly a thousand and five hundred years old ; also fragments of the lead, wood, and nails, which are remarkable.

5. Read my Lord Archbishop's sermon at the coronation of the Queen (which his Grace gave me yesterday) before prayer ; then to visit worthy Mr. Gale, the late excellent Dean's son, and the very obliging Precentor, Dr. Fall, who kindly presented me with a pious treatise of the primitive Archbishop Leighton's, which himself published the last year, having a great veneration for that pious prelate's memory, who died about 1674.   His pious mother-in-law, Madam Leighton, was a benefactor to this parish, &c.   Then at Mr. Gyles's to see a noble window that he has painted most exquisitely for Denton-hall, my Lord Fairfax's.   After dinner again to consult Mr. Empson, with whom, in the Consistory Court at the trial, had the desired success, in what all seemed to apprehend reasonable as well as just.   Then for several hours engaged in the perusal of manuscripts in Mr. Empson's office, was particularly pleased, that after much seeking in

* One of the artists employed by Thoresby in his *Ducatus*. See Walpole and Granger.

Archbishop Thoresby's Register, temp. Edward III.
I found a record concerning that pious prelate's so
memorable exposition of the Lord's Prayer, Creed,
and Ten Commandments, in the English tongue,
which he required all the clergy in his diocese to
read unto their parishioners;* as also with a more
modern manuscript of the clergy's subscriptions;
whence I found the colleges where Mr. Wales, &c.
were educated, as well as the times of their taking
holy orders.   Afterwards visited good Mr. Hodgson,† (the charitable Lady Hewley's chaplain,) and
the obliging Sir John Middleton, who having found
the two original letters of King Henry VIII.'s writing,
which his father-in-law (the last heir male of the
ancient family of the Lamberts of Calton) promised
me, has laid them aside for my collection : had also
his ingenious chaplain Mr. Leach's company.   Evening sat up too late with a parcel of artists I had
got on my hands, Mr. Gyles, the famousest painter
of glass perhaps in the world, and his nephew, Mr.
Smith, the bell-founder (from whom I received the
ringing, or gingling spur, and that most remarkable
with a neck six inches and a half long;) Mr. Car-
penter, the statuary, and Mr. Etty, the painter, with
whose father, Mr. Etty, sen. the architect, the most
celebrated Grinlin Gibbons wrought at York, but
whether apprenticed with him or not I remember
not well.   Sate up full late with them.

* Thoresby afterwards committed this to the press.   It forms the
seventh article in the Appendix to the *Vicaria*.

† Timothy Hodgson, a son of Captain John Hodgson, a Parlia-
mentary officer, whose Memoirs were rinted at Edinbur h. in 1806.

6. In return, visited Dr. Barwick Fairfax at Newton, and Major Fairfax, who being upon a journey, prevented my designed quest about the Roman antiquities at Newton. Rode by the house there where Bishop Oglethorp, of Carlisle (who crowned Queen Elizabeth), was born. From Bramham-moor I rode in pursuit of the Roman highway, by Potterton, where it appears in one part of the lane for a considerable space, pointing directly to Berwick ; through mistake of the way, I went to Beckay Grange, which seems to have been a considerable place ; where the remains of the hall stands, deep trenches ; and I was told by an intelligent person I met with, that there is another ridge very visible in some parts of Beckay grounds, which comes directly from the great ridge at or about Aberford, westward towards Potterton, &c. but could not come at it on horseback : at Berwick, inquiring after the ruins or rubbish that Camden mentions, whence he supposes that the town was walled round, I was directed to a most remarkable agger on the north side of the town, partly opposite to the hall-tower-hill, till divided from it by the road into the town from Leeds, and this doubtless is the Windle-hill. I left my horse and clambered to the top of it ; it is to this day so high and steep on either side that I was almost afraid to walk it in my boots, &c. yet walked upon the top of it about three hundred paces, till interrupted by cross hedges at one end and buildings at the other, where it enters upon the town, but was never designed as a wall to it, for it

terminates at the nearer end of it, but seems to have
turned towards the Hall-tower-hill.   By so much of
it as I could then trace under so great inconveniences, shows it plainly to have been circular ; and if it
has not received its denomination from panȝ, (wang-
hill) *campus, ager,* I should think it so called from its
turning, Wenðel hıl as Wenðel ɼæ (the Mediterranean
Sea)—(it is called Wendel-hill to this day)—from
penðan *vertere,* whence to wind or turn is continued
to this age, in the same notion.   From Berwick I
rode by Barnbow-hall, forte à Beapn, *Primus, Princeps,*
(Noe sic dictus,) the seat of a very ancient family
of the Gascoignes.   Sir Thomas was there now, but
I could find nothing of the Roman rig amongst the
inclosures, till I came to Whitkirk-moor, where
upon that part commonly called Brown-moor, it is
very apparent quite across the whole moor ; it seems
to come from Berwick and Barnbow, by Marston to
this moor, and thence directly in a line in the enclosures, where in some places it is visible without
alighting from the horse, till we come at Swillington-
moor, but whether it turn thence by the top of
Newsom-green by the bank close, or go quite over
that moor where I traced a ridge to Bullay-grange,
and so go down to the bottom of Newsom-green, I
know not; but in endeavouring to find this, had
almost lost myself.   After a visit to brother Hough's,
at Newsom-green, in the fields below which I have
traced the ridge on foot, I returned by Pontefract-
lane.

12. Got to York in due time and without inconvenience, though much rain in the night; was with Mr. Empson, &c. about administration; and then with the Chancellor, Dr. Watkinson, about ditto. Afterwards, at my Lord Archbishop's Register-office, transcribing part of Archbishop Thoresby's serious Treatise in old English, to oblige the clergy to instruct their parochians in English. Afterwards visited Dr. Cotton and Mr. Hodgson.

. 13. Walking in the minster till the office was opened; when busied again in transcribing what I could of ditto excellent MS. out of the original Register, till past twelve. After dinner returned by Tadcaster, and finding the minister by the old mount, at the town-end, discoursed him relating to their antiquities; he showed me the place, now at the far end of a large field, that yet retains the name of Kel Bar, whither they suppose their old Calcaria reached, one part of which field is so impregnated with the lime, that it brings forth excellent corn without manuring. They have a tradition of Todcastle standing upon ditto hill.

16. With W. P. and another Quaker about business, found, under a pretence of a holy simplicity, downright treachery, was tricked out of two guineas. Lord, pardon them! Sent for by Mr. Arthington, of Arthington (lately admitted into the list of the Royal Society), who gave me the inscription upon a Roman monument lately discovered upon Adle Moor, where the continuation of the Roman

via vicinalis that I discovered at Haw-caster-rig, upon Black-moor is visible, and they apprehend tends to Ilkley.

17. Writ to Dr. Sloane, Sec. Royal Society.

18. At Mr. B.'s with Esquire Hutton, of Popple-ton ; then at the christening of Mr. Mawd's son ; had the vicar's, and rest of the clergy's good company, but all melancholy at the news of the dangerous illness and yet more dangerous hardness of a certain lord, to whom good Mr. Thornton, after he had made his will, most piously and affectionately minded him of eternity, desiring that Mr. Killingbeck might be permitted to attend his lordship, to which the pite-ous reply was, Mr. K. was a good man, but he was not weak enough for that, and since when he has had little sense of any thing.   Lord, in much mercy, open blind eyes!   Some other piteous cir-cumstances of a past life and approaching death made me tremble.

19. Drawing the figure of an ancient and very odd spur for Dr. Woodward, to transmit to Mon. Sperlingus, who is writing a tract *de armis veterum.*

20. Writ to Dr. Woodward, at Gresham College ; evening, transcribing the pedigree of the Lord Ir-wins from Mr. Hopkinson's MS.

24. To three clergymen (Mr. Robinson, &c.) procured their attestations for brother Idle, to be transmitted to Sir J. Levison Gower, Chancellor of the Duchy.   Afternoon, rode with Mr. Barstow to

visit my dear friend, Mr. Kirk, at Cookridge, to see his curiosities bought lately at London.

25. Rode to the Spas at Harrowgate, to visit and consult dear Mr. Thornton, with whom, and Mr. Dwyer and Mr. Denison, spent rest of day and evening, upon the forest; which, although now not a tree scarce for a way mark, did of old so abound in wood, that it was so called from the Saxon heaꝑȝ, or hæꝑȝ, *lucus;* yet, for want of such a guide, and what the excessive rain and hail, which almost blinded me, I missed the way, and got cold. The place itself is so altered with new buildings, from what it was when I knew it formerly, that it helped to deceive me.

26. Rode through Knaresborough, Flasby, and Allerton Maleverer, over Marston, or Hessay Moor, (where the bloody battle was fought in the late unhappy wars,) through Akeham to York. Went immediately to Mr. Empson, and with him to the Chancellor, to certify him of the falsehood of the opponent's allegations; then transcribing ditto the memorable old English paraphrase of Archbishop Thoresby's, of the Creed, Lord's Prayer, Commands, &c., which that pious prelate's zeal to rescue poor creatures from the predominant ignorance of that dark age, enjoined the clergy to read through his province. Writing ditto from the original record till two, then at the Court, succeeded in what I apprehend equitable and highly reason-

able, as well as legal. Evening, visited Mr. Hodgson, the good old Lady Hewley's chaplain, who has now actually endowed her lately-erected hospital with 60*l.* per annum, for ten widows.

27. Rode to Bishopthorp; dined with his Grace, who would have presented me with a Coronation medal, which I thankfully refused, having one before. Returned well home; though thunder and rain on every side, got little of it, blessed be God!

July 8. Drinking our Leeds Spa waters; after sent for by Mr. S. Hickson, whose wife, (the late Dr. Neal's relict,) lay a dying, but very sensible; persuaded her to make her will, which, with other writings to settle her concerns, prevented me both forenoon and afternoon of attending the public prayers, as also of Mr. Kirk's company, who sent for me about business, as he went to the funeral of the late Lord Irwin. Rest of the day transcribing MS. pedigrees.

11. Drinking the waters; after at the funeral of Mrs. Hickson.

17. Received a kind visit from Mr. Smith,* the pious author of the True Notion of Imputed Righteousness and our Justification thereby, to whom showing books, &c., but unhappily prevented, as frequently this week, of attendance upon the public prayers. Lord, pity and pardon!

* Matthew Smith, a Nonconforming minister, in the neighbourhood of Halifax and Bradford.

21. At the Spas; after rode to York, with vast numbers to the election of Knights of the Shire for the ensuing Parliament; waited of my Lord Fairfax and Sir John Kaye: afterwards sent for, with Mr. Kirk, by some ingenious gentlemen, Sir Godfrey Copley, Mr. Molesworth, (who wrote the State of Denmark,) Mr. Arthington, and Mr. Kirk; one of company observed, that being but five in company, all were Fellows of the Royal Society; might have added all that were in the county, and of it, except Dr. Lister and Dr. Bentley, who are in the south. Was afterwards with my Lord Fairfax, Sir Walter Hawksworth, and some members of Parliament, till pretty late. Had Mr. Fenton's company.

22. At the Castle-yard, where was a general discontent visible in the countenances and expressions of all persons at my Lord Fairfax's declining, as being too late in his applications; came but into Yorkshire on Saturday last, though people generally apprehended, if he had but appeared this morning, he would have been one. I was again with several gentlemen to wait of him, but, upon his resolution to desist, the Marquis of Hartington and Sir John Kaye were elected.

28. With Mr. Fenton, from whom, and a person that gathered it, received a parcel of the reputed wheat that was rained on Lord's day last, betwixt Hunslet and Middleton, but 'tis rather seeds of ivy-berries, or other plants.

31. At the Spas; ended Bishop Patrick's Friendly

Debate, wherein are some things jocose, **and** some censured as severe, but many solid arguments against separation.

August 3. Begun the answer to the Friendly Debate, called, The Humble Apology ; concluded Mr. Gibson's, Bishop of Lincoln, Synodus Anglicana, a most curious and excellent treatise ; the ingenious and industrious author's present, who, from the registers and journals printed from the original MSS. draws so pertinent and judicious observations, as I hope will put an end to the controversy betwixt the Upper and Lower Houses of Convocation. Afternoon, with the Lords of the Manor for fee-farm-rents ; prevented thereby of public prayer. Evening, with nephew Wilson, and Mr. Witton, of Gray's Inn ; and after to visit Alderman Milner indisposed : the doctor was apprehensive of a fever.

8. Writing to Dr. Cay. Getting in hay, which came so unhappily as to prevent attendance on public prayer. Evening, concluded the Humble Apology for the Nonconformists, wherein are some too severe reflections upon the Bishops and Conformity itself ; but there are also some modest and healing concessions ; and if that proposition, p. 131, could be made good, that for laying aside the ceremonies, the Church might gain thousands and ten thousands of our brethren, I should rejoice to see that happy day : with this proviso, that as the observance of them should not be imposed upon some, so neither denied to others who could not be satisfied in the omission :

and to my own particular case, as I should have
some ease thereby, as to the cross in baptism (which
though I think lawful, yet had rather omit) and taking charge of my own child in that ordinance, either
singly or jointly with some conscientious friend who
would assist me, and after my death look upon themselves as obliged in conscience to see to the education
of the orphan ; so on the other hand, as I should not
omit the monthly celebration of the Lord's Supper, so
neither the usual gesture, the Church declaring so
fully against the abuse of it, nor should I ever, I
hope, as long as I am able to walk, so far forbear a
constant attendance upon the public common prayers twice every day, in which course I have found
much comfort and advantage, and do from my very
heart bless God for those happy opportunities, the
loss of which is almost the sole reason that keeps me
from a solitary recess into the country, for a greater
freedom in study and meditation. But an All-wise
God has determined the bounds of our habitations,
who knows better what is good for us than we do
for ourselves. Blessed be his name for all mercies !

12. Visited by Mr. Midgley, of Brearey, and some
other mathematicians from the country, desirous to
see collections. Received a kind visit from Mr.
Brearey, Fellow of Jesus College, Cambridge, and
Lawyer Foster, to whom showing library and MSS.

13. Walked over the Black-moor ; had Haw-caster-rig and Tuninghal (or hough, rather) hill, on the
left hand, and Moor-Allerton, and the Street-lane on

the right; to Allingley, (in old writings, Alwoodley),
whence Mr. Midgley walked with us to Eccup Moor
and Adle, to direct to the place where the heaps of
ruins were lately discovered.   After a transient view
went to the mill below; discoursed John Robinson,
an intelligent person, who having occasion to plough
a parcel of ground he had leased of Cyril Arthington, of Arthington, Esq. lord of the soil, was the
happy occasion of this discovery of a Roman town,
which by the ruins seems to have been very considerable; they have got up so many stones, though they
have dug no deeper than necessity obliged to make
way for the plough, that they have already built
therewith two walls, one a yard high and twenty
seven rood long, the other a yard and a half high
and fifty-two rood long; these are rough stones
the foundations of houses, many of which were three
or four courses high, undemolished, being under the
surface of the ground. We took as particular a view
as the present circumstances will admit of, and found
fragments of urns of a very large size; but what is
most remarkable, are the remains of two funeral monuments, one has PIENTISSIMA, very legible; another a larger inscription, D.M.S. CADIDINIÆ FOR-
TVNA PIA V.A.X. (vixit annos x.)* I returned by
Adle to see the head, which is all that remains of a
noble statue the full proportion of a man : discoursed
the old man who digged it up some years ago, as also
a stone with an inscription, which I could not retrieve,

* These remains are engraved in the *Ducatus,* p. 162.

but hope to have these brought hither in carts the next week, with one of the little mill-stones found also amongst the ruins not far off. I viewed a Roman camp which is yet very entire : there is another somewhat less upon the said moor, and a third upon Bramhope moor, which I had not time now to survey, it turning to rain, that we were severely wet ere we reached home, but putting on warm and dry apparel, got no harm, blessed be God !

14. Consulting Burton's Comment upon Antoninus's Itinerary, where, if Selegocim, or Agelocim, as it is elsewhere writ, had been the station on this side Danum, I should have concluded this had been the place, and should have read it as Camden himself once did, (when he made that station at Idleton,) Adellocum (the ancient name is Adel in the Monastic. p. 857,) much of which old name is yet retained in the present name of Adle, or Adel ; and this very author refers, p. 247, to a transposition of two stations, Nidum before Bomium ; and why may not Danum be misplaced before Adelocum ? or why might there not be two several Adelocums, as our late learned Dean of York, Dr. Gale, (whose assistance I greatly want in this matter,) apprehended from the Roman altar in my possession, that there were two Condates : this Adelocum, or what other station soever it has been, seems, by the blackness of the earth, and remaining burnt coals and cinders, to have been burnt down by the Brigantes, in some of their revolts from the Romans, perhaps in Ha-

drian's time, when Julius Severus was called out of Britain, where he was President, to go against the Jews, who then also rebelled. Was ruminating and searching authors about these matters, till ten at church.

16. Read Bishop Usher of Self-Examination, wherein, through mercy somewhat affected, being concerned (though, alas! infinitely short of what I ought,) for the mispence of my life hitherto, having this day completed forty-four years: alas! that I have lived so long, and done so little to any good purpose; Lord, pardon by past sins, and in much mercy, give me power against them for the future, that the little yet remaining may be spent after a more holy and exemplary manner, that I may be more useful in my generation!

19. Ended Bishop Patrick's Appendix, in defence of himself, wherein are many things instructive, particularly as to the *Chor-Episcopi* and Suffragan Bishops, as well as some things reputed sharp. Lord, heal our piteous breaches! Then writing to Mr. Evelyn.

20. Received a visit from the Lord Irwin and his tutor, Mr. Ingram, of Barrowby, to whom showing the collections of coins and natural curiosities.

21. Writing a little, till sent for by Mr. Kirk, who being for Temple Newsom, I took that opportunity to wait of my Lord Irwin, and Mr. Machel, (a noted member of Parliament,) his grandfather. After dinner, to view the hall and gardens; some

pictures in the gallery are considerable, particularly St. Francis, said to be worth 300*l*.

25. Walked to Mr. Kirk's, but prevented of surveying the Roman camp at Adle, by the coming in of Mr. Arthington and other gentlemen; so that I accepted of my Lord Irwin's kindness, and came home with him and Mr. Machel in the coach.

29. About poor ministers' concerns; then showing collections to Mr. Hotham, &c. After, preparing for a journey. Lord, grant thy gracious presence, protect thy poor unworthy servant from sin, the greatest of all evils, and from the calamities that might justly befal me for sin, and preserve thy handmaid and the poor children thou hast entrusted us with, and the poor orphans thy Providence has committed to our charge;* charge thy good angels with all of us, and whatever appertains unto us, for thy mercy's sake! My kind friend, Mr. Kirk, having sent his man and horses for me, I rode thither in the evening, and enjoyed his acceptable converse; was looking amongst his books, &c.

30. Rode with Mr. Kirk and family to their parish church at Adle. Afterwards rode with this good company to Arthington Hall, and thence after dinner again to Adle church. After prayers at the parsonage-house, with ditto good company, attesting the writings about his induction, &c. Evening, returned to Cookridge.

---

* These were the children of his brother, Jeremiah Thoresby, who died in the early part of this year, leaving a family wholly unprovided for.

31. Began our tour from Cookridge, which I am
apt to think received its denomination from the
Roman rig or ridge, which passeth by it in its course
from Blackmoor, in the parish of Leeds, Alwoodley,
and the lately discovered town and camp near Adle-
mill to Olicana, &c. *Mon cher ami*, Mr. Kirk, rode
with me to several places in his grounds there where
it is not only visible, but points directly to the said
camp. Further on, upon Bramhope-moor, in the
place now called Stadtfolds, we saw another large
camp, but this has a double agger, though by its
squareness and the leading of the via vicinalis thereunto, it seems also to have been Roman ; here also
we saw the nameless head of our Sheepscar beck;
upon which, in so small a distance, are seven or eight
mills before it joins with the river Aire at Leeds.
Thence we rode to the highest point of the Cheven
(in British, the ridge of the mountain, as Camden
tells us) ; had a large and noble prospect of Wharf-
(vulgo Wharl)-dale, *viz.* of Mensington or Menston,
(the seat of my honoured friend Thomas Fairfax,
Esq. now of Leeds, for the convenience of the church,
which he duly and piously frequents with his lady
twice every day :) his father, Mr. Charles Fairfax,
third son, who survived the first Thomas Lord Fairfax (for his two famous brothers, captain William
and John Fairfax, were slain in the Palatinate) was
an eminent antiquary, wrote Analecta Fairfaxiana,
&c. and the first of Menston : Burley-wood-head
and the lordship thereof, the seat of Mr. Pullen :
Ilkley, (the Roman Olicana,) Middleton-lodge, Beth-

mesley-beacon, and Nessefield-scar, all three belonging to the ancient family of the Middletons of
Stockeld, which is within the constablery of Middleton, though near a dozen miles distant : the manor
of Denton and Askwith, both which appertain to
the Right Honourable Thomas Lord Fairfax, of
Denton-hall, a strong and stately building, as is
also Weston, the seat of — — Vavasour, Esq.; Newhall, of Mr. Hardisty ; Farnley, the pleasant seat
of Thomas Fawkes, Esq. my dearest father's friend
and mine ; his son, Mr. Francis Fawkes, is also
ingenious and obliging : between Farnley and
Leethley, Washburn falls into Wharfa. Leethley
is the seat of Mr. Hitch, whose grandfather was
Dean of York ; Lindley, of the noted member
of Parliament, William Palmes, Esq. my father's
special friend, and yet living in the south, to
whom also appertains Stainburn. The next thing
in view are the two famous crags of Ames-
cliff, in some old writings called Aylmoys *ut dici-*
tur, but have yet seen nothing memorable of it,
saving its remarkable lofty situation ; Rigton, the
possession of the Duchess of Buckingham, but in
reversion my Lord Fairfax's ; Casley, where Mr.
Robert Dyneley, the second son of my late good old
friend Robert Dyneley, Esq. has built a seat : Weeton, Dunkesswick, Weerdley, the Manor of Harwood,
its ancient castle and church, all appertain to my
honoured and kind friend John Boulter, Esq. of
Gawthorp-hall, who has brought me several curiosities from beyond the sea, and (which will make him

justly famous in succeeding ages) has given 50*l.* per
annum to the church at Harwood, and 10*l.* or
12*l.* to the school, &c.: Kirkby-overblows to the
Duke of Somerset, who is patron of the living, worth
350*l.* per annum (as also of Spawforth, worth 400*l.*
or near 500l. per annum) and Lord of both the
manors: Swinden-hall to the Bethels, of which
family Dr. Bethel and the late Sheriff of London,
Slingsby Bethel, author of a Treatise called . . . . . .
Had also a view of the noble edifice at Arthington
built by the ingenious Cyril Arthington, Esq. F.R.S.
Lord of the manors of Arthington, Adle, &c. to the
reputed value of 2200l. per annum. Bramhope, of
John Dyneley, Esq. whose famous grandfather built
and endowed the chapel there: Poole to Madam
Thornhill; Caley-hall, to Mr. Benjamin Atkinson of
Leeds; and Cookridge to my honoured and dear
friend Thomas Kirk, Esq. F.R.S. whose wood there
has the most noble and curious walks, containing
above three hundred views, that ever I beheld. I
had almost forgot what is most in view of all the
places, being just at the foot of the Cheven, *viz.* the
market town of Otley, which belongs to my Lord
Archbishop of York, who has power to appoint
Justices of the Peace for that Liberty, which also
comprehends the whole parish of Otley, Cawood,
and Wistow. From this top of Cheven, where we
had this noble prospect, we descended to Guiseley,
a country vill, but valuable living, worth 300*l.* per
annum, but the presentation now controverted be-

tween Sir Nicholas Sherburn (a Popish recusant)
and Trinity College, Mr. Hitch and Dean of York.
Upon the church steeple is a monument for John
Myers, the memorable parish-clerk there for fifty-
four years, yet was quite outdone by the good old
Mr. Moore, who was minister there sixty-three years.
Thence, leaving on the left hand Esholt, (perhaps from
Ash and Holt, wood) formerly a nunnery, now one
of the seats of Walter Calverley, of Calverley, Esq.
a worthy gentleman, and honour to that very ancient
famliy, we came to Hawksworth, where we dined
with the ingenious Sir Walter Hawksworth, who is
making pleasant alterations and additions to that
ancient seat and gardens, &c.; he entertained us
agreeably with Roman histories, &c. wherein he is
well versed, and accompanied us several miles in his
own demesnes; *inter alia*, he showed us a monumental heap of stones, in memory of three Scotch boys
slain there by lightning, in his grandfather's, Sir
Richard Hawksworth's time, as an old man attested
to Sir Walter, who being then twelve years of age
helped to lead the stones.   We left Baildon on the
left hand, anciently the seat of a family of that
name, now of Mr. Thompson of Marston, who married the heiress of that accomplished gentleman,
Bradwardine Tindal, of Brotherton, Esq.   We rode
through part of the populous parish of Bingley, in
which are the seats of Mr. Benson of Wrenthorp,
near Wakefield, who is also Lord of the manor of
Bingley; Mr. Farrand, a Justice of Peace; Rish-

worth of Mr. . . . . . . Thence through Morton
to Ridlesden, the seat of Mr. Edmund Starkie,
where we parted with the pleasant and populous
Wapentake of Skireake, and having passed the river
Aire, we entered upon Staincliffe and lodged at
Kighley, anciently the seat of a famous family of
the same name, of whom Sir Henry Kighley lies
buried in the church, but the date of his death not
legible; one of the heiresses was married to the
Lord Cavendish; and the Duke of Devonshire is the
patron of the living, reputed worth 150*l.* per annum.
We lodged with the modest good parson Mr. Gale,
who has made some curious mathematical instruments, and drawn some good figures with Indian
ink, being an ingenious and obliging person.

Sept. 1. Retired, but alas! too frequently prevented in the evenings for want of convenient privacy upon journeys. Had good Mr. Gale's company
about two miles; he showed us a free school lately
erected by . . . . of Kighley, now living, who will
settle the whole of his estate upon it at death. We
rode about five miles over the hills in Kighley parish,
till we entered Lancashire, at a heap of stones as
a boundary; having, on the left hand, Haworth, a
church or chapel within the vicarage of Bradford,
though at so great a distance as the skirts of Lancashire; where nothing appears for many miles but
hills and rivulets descending to the dales; and here
it was observable that in a very small distance, the
heads of rivers and springs we passed at the height

of this mountainous tract parted to the two contrary
seas, some to the East, others to the West Sea.
Upon the height of the mountain stands Camil Cross,
which we left upon the right hand, designing for
Burnley; but after we had left the lime-kilns below, and ascended a steep and dangerous precipice,
the road dwindled away upon an ugly boggy mountain, where we wandered in sight of distant houses,
to which we could find no road. At length, through
the enclosures, having come at one, we were surprised to find that, though a large house and substantial people, (bringing us a large silver tankard of
ale) yet had no horse-road to the market town; but
pulling down part of a dry wall, we passed through
his and his neighbour's grounds till we recovered a
blind lane, and rode through a continued thicket,
several times passing the beck, till at length we met
a more open road. We had a view of Emmet, a
handsome seat lately sold by a gentleman of that
sirname, near to the market town of Coln, which I
am apt to think was a Roman station, and very probably their Colunium, as Mr. Hargraves has it from
a curious itinerary of our late learned Dean Gale's,
and Dr. Leigh's objections are not convincing to me.
I was at a loss for Mr. Blakey, (who married my old
friend Mr. Brearcliffe's daughter) who were enquiring
for me at Leeds, when I was for them at Coln; but
Mr. Tatham, the minister, gave me satisfaction in
many things. I transcribed some old inscriptions in
the church, and first observed a large cross of five

deep steps round it in the church-yard; where I.H.S.
with crosses are upon several modern grave-stones.
But I was best pleased with his account of Caster
Cliff, about a mile from Coln, where is a regular
camp visible to this day, and the " Caster" is a sufficient evidence of its Roman antiquity. After dinner, we rode through Burnley, where was another
cross in the church-yard, but with the addition of a
new stately cross erected above the steps. We were
now near what we had seen in Yorkshire, Pendle
Hill, one of the most eminent hills in our Appenine,
but we had the favour to see it without its cloudy
cap, so that we had a clear prospect of Houghton
Tower near Preston; but we stayed not at Burnley, hastening to Townley, where we were very
kindly received by that famous mathematician and
eminent virtuoso, Richard Townley, Esq. and his brother Charles, (the Governor) my old correspondent;
had also the converse of Mr. Trafford, of Trafford,
Dr. Prescot, &c.

2. Then viewing the mathematical curiosities of
Mr. Townley, particularly that for observing the
quantity of rain that falls there, having thoughts of
doing the like at home, but am discouraged with the
charge and tediousness: the chariot of his own contrivance, to pass over those mountainous tracts of
stones, &c. is very curious; as also a dial in the
garden, where are also great plenty of very fine firs,
which they have learnt to propagate by slips; he
showed us also Mr. Adams's curious instrument, a

vast large brass quadrant, that he used when he surveyed England and made his curious map.   But I
was best pleased with the collection of original letters that passed through Mr. Christopher Townley,
the antiquary's contrivance, between Mr. Gascoigne,
of Yorkshire, and Mr. Crabtree and Mr. Horrax of
Lancashire, whereby it plainly appears that the said
Mr. Gascoigne, in the reign of King Charles I. was
the first and genuine author of the invention of
dividing a foot into many thousand parts for mathematical purposes, which Monsieur Auzout values
himself as the supposed first inventor of in the present age.*   We saw also some ancient manuscripts
in his library, and several curious modern prints, &c.
he bought in his travels at Rome, &c, : but could
not find the old writings of the Abbots of Kirkstal,
nor procure King James II.'s coronation medal.   Mr.
Charles Townley showed me some curiosities in his
apartment, and presented me with a MS. catalogue
of the Irish nobility, with their arms in colours, &c.
The rest of the day was spent there (after we had
viewed the new apartments in this college, or castle-
like house,) in converse with the three brothers,
Mr. Trafford, and other strangers, in the garden-
house, in the midst of the fish-pond in the garden,
except that I stole a little time to peep into some

* Crabtree, and Horrax or Horrocks who died when he had advanced only one or two steps in what would have been a brilliant
career, are names known to the history of mathematical science. Less
is known of Gascoigne, for whom see the Correspondence.

volumes of Mr. Christopher Townley's, MSS. of
pedigrees, whence I transcribed that of the Lang-
tons. Mr. Townley's own pedigree upon skins of
parchment, with the matches, &c. blazoned, and the
old short deeds inserted, is most noble and curious,
and attested by the King-of-Arms, being drawn from
original writings, &c.; and was proposed as an ex-
emplar by Dr. Cuerden, in his designed Brigantia
Lancastriensis, which is feared will now perish by
the author's death.*

3. Having taken leave of the obliging and ingenious family at Townley, we returned by Burnley,
and thence, in our way to Padjam or Padingham,
we had a distant prospect of Hapton Tower, which
stands melancholy upon the mountains on the right-
hand, and Townley Royal on the left. We stepped
aside to see the Lady Shuttleworth's turretted house
at Gawthorp. Thence by Altham church, to which
only one house in view, though more afterwards at
a distance, through Dunkenhalgh, which has nothing
remarkable but the hall of Mr. Walmesley, which
seems considerable, but like most seats of the gentry
in these parts, has so many out-buildings before it,
as spoils the prospect. Thence to Blackburn, a market-town, which gives name to the whole hundred,
the third of the six in Lancashire ; here, while the

* Dr. Cuerden made very considerable collections for this work.
One large volume, full of very useful information, but like gold in the
mine, is in the library of Chetham College at Manchester. Other
portions of his collections are said to be in the library of the Heralds'
College.

dinner was preparing, we viewed the church and town, but found nothing remarkable as to the modern state: of old, William the Conqueror gave Black-burnshire to the Ilbert de Lacy, grandfather to Henry Lacy, who built Kirkstal Abbey, anno 1159. Thence by Houghton-tower, which gives name and habitation to an eminent and ancient family; Sir Charles Houghton is the present possessor; its situation is remarkable, being upon a very steep hill, almost a precipice on three sides, and so high that it is seen at many miles distance.   Then through Walton, which seems to have been a Roman station, and where we are told the noted Kelly* was born, but is now chiefly famous for the manufacture of linencloth: we saw vast quantities of yarn whiting.   In the vale we saw another good house that belongs to a younger branch of the family of Houghton Tower. We passed the river Ribble (which rises in the Yorkshire hills) to Preston, which was now extremely crowded with the gentry as well as commonalty, from all parts to the Jubilee, as we call it, but more rightly the Guild: we were too late to see the formalities, (the several companies in their order, attending the Mayor, &c. to church; and thence after sermon, to the Guild-house, to the feast, &c.) at the opening of the Guild, but were in time enough for

---

* Kelly was one of the Alchemical Philosophers, a friend of Dr. John Dee. Wood says, that he was born at Worcester. His name is, however, connected with Walton and Lawchurch, by some very extraordinary proceedings there, of which an account may be seen in Weever's *Funeral Monuments*, p. 45.

the appendices, the pageant, &c. at the bringing in
the harvest, ushered in by two gladiators in armour,
on horseback, &c.   The Queen discharged her part
well, but the King was too effeminate.   I was best
pleased with a good providence that attended a
fellow clad with bears' skins, &c., who running
amongst the mob in the Low-street, by the church-
yard, happily chased them away just before the wall
fell, whereby their lives were saved.   Had afterwards the company of several Yorkshire and Lancashire justices, with whom went to see the posture-
master, who not only performed several uncommon
feats of activity, but put his body instantly into so
strange and mis-shapen postures, as are scarce credible, &c.   Disturbed with the music, &c., that got
little rest till three in the morning.

4. Morning, retired, &c.; then walked with my
dear friend, Mr. Kirk, to view the town, wherein are
several very good houses, but none so stately as that
where the Duke of Hamilton usually resides, who is
now abroad; but there was one Mr. Hyde, a very
proper gentleman, said to be the Queen's cousin.
We after went to the top of an adjoining hill, where
we had a distant prospect of the sea; but the chan-
nel up to the town is broad and shallow, that they
have little commerce that way, and no merchants or
manufacture, the town chiefly depending upon the
quill; here being kept all the Courts relating to the
County Palatine of Lancaster, as the Court of Chancery.   We went to the Town-hall, where the Mayor

showed us their book of privileges, and transcript of their charters for the Guild, (and inspeximus's), as old as Henry I. as I remember. They made us a compliment of our freedom, but we thought our-selves more free without it. An alderman attended us to the Guild-house, where we were treated at a banquet and choice wines.

We then walked to the fields to an eminency lately purchased by the town, where is a very curious walk and delicate prospect; then went to view the church, but found no inscriptions either for the family of the Houghtons (though Sir Richard was buried there,) nor good Mr. Isaac Ambrose. Dined at Lawyer Starkey's with Justice Parker, and much good company. Afterwards at tavern involved in more; to avoid inconveniences, Mr. Kirk and I went with the ladies to a play; which I thought a dull, insipid thing, though the actors from London pre-tended to something extraordinary, but I was the better pleased to meet with no temptation there.

5. Morning, rose by five, having got little rest; the music and Lancashire bag-pipes having con-tinued the whole night at it, were now enquiring for beds. From Preston we rode through some country villages in Anderness, or Amounderness, to Rib-chester, to view the antiquities of that ancient Roman station; had the kind assistance of Mr. Hargraves, the minister, who, having showed us the church and adjoining library over the porch, lately given by Mr. Hayhurst of that town; went with me

to the adjoining Anchor-hill, where are frequently
found nails and rings belonging to boats to pass the
adjacent river Ribble; we then went to the shore,
picked up some fragments of urns, &c. there; found
CAES upon the pillar Dr. Leigh mentions as without
inscription; found another inscription in the wall of
a house, which the Dr. supposes an altar to Caligula
(because he found CA upon it, which is only part
of CAE for Cæsar,) but I conclude to have been
a funeral monument; for though the inscription
is imperfect, and we also differ in the reading, yet
both have VIX upon it. I brought thence one of
the iron nails and fragments of different coloured
urns, one of a whiter clay than ever I had seen any,
and tiles, with scores or lines upon them, different
from what I had before; the place seems to have
been eminent amongst the Christian Saxons; a chapel, now one of the side isles of the church, has a
place for a bell to hang in it, quite distinct from
the modern belfry; fragments of Roman vessels are
found even in the churchyard, which was probably
a camp or place for devotion or sacrifice. Langrig,
Langridge Chapel, &c. in these parts, seem to have
been denominated from their situation near the
Roman road. Upon Anchor-hill we had a prospect
of Osbaldston, the seat of an ancient family of that
name, the present heir thereof, with other Lancashire gentlemen, justices, parliament-men, &c. I
had the names of in my travelling album at Preston,
which beautiful town is said to have risen out of the

ruins of Ribchester. Upon the road we had a distant prospect of Browsholm, the seat of Justice
Parker, who was very obliging at the Guild ; gave
us a letter of recommendation to Ribchester ; and
rode close by Sir Nicholas Sherburn's pleasant seat
at Stonyhurst, which is deservedly esteemed one of
the best houses in Lancashire. I was extremely
desirous to have called to see the Roman coins (of
which he has a vast quantity) lately found within
his territories at Chippin, but there were some
reasons to believe we should not be grateful to him,
who is reputed a stiff Papist, and Mr. Kirk setting
out a militia horse for him. We passed by Mitton,
seated near the confluence of Ribble and Holder,
which belongs to our countryman, Sir Walter
Hawksworth, of Hawksworth, through Clithero ;
had a view of the ancient castle built by the Lacys,
of which very little is now remaining, but had not
time to see the church, though desirous for Dr.
Webster's sake, who has a very odd epitaph there ;
besides his Display of Witchcraft, he published
Metallographia (dedicated to Prince Rupert), Ex-
amen Academiarum, several sermons preached at
Alhallows, Lombard-street, and a little piece called
his Saints' Guide, as informed by a minister who
married his widow. We had a distant prospect of
Waddington, where Mr. Parker, of Carlton, has
erected an hospital; and of Waddaw, a very pleasant seat (with some walks in the wood) of the late
Mr. Wilkinson, now of Mr. Weddell, of Bradford or

London.   It was almost dark before we reached
Downham, so that I could procure none of the
diamonds there found; and now, having happily
attained Old Yorkshire, I resigned my government
to my fellow-traveller, who is now to have it with a
continuendo, not as this afternoon, for a few hours as
we passed in and out the indented skirts of the two
counties; but this joy was somewhat allayed with
the dark evening, in which it was uncomfortable
travelling the Craven hills; but having reached
Newbiggin, we met with a very kind reception from
Mr. Lister (my cousin Lodge, the ingenious artist's
nephew) and his Lady, the third of the three sisters,
Mrs. Parker, of Browsholm, and our neighbour, Mrs.
Ashton, being the other two, all discreet and aecom-
plished gentlewomen.*

6. Die Dom.   Left this pleasant seat, and rode to
church at Carlton: in our way we passed through
Gisburn, where nothing worthy notice but Justice
Marsden's house, whose co-heiresses are married to
Colonel Pudsey, Parliament man for Clithero, and
late High Sheriff of the county, and to Mr. ——.
Thence, through Marstons ambo and Broughton to
Carlton, just as ringing in.   The minister made a
very good sermon, though almost half of it Latin
sentences; but I was more than ordinarily affected
with the prayers, blessed be God! found my heart
enlarged in his service, and concerned that any part
of his day should be spent in travel, but besides my

* Daughters of John Parker, of Extwisle, Esq.

too strong desires to be at home, for fear my dear
or children should not be well, I thought there
was less danger therein than in the excessive kindness, &c. (manifested by too great plenty of wine,
&c.) of our hospitable friend. We dined at good
Mr. Parker's, who has erected an hospital at Waddington, in Yorkshire, for ten widows, and a chaplain to read prayers to them forenoon and after,
and endowed it already with 50*l.* per annum, which,
he told me, he designs to increase the salary of at
his death: they have already received 50*l.* per annum for several years, agreeable to his motto in my
album, " *bis dat qui cito dat.*"   After dinner, we saw
a few of his curiosities, particularly the pedigree of
King James from Adam, with the pretended coats
of arms; and a large silver seal, for the approbation of
ministers in the late times; but the key of his cabinet of coins (formerly Mr. Brearcliffe's, of Halifax)
could not be found.   Afternoon, we rode through
the skirts of Skipton, over Rumbals Moor, where we
had a fair prospect of Skipton, with the church,
castle, and park, (belonging to the Earl of Thanet,)
which has several pleasant walks in it; upon the
heights we had a distinct prospect of Bolton Abbey,
Bethmesley, &c.   We left Wingate Nick, whence
we have our largest millstones, on the right hand,
as also Rough Robbins, (though his name is Will.)
who would be thought a noted astrologer; but, I
believe, by my friend's account of him, is no con-
jurer.   I passed Long Addingham patiently enough,

but was concerned that I had not a convenient time
to view the antiquities of the Roman Olicana; the
nymph Verbeia was so surly, we durst not pass her
without the help of the bridge, that we had a great
deal of rough way along her banks, which made us
late ere we reached Denton Hall, but were kindly
received by my Lord Fairfax and his good family;
and I was glad to observe the continuance of so religious an order in the family, all the servants, &c.
being called in to daily prayers.

7. Morning, retired, &c. then viewing the house
(wherein my Lord is making several alterations,
which are both noble and convenient) and gardens,
the hawks, horses, brood-mares, and foals, (for four
of which 80*l.* has been refused;) but I was best
pleased in the old library, for which my Lord is preparing a new place, &c.   My Lord very kindly bestowed upon me an original letter of Prince Rupert's,
and other valuable autographa of Horace Lord Vere
and his pious lady, Bishops Hutton, Wickham,
Matthew, (concerning the Hampton Court conference,) from the Earls of Huntingdon, Newcastle,
Essex, (his Instructions about the war, &c.) commissioners of both kingdoms, &c. with the finest
medal I have of King Charles the Second, most accurately performed by Simons, the famous artist;
and, after all, would oblige us to stay another night
there, when the same pious order, family called into
prayers.

8. Morning, *ut prius*, observed the solid stone,

wherein, when sawed asunder, was found a living
toad, as large as to fill the whole cavity in the middle, a chimney-piece of Yorkshire marble, which
admits a good polish, and looks very well. My
Lord very kindly rode with us part of the way, and
showed us four of his oxen, that are the largest,
finest beasts that ever I beheld. The waters were
yet out, that we rode through Askwith, and by Mr.
Vavasour's, of Weston, which is a very noble building, and seems to have fine gardens, &c. and Newhall, which looks well, over the bridge to Otley,
where the first thing I observed, was the ruins of
the Archbishop of York's palace there; then a modern school, founded " by gift," as the front tells us;
but, I suppose, of many private benefactors, because
none named. In the church are some monuments
for the ancient families in these parts; the stateliest
is the Right Honourable Thomas Lord Fairfax, the
first Baron of the family, and a very memorable
person; near which is a pretty little one for Mr.
Fawkes, which I transcribed; an ancient tomb of
the Dyneleys, (Sir Robert, if I mistake not,) the
Lindleys of Lindley, now succeeded by the Palmes's,
and some modern for the Barkers, wherein a slender herald will find the mistake in placing the
mother's coat instead of the father's in a lozenge for
a maiden daughter : upon the capital of a pillar was
cut Sir Simon Ward's cross, once a most famous
knight in these parts, now scarce remembered ; *sic
transit gloria mundi*, &c. We mounted the mighty

Cheven, and rode to Rawden, once the seat of an
ancient family of that sirname, of which the famous
Sir George Rawden mentioned in my notes in the
late edition of the Britannia, and of which family
there is yet a Baronet in Ireland, now of a memorable old gentleman, Henry Layton, Esq. a good
historian and accomplished gentleman, who has
printed many tracts against pluralities : his observations about money and coin in general, but especially
those of England, 4to. 1697, which are curious, and
show much reading in his younger years, and a
strong memory in his elder, now he is blind ; but
must always own my dissent from his heterodox
notions of the soul's sleeping with the body till
the resurrection, being abundantly satisfied in my
own conscience, from Scripture and reason, that
the soul of man is abundantly capable of subsisting
and acting in a state of separation from the body.
Lord, prevent the growth of this error, and preserve
especially the young gentry in these parts from the
contagion thereof. This ought to be added in behalf of the ingenious, and, in other respects, religious
old gentleman, that he lives piously under the power
of a practical belief of the Resurrection at the great
day of judgment, &c. After dinner, and discourse
with Mr. Layton and his two nephews, my dear
friend and Mr. Robinson, returned through the pleasant walks in his wood to Cookridge, having in
all our journey not travelled one mile twice over,
except that betwixt Townley and Burnley, in

Lancaster, where there was no other road. I stayed
little there, hasting home to my dear wife and children, whom I found very well, blessed be the God of
all our mercies ! I desire particularly to bless my gracious Protector, for preserving my dear friend and
self upon our journeys, and bringing us comfortably
to our respective habitations. Oh, that we may live
more and more to the praise and glory of his great
name !

12. Throng in getting in the Roman monuments,
lately dug up near Adle mill, and brought me in two
carts, the gift of the ingenious and obliging Cyril
Arthington, Esq. ; getting them into the library,
and preparing place for them.

17. Received a visit from Mr. Barlow, of Middle-
thorp, near York, which very curious house he built
after the Italian mode he had observed in his travels
to Rome ; showing the collection of Roman coins,
which, he says, are rare to be got in Italy, that are
genuine.

22. With Mr. Dwyer at Town-end; stayed full
late ; some of the company coming late from the
famous horse-race at Bramham Moor, the Earl of
Carlisle (of Hinderskelf Castle, in the North Riding,)
won the gold cup of 100*l.* value, that her Majesty
appointed for that end.

25. Concluded Mr. Calamy's Abridgment of Mr.
Baxter's Life, with additions, wherein are many
things curious and agreeable, especially the moderate
characters and memoirs of some eminently pious and

learned divines, and some arguments, especially relating to private persons' stated communion with the
Church of England, that in my poor judgment are
not conclusive ; for, though he holds occasional communion not only lawful but expedient, and, in some
cases, absolutely necessary, yet would deny the
other ; his deserved praise of the Bishop of Salisbury, (to whom I am particularly obliged for the res-
peets his Lordship has showed me,) will, I fear, make
some rage the more against him. What a deplor-
able case are we reduced to, that so many attempts for
reformation [comprehension] have been unsuccessful,
particularly that most famous in the beginning of the
late reign, 1689, when so many incomparable persons, of primitive candour and piety, were concerned
therein, of which my Lord Archbishop of York has
spoke to me with deep concern ; for which disappointment all good Christians have the deeper cause
of sorrow, because we are positively told (page 655,)
that in all probability it would have brought in two-
thirds of the Dissenters in England. Lord, send
thy holy and peaceable Spirit to influence the hearts
of such as have power in their hands, to heal our
piteous breaches in thy due time !

26. Walked with Mr. Fairfax, per Kirkstal Abbey ; stayed a little to view the stately ruins; per
the forge, pleasantly along the bank of the river,
which is very well wooded on both sides; per New-
ley-bridge, to Mr. Pollard's, at New Lathes, to visit
Madam Rawden, of Rawden, sister to the famous

Sir George Rawden, who, being in England at the beginning of the Irish massacre, 1641, hasted, through Scotland, to that desolate country, whence they met whole multitudes of poor naked men and women : when he arrived at Lisnegarry, (now Lisburn,) he found but forty-seven muskets in the whole town, and but little powder, &c., but a poor distressed people, who met him with their prayers and tears, and resolution to sell their lives at the dearest rate they could, even the women, with spits and forks ; but before he could get matters in so good order as he designed, the cruel cut-throats, under the command of Sir Philim O'Neale, came (the very next morning, as I remember) to burn that town and massacre the inhabitants, as they had done thousands of poor Protestants elsewhere, where, meeting unexpectedly with so brisk an opposition, they were the more enraged, crying, George Rawden sure was got from England ; and afterwards, when his horse being shot under him, he was dismounted, they set up a terrible shout, hoping he had been slain ; their little ammunition being almost spent, he dispatched away an express, and got a small supply of powder, (from Belfast, as I remember,) which happily arrived in their extremity, the very first shot of which made fresh havoc amongst the Irish, and so animated these poor Protestants, that with less than 200, in which were but forty-seven muskets, he repulsed Sir Philim O'Neale, at the head of an army of those cruel rebels, of about

7,000 strong, who never appeared again in any considerable body in those parts of Ireland, which were thus miraculously saved by this worthy gentleman, who was born here at Rawden, whose picture this lady (who is the last of the family in these parts, but there is a Baronet, his grandson, in Ireland)* presented me with, &c. She told me this story, the substance of which is related also by Bishop ———, in the funeral sermon for another of our famous countrymen, Archbishop Margetson, who was born at Drighlington, where he has built and endowed a free school, &c. This good old lady (who is above eighty-one years of age,) entertained us pleasantly with these discourses. Mr. Pollard also showed me the Abbot of Kirkstal's stirrups, which are prodigiously great, and of a very antique form. We returned along the river side, and had a very pleasant walk, blessed be God for all mercies!

29. After dinner with the Lords of Manor; was at the Court, where a new Mayor and common councilman were chosen. I was glad a proud haughty man was prevented, and our good Vicar's brother elected. Received a kind visit from my dear friend, Mr. Kirk, with whom and Sir Walter Hawksworth, at the Mayor's treat till past ten.

Oct. 2. Received a kind visit from Mr. Skipper, who brought my Lord Archbishop's son, to be educated at our school under good Mr. Dwyer, who has also the Lord Mayor of York's son.

---

* From whom descends the Marquis of Hastings.

Nov. 5. Walked to Adle Church, transcribed Esquire Arthington's epitaph, &c. before prayers, and after walked to the mill; had honest J. R's. company in viewing the vestigia of the lately discovered Roman town, which seems to have been considerable by the remains of the aquæduct, fragments of pillars, and monuments, &c. with the scars of different coloured urns, some even of the Coraline. It seems to have perished in the wars betwixt the Britons and Romans in some of the insurrections of the natives; we measured the camp at the town end, which is about five chains (one hundred yards) on each of the four sides; the agger is yet twenty-two feet high, and each chain is twenty-two yards long, but we could not be so accurate as I wished by reason of the extremity of the season, hasting to the mill for shelter. Afterwards, walked with Mr. Marsh to Cookridge, because Mr. Kirk had left my Lord Fairfax, &c. to meet me, and consequently, obliged to stay all night with my good friend, in the drawing of whose pedigree from writings and his own remarks, we found that my grandmother Thoresby's mother, and his grandfather's (of both his names) father, were brother and sister, Gilbert and Frances Kirk, son and daughter of Thomas Kirk, of Buslinthorpe, whose elder brother Gilbert was the first of Cookridge, where he purchased the estate now in the possession of my said dear friend, for dying without issue, he gave his estate there to his nephew Gilbert, *proavus* to the present Justice, and gave a

legacy of 26*l.* 13s. 4d. to the said Frances, my *pro-
avia*, &c.

6. Got an opportunity of retirement, which I had
not, or improved not last night. Lord pardon! Afterwards, transcribing ditto remarks, and drawing a
pedigree of the family; then rode to visit Mr. Boulter, of Gawthorp Hall; in our way viewed the remains of the Roman rig, which from the said lately
discovered town and camp, comes directly through
Mr. Kirk's ground at Cookridge, or Cuckerigge, as it
is writ in the letters patent, &c., which I am apt to
believe, received its denomination from the said
Roman rig that passeth through it, near one Dri-
ver's farm, in which was dug up an old stone with
an inscription manifestly Roman, by the letters remaining as I M . . . but so obliterated, as not to make
out the sense of it : Mr. Kirk has the original.
Thence over Blackhill, through Eccop and Werdley
Hollins, to Stank (from *Stagnum*), where is an old
camp, .to Gawthorp Hall; enjoyed Mr. Boulter's
company till towards evening; then returned to
Cookridge, where lay all night with ditto friend;
guilty of same omission.

7. Perusing Archbishop Cranmer's Letters Patent from King Edward VI., and transcribing what
relating to the parish of Leeds, which kept me
there till noon, as stress of weather after dinner
did till almost night, that rode home; found all
well, blessed be God !

30. Received a visit from the ingenious Mr.

Mauleverer,* who lent me the pedigree of that ancient family, of which one branch flourished at Potter Newton, in this parish, for several generations;
he presented me his curious treatise, Europa Libera,
which being communicated in MS. to a prime Minister of State (my Lord H—x.) was not only approved
of by him, but in many particulars put in practice,
though under the notion of his own project, and
seems to have had an influence upon our happy success at Vigo, &c.

Dec. 9. Got not to church; read Mr. Mauleverer's Europa Libera, which seems to me, not only
honestly designed for the public good, but to be very
well performed, and is thought by more competent
judges than I pretend to be in state affairs, to have
had a happy influence upon our good success in respect of the Spanish plate fleet, and the attempt at

* Nicholas Mauleverer, a name scarcely known in the history of
General Literature or Political Science. A pedigree in which he appears may be seen in the *Ducatus;* and in Thoresby's Biographical
Adversaria, I find respecting him, that he was born at Letwell, on the
southern border of the county, where his family had been long seated:
was of St. John's College, Cambridge, of Gray's Inn, and called to the
Bar. He resided at Leeds many years, and there wrote the treatise
mentioned in the text. He was the author of two anonymous tracts,
in which he recommended moderation to the parties in Church and
State. In the latter part of life, having lost his only son, he lived at
Burton, near Ferrybridge, where we shall find Thoresby visiting him.
He died in May 1712.

A brother of this Mr. Mauleverer, named John, was also a scholar
and author. He has verses in the *Threni Cantabrigienses,* on the
death of the Queen-Mother, and translated by M. Fleury, concerning
Education. He was a Fellow of Magdalen College, Cambridge,
which he ceased to be at the Revolution, refusing to take the oaths.
He died in March 1695.

Vigo, and 'tis now said, that the Duke of Ormond is
again going out with the fleet upon some great eu-
terprise that is yet kept secret, but perhaps to attempt some place in the Indies to gain possession of
some of the American mines, to which the English
are at liberty by the sixth article of the Alliance,
which was procured some months after the first edition of this treatise, which had before that been communicated to, and approved by, several of our good
ministers of state.

11. Transcribing Scotch journal of my dear friend,
Mr. Kirk ; concluded Bishop Burnet's most excellent Pastoral Care, wherewith extremely pleased.
What a glorious Church should we have if it was
duly practised!

23. With Mr. Blythman about house-letting ;
he told me a remarkable deliverance the Duke of
Leeds had in his childhood : when his father, being
Vice-President of the King's Council in the north,
lived at the Manor-house at York, the nurse having
dressed the child sent him after his brother to the
schoolmaster, who taught them in an apartment of the
said manor-house ; as he was going through a great
room he met with a little cat, and fell a playing with
it instead of going into the school, which else had
probably been as fatal to him as it was to his elder
brother, who was slain at that very juncture by the
fall of the roof, which crushed down the room where
they were, being blown down in a storm that then

happened, by which accident this eminent statesman was preserved.

24. Writing for Mr. Mauleverer; after to visit ditto ingenious gentleman ; presented him with a correct pedigree of that ancient family, partly from his own, partly from Mr. Hopkinson's MS. ; he showed me the autograph of his brother John (late Fellow of Magdalen College, Cambridge) in a pocket-book, wherein he had recorded his remarkable dream of his being wounded in the head by the fall of part of the roof of a house as he walked the streets, which shortly after came to pass, *anno* 1694.

A.D. 1703.

February 1. Finished the perusal of Mr. De la Pryme's* MS. Catalogue of the Manuscripts he has collected, which are many and valuable, particularly his History of the Antiquities, &c. of the town and county of Kingston-upon-Hull, in four volumes, in folio, which the author left with Mr. Thornton, for my perusal, being then in Lancashire.

8. Visited cousin Whitaker, who told me of the

---

* Abraham De la Pryme, F.R.S. a clergyman, lecturer at Hull, and minister at Thorne, where he died at an early age. His pursuits resembled those of the Leeds Antiquary, but he engaged in them with more earnestness, and more assiduity than even Thoresby himself.   De la Pryme also left a Diary, (for this was the age of Diaries,) in which I find him lamenting his disappointment at not meeting with Thoresby, on the visit to Leeds here mentioned. A pretty full account of his life and studies, may be seen in *South Yorkshire*, vol. i. p. 179.   See a notice of his death in this Diary, under June 20, 1704.

death of my kind friend and benefactor to my collection of natural curiosities, Dr. Cay, of Newcastle;*
sense and seriousness filled his last hours, as Mr.
Bradbury's† expression was. He died 22d January.
Lord sanctify all mementos of mortality !

9. Finished the perusal of the excellent Dr. Gibson's, now Bishop of Lincoln, Answer to the Pretended Independence of the Lower House of Convocation upon the Upper; am sorry to observe that
such contempt should be poured upon such excellent
Bishops, as the good providence of God has bestowed
upon us, than whom I think this nation never enjoyed more learned and pious prelates, nor more of
them, yet strangely affronted by the high-flown
party who pretend a veneration for that order, their
practices seem to undermine.

10. Finished the transcript of Mr. Hopkinson's
MS. folio of the pedigrees of the Yorkshire nobility
and gentry of the West Riding, with additions and
continuations, in many places, by the excellent Mr.
Thornton, who favoured me with the loan of it,
wherein are many things absolutely necessary to be
inserted in my designed History of Leeds, which
may be admitted as an apology for the expense of so
much of my time, (the original containing above

* Dr. Jabez Cay, a physician of eminence there, who has been frequently mentioned in this Diary.

† A Dissenting minister, then living at Newcastle, but afterwards
of London. He was for some time assistant to the elder Whitaker,
at Leeds. See under Nov. 14, 1703.

eight hundred pages, in folio) and my circumstances will not allow me an amanuensis.

14. Begun Mr. Clark of Communion with God, at the end of his Analytical Survey of the Bible, which I concluded yesterday, in the usual course of family duty, together with the old translation of the Bible and the marginal notes, of which I have neither so towering an opinion as some, nor so mean as others, who depreciate them too much because of some secret and supposed reflections, which had, indisputably, been much better omitted; but there are certainly many useful and plain notes, for the assistance of poor families, which want better, with which this age abounds (blessed be our good God!) but nothing symbolizing with the Arians or Jews, touching the divinity of Christ and his Messiahship, as they were causelessly traduced by a Hyper-conformist. They were printed with a general approbation above thirty times over, and were certainly the best that our nation and language then afforded. Read worthy Mr. Clark's Annotations upon second chapter of Genesis, whose memory I honour for his excellent works, and am in love with an expression I find in an original letter I have of his to Mr. John Humfrey: "the truth is, I find little savour or relish in dry, crabbed notions, which have no influence upon practice. Now I grow old, such discourses as may prepare me for eternity, help me to further acquaintance and communion with God, and stir up my sluggish

desires after him, are more suitable both to my necessities and inclination." This suits my own temper so much, that I could not forbear transcribing it from the original, given me by ditto Mr. Humfrey.

16. Abroad about poor ministers' concerns, most of day (except usual walks to the church); within, transcribing Dr. Woodward's directions about keeping a register of fossils, &c.

23. Heard the melancholy tidings of the death of my good old friend, the Rev. Mr. Milner, late vicar of Leeds, and author of several learned tracts, who died at St. John's College, in Cambridge, about the 19th of this month. Lord prepare me to follow him!

March 12. Sent for by Monsieur Permentier, who obliged me to sit for my picture.

13. Preparing for a journey with my dear friend, Mr. Kirk. Lord preserve from sin and all dangers, at home and abroad, for thy great mercy sake! Rode by Halghton and Whitkirk to Preston-super-le-hill, where most courteously received by Sir William Lowther, a native of Leeds, and noble benefactor to the library, whose house is pleasantly, but very strangely, situated; they go up stairs to the cellars, and down stairs to the garrets: from a tower he has built there, York Minster may be seen, and a pleasant prospect of this country round about. After dinner I transcribed the twenty-eight families they have matched into, and had the perusal of some original letters to himself, from eminent hands.

From thence we rode through Allerton, "juxta aquam de Eyre" (Aire), over Castleford-bridge ; viewed the new lock lately made by the undertakers for the navigation ; thence not far from the glass-house at Houghton ; after, upon the ascent, had a fair view of the ruins of the once celebrated castle, at Ponte-fract, with the high church, and Dr. Johnston's house, and a little after of Newhall, which belongs to the Pierrepoints. Thence by Darrington and Stapleton Lees to Wentbrig, beyond which, upon the heights, may be seen York Minster, and it is said, also, that of Lincoln, but it was too duskish for us to do it ; what I was more intent upon was the famous Roman highway, which is not only visible for several miles, but its complete dimensions, near which we drank at a curious spring, which receives its deno-mination from Robin Hood, the noted outlaw ; after which we left the common road to Doncaster, and followed the old one, as is evident from the said Roman rig, which we followed for some time, in our road to Sprotburgh, the noble seat of the Honour-able Sir Godfrey Copley, who received us kindly, but having left his lady and family at London, whither he is obliged to return in a very few days, being a chief commissioner for taking the public ac-counts, we lodged and dieted with him at Mr. Lamplugh's, the parson's, where he had also his uncle, Mr. Arthington's company. Evening, enter-tained with the relation of some remarkable trans-actions as to the public account, but, as is too com-

mon upon journeys, had not a conveniency of retirement for prayer : Lord pity and pardon!

14. Having quitted my bed-fellow and fellow-
traveller, got an opportunity for prayer. Afterwards
walked to the hall; had Sir Godfrey's company to
the church, where Mr. Lamplugh preached very
well, but had not the conveniency of writing the
heads of the sermon ; was sorry to observe so slender
an appearance (scarce to be called a congregation).
In the afternoon, after prayers, I viewed the monuments of the Fitz Williams, whose arms are painted
in several of the windows; and there are two
ancient statues, to the full proportion, in the south
wall of the church; there is a tomb in the choir for
one of the present family of the Copleys, of which
Sir William Copley married Dorothy, daughter and
co-heir of Sir William Fitz William, the last heir
male of that ancient family of which William Fitz
William came in with, and was Marshal to William
the Conqueror. Afterwards, walked with Sir Godfrey and the other gentlemen to his new canal;
then inevitably engaged in company, Mr. Copley, of
Doncaster, and Mr. Battie of Warmsworth, making
a visit to Sir Godfrey, with whom till evening;
again prevented of privacy.

15. Reading some remarkable papers relating to
the public accounts of the nation ; afterwards viewing the most pleasant gardens and curious fountains,
statues, &c.; then assisting Mr. Kirk and Mr.
Arthington in taking a level for the new canal that

is now making from the water-engine (which is very
curious, and conveys water to a large lead cistern
upon the roof of the hall, a vast height from the foot
of the hill) to the corn-mill, whence he can go by
water to Coningsburgh Castle on one hand, or Doncaster ou the other ; then viewed the salmon-heck ;
then received a visit from the ingenious Robert
Molesworth, Esq. (since Lord Molesworth,) his late
Majesty's Envoy at the Court of Denmark, so that
all the five members of the Royal Society, in this
county, were met at Sprotburgh.   After dinner,
walked to Warmsworth, to visit Mr. Battie and his
brother Copley; got a sample of some fine spar, or
selenites, found in a bed of plaster, as they were
digging near his new house, which is very pretty for
the size, but scarcely finished ; he gave me samples
of very curious Derbyshire marble, well polished.
Spent evening with Sir Godfrey, &c. at Sprotburgh ;
had a remarkable account from Mr. Barrowby, of
Burrowbridge, of a little image, and other Roman monuments himself found under the walls of Aldburgh,
&c. which Sir Godfrey has promised me.

16. Perusing the Register for town and parish of
Sprotburgh; then rode with Mr. Kirk to meet Mr.
Molesworth at his wood, where is making a curious
walk, formerly set out by my said friend, Mr. Kirk,
which we now marked through another wood, &c.
within his lordship, which, when finished, will,
perhaps, be the noblest in England, being near two
miles long, in a direct line, and, for the most part,

stately high trees on each side. After this was
finished, we were conducted to his house at Edling-
ton, which is an ancient fabric, lately the seat of Sir
Thomas Wharton, but stands conveniently, and has
a good prospect ; he entertained us with a variety of
choice wines and delicates, but I was most taken
with his own conversation ; he presented me with
his account of Denmark, as it was in the year 1692,
when he was Envoy at that Court from the late
King; his Lady also, who is the Lord Coote's
daughter, sister to the Earl of Bellamont, gave me
an Indian fan, with a gilded inscription in the native
characters and language, being said to be a hymn or
prayer to their reputed gods.   Spent the evening at
Sprotburgh, with Sir Godfrey Copley, who entertained us with some memorable passages relating to
the public affairs of the nation, as also of the Royal
Society, and our friends there.

17. To wait. of Sir Godfrey, who showed us the
several apartments of his noble and spacious house ;
the stair-case is curiously painted by a good hand,
the gallery adorned with some original pictures of
Sir Anthony Van Dyke's, and other great masters ;
his closets with choice curiosities, amongst which I
took notice of a Pope's bull, a large snake, a delicate
unicorn's horn, a speaking trumpet and other mathematical instruments, wherein he is well versed ;
showed me also some things of his own painting and
drawing, in crayons, casting, &c. with heads also
and busts seemingly of stone, but really pasteboard.

He presented me with his own picture, the prospect of his noble seat at Sprotburgh, with the fountains, canals, woods, and gardens, wherein I forgot to take notice of one natural, as well as many artificial, curiosities, statues very well performed, viz. the jaw of an unknown but prodigious large fish, . . . yards long, much higher than the walls, &c. Afterwards, took leave of this obliging Baronet, some of whose speeches are in Sir John Fenwick's Case, which he presented me with, and a coin of Antoninus Pius, which proves a different reverse from all I had before. In our return, we rode by another seat of Sir Godfrey Copley's, formerly Sir Thomas Adams's, and after, had a distant prospect of Mr. Washington's at Adwick, of which family was Mr. Robert Washington, merchant in Leeds, where he died, and where his son Joseph was educated, and I think born, though registered at Tinglaw, the old gentleman being an eminent member of that Society; this Joseph Washington, Esq. published the most correct and exact abridgment of the statutes and other tracts hereafter to be mentioned amongst our Leeds authors (Deo volente); then along the famous Roman rig we had the view of Skelbrough, lately a seat of one of the Copleys, and Elmsall, now of Sir John Wentworth, and other towns, at a little distance to Wentbrig, where saw the ruins of a house lately burnt down by lightning, as a gentleman in our company (Mr. Parker, of Roch Abbey) informed me, who was travelling in the same storm, and saw it

burning; at Ferry-bridge parted with my dear
friend Mr. Kirk, and the other gentleman who went
to the Assizes. I took up at Brotherton to visit
sister Rayner, being near her hour of travel. After
dinner, rode with brother about his concerns, almost
to Knottingley; took a particular view of Sir William Ramsden's Hall, at Byram; afterwards, perusing some old papers of father Sykes', found some
remarkable letters, &c. in the late times. Evening,
visited Parson Daubuz,* who gave some original
papers subscribed by eminent statesmen of the
French nation, and one by Lewis le Grand himself, &c.

* Mr. Daubuz was the Vicar of Brotherton. Thoresby has preserved some particulars respecting him, which escaped the researches
of Dr. Zouch, and of other persons who have attempted to collect the
incidents of the life of this truly learned divine. Charles Daubuz
(son of John, Doctor of the Civil Law,) Minister at Nerac, and Pro-
fessor in Divinity at Montauban, author of several learned tracts in
Latin and French, was the father of Esay Daubuz, who was also
Minister of the Reformed Church at Nerac. Esay Daubuz was the
father of Charles, who was brought to England in 1686, by Julia
Daubuz his mother, who, with her family, fled to avoid the persecution to which the Reformed were at that time exposed. The son was
born in July 1673, at Agen, and, on the arrival of the family in
England, was sent to a private school at York, from whence he passed
to Queen's College, Cambridge, where he took the degree of A.M.
Early in life he was Master of the Grammar School at Sheffield.
From Sheffield he removed to Southwell, on being appointed one of
the Vicars Choral. He had, afterwards, the Vicarage of Brotherton,
where he resided till his death, in 1717. In 1706 his Treatise was
published, *Pro testimonio Flavii Josephi de Jesu Christo.* In 1709,
The Maxims of Popish Policy in England, translated from the
French; and Thoresby adds, that he is writing *The Revelation of
St. John, Explained by a Perpetual Commentary,* which was published after his death.

18. Again engaged in ditto old chest for autographs, till called for by the obliging Mr. Daubuz,
with whom till near noon; retired. After, took
leave of relations, and returned through Fair burn,
(or water,) by Ledston Hall to Kippax, but missed
of honest Parson Baynbrigg; crossed the Roman rig,
or Via Vicinalis not far from Barrowby, which,
perhaps, received its name from some of the Roman
tumuli, or barrows. Betwixt Hawton and Wikebridge is a remarkable bank that points towards
Leeds; which, though upon the top of the hill is
called Slack Bank, therefore not from its situation in
a bottom, or slack, but rather from the Saxon ꝼlaᵹ,
bellicum, c and ᵹ being often used for each other, as
þonceꞃ, þonᵹaꞃ, *cogitationes*. The situation of the
place, and the convenient distance from Ossinthorp,
the *regiam villam*, or cẏnınᵹeꞃ boꞇl, as King Alfred
renders it *in Regione Loidis*, argue it to have been
a convenient place for a signal or warning in time of
danger or war, as the name signifies; and this village being written in ancient MSS. four or five
hundred years ago, Halghton, or Holy Town, (for
halᵹa is holy, whence the tabernacle is called halᵹan
ꞃꞇop, or *sacer locus*,) why may not this be the place
which was *in Sylva Elmetæ*, which Bede refers to,
(lib. ii. chap. 14,) where the altar was preserved
even to his time, that was brought from the ruins
of Almanbury, when the King's palace and church
there were destroyed by the Pagans, which is the

more probable, because so near Ossinthorp, where the succeeding Kings boŧl poꝺhŧon on ꝺam lanꝺe ꝺe Loiꝺiꝛ haŧen, *Regione Loidis* as Bede has; and, therefore, rather there than in the very town of Leeds. Enquiring after the name of this Slack Bank, &c. I heard of another, not far from Wykebeck, called Deyns, which I had not time now to view, but suppose it some Danish work.

19. Transcribing Sir Godfrey Copley's pedigree, which I promised to send him.

20. Writing to Sir Godfrey Copley; then, entering benefactions to my collections, which was also augmented by some Roman antiquities and MSS. from Chester, now arrived, which kept me employed the rest of day, except usual walks to the church.

30. With honest J. R. of Adle Mill, who brought me the old Roman head, mentioned in the Phil. Trans. number . . . . and some fragments of Roman pots, &c.; received also from Mr. Pollard, the Abbot of Kirkstal's very antique stirrup. Sent for by Mrs. Morris about Mr. Morris's MS. designed for the press.

31. Received a kind visit from Sir William Lowther, with whom I dined at Mr. B.'s; had discourse concerning that ancient family, of which have been, he says, thirty-one knights successively. His father married Mr. Busfield's daughter, of this town, (where this Sir William was born,) was a merchant here, and afterwards, Parliament man for sixteen years, till his death, and one of the council in the north.

Sir William designs to oblige me with original letters to him from several persons of honour.

April 5. Retired to private prayer, but, alas! had
not time to read, being the great court day; sent for
by Alderman D. about the manor concerns, only
obliged to steal so much time as to show collections
to Mr. Boulter, of Gawthorp, and his friend, and to
write to Sir William Lowther, to make an acknowledgment for the fifty autographa sent me per post;
but rest of day and till too late at night with the
Mayor, &c. (invited to the court dinner.)

7. Rode with my neighbour, Mr. Br. to the General Quarter Sessions at Pontefract, to vindicate
his reputation, that is attacked by a villain, who,
upon better consideration, durst not bring it before
the Justices, with whom in the evening walked to
view the remains of the famous castle and ruins of
the church, which is a piteous sight. Afterwards,
went to see a remarkable grotto in Mr. English's
garden, hewn out of an entire rock, out of which
solid rock are cut a pair of winding stairs, the roof,
sides, and steps, all of a piece, at the bottom of
which is a little fountain, or well: we counted sixty-
nine steps up again into the garden, formerly called
Fryer's Wood.

8. Went to view Dr. Johnston's collection of
natural curiosities, which has been very considerable:
there yet remain some things that are remarkable,
but in very ill condition, exposed to injuries in more
respects than one. Afterwards, with Sir Walter

Hawksworth, Sir William Lowther, who came to the end of the bench to tell me he had some other autographa for me; but missed of Mr. Molesworth. Afterwards, had Mr. Harwood's company, (an ingenious schoolmaster,) who gave me the printed effigies and autograph of Monsieur Beverland, his acquaintance, who published the famous Isaac Vossius's Observations upon Catullus, and wrote a piece De Peccato Originali, and another De Fornicatione Cavendâ. Afternoon, returned home, had a pleasant journey, and found all well, blessed be God.

14. Finished the perusal of Dr. Hicks' Devotions, in the ancient way of Offices, with psalms, hymns, and prayers, originally written by Mr. Austin, a Romanist, but reformed by a person of quality, and published by Dr. Hicks; and in this dress is not only useful and edifying, but very affecting, as I have found by experience in the perusal of it. Lord! help to improve all advantages.

28. Finished the second perusal and the excerpta taken from Dr. Grew's Cosmologia Sacra; wherein the learned and pious author does admirably and most ingeniously demonstrate the truth and excelleney of the Bible, evincing it beyond all the objections of pretended critics and supposed wits; and makes so useful and pious reflections upon natural curiosities as was mighty pleasing to me, such as relate to any in my collections I have transcribed. Afterwards, in my walks to the garden, ended Mr. Molesworth's, now Lord, most instructive account of

the Court of Denmark, as it was anno 1692, when his Honour was Envoy at that Court from King William ; it was the most obliging author's present, and is the most impartial (if not too severe in some passages) and excellent account of those northern parts of Europe that ever I read ; and argues the author to be an excellent statesman, as well as accomplished gentleman and virtuoso. Was rest of day making additions to Mr. Ray's local words, at that ingenious gentleman's request.*

May 13. Perusing a MS. of our late Town-clerk, Mr. Castilion Morris, wherein are both historical notes of his own time, and the History of Pontefract Castle, which his father, Colonel Morris, held out for King Charles the latest of any in England. This part was designed for the press, only prevented by the author's death. After, with Mr. Arthington, Mr. Kirk, and other justices, who visited me to see an ingenious young man (from Lynn) who rung all our eight bells, (two of which were, in a great measure, the gift of my late cousin Lodge, the ingenious traveller and painter,) and played very artificially the several changes upon them, with Lilly-bul-lero, and several tunes very distinctly, as if there had been a man to each bell. Mr. Kirk and I went aloft to the height of the steeple, to see how he had fixed the ropes to the clappers of each bell, whence they were brought into the ringing-loft,

---

* These were afterwards published in a volume of Ray's Correspondence.

where he screwed them down in a semi-circle and sat upon the floor in the midst of them, touching some with his hands, others with his arms, and the great bell generally with his elbow, but varied very dexterously according to the several tunes.

15. Evening, finished the perusal of Mr. J. H. (perhaps Mr. John Humfrey's) View of Antiquity, presented in an account of the fathers within the three first centuries after Christ, wherein he gives a very judicious and learned account of those famous men, well distinguishing their genuine works from such as are falsely ascribed to them ; with which I collated our learned Vicar, Robert Cooke's Censura quorundam Scriptorum, wherein he most accurately distinguisheth the doubtful and supposititious from the genuine works of these venerable authors, a book, never to be named without honour, of that pious and learned person, the glory of our Leeds writers, of whom *vide plura* in my MS. Essay to the history of this town and parish.

17. Began my journey to Newcastle, in company of my honoured and pious friend Alderman Milner: the first place out of our own parish worthy of note was Harwood, which I presume may have received its denomination from some eminent battle from Hepe *exercitus legio ;* thus Hereford is *exercitûs vadum,* and our Harelow-hill, or the Battle-hill, &c. This, I am the rather induced to believe, the true etymon of the name, because of a remarkable camp, that Mr. Boulter showed me (of which vide a former

Diary,) who is the Lord of Harwood, where he has lately erected a stately column in the midst of the market, which is one of the most remarkable for calves in these parts; we met several scores for Leeds alone, but this worthy gentleman, John Boulter, Esq. has been a grand benefactor to the public in other respects, having endowed that vicarage with 50*l.* per annum, and given 12*l.* or 14*l.* yearly to a school; and I lately saw my neighbour Atkinson engraving two pieces of plate that he had bought for the service of the communion in that church, and in gratitude I am obliged to add, he has been a kind benefactor to my collection of curiosities by the addition of several ancient Roman coins and others of modern times. We passed by the remains of the castle which Camden justly notes for its frequent change of owners, and passed the river Wharf to Kirby Overblows, or rather as I find it in some ancient writings, Ore-blowers, for the neighbouring forest of Knaresborough did abound with minera ferri, *vide* my excerpta from my dear friend Mr. Thornton's manuscripts. Here we were kindly received by parson Rogers, whose furious dog I was the less concerned for, because of his master's art, who when a young spark at the University has frequently boxed the fiercest mastiffs they could set upon him, and can even yet by a peculiar cast of his eye make the stoutest turn tails, or if by chance one madder than ordinary venture to encounter him, a few cuffs make him retreat yelling, &c. We

had a distant prospect of another fat living, Spawforth (said to be worth near 500*l.* per annum) both
which are in the Duke of Somerset's gift.   This
forest was once so woody, that I have heard of an
old writing, said to be reserved in the chest at
Knaresborough church, which obliged them to cut
down so much yearly as to make a convenient passage for the wool-carriers from Newcastle to Leeds,
&c.   Now, it is so naked that there is not so much
as one left for a way-mark, such a consumption did
the blasts make, of which I have seen great heaps
of slag or cinders, overgrown with moss, &c. now
often dug into for mending the highways.   Upon
the forest we had the prospect of the Spa at Harrowgate (lately much improved in convenient buildings for reception of strangers): of the name of the
place, *vide* my manuscript papers, and of the four
so different springs, *viz.* the spa and sulphur-
well at this Gate through the heaჳ, *lucus,* &c. the
petrifying well at Knaresborough and St. Monga's
at Copgrave, *vide* the additions in the new edition
of the Britannia.   Upon the road, we had the prospect of Plumpton tower and tree, Mr. Stockdale's
seat, (late Parliament-man for Knaresborough), and
Scriven of the Slingsbys, for which ancient family
there are several stately monuments in the church
here.   But we passed through the town without the
least stay, as we after did through Feronsby and Myn-
skip to Burrowbridge, *pons burgi* in old fines, where
we dined.   There is now a good stone bridge, where in

Edward II.'s time was one of wood, through a
chink of which Bohun, Earl of Hereford, was thrust
through with a spear by a soldier, who lay in am-
bush under the bridge.   After a comfortable refresh-
ment, we passed in view of several country villages
by Dishforth to Topcliffe, of old the seat of the ancient family of the Percies.   I saw nothing remarkable in our hasty passage through the town, but the
church and bridge over the river Swale, except Mr.
Newsome, the minister, (who married Mr. Garnet's
daughter of Leeds,) be the author of the Defence of
the Gentlemen's undertaking at York at the Revolution 1688, which piece was then much in vogue,
and by some ascribed to Judge Rokeby, by others
to Mr. Newsom.   Along the banks of Swale, are
the very pleasant gardens of Sir William Robinson,
lately Lord Mayor of York, but a few miles after a
more doleful object of Mr. Busby hanging in chains,
for the murder of his father-in-law, Daniel Anty,
formerly a Leeds clothier, who having too little
honesty to balance his skill in engraving, &c. was
generally suspected for coining, and other indirect
ways of attaining that estate which was the occasion of his death, even within sight of his own
house.   Thence through Sand Hutton, and both the
Otteringtons to North Alverton, where we lodged.
Upon the road we had a distant prospect of Ouns-
berry or Rosemary Toppin, a remarkable height,
being a mark for the mariners, and a nigher for the
growing market town of Thresk, which sends bur-

gesses to Parliament, as also does North Allerton—
witness " Parliamentarius" upon a tomb in the church,
for the inscriptions whereof *vide* the later book of
my collections.   Was pretty much out of order by
the excessive heat, and too unadvisedly drinking a
hasty draught of new milk; but after prayer and a
tolerable night's rest, was better in the morning,
blessed be the God of my mercies!

18. Went to view the town; found an hospital,
called the Earl of Carlisle's, but was the benefaction
of another family they matched into, and is only
paid by them : it is for four persons, who have each
fifty shillings per annum : transcribed some epitaphs
in the church, of which Mr. Francis Kaye was thirty-
two years vicar, who left 10*l.* per annum to four
widows.   I inquired after Mr. George Meriton, an
attorney of North Alverton, who writ Anglorum
Gesta, Landlord's Law, Nomenclatura Clericalis, and
somewhat of the northern dialect, &c., but could not
hear any thing further, than that he removed into
Ireland, where he was said to be made a Judge, but
whether alive or dead, unknown.   From North Allerton, we passed by several country villages, but of
no great consideration, till we passed the river Tees,
in a fruitful country, which produces very large
sheep; we stayed little in Darlington, hasting to
Durham, where I found myself under a great disappointment, the ingenious Sir George Wheeler
being at London, and also the Bishop; but, after
the prayers, we were very kindly received by the

most obliging Dr. Smith, one of the prebends of that
church, who was concerned for the Bishopric, in the
late edition of the Britannia, who showed me some
original MSS. of that great benefactor, Bishop Co-
sins ; but we had not time to view the famous collection of the charters of the Scots' kings, which the
Bishop of Carlisle wrote me were the fairest that
ever he saw, the seals very entire, &c. At Chester-
in-the-Street we called to visit our good old aunt
Thoresby, (Alderman Paul Thoresby's widow,) who
is about ninety years of age, yet her memory and
other senses very perfect, and she discoursed piously
and prudently, though at present with difficulty, because of her present weakness. In this church, I
formerly saw the monuments of the Lords Lumley,
of Lumley Castle, in this neighbourhood, but had
not time now ; they are descended from Liulphus, a
nobleman temp. R. Edwardi Confessoris : the present heir was, by King William III., made Earl of
Scarborough. From Chester, over the Fells, which
were so high, and the clouds so low, (an ugly
Scotch thick fog,) that we seemed to be enveloped
therewith ; but, blessed be God, we got well to our
journey's end, but too late to do any business that
night.

19. To inquire for Mr. John Cay, brother to my
late ingenious friend and kind benefactor, Dr. Jabez
Cay, whose death was a public loss, as well as to me
in particular. Then to visit good Mrs. Manlove,
(who gave me some original papers of the late Doc-

tor's,) to her brother Bennet; and after, to visit the
widows of Dr. Gilpin, (the pious author of Dæmono-
logia Sacra, &c.), and his son-in-law, Dr. Cay; then
visited Madam Clavering, daughter and co-heir of
the late Esquire Hardwick, of Potter Newton Hall,
parochiâ de Leeds; she was very obliging and ingenious, but the pedigree which I designed to transcribe was at their country seat. Afterwards, cousin
Milner and I went to see the town-house upon the
Sandhill, to the building of which Mr. Warmouth
gave 1,200l.; took an account of some other benefactions there and at St. Nicholas's Church; transcribed some epitaphs there and at another church;
went to visit Mr. Hutchinson, Parliament-man for
Berwick, almost purposely that I might once again
see the house where my honoured uncle, George
Thoresby, and his virtuous consort, lived exem-
plarily, and died piously. Cousin Milner went with
me to Mr. Ord's, to pay rent for poor brother Jerry's
house; we walked upon the quay to see the ships
laded with corn and other merchandize, the life of
the town; after, to see the house built for the
Mayors of Newcastle, to keep the mayoralty in;
saw the remains of a noble statue of King James II.
part of which is already used for bell-metal, &c.
After, walked to the very curious bowling-green,
built at a public charge, and where are the best
orders kept, as well as made, that ever I observed.
Evening, with Alderman Fenwick, at whose house
we lodged, and Mr. Banson, an ingenious writing-

master, who has lately printed the Merchant's Penman, or a new copy-book, &c., who went along with me to Mr. Rudd, who teaches the Grammar school, an ingenious, modest, and obliging person, (see Dr. Gibson's Preface to the New Britannia); rest of evening with ditto Alderman Milner till bed-time.

20. Sent for by Madam Clavering, to see a curious pedigree of the Dudleys, her husband's relations; took leave of Mr. John Cay and Mrs. Manlove; took leave also of the place in a sad rainy day, the people as morose at the loss of so many horse-loads of money, (the old Earl's of Northumberland, now Duke of Somerset's, rents,) as my cousin Milner returns twice a year, with which we made the best of our way, (without coming at Durham); was mightily pleased with some remarkable providences that have attended this worthy magistrate, who is of a good family; his grandfather was chief magistrate of Leeds, yet begun the world with little, being the youngest son; but as the Earl of Cork, who was a younger brother [son] of a younger brother, used to inscribe on the palaces he built, " God's Providence, mine inheritance;" so may this worthy and pious person, who, with a thankful heart to God, recounted to me (with which my heart was much affected,) the various steps of his growth; the first year he had commissions for 5,000*l.*; the second for 10,000*l.*; the third for 15,000*l.*; the fourth for 20 or 25,000*l.*; and has now dealt for 80,000*l.* per annum; and as an acknowledgment of

his gratitude to the grand Benefactor, he designs to
leave a considerable sum to pious uses, &c.; of his
carriage during his mayoralty, and extraordinary
activity in procuring the Act of Parliament for
making the rivers Aire and Calder navigable, see my
notes elsewhere.   We passed by Sunderland-bridge;
from whence, to another bridge, at a little distance
two persons rode a course, which was so near run
that both jumped with that force upon the bridge,
that one of the horses and his rider tumbled down
the battlement of the bridge, and fell both down together with the stones, yet received no damage.   It
is yet discernible how much of the bridge fell, by the
difference of the lime, in memory of which, there is
engraven upon the cope-stone, Sockeld's Leap, 1694.
We baited at Ferry upon the Hill, which answers
Kirk Merington (in the other road,) as to its lofty
situation, and got in good time to Darlington; viewed the town, where, by the encouragement of the
late Queen Mary, is settled the linen manufacture;
they make excellent huckaback and diaper, and
some damask, &c.   Went to transcribe what monuments I could find in the church; was pleased to
find there several young persons met to sing psalms,
which they performed very well, with great variety
of tunes, &c., but was concerned to see the adjoining
house of the Bishop of Durham converted into a
Quaker's workhouse.   There being a funeral, we
had the happy opportunity of public prayers, which
was comfortable.

21. The river Tees not being fordable by reason of the late rains, we went about by Croft bridge, where Sir William Chater has a seat, by which means we had the convenience of seeing the Hell-kettles, the best account of which, is in my late kind friend Dr. Jabez Cay's letter, inserted by Dr. Gibson in the new edition of the Britannia, p. 782. We baited at North Alverton ; thence we rode by Sand Hutton, Topcliffe, &c. to Burrowbridge; had wet weather and one smart thunder shower, but blessed be God, without any prejudice. After supper we walked to Aldborough, the ancient Isurium Brigantum, where Mr. Morris, the minister, showed us a cornelian signet lately found (for which he gave 3s. 6d.) with a ball of stone found in the Roman wall, part of a white wrought glass vessel, which he kindly presented to me. Mr. Gilberts, related to the late master of the free-school at Leeds, and one of our authors (whose father was vicar of Aldburgh) showed us a tesselated pavement of small stones not an inch square; this is composed of dark coloured chequered stones, partly circular; there have been found of these wrought in flowers, &c. eight yards long. I met with one old Mr. Thoresby, who gave me two of the red chequered stones, some of the town brought of the old coins and one signet, but meanly engraved and preserved, yet at excessive rates, that I bought none. After return to Burrowbridge looking for the inscription Dr. Lister mentions, *Phil. Col.* No. 4, p. 91, which I read somewhat differently, but

whether way soever we read it, it seems to be the remains of a funeral monument : it is now làid sideways in the garden wall ; there are also at the same place different sort of bricks or pavements, rather more than three inches square, exactly like those I had from Kirkstal Abbey, save that these are a quarter of an inch thicker and a hollow·in the lower side to fix more tightly in the cement or plaster in which they were laid.

22. Walked into the fields at Burrow-bridge to see the celebrated Roman Obelisks, commonly called the Devil's arrows ; that which I measured was about three fathoms round, rather more, and perhaps eight or nine yards high : a second is about the same dimensions ; the third not so tall but much thicker : the fourth is broke, and removed for a foot bridge, somewhere about the town : the greatness of the stones might surprise Mr. Camden, and make him conclude them artificial, yet upon the strictest observations I was able to make, they seem to me to be natural, and such as the far greatest part of the Roman monuments in these parts are evidently ; to those mentioned by Dr. Lister in the place beforementioned, may be added the funeral monuments lately discovered at our Adellocum, amongst the ruins near the Roman camp, by Adle mill, now in my possession, and I was told by Mr. . . . ., a sober and intelligent person, that at Bracasty Wood, near Ripley, within eight miles of Burrowbridge, there is a delf of stone that will produce as long obelisks as these,

(which is but half the way to Ilkley,) and I have
seen some coins found in ruins there, which evidence the Romans were particularly resident in
those parts. From Burrowbridge, we returned
through Knaresborough town and forest, by Kirkby-
Ore-Blowers, and Swinden, the seat of Madam
Bethell, to Harewood-bridge, (the river Wharf not
being rideable) over the edge of which the present parson Cheldrey and a boy fell, in a dark night, and were
wonderfully preserved upon the piers that the bridge
is built upon, till help got to their relief ; the relation whereof I had not from common fame only, but
the persons that were eye-witnesses, and assisted in
drawing them out of the water. We got home in
great time and found our families well ; blessed be
our good God for all his mercies, both to us upon
our journeys, and our families and habitations in
our absence! I got in time enough to the prayers
at church, and was, I hope, truly affected with the
goodness of God. Was afterwards concerned at
the indiscretion, or malice rather, of two neighbours,
who having, to use their own expressions, fished it
out that it was on my account that Mr. Peters
prayed for one going a journey, made it their full
employ from the cloth-market in the morning to the
shambles, corn-market, taverns, ale-houses and coffee-
house, (though one of them scarce appears there in
twelve months but upon this occasion) in all companies to whom it would be ungrateful, to ridicule
it with such unworthy taunts, and also bitter and in-

tolerable reflections upon the public prayers as has
been extremely to my disadvantage, that I cannot
pass the streets, or come into any company, without
taunts from younger, and frowns and reproofs from
graver persons, for giving occasion for such reflections upon the public worship; whereas the Lord
knows I did it in simplicity of heart, because there is
no particular prayer for the like occasion appointed
by authority; and if I had put in a ticket (as is not
unusual in the churches at London,) to the curate,
I have reason to believe it would have been rejected,
as my request was, to return thanks for my dear
wife's recovery from the fever; and how piteous a
case are we in, who being exposed to continual dangers, and have so many instances of such as never
return home, one merchant of this town lately cast
away, and another (the father to one of these scoffers)
within a mile of the town fell sick and was brought
home dead, and yet cannot desire the prayers for the
merciful protection of God, but must be ridiculed,
not by the commonalty only, but even by such as pretend to be zealots in religion, who yet rather than
not gratify their little private grudges, will strike at
religion itself. Lord, pity and pardon mine and
their sins, for thy mercy's sake!

31. Evening, sent for per parson Plaxton, presented by the Lord Gower (as Chancellor of the
Duchy) to the great living at Berwick in Elmete;
he showed me a piece of British gold, and a noble

statue of Hercules in bass-relief upon an onyx stone.

June 1. To the ingenious Mr. Plaxton, who has promised to procure me one of the ancient clogs, or perpetual almanacks, described by Dr. Plot in his History of Staffordshire. Sent for by Mr. Thornton to Dr. Richardson, with whom till evening at the Club; where again baited by my friends for what my unkind neighbours have ridiculed me, if not religion through my side.

5. Visited by the famous artist, Mr. Henry Gyles, of York, who has been setting up for my Lord Fairfax, at Denton Chapel, the noblest painted glass window in the north of England; he painted the celebrated window at University College in Oxford, and is now for making one for Katherine Hall, in Cambridge.

9. At cousin J. Sympson's, making trials upon the stones voided by siege, with spirit of nitre and oil of vitriol.

10. A little with the ingenious Dr. Richardson; then perusing a MS. Mr. Rockley brought me, and transcribing the pedigree of that ancient family, some of which resided at Rockley Hall, in Leeds, and had a quire in the old Church, in old writings called Rockley Whear, of which family this gentleman, now a retainer of Sir John Kaye, is the last heir male.

12. Visited by three descendants of the famous

Archbishop Toby Mathew : viz. Mr. Mauleverer, his sister Dyneley, (who presented me with some of the needlework of that excellent Archbishop's lady,) and cousin Robinson, to whom showing collections.

July 1. Rode with nephew Wilson and Mr. Hickson to visit Dr. Sharp, of Horton, and his uncle Abraham, the famous mathematician, who showed us some curious instruments and most ingenious contrivances of his own invention; was pleased with the sight of some original letters of 'Mr. Flamsted and Mr. Halley to him, &c.

-- 12. Afternoon at the Court, where some things were proposed for the benefit of the Corporation, to be consulted about at the Assizes; then showing collections to cousin Thoresby, of Chester-in-the-Street, and his wife, of the ancient family of the Lumleys; the second match into that family, John Thoresby (the younger brother of Christopher, from whom we are descended,) marrying Margaret, daughter to the Lord Lumley, in Henry the Seventh's time.

13. Drank but little, the Spa-well having been flooded yesternight with the thunder-shower, which yet reached not so far as Alderman Ivison's, where they made hay in their shirts all day, yet was so violent here that in less than an hour's time Sheepscar-beck rose a yard and a half in perpendicular height.

This thunder-shower was ordered by Providence, for the detection of a murderer, John Brown, *alias* Clement Foster, who had fled from the North, where he had slain an exciseman, and skulked at Runder's upon the Moor, into whose house the violence of the storm forced Mr. Routh, the stapler, who overheard the fellow say he was brother to such-a-one, Mrs. Brown, in the North; he came the next morning to read the Gazette at Leeds, where Mr. Routh got him apprehended, for that such-a-one's brother had slain a man, and was fled; he denied all, but being sent to Newcastle Assizes, it was proved upon him, and he was executed for it: it is said he died penitent.

14. Sent for by Mr. Edmondson, of St. John's College, Cambridge, who brought me an obliging letter from Dr. Gower, the master, concerning the learned and pious Mr. Milner, one of the most famous of our Leeds authors.

15. Received a visit from Mr. Kirk and Monsieur Corbiere, of Geneva, to whom showing collections. After, sent for per Mr. Monckton, Parliament-man for Aldborough, who brought me a kind salutation from the Bishop of Norwich, &c., with whom and Mr. Benson, of Wrenthorp, &c.

20. Rode with Alderman Barker, &c. to York, where met with my kind friend, Dr. Barwick Fairfax, with whom went to the Minster. Evening, with Mr. Kirk, Mr. Arthington, Mr. Thompson, and other ingenious gentlemen, late enough, and, which was worse, prevented of an opportunity of retirement.

21. Left my dear friend (Mr. Kirk) in bed; re-

tired ; then went to meet cousin Johnson about the
poor orphans' concerns ; was disappointed.   Then
visited worthy Mr. Hodgson, the charitable Lady
Hewley's chaplain ; then at the prayers at the Minster ; and after rode to Bishopthorp, where (it being
a private day,) I had the opportunity (after prayers)
of private discourse with my Lord Archbishop in
his walks in the garden, and made known my circumstances in several respects, and had the comfort
and happiness of his Grace's advice and consolation,
with the tender of some kindnesses I thought not
convenient to accept of, but was much comforted
by his Lordship's application of some Scriptures ; as
when I objected my deep concern for that of the
wisest of mere mortals, " when a man's ways please
the Lord, he makes even his enemies to be at peace
with him," whereas even my relations, &c. are at
enmity with me, which has caused me much thought
of heart ; but his Lordship reminded me of that of
David, " my own familiar friend, in whom I trusted,
has lift up his heel against me;" and that of Job,
"my brethren are far from me, and mine acquaintance
are estranged from me, my familiar friends have forgotten me," &c.   After a more than usually importunate and kind invitation to stay all night, which
the poor orphans' business would not permit of, I
returned to York, where I met with an uncomfortable couple, cousin Johnson and his wife, at suit
together, and as untoward dealings with the poor
orphans, they having opened the locks of a trunk

and all the four boxes, taken out the best linen, six
gold rings, (whereof one or two had precious stones
in,) a silver box, with some gold in it, &c., of which
I had three voluntary witnesses, who were present at
the opening of the boxing, either not knowing, or
being pretendedly ignorant, that my poor brother
and his children were as much interested therein as
these relations, friends I cannot call them, who have
not left so much as will quit the charges of my
journey.

22. At cousin Sympson's, to desire her assistance
in dividing the linen, but had little need of it, the
boxes being not half full, and nothing but refuse
left. After, visited good Dr. Colton, who made me
a present of his Ships of Tarshish, &c. ; then at the
prayers at the Minster ; took leave of the pious Dr.
Fall and other good friends, but, being full late, was
prevailed with to stay till to-morrow. After dinner,
waited of old Esquire Hutton, at his son-in-law's,
the Lord Mayor of York ; took the inscriptions
upon all the swords of state used upon different
occasions ; was much pleased with the obliging Mr.
Banks, of Hull. Was at Mounty Gyles', to inquire
what has been lately found as digging for clay in
the Roman burying-place, and he gave me a brass
key, fixed to a ring, to be worn upon the finger, and
other curiosities, lately dug up there. Made a visit
with Alderman Rookes to Dr. Ashendon ; looked at
his Phil. Trans., but found none of the five I want ;
supped at the Chancellor's, with excellent company,

his son Pearson, Drs. Fall, Deering, our Vicar, &c. After, went to the Hall, where the Judge and Court were sitting, with candles, almost at midnight, to inquire of my dear Mr. Thornton's health, which, alas! is nothing to boast of. Lord, spare such as are useful!

23. With Mr. Kirk to visit Mr. Sturdy, the quondam famous schoolmaster of Bradford, whose account of the Hœmatites wrought into iron, is registered Phil. Trans. 199; but alas! he was seduced to the Romish church. Then with ditto Mr. Kirk, at a venison feast at Mr. Thompson's, who yet treated me more agreeably with some autographs of King James II. and above twenty judges, &c. Then at the Minster, transcribing the epitaphs of the Earl of Strafford, from his most noble monument lately erected, and that of my useful and kind friend, the excellent Dr. Gale; then to visit the ingenious Mr. Lumley, (brother-in-law to my cousin Thoresby, of Chester,) an excellent artist in many respects, paints excellently, japans incomparably, and, what I was most pleased with, works mezzotinto plates very fine; he made me a kind present of the lady Fenwick's, Dean Comber's, and Czar of Muscovy's, pictures of his own doing. After dinner returned with the courteous Dr. Barwick Fairfax, to Tadcaster, and thence, in tolerable time, to Leeds: found all well, blessed be God!

24. To visit Mrs. Boyse, from Dublin, who brought me her husband's kind present, of his "Vin-

dication of the True Deity of our blessed Saviour,"
in answer to his quondam colleague, Mr. Emlyn's
pernicious pamphlet, which was a great affliction to
this good man.

August 14. With Mr. Robinson, of Rokeby, who
had kindly searched the register at Bernard Castle,
for some of our family; he told me of the benefaction of Mr. Robinson, since Bishop of London, her
Majesty's resident at the court of Sweden, who
being a boy of pregnant parts, though of a private
house, was educated by Mr. Robinson, minister of
. . . . .; this worthy person has either built from
the ground, or considerably repaired a ruinous
church, at the place of his nativity, near the river
Tees, but on the Yorkshire side; for he was " Ebora-
censis nat.,". and allowed ten shillings a sermon, for
many years, till he could find a convenient purchase
to endow it with.

18. Afternoon, with cousin Cookson, collecting for
Mr. Dwyer; was pleased with the sight of some very
curious flutes, flageolets, &c. made by Mr. Dickens,
an attorney, who took them up of himself. Evening, read Dr. Colton's serious sermon; was especially pleased with his notion, that Cadiz was of old
called Tartessus, with reference to which, we so
frequently, in Scripture, find mention of the ships of
Tarshish; *vide* also Mr. Hirst, in his Annotations
upon Ezekiel, in continuation of Pool.

23. Rode with cousin Cookson, to meet Mr. B. of
B., at Kirkstal-bridge; walked to view the ruins of

the once famous Abbey, and after dispatch of the accounts and business, walked with Mr. T. Dinsdale to his farm, beyond the bridge, to see some old works in the Fall, which seem, by the roundness and smallness to have been Danish, but by the vast quantities of leaves from the wood which yearly fall and turn to earth, are much filled up, that they cannot be so distinctly discerned, except the highest camp, which is circular; there is also a noted well in the said Fall, near which they say lead-pipes have been found, whence they conclude that this fine water was conveyed beyond the river, for the use of the Abbey, which stands directly opposite to it.

27. Invited by, or rather in the name of the Marquis of Hartington to a treat; but some of the company were so offensive to me by their oaths and bumpers, that I stayed not a quarter of an hour; this is not designed in derogation of his Lordship, who has the repute of a sober and excellent person, but in commiseration of our piteous circumstances, that a person must either be rude (at least so reputed,) or run the hazard of wounding his own spirit, by sinful compliance, in most public treats.

28. Received an unseasonable visit from Mr. B. D. which prevented my going to church; was reading his surrenders from the Prior and Convent of Trinity, in York, concerning an estate in this street, which court, after the Reformation, is in the name of the Darcys, then of Queen Elizabeth, and then of the Ingrams, Sir Arthur purchasing Kirkgate-cum-

Holbeck of King James the First; it is now Edward Machel, Lord Ingram's, Viscount Irwin, the fifth in a lineal descent.

Sept. 4. Perusing a MS. relating to the town about one hundred years ago; wherein pleased with the punishment of offenders in time of divine service; order of sessions (from the Justices at large, for the town was not then incorporated,) for suppressing disorders on the Sabbath, the encouragement of exercises; then were the churches so full that they were constrained to build new seats and lofts, "because they had no room any where in the church to sit in," as are the express words of the famous Mr. Robert Cook, Vicar of Leeds. Oh, thrice happy days!

9. Walked with the Lords of the Manor to Sheepscar, to cousin Walker's, whence begun our survey of the manor of Leeds, which contains the Main Riding, viz. from Great Wildikes by Sheepscar and Buslinthorp by the top of Lorybank to Scot Mill; thence including the Car, &c. all along Sheepscar-beck to the Ridge Mill (old Thomas Vaux's) which is within the Manor, which beck divides the Manor of Leeds from that of Esquire Savile's, of Methley. At the end of a pasture beyond the said mill, we mounted Pykeman ridge, where a noted hedge, that carries us to Wreghorn stile at Woodhouse, is a boundary betwixt this Manor and the Earl of Cardigan's (formerly the Earl of Sussex's) Manor of Hedingley, to which belong also Burley and Kirkstal, all with-

in the parish of Leeds.   Having refreshed ourselves
at J. W.'s, our bailiff's, who run the measuring-wheel
during this perambulation, we went along the west
side of Woodhouse-Moor to the south-west corner ;
thence, including the new church land, to a small
lane that leads to Greystone, in the highway to
Bradford ; thence, including North-hall wood, &c.
down Mr. Banister's ground to the river Aire, against
Giants-hill, which, with the ground beyond the
river, is in Armley Manor, formerly Sir Ingram Hop-
ton's, now Sir John Ingleby's ; thence along the
river by Spring-garden and Mr. Lowther's house,
(*olim*, Dronylath) to Bene Ing, or Prayer Ing, (probably given to pray for the soul of the donor,) which
is $3\frac{1}{2}$ furlongs long, and Monckpits, to sister W.'s,
where we dined.   Afterwards, by the Highdam
closes, which part this from my Lord Irwin's Manor
of Holbeck ; thence, crossing Water-lane, we passed
by the side of Holbeck-beck beyond Austrop-hall,
the Hall Ings, &c. to Meadow-lane, and thence over
the enclosures to Hunslet-lane ; thence, by a long
dike which is oddly indented, (running under the
present Mayor's kitchen,) to Woodersome deep in
the river Aire, which same dike divides not only this
manor from that of Hunslet, but this wapentake of
Shire-ake from that of Ake-bridge and Morley.
Having walked about seven miles, we left the resi-
due to a further opportunity, Russell (commonly
called Admiral Russell) conveying us over the river.

Oct. 2. Received a kind and acceptable visit from

my honoured friend, Dr. Bryan Fairfax, Secretary
to the Lord Archbishop of Canterbury, who told me
good news in reference to our common friend, Dr.
Gibson, upon whom the Archbishop has bestowed
the living at Lambeth, worth three or four hundred
pounds per annum, besides other preferments, as an
encouragement to, and reward for the great services
he has done the public by his writings, &c.   Spent
the evening with my Lord Fairfax, the Dr., and his
ingenious son, Mr. Kirk, &c.; was pleased and instructed by ditto excellent Dr.'s converse, who in
discourse concerning the present Scots' affairs, told
me somewhat of his private message from the old
Lord Fairfax to General Monk, to whom he went
in such privacy, that he never saw Scotland, though
he dispatched that great concern with him there.*

Nov. 1. Walked to Cookridge, and thence (after
Mr. Kirk) to Adle; took the draught of a very ancient history in bas-relief upon the capitals of the
pillars in the church, representing most rudely the
baptism of our Saviour by John the Baptist; the
opposite seems to be of the Crucifixion.   Over the
great door is the figure of the Holy Lamb, and below it four figures designed to represent the Evange-
lists.   The door has been richly adorned with brass;

---

* In the *Review*, this remarkable passage stands thus: " Was especially pleased with the relation of Dr. Fairfax's secret transactions
with General Monk, to whom he went from the old Lord Fairfax, into
Scotland, where he conducted that great transaction about the Restoration of King Charles II. yet with such privacy, that he never
saw Scotland, though the matter was transacted there."

the heads of the nails covered with large bosses, &c.
Dined at the ingenious parson's, Mr. Jackson's. Afterwards, had Mr. Arthington's company till towards
evening; returned to my dear friend's at Cookridge,
read him my manuscript notes relating thereto ; but
before we could proceed therein, and compare them
with his writings, &c., ditto Mr. Arthington called
there, and staying all night prevented further progress therein.

2. Writing an account of the benefactions of
the late Mr. Kirk, of London.   Afterwards returned,
read Historian's Guide, in walks, till came to
Hedingley Moor, when turned aside to take a
more particular view of Harelaw, which is to this
day a suitable place for the occasion that gave it
the name of Battle Hill ; it has an ascent upon
three sides, and is well fortified on that towards
Monkbridge and Bentley, or the field of prayer or
supplication, which was the miraculous occasion of
the wonderful victory, as is expressly mentioned by
Bede, and all historians who treat of that admirable victory.   My heart was truly affected in remembrance of so signal a deliverance as the divine providence vouchsafed to our forefathers, his poor distressed Christian servants from the insulting Pagans.
That side of the hill towards Bentley, and consequently to Winmoor, &c. seems to have had a
triple fortification.   I measured a place in the highest to be yet about five yards deep to the middle
of the trench ; there are other two lower upon the
hill nearer Monkbridge, which is over Sheepscar-

beck, which is shaded with trees, and fronted with a steep craggy ground.

4. At the Lord Mayor's [at York] to take a more particular notice of the inscriptions upon the swords. After to visit Mr. Harrison, who showed me some very fine artificial curiosities of his father's own handy work, who appears to have been a most ingenious artist, by the very curious pictures in miniature as well as oil-colours, several things of turned or thrown work admirably fine, in ivory transparent, and some MSS. in heraldry (one of which was sold for 20*l.*) and in physic.

5. With cousin Milner to visit Major Wyvil, (son to Sir Christopher, the author of some learned tracts against Popery.) The Major being concerned in the late Mint at York when the old monies were called in, I desired an account of what monies were coined at the Mint, which by his books he showed me was 312,520*l.* 0*s.* 6*d.*

10. Writing to the learned Dr. Hicks, about Saxon coins for Sir Andrew Fountain, to be inserted in his great work.

12. Perusing Saxon coins to be lent Sir Andrew Fountain. Taking Constables' accounts, and took notice of the mittimus to send John Brown *alias* Clement Foster, to York Castle (20th July) for suspicion of murder : this was the fellow that was providentially discovered near Leeds, was convicted and executed at Newcastle the last assizes.

14. Finished the perusal of Mr. Bradbury's pious and ingenious sermons, some whereof were preached

at Leeds, when he was in my cousin Whitaker's
family, to whom they were dedicated. I ought to
make one remark in his commendation, that when
here he used once a week to instruct the youth to
sing in their chapel, which succeeds so well, that
that congregation perform that the best of most, if
not any, in these parts, which is the more remarkable, because some of that denomination are too
scrupulous in singing in what they call a mixed
congregation. He had afterwards a call to Manchester, subscribed by the Lord Willoughby and the
chief of that church; was courted for his known
moderation by a party at Mill-hill to succeed Dr.
Manlove; had calls to several other places; was for
a time at Beverley, and after at Newcastle, whence
he lately removed to London.

Dec. 20. With the other feoffees, went to Great
Woodhouse, distributed part of great-grandfather
Jenkinson's dole to poor housekeepers there, and at
Leeds town and Quarry-hill, Mabgate and Marsh-
lane.

22. Was all day with the feoffees, distributing the
rest of the pious benefaction (ten pounds per annum)
to poor housekeepers, &c. as the donor himself had
used to do in his lifetime.

A. D. 1704.

February 24. Drawing the pedigree of the Lord
Irwin and Mr. Ingram's family, before I took a walk
to Barrowby to the funeral of Mr. Thomas Ingram,

the eldest son of Arthur Ingram, Esq. brother to the first Lord Irwin; heartily sympathised with the good old gentleman, and the prudent and pious reliet of the gentleman deceased in the prime of his days. Afterwards in return transcribed the monuments in Whitkirk.

March 6. Finished my manuscript extract of the Bishops' register of the ministers' subscriptions; this first volume is from 1606 to 1627, the time that the most excellent Archbishop, Toby Matthew, continued in the see of York, whereby I have discovered what I sought in vain from the registers at Cambridge, viz. the particular colleges where several of our famous writers were educated, together with the dates of their entrance into the ministry and several removes, &c. The contemplation of one generation succeeding another was affecting, and furnished my meditations both with suitable arguments for preparation for approaching death, and of admiration of the goodness of God in raising up a continual supply for the instruction and guidance of his church and people.

20. Collecting memoirs of the excellent Archbishop Matthew; with Lords of the Manor; then sent for by the Mayor and some of the Aldermen to consult more particularly concerning the Judges' entertainment.

21. Finished my cursory perusal of George Fox's journal, to find what he says of William Dewsbury, an apprentice at Holbeck, and one of their celebra-

ted friends in the ministry ; was troubled to observe
how confidently they ascribe their vain imaginations
to God, " The word of the Lord came to me," " I
was commanded of the Lord," &c. Rode with the
Mayor and rest of corporation in their formalities to
meet the Judges, (Tracy and Smith) who with the
lawyers, &c. were treated by the corporation, but was
pleased to see all grave as judges, without the least
intemperance in the whole company.

22. Showing collections to the Judges, favourites,
&c. Was especially pleased with the obliging Mr.
Stephens, who has published a volume of Letters
(from the originals) of the famous Lord Chancellor
Bacon.

29. Riding with the Vicar, Mr. Thornton, Mayor
and Aldermen to Temple Newsome, where most
kindly received by my Lord, the Lady Dowager, &c.
Received an account of some benefactions, &c. relating to that honourable family from Mr. Roads,
one of the trustees during his Lordship's minority,
to whom his Lordship referred me ; found the ways
very bad that I rode as usually in fear, but received
no harm, blessed be God !

April 3. Concluded the first volume of the most
industrious Mr. Fox's Acts and Monuments of the
Church, wherein if there be some things less accurate
and nice, I am sure there are many excellent, wherein he shows both the cruelty of the Romish Church
and the constancy of such as endeavoured a reformation in all ages, and it is a noble as well as just

character that Bishop Burnet gives of this author, that having compared his Acts and Monuments with the records, I have never been able to discover any error or prevarication in them, but the utmost fidelity and exactness.

8. Concluded Mr. Briggs, of Catholic Unity and Church Communion, the reverend author's gift, some part of which is done with that candour and temper that seems wanting in others, close arguments and soft words being most attractive; but his zeal to the public establishment influenced him to what charity must call a pious zeal in a good cause, which suits with Mr. Shaw's motto before his Treatise, "No Reformation of the Established Reformation," "*Qui non zelat, non amat.*"

12. With Mr. Mortimer, one of the late excellent Lord Wharton's trustees about poor ministers' concerns; dined with him at Mrs. Hickson's; was rest of the day running over an old trunk, full of papers, for autographs, late Mr. Belton's and Dr. Neal's.

13. About Mrs. Hickson's concerns, to consult Alderman Milner, with whom walked to Giant's Hill, a Danish fortification, upon a precipice on the south side the river Aire, which has a good prospect and command of the river. He discoursed me again concerning his intended benefaction, build a house for the lecturer, and a monthly lecture, or preparation sermon before the Sacrament.

14. Rode with Alderman Barker to Wakefield, upon good Mrs. Hickson's concerns; viewed the

new market Cross, with the convenient archives for the public writings; and after we had done our best with the Normanton gentleman, viewed the church.

16. Concluded Mr. Boyse's Family Hymns, (taken out of the Psalms,) which I take to be the best, in all respects, that are extant, because the pious author observes a due medium betwixt the flatness and obsolete expressions of the old version, and the fanciful strains and conceits of some newer.

19. Heard of the death of Mr. Ferrar, formerly master of our Free-school, at Leeds; whence, for the happiness of Mr. Dwyer's assistance here, he was transmitted to Pocklinton, where he now died, having been a benefactor by recovering a considerable revenue out of the late Sir John Reresby's estate, due to that school.

26. Rose pretty early; took a walk, designing for Bishopthorp; the Lord grant me his merciful protection and direction. Began my walk about six; when I came upon Bramham Moor, took a ramble upon the right hand to meet with the Roman rig, or military highway; was fit for a bait by that time I got to the Street-houses; got to Bishopthorp in good time. After more general converse, had the favour of private and affectionate discourse with his Grace in his library: the Lord direct to what may be most for my spiritual and eternal interest, as well as my temporal advantage.

27. At the family prayers in the chapel; after, in Mr. Deering's apartment; then, transcribing some

memoranda from Mr. Torre's MSS. After dinner,
with Mr. Finch, Mr. Talbot, and rest of ministers;
took leave of his Grace, &c.; went with some of the
company by coach to York; was pleased with Mr.
Noble, minister of Crux; had his company at Mr.
Gyles's, viewing his curious workmanship; then, to
visit Mr. Townleys, of Townley, (the two ingenious
brothers;) and, after a little, at the pious precentor's,
Dr. Fall's, where met with the Dean and his brother
Finch.

28. Ere I was well begun my journey, got a
smart shower, that drove me into the church porch
at the Dring houses; was troubled to see an ale-
house at one end, and tavern at the other, joined
close to the edifice; had small showers most of the
forenoon, but it afterwards cleared up, that I had
more comfortable walking, and finished the perusal
of the Historian's Guide, which seems very partial
as to the affairs in King James the Second's time,
in whose reign it was printed. Got Mr. B.'s good
company the latter part of the journey; returned in
time for the church, where my devotions were somewhat enlivened in sense of the great goodness of my
merciful Protector; found all well at home, blessed
be the God of my mercies!

May 4. Drawing pedigree, &c.; rest of day sorting original papers, &c. except when before the Commissioners, to whom in vain appealed for relief in
the land-tax, which is advanced by the present as-
sessors, who, with the Justices, little know the

circumstances of my family, else I believe I might have had the redress I could not obtain, though I told them as much as was convenient; the Lord give me a contented heart in all conditions! was rest of day too much dejected in spirit; the Lord support me!

6. Was all day (except at church) ruminating upon, and endeavouring to draw up the arguments for and against a change of my condition; with prayers and tears besought God for the guidance and direction of his Holy Spirit in a matter of so great moment to my own soul and the souls of others.*

8. Began to revise the little Greek I once had; Lord, succeed my endeavours!

10. Read Mr. Colton's fast sermon, a present received yesterday from its reverend and pious author, to whom and Mr. Hodgson writing; afterwards, sent for by Mr. H. of P. about the late Sir Richard Lloyd's copyhold fine; then at cousin Cookson's about ditto, and with his brother before his voyage for Sweden.

29. Finished the perusal of our famous Vicar, Mr. Alexander Cook's History of Pope Joan, which is a learned tract, and shows the author a man

---

* This relates to a suggestion of Archbishop Sharp on his late visit, that "he would have made a good minister." It did not appear even then too late; but, after a serious deliberation, he decided against the change. "Upon the whole," he says in the *Review*, "I durst not adventure upon that weighty office in my declining age, having spent the prime in secular concerns; but it was afflicting to me that the opportunity was lapsed wherein I might possibly have been a little useful in my generation."

of great reading and industry; that this was generally believed amongst the Papists themselves before
the Reformation is evident from my MS. Scala
Mundi, where she occurs without interlineation.

June 2. Wrote Memoirs of Dr. Manlove.

4. Finished the perusal of Bertram's learned Treatise concerning the body and blood of Christ in the
Sacrament, which is a clear evidence that even
during those darker ages, near a thousand years
ago, there were learned and holy men of contrary
sentiments to the Romish Church in that moment-
ous point.

6. Concluded the excellent Bishop Stillingfleet's
Origines Saeræ, an incomparable treatise, wherein
the learned and pious author shows a truly great
genius, and vast reading, which he makes subser-
vient to the best purposes, in asserting the truth and
divine authority of the Scriptures. Lord, teach me
to profit!

19. Walked to Holbeck to visit good Mr. Dennison, the minister, take inscriptions in Mr. Fallow-
field's house and garden, to enquire farther concerning that author, at his kinsman's, who has presented
to me the original MS.; was at the chapel, writing
the epitaphs; then, to visit good old Mr. Isles, the
benefactor, and to enquire of some old writings.

20. Showing collections to Dr. Bernard, Alderman Barker and brother, with whom rode to Barrowby, to visit Madam Ingram, which took up rest
of day. Was much concerned to hear of the death of

my kind friend Mr. Abraham de La Pryme, Minister
of Thorne, who, visiting the sick, caught the new
distemper or fever, which seized him on Wednesday,
and he died the Monday after, the 12th inst. in the
prime of his age; he was a Fellow of the Royal
Society; has several letters in the Transactions;
had made a great collection of MSS. compiled the
History of Hull, in three vols. fol.   Heard also,
lately, of the death of another kind friend, Mrs.
Madox, aged sixty-seven, an ingenious and pious
gentlewoman, who brought me several curiosities
from Conigsberg, Prussia.   Lord! sanctify afflictive
providences.

21. To visit Dr. Russel, see his MS. Le Merite
Infortuné.

24. Concluded my Lord Archbishop of York's
excellent volume of Sermons, his Grace's gift; was
often much affected in reading them.   After, to
consult Mr. Thornton about Mr. Ibbetson's concerns, being abominably dealt with, and, instead of
receiving my moneys, threatened to be paid with a
chancery suit.

27. Begun to read Bishop Stillingfleet's additions
to his Origines Saeræ, in the new edition, published
by our countryman Dr. Bentley.

29. Within, making an Index to my own collection of epitaphs, &c. where I have travelled.   Received a kind visit from Dr. Kirshaw and his Lady,
(Sir Griffith Boynton's only sister,) and other relations.

July 3. Writ per post to the obliging Mr. Stephens, in return for his excellent book.

4. Making an Index to ditto, Mr. Stephens's Memoir of Lord Bacon.

5. Perusing Mr. Hopkinson's MS. of the Lancashire Pedigrees, lent me by my kind friend Mr. Thornton.

7. With the corporation and clergy, at the public rejoicing for the Duke of Marlborough's late victory in Germany. Lord, help us to do it in a more spiritual manner! was displeased at misspence of both time and money.

13. Evening, concluded our famous Vicar, Mr. Alexander Cook's, More Work for a Mass Priest, whereby he appears to have been a very learned man, and extremely versed in those controversies.

24. Was all day within, making cases for the English coins.

29. Ended Mr. Cook's Abaitment of Popish Braggs, in answer to several of their pamphlets refuted by him.

THE REVIEW.

December. All the diversion I had to keep me from melancholy despondency* was in my library, and the happy society of dear Mr. Thornton, Mr. Dwyer,† &c. at the Town-end Club once a

---

* Arising out of the distracted state of his affairs, particularly his difference with Mr. Ibbetson, of whose treatment he complains in terms of great bitterness.

† Thomas Dwyer, B.D. Master of the Grammar School, a native of Ireland, Fellow of St. John's College, Cambridge. He was afterwards Master of the School at Sedburgh.

week : this was so coveted that Mr. Fairclough
gave for his admission a guinea towards our charity-
stock, out of which we gave forty shillings towards
the erecting the minister's house for Armley Chapel ;
but the remembrance of this also is now bitter by
surviving every one of them, not only the two excellent persons before-mentioned, with Mr. Dennison
and Mr. Pawson, but Mr. Nevile and Mr. Skinner,
who paid more for forfeitures than their sixpenny
clubs would come to.

A. D. 1705.

Jan. 15. I rode to Bradford, to the funeral of
Dr. Sharp, the only son of the late excellent Mr.
Sharp, my dear friend and incomparable preacher;
was much troubled for the loss of so hopeful a gentleman, who died in his prime. I lodged at Mr.
Waterhouse's, and sat up till two taking extracts from
the registers of the nativities of the Archbishop and
other noted authors. I was not long after at the funeral
of an ancient friend, Mr. Adam Hargrave, sen. : the
Vicar preached excellently, though death delay till
87, yet it comes certainly. Was also affected with
his admirable sermons upon Christ's coming to
judgment, and in drawing up the Memoirs of the
pious, as well as valiant, Captain Wm. Fairfax,
drawing the pedigree of the descendants of the two
sisters of our famous benefactor, Mr. Harrison, in
order to distribute his charitable bequests (at the
request of his nephew, Mr. Robinson,) and engrossing

it upon parchment, cost me much time; but I cannot do too much for so grand benefactors to the town of my nativity. I wrote, also, at Mr. Robinson's request, an account of his excellent father, once Vicar of Leeds, and at Dr. Kirshaw's, of his grandfather, Parson Sikes, of Kirkheaton, both since printed in Walker's Sufferings of the Clergy: they were both very pious as well as loyal clergymen.

I was also well pleased in serving dear Mr. Thornton, in transcribing some extracts from Domesday-Book, and other matters from MSS., relating to the Manor of Wakefield, which he durst not intrust another person with the notice of, which cost me several days' labour; but I cannot do enough for that best of friends.

The election of knights for the Shire, obliged me with many others to ride to York; I took Bishopthorp in my way, and was most kindly received by his Grace, but found too much company upon this public occasion. The Earl of Carlisle promised me an original letter of Count Tallard, now prisoner in England, but his non-performance showed him too much a courtier. I lodged at Mr. Gyles's, with dear Mr. Kirk, with whom I went to wait upon the two candidates. I met with many learned and ingenious gentlemen; Mr. Molesworth, now Lord, Mr. Gale, who are both for publishing some rare MSS. and after with Dr. Watkinson, Dr. Fall and Dr. Pearson, since removed to their eternal habitations.

I went also to see the house (in Oldwork) where the famous Mr. Pool* was born.

During the season for drinking the water at our Leeds Spa, I made several sallies upon the moors and other parts of the parish, whither the remains of antiquity, in the names of places, induced me to view them, as Coning-shaw (or the King's-grove) near Ossinthorp, the *Regia villa;* the Deins and Hell-dike ; which are since published in the Ducatus Leod : as also the Mosses ; walked also to discourse with a descendant of the Claphams, concerning Sir Sheffield Clapham, a famous warrior, born in this parish.   I rode also with Mr. Thornton, to see How-ley-hall, where was a stately entrance from the Por-ter's-lodge to the front of the hall.   I took copies of the inscriptions, but was disappointed of the family pictures, as the famous Sir John Savile, first Alder-man of Leeds.   This hall is since demolished, and the materials sold, *omnia vanitas!*

July 22. Mr. Hodgson, of Christ's Church, and chaplain to the Earl of Derby, preached excellently at Leeds, where were present also Mr. Neville, of University College, Mr. Jackson, minister of St. Alban's, in Hertfordshire, who, with Mr. Killingbeck, the vicar, are all natives of the town or parish of Leeds. There were also two-and-twenty couples *spurred*, (to use the local word) in order to marry this day : but it was a more melancholy reflection that was occasioned by my computations of the

* Matthew Poole, author of the *Synopsis Criticorum.*

numbers of the births and burials, with the mar-
riages in several decads, that either the town and
parish is not so populous as forty years ago, or the
registers are not so carefully kept.

August 16. Being this day forty-seven years of
age, I do heartily subscribe to that great truth of
the inspired preacher, vanity of vanities, all is
vanity ! which must be owned by all men, being ac-
knowledged by persons of contrary extremes, as here
by King Solomon, who owns he had got more wisdom than all before him, and now by one who must
confess surely I am more brutish than any man, and
have not the understanding of a man, yet have I
learned this by dear-bought experience, that all is
vanity, not only of carnal pleasures, which indeed
deserve not to be put in the balance, but those more
refined of learning and study, except what is some
way or other directed to the supreme end of all,
viz., the glory of God and salvation of the never-
dying soul.

In this interval I read the excellent Bishop
Usher's Annals of the Old and New Testament, a
very useful work, but this English edition incorrect;
Josephus; Selden's Titles of Honour, a very learned
and curious work; Wood's Athenæ Oxonienses, a very
useful, yet injudicious work; Sir John Spelman's
Saxon Psalms, wherewith I have been often much
affected, in gratitude for the Divine goodness, in
affording our forefathers, in these remote isles of the
Gentiles, the Scriptures in their native tongue, and

with the fulness and significance of the expressions;
and in manuscript, Mr. Morris's Account of the
Siege of Pontefract Castle, the last that held out for
King Charles I., and first that declared for King
Charles II., Dr. Sampson's MSS. wherein are re-
corded many remarkable providences.

I generally read the printed authors in Divinity
or History till light, and then digested loose papers,
autographs, (of which I received many learned foreigners' from Dr. Hudson) till church-time, ten before and three or four in the afternoon, except when
diverted by visitants to see the Museum, from almost
all the counties in England, and some from Scotland
and Ireland, with others from Hamborough and
other transmarine parts, that being stinted for time,
I only took a mere cursory view of Dr. Hicks's noble
Thesaurus.

Amongst the many visitants were Sir Thomas and
Lady Willoughby, since Lord, and at another time,
Bishop Nicholson and his cousin, Archdeacon Pearson, with the vicar and many clergy in the forenoon,
and Judge Bury, with many of the long robe and
the magistrates, in the afternoon; with whom, at
the treat, till near nine, and was invited by the
Judge in the next morning, who expressed great
satisfaction; but I was most pleased with the instructive conversation of my old friend, the Bishop
of Carlisle.

I must not omit, that this year the new charity
school in this town was finished, and furnished with

forty poor children, decently clothed in blue, and
wholly maintained, who first appeared in public,
March 24, 1705, the second Easter in the same
year. Lawyer Wilson condescended to be a collector with me : it cost me much time, but seemed
a necessary employ at first, for the encouragement
of so necessary a charity.

But I endeavoured to ease myself of another matter, and accordingly made a resignation of my place
in the corporation. The officers watching my going
to church, used to serve their summons to court,
when I had much rather have been at my study
than at their extravagant treats ; but, after a quarter of a year's fruitless endeavour, I was constrained
to continue in my station, under pretext of a useful
man, whereas, I am fitter for an obscure cloister, (if
for any thing at all,) than a public station : at long
run, having got it under the hands of two-thirds of
the court, that I should never be advanced, without
my consent, I thought myself secure, (not fearing
Alderman Milner and some of my best friends, who
yet refused to subscribe the paper.) I continued
for some years, and was not wholly unserviceable ;
but after some years, by the deaths of some, and
unexpected removal of others, I was in danger from
the adverse party, and therefore getting a resignation strictly drawn by dear Mr. Thornton, and
duly attested, I sent it to the court, and though it
was at first rejected, the messenger turned out and
door locked, yet it was at last accepted, and, upon

my payment of 20*l.* fine, I was dismissed, though a new order had made it 50*l.* for every one that resigned his gown.

I had now more leisure and more freedom in distributing the Lord Wharton's Bibles, which, by experience, I found to be a troublesome but very useful charity. I sometimes catechised above fifty poor children on a Lord's-day night, and afterwards heard two sets of them the appointed Psalms, that I have been fatigued and almost stifled, but revived to see the zeal of so many, some of whom came many miles.

I ought to mention one thing, for the information of my poor children, that the two closes at Sheepscar were not sold for any debt of my own, but upon the executorship account, for which I had advanced more monies than my proportion came to ; but brother Rayner and brother H. either could not or would not advance theirs, and I being joint executor, was liable to be sued in Chancery, that they were sold for the discharge of father Sykes's bonds. Others took advantage of my natural temper, and dread of suits ; but I had more peace within.

A. D. 1706.

I had now read over the entire Bible, with notes, eight times since our marriage, and have in some measure made it the rule of my life, and humbly beg divine assistance to improve ordinances and providences. I was more than ordinarily concerned for the death of dear Mr. Kirk; in his sickness I took a walk to visit him, and discourse with him about soul affairs, (as we had often done about matters of learning and curiosity, he being F.R.S.) and was pleased with the motto I found in some books υ. devotion in his closet, *nulla dies sine prece.* I was jealous, lest his uncle Layton's heterodox notions about the soul's dying with the body might have influenced him. But in his last sickness, he said to the minister, " My faith, I thank God, is firm and orthodox, and my repentance, I hope, sincere," a far more comfortable expression than the more positive (though often too groundless) of many others. Of his ingenuity and his writings, see his memoirs elsewhere :* in walk thither, read Mr. Husler's Chronicle, written at Leeds.

My dear and I rode to Berwick, to oblige Parson Plaxton† and family with our child's company, and myself with his, and perusal of the registers of that church, and some ancient MSS. various editions of the Common Prayer and Bible; as also those at Spawford, at Dr. Talbot's. I rode also with them to the meeting of the neighbouring clergy at We-

---

* These Memoirs were intended by Thoresby, for what he calls The Historical Part of his Leeds Topography, which was never completed. Portions of the manuscript of this work have been preserved, but not those in which the memoirs of Mr. Kirk were contained. His name often occurs in the *Ducatus,* as does that of his uncle, Mr. Layton, of whom we have had an interesting notice in this Diary. The day of Mr. Kirk's death was April 24, 1706.

† George Plaxton, Rector of Berwick in Elmete, some of whose amusing letters will be found in the Correspondence.

therby, where the Doctor and several rectors and vicars read, subscribed the orders agreed upon, and after discoursed very well of matters relating to their own province ; but death has made a sad alteration since, Dr. Talbot, Mr. Killingbeck, Mr. Plaxton, Mr. Rogers,—all dead.

The satisfaction I had in seeing their libraries made me more willing to gratify others with that of my own, where I had plenty of visitants from London, Newcastle, and others from Holland, Ireland, &c., which cost too much time, to the omission of prayer. Lord pity and pardon ! Notes relating to Castle Cary at Aberford, the once noble seat of the Percys, Earls of Northumberland, are entered elsewhere.

Aug. 16. I was pensive, for having misspent forty-eight years : the last anniversary of my nativity I was with dear Mr. Kirk, who is since dead, and Sir John Kaye, another friend, was buried this week ; useful men are taken away, and useless cumber grounds left behind. Lord, help me to bring forth better fruit in my old age !

The next month began with an excellent sermon of Bishop Sharp, who afterwards confirmed betwixt 3 and 4000 : in the evening I was with his Grace and much good company at dear Mr. Thornton's. The same month, I received a kind visit from the Lord Fairfax and his ingenious kinsman, B. F. Esq. ; and a few days after, our three lawyers, and a fourth from Ripon.

Since the last mentioned authors, I have perused the three volumes of the Lord Clarendon's History written with a commendable freedom, discovering the springs of many of the transactions of that age, that are not to be met with in common authors, and is very copious and free in the character of persons concerned on both sides; only the Presbyterians apprehend him not full in acknowledgment of the assistance they contributed to the great Revolution, *an.* 1660, wherein they were eminently concerned; Test. Tho. Dom. Fairfax et patre meo;* the second and third (the first before) volumes of Fox's Martyrology, solid, useful, notwithstanding the clamours of some bigots against it; Burton upon Antoninus's Itinerary, wherein is abundance of learning, though in a crabbed style, though absolutely necessary for such as would fully understand the Roman affairs in this island; Lisle's Saxon Treatise, by which it is evident how much less that church was corrupted than the Roman afterwards.

A. D. 1707.

Read also Junius and Marshal's accurate edition of the Saxon gospels; I was also much affected in

---

* This censure of Clarendon might be borne out by an attentive comparison of the account he gives of the proceedings of General Monk with historical evidence, arising from other quarters. But it is not Presbyterians only who have reason to complain. There is *one person*, not a Presbyterian, a man of eminent rank, who performed a signal service at that time in the Royal cause, and a service as signal on another occasion, whose name is not to be found in Lord Clarendon's History.

reading Brerewood's Inquiries, in consideration of the slender part enlightened by the Gospel; that, dividing the known regions of the habitable world into thirty equal parts, the Christian part is but as five, while the idolaters have nineteen, and the Mahometans, six. Dr. Pearson's Case of the Curate of Penrith's taking on him the office of churchwarden (the pious and ingenious author's gift) is written with great judgment, and variety of curious learning in a very uncommon case ; the late Mr. Bridges' Christianity no Enthusiasm, discovers him to have been a learned and judicious divine, very well read in the ancient Fathers and Church history, and which was more troublesome, conversant in the writings of the enthusiasts, ancient and modern. I perused also the registers at Ripley, and other churches, as I had opportunity, and Archbishop Neal's book of subscriptions, having the original lent me by Chancellor Watkinson, to whom I restored it faithfully, having taken extracts ; read also good old Mr. O. Heywood's, MS. Diary, whereby it appears he preached in one year a hundred and five times, besides Lords' Days, kept fifty fasts, and travelled one thousand four hundred miles in his master's service.

These were most of the printed and manuscript books I got time to peruse, without intrenching upon the usual portion of scripture before prayer, with Annotations: Solomon's description of a good

wife, which, fell in discourse, gave me occasion most
thankfully to praise my good God for giving me such
an one, who is the great comfort and happiness of
my pilgrimage and support under all troubles, domestic and others.

I was also much affected when, in bespeaking a
grave for a friend, good Mrs. Hickson, at the new
church, I saw the remains of two eminently pious
ministers, Mr. Wales and Mr. Sharp, turned to pure
dust, except the larger bones, a melancholy sight,
was it not for the comfortable prospect of a glorious resurrection, when these dry bones shall live;
and what was sown in weakness, shall be raised in
power.

I should scarce mention here a journey to Sheffield, which was undertaken for the sake of J. A.
Esq. a good widow's only son, was it not that I had,
by Mr. Drake, the vicar's, favour, the opportunity to
gratify my melancholy constitution in a particular
survey of the vault where the famous Earls of
Shrewsbury were entombed with their ladies; the last
of which being neither wrapped in lead, nor placed
in a stone coffin, but that being of wood, covered
with a velvet pall, (which had as little of the black
left upon it, as the Countess's had of white) I had
the opportunity to behold and consider how little
difference there is betwixt human bodies turned to
dust, and that we tread upon, and are composed of;
a pugil of this in the museum may be a mortifying

object to such ladies as have never seen the like unmixed with common earth.

Upon my return I was honoured with a visit by
the obliging and learned Dr. Hudson, head-keeper of
the Bodleian library at Oxford to see the MSS. and
other scarce books, and another time the coins and
medals, he afterwards sent me autographs of several
learned professors in foreign parts. The Earl of
Westmoreland and his brother and chaplain came afterwards upon the same errand, and the Lord Irwin
with his uncle and his son from Turkey ; and at
another, one of my best friends, John Boulter, Esq.
whom I most gladly obliged with some original writings, to fence against a contentious neighbour ; as at
the same time good Mr. Strype with two sets of
subscribers. But the quality and multitude of visitants occasioned a complaint of a sad week, wherein
but five times at church betwixt Lord's day and
Lord's day ; the Swedes and other foreigners not
being able to come at other times.

But the Lord's days' evenings could not be alie-
nated, having often fifty or sixty poor children (with
their parents) and orphans, to repeat the catechism,
and appointed Psalms, in hopes of the Lord Wharton's Bibles.

Afterwards, Archbishop Tillotson's sermon of Res-
titution, which if effectually put in execution, even
by some who have ability enough, would be better
for my poor family by many hundred pounds. The

last thing worth note is, that the excellent Mr. Thornton was elected Recorder *nemine contradicente*, and was a great and public blessing.

About this time I bound up twelve volumes of letters from my friends and correspondents, that I might more readily find the useful contents of many, intermixed with others almost useless as to learning.

THE END OF THE FIRST VOLUME.

LONDON:

PRINTED BY S. AND R. BENTLEY,

Dorset Street, Fleet Street.

ND - #0128 - 020924 - C0 - 229/152/26 - PB - 9781331961659 - Gloss Lamination